- IN THE NAME OF GOD -

Defending Apartheid

Michael HH Warren

My story, *In The Name Of God: Defending Apartheid*, is about people and events that are real. Original names of places and organisations are used, and for the most part, I have used people's real names. Those identified by only their first or last names are done so for personal reasons. In rare instances I have changed names to prevent confusion or preserve anonymity. Places, businesses, institutions, incidents and events evident and occurring in public domain source documents and resource repositories are true to life and therefore factual.

Any factual inaccuracy in this account is the fault of memory loss or past and present social orders influence, or both. Should a suspected lapse in basic intelligence on the part of the author be detected, I hope the reader will interpret the oddities with humour and relevance. Accordingly, the author hereby absolves himself from any libellous action or responsibility for any unintentional errors or omissions.

Editing, layout & design: Clockwork Books

FIRST EDITION 2012
SECOND EDITION 2016

ISBN-13: 978-1470128395
ISBN-10: 147012839X

Printed in the United States of America

Contents

Acknowledgements

Dedication

I dedicate this book to the men who were conscripted into the SADF as national servicemen who remain silent voices today, their stories untold and unheard. This work is my tribute to you.

To those I suffered and served with: I salute you.

Also, to my wife, Alison, and our two children, Kelly and Caden, who allowed me times of self-absorbed recollection and long hours of writing.

Author's Note

The old South African flag unfolds to tell a story over twenty-five years old, a story of a forgotten time that continues to influence the memories and minds of many. It is my story, a story worth telling.

Michael HH Warren
February 2012

Prologue

I lean my forehead against the cool glass of the bus window, feeling the vibrations as we ramble past familiar landmarks: the public swimming pool with its patriotic variegated red, white and blue stained glass window above the entrance door, the park with its swings and roundabouts and, of course, the little leaguers' baseball diamond where kids hang by their fingers from the mesh fence to chat between innings. I've always admired the neatness of the residential properties we pass. For five years I've been catching this 07h00 bus; five years I've ridden this route from the "burbs" of my new hometown in the State of Pennsylvania to the city centre; five years since I packed up my family and left South Africa shortly after the first democratic elections for the United States, the land of the brave and free and the bastion of democracy.

As I step off the bus a block from my office, I am confronted with the sight of graffiti, obscene and revolting to me, on the nearby motorway overpass, evidence left in the wake of gangs of poorly educated white and black boys. They seem to detest each other. I think they detest themselves more. The dim recesses below are strewn with the plastic sheeting and cardboard boxes of the homeless. The stench emanating from this rat-infested grotto is overpowering. *What a pity*, I think. This once-vibrant city centre is steadily sliding into decay.

And then it occurs to me: a way to deal with this repulsive sight ...

My day at the office seems to drag on indefinitely. I watch the clock, distracted by my plans. With just over an hour to spare before the bus arrives to carry me home, I leave the office and walk in the opposite direction to the bus stop. A block and a half away, I enter a small paint and hardware store, a little bell ringing my presence as the door swings shut behind me. I sweep up and down the aisles: a portable high-pressure paint cylinder apparatus with spray gun and back harness, gloves, a protective mask. I dump the goods on the counter.

"Two gallons white wall paint, exterior," I bark at the youth behind the counter.

Five minutes later, I return to the bus stop lugging the newly-purchased paraphernalia. Slipping behind the concrete column, out of sight of passers-by, I fill the cylinder, fit the contraption to my back, adjust the gloves and

1

mask. As I prime the spray gun, I catch a glimpse of myself in the window of a parked car. I look like a moonwalker.

I make good progress. With each alcove I cover the repulsive graffiti quicker and more completely. It's satisfying to watch the multicoloured and unsightly scrawls dissolve into white. I lose track of time.

Just as I start on the third alcove, I hear profanities being shouted, footfalls echo off the concrete around me. I look up and see two security guards bearing down on me, their abuse aimed at me. They wear black pants and grey shirts. Bright red star insignias are visible above their left breast pockets and on each shoulder. I recognize them as part of the town's newly-mobilized street-patrol syndicate, comprised of foreigners, hired by the city to assist the local police enforcement agency to rid the city of petty crime. I've heard that they have become a law unto themselves.

I drop the paint cylinder and the spray gun and run. I cross the street and pass behind a departing bus. It's after 17h00. That's my bus.

A billy club narrowly misses my head and thumps against the back of the bus. These guys are serious! I don't stop. I mount the sidewalk and keep going, arms pumping. Homeward-bound workers, eyes wide at the sight of me running, jink left and right to get out of my way. It's hard to breathe.

I rip at the gloves without losing speed, drop them, and begin pulling at the mask. It comes off my face and I gulp at the air. As long as I avoid being caught, they need never know who I am.

Street after street, block after block, I run. My feet barely touch the ground, my chest aches. I am not as fit as I thought I was. Turning a corner, I glance backwards. Although there is quite a gap between me and my pursuers, I know I can't keep up this pace for much longer.

I've left the business district and find myself in the old, stately suburban area abutting the city centre. Shadows are starting to lengthen. I search for a place to hide in the quiet streets. I run past high walls and towering gates and begin to despair. At last I come across a tall, thick hedgerow bordering rolling green lawns. I scramble under the hedge, panting, my ears alert for footsteps.

Just a few meters from where my hands rest on tangled roots, a gate squeaks open. A pair of slippered feet steps onto the sidewalk. There is a sound of crackling static. I lean forward to get a better look, peering through gaps in the leaves and branches which cover my hideaway. An elderly gentleman stands with one hand resting on the gate. He is dressed in a monogrammed silk robe.

The static becomes a tinny voice. The robed man scowls. He shouts into

2

what I realize is a two-way handset: "How you could let him escape?" I try to place the accent. "You know vot it means to me!" I'm sure I know the voice. "Find me zat bastard!"

My brain whirls. This is the town's mayor! A wealthy, well-educated Russian immigrant who recently stood for office, sweeping voters up with his affable gusto and piles of cash. I remember his electioneering: *"America is best! Look at me! A foreigner! And you haf treat me so vell since I come to your beautiful country of freedom. Elect me, and I vill treat you vell also."*

I know he is calling for my head. I try to think. Why? Why was I chased by the guards when gangs of hooligans are left to deface the town with curse words and crude signs? Why does the mayor want me found?

My two pursuers arrive at the gate, breathless. "Are you stupid? Vere he is?" They are bent over double, hands on their knees. The mayor's face is growing redder. "How dare he? Who he is?" They shake their heads. "I must to have these last buildings! You hear? No vone must interfere vis my plans!"

It becomes clear to me, now, why the town has grown so scruffy and shabby in so short a time. How could these down-to-earth locals have voted for such an obvious con? I want to hear more. I back cautiously out of the hedge, inch closer along the other side, unseen, towards them. I hear footsteps on the pavement on the other side of the hedge and flatten myself on the grass.

When I lift my head, the group of men surrounding the mayor has grown. Two olive-skinned men, conversing rapidly and animatedly in an Oriental dialect stand a little to one side, watching the others with suspicion. North Korean or North Vietnamese, I surmise. Some dark-skinned Latin American men, almost certainly Cuban, in khaki jackets like battle fatigues, are loudly questioning the guards. A sharp-suited man is shouting at the mayor with a thick Germanic accent. I try to fit these pieces of a puzzle together.

Suddenly a powerful hand grips my shoulder. A faintly accented whisper speaks words belonging to another time, just behind my left ear.

"Don't make a sound, lieutenant." I turn my head and look into a darkly black, earnest face. He puts a finger to his lips, then beckons with his hand, "Follow me." Then it dawns on me. It's Phiri. The same Phiri I'd trained in the South African Defence Force, so many years ago.

There's no time to think. No time to question why Phiri would be here. Or if I can trust him.

The two of us back up and crawl away from the Russian and his cronies.

Spying a retaining wall at the far end of the garden, we pick up pace, lope towards it with our heads down. We are almost there when I hear the familiar click of a gun being released from its safety-catch. The raw taste of fear fills my mouth. Who will die first? Will I even hear the shots ring out before I die?

I wake to find myself drenched in sweat, my heart pounding in my ears. It was all so real. Could it really have been just a dream?

My breath slows as I regain my composure. I lie in the darkness thinking ... I'm reminded of a time so long ago ...

Chapter 1

Coordinates: 33°34'52.56"S 22°11'29.59"E

Through the windshield of Derick's car I could see the statue of an infantryman. He stood atop a large rock on an island in the middle of the road in front of the main gate to Infantry School. He faced east, his right hand thrust skywards. In his fist, his trusty R1 automatic rifle. His sleeves were rolled up, a helmet on his head. His mouth was open, urging his brothers-in-arms onwards. Sentinel and protector, he was the epitome of the South African Defence Force soldier: Here to win. Never give up. Forwards and onwards!

A hollow feeling gnawed at the pit of my stomach.

We arrived at Infantry School main gate on time on the morning of Monday 13 January 1986, fearing punishment if we were late. In silence, we inched past the infantryman for the last time as free men and drove slowly up to the guard house at the entrance. Stopping there, I studied the Infantry School shield on the wall: two gold swords crossed on a dark green background enclosed by a border of intermittent black and gold. Inscribed below, the motto: *Exerce Perfectioni*. My basic Latin was sufficient to translate, "Strive for excellence". Derick cocked his head without looking at me.

"Huh?" He said. I hadn't realized I had spoken aloud. I shrugged. "Nothing," I said, and returned to my thoughts.

Although a part of me was nervously curious about what lay ahead, I desperately wanted not to be here. I found myself daydreaming about happier times.

I had been skydiving for the first time just a few months before. Some school mates had been doing it for a while, and when they suggested I join them, I jumped at the chance to leap from a plane.

We made an occasion of it. Allan, Anthony, Dave and Thomas, the experts, were joined by Alan, Stefan and me, the novices. The love of my life, Kimberly, and several of her friends came along for the ride. We drove up to Pietersburg in the Northern Transvaal on Friday and stayed over at the skydiving club which was perched on the edge of a small airfield southeast of town. The club was managed by Titch and his wife Debbie.

Alan, perhaps wisely, declined to jump from a perfectly good airplane, so it was just Stefan and me who spent Saturday morning with Titch, who took us through the dry drill, over and over. Later, we jumped several times from a high platform in a shed to simulate a landing. On Sunday morning we enjoyed an early breakfast of eggs, bacon and coffee before donning our jumping overalls and clambering into the powerful single-prop plane.

At 3 500 feet I jumped. My feet left the reassuring solidity of the aircraft, and for a moment I felt as though I was suspended in space. Soon I noticed the air rushing past me, buffeting my body as if I was a feather. As I floated earthwards, I whooped and whistled as the adrenaline rush kicked in. But my joyful racket just disappeared above my head, leaving me surrounded in silence to contemplate the bush-dotted savannah below. What an experience!

The C-9 parachute I made my first jump with is not particularly known for its manoeuvrability, but I made a reasonable landing close to the drop zone. Buoyed by the rush, I felt unstoppable, and when Titch asked if I wanted to jump again in the afternoon, I readily agreed. After lunch the wind picked up. I wasn't afraid. I didn't know what to fear.

As I took my second jump from the craft, my right hand held onto the support strut of the upper wing a fraction too long. When the rushing air got hold of me and pulled me free of the plane, the chute – being on a static line – trailed behind me on an arc, and seemed to catch the back wing. By the time I realized I needed to execute the safety drill, my neck was pressed forward at an awkward angle, the lines above me twisted into a roman candle.

I took a deep breath and gripped either side of the fouled lines. Giving them a mighty pull to unravel the entwined mess, I spun in the opposite direction to the twist, sending the landscape below into a frenzied whirl. At just under a thousand feet, the whole chute sprang open with a jolt. My feet scrambled across the earth several hundred meters from the drop zone, and I fell to the ground with relief. I was almost veld fodder: I would have "bounced", as skydivers say when one plummets to the ground without a fully functional chute.

Stefan jumped just after me and had witnessed the whole episode. He came running over with his parachute.

"Hey," he said, breathlessly. "Are you okay?"

"I'm okay. I'm okay." I repeated dully. Then, "I held on a bit too long."

"I saw that!" Stefan's eyes were wide. "It looked like you came out of the plane horizontally, man!" By now the others had driven the bakkie over to where I had landed. I rubbed my face and suppressed a manic laugh.

"Whew!" I looked at Stefan, shook my head. "Fortunately, I dipped under the back wing."

"Just in time, too!" He said. He held up his thumb and forefinger, a centimetre apart. "You were this close to big trouble!" He broke into a huge, relieved smile.

"Let's get out of here," I said.

***

"*Uit die motor uit, asseblief.*" A guard stopped us at the boom and asked us to exit the vehicle. I watched as he searched the Honda thoroughly, running his hands under and between seats and rummaging through the boot. A second soldier walked around the car with a mirror on an extended pole, checking beneath the car. A third stood a short distance away, casually indifferent to the goings-on, R4 assault rifle at the ready.

"What are you looking for?" I asked the first guard as he shut the boot. "Contraband," he replied. "Booze, drugs, firearms." He nodded to the guard with the mirror, "He's looking for contraband and explosive devices." I realized I was about to enter a whole new world.

Search complete, we pulled slowly through the open boom. A genial corporal told Derick where to park his car and sent us to report to an administrative cabin alongside the parade ground where we joined the already long queue of raw recruits. I spoke to the head in front of me: "So, where are you from?" I asked.

The broad-shouldered youngster turned to me. "Natal," he said. "You?" He seemed as keen to chat as I was.

"Pretoria. You get here by train?"

"Yep," he replied. "Not a five-star journey!" He grinned.

"So I hear," I said, silently offering up thanks for my ride with Derick. "When did you get here?" I asked.

"Last night," he said. "Man, it was awful! We were met at Oudtshoorn station by these PF corporals, right?" PFs were permanent force members – notorious even to us newcomers. "The first words out of their mouths are *Bid, rower, bid! Jy sien jou ma nooit weer nie!* and *Julle gaan kak!*" The PFs had greeted the poor, anxious arrivals by shouting, "Pray, recruit, pray! You're never going to see your mother again!" and "You're gonna shit!" I shook my head.

"Nice welcome," I said.

"I'll say," my fellow conscript snorted. "I thought I was in for a *roof*-ride!" A *roof*-ride was when a new recruit was handled with disdain and made to do unsavoury things while being transported in a military vehicle. We'd all heard the stories from the *oumanne*. "Anyway," the Natalian continued. "They load us into a bunch of SAMILS, right?" SAMILs are the ubiquitous brown South African Military trucks we would come to know well. "And we drive here to the base camp. We all get off, and the PFs shout, *Wie will grens toe gaan?*" ("Who wants to go to the border?") The youngster chuckled at the memory. "So a bunch of eager guys raise their hands, right? And the PFs shout, *Daar's die grens van die kamp, hardloop soontoe!*" I laughed at the story of the eager beavers being made to run to the border of the camp, but I learned a valuable lesson then: In the army, never volunteer for anything. Ever!

The recruit from Natal went on to tell me how he and his fellow arrivals had undergone some basic administrative processing before forming up outside the quartermasters stores in the early hours of the morning. They were marched off to barracks where they were assigned beds with clean but stained mattresses and no bedding. At dawn they were awoken for breakfast and further processing.

I stood listlessly in the queue outside the admin cabin waiting to *klaar* in. Some of the newcomers decided to take a load off and stretched out in the sun on the grassy mound at the head of the parade ground. All at once, a ferocious roar reverberated around us, and we all jumped. *"'n Mens lê nie op jou gat in die weermag nie!"* ("A person does not lie on their backside in the army!"). The scolding emanated from a stocky non-commissioned officer (NCO) with the red face of a Uakari monkey. With typical PF mentality, he was trying to show us who was boss around here. It occurred to me that this routine was probably repeated every year: fresh young recruits intimidated by the PFs as they honed their *kak* ways into a fine art, a preparatory step in breaking us down so that they could rebuild us to their requirements.

I was reminded of my first encounter with the military as a kid. I couldn't have been more than eight years old. I had accompanied my father, an avid sportsman and cricket player, to a weekend cricket match his team, the Harlequins, were playing against a defence team at Voortrekkerhoogte, an army base in Pretoria. I had been playing with a bat and ball with some other youngsters next to the field, when, late in the afternoon, I decided to go in search of a drink to quench the thirst I had worked up.

A bit scruffy from games in the heat and dust, my shirt hung out at the back and my socks had slipped down my scrawny pins and come to rest on my dirty shoes. I entered a little canteen near the cricket field and approached the man in browns behind the counter.

"Please, sir, may I have a Coke?" I asked. The man stared at me icily for some time before answering me in Afrikaans.

"*Wat die donner?*" He demanded of me. "*Hoekom lyk jy soos 'n vark?*" ("What in the blazes? Why do you look like a pig?") My Afrikaans wasn't great and I didn't understand him.

"Pardon me?" I enquired.

"I will not serve you looking like that!" He barked at me in heavily-accented English. "Go outside and clean yourself up, *Engelse!*" Taken aback, I left the canteen to find a tap. I washed my hands and face, and pasted my hair down with wet fingers. I tucked my shirt into my shorts and pulled up my socks. After rubbing my shoes up and down against my calves, I re-entered the shop and approached the counter. Without so much as a nod to acknowledge my attempts at sprucing up, the man reluctantly banged my bottle of Coke down on the counter, bitter resentment etched into his face.

During my time in the army, I would come to despise the arrogance of the PFs. I regarded them as has-beens and rejects, men who would never have cut it in civvy street.

After being processed by the admin officers, we were given the order to assemble on the main parade ground. There, hundreds of young men gathered together in the baking summer heat of the Little Karoo, to be welcomed by a senior commissioned officer – first in Afrikaans, then in broken English. I could just make out the English version through the thick Afrikaans accent:

"Here," the officer said. "Yous will be treated firmly, but fairly." He spoke with great drama, a performance full of pauses and meaningful looks. "I expect yous to be mature men. Many of yous is older. Yous has studied before coming to do your national service here. Remember, yous is fortunate. In other SAI *kampe*, the non-commissioned officers would of give you a hard time." The officer's voice rose, "They would of *moer*ed you!" He said. "They canst there break you *rowers* ... I mean, recruits. Break you down verbally and physically."

"Yous must regards *Infanterie Skool* as an honour and a privilege," he went on. "If yous doesn't like it here, yous must tell me. But remember," he paused and lifted a finger for emphasis. "Yous is in the army now. And the army isn't for sissies!" The officer's wagging finger moved to point towards us. "If yous doesn't obey orders here," he said. "Then yous can only blame yourself for what will come. Disobedience will be punished, I promise you that. *Hier gaan ons al daardie* civvy *kak uit julle kry.*" All around me I heard the awkward shuffling of feet as the conscripts contemplated the consequences of "all the civvy shit" which would be "taken out" of them. *"Die* army *is nou jou ma en pa, rowers!"* By telling us that the army was now our mother and father, I took it to mean that we should leave our previous lives behind. I found the message a bit disconcerting.

I never quite worked out the meaning and intention behind the Afrikaans word for "recruit". A direct translation of the word would be *rekruut,* but it was never used. *Rower* is a brigand; a robber, thief, mugger or thug, and the colloquial term *roof* or *rofie* means "scab". I guess that's what they meant by our label: We were worthless degenerates; *suurstofdiewe,* "oxygen-thieves", not yet fit for the army. Crusty blemishes on the fine skin of South Africa's military elite.

Chapter 2

Like all white South African boys, I had registered for *Nasionale Diensplieg* at the age of sixteen, halfway through high school, as was required by law. The dreaded annual call-up papers addressed to *Rifleman Michael HH Warren, SADF No. 79551743 BG* seemed calculated to inflict cruel and unusual psychological punishment on me. How were sixteen-year-olds meant to process this mentally? The papers usually contained the name of some training base in a remote and disagreeable place – for the first few years, mine had me posted to Walvis Bay in what was then South West Africa. Walvis Bay was indeed a godforsaken place: a bleak town on the arid West Coast, infamous for its rank smelling trade – fish. It was made even worse by the tales spun about it.

SADF No. 79551743 BG would eventually become a second identity number for me, forever a part of my life.

To be fair, good fortune had smiled on me more than many of my peers. I'd planned to go to university before national service, knowing that the SADF would consider me as officer material thanks to my qualification. Those who had qualified as engineers or medical practitioners were usually sent straight to those units which would most likely be in need of their skills. My natural sciences degree virtually guaranteed I would be joining the teachers at the School of Infantry in Oudtshoorn.

When I finally let the powers-that-be know that I was about to finish my degree, I received the dreaded final call-up papers. My time had come – I was on my way to Infantry School. I was not to know that my sheltered, youthful innocence was soon to be blown away by the harsh reality of national service.

It was the mid-eighties and South Africa was burning. In the townships, the oppressed were taking to the streets in violent protest against their inhumane treatment at the hands of the Apartheid government. As if the government didn't have its hands full internally, it was embroiled in a full-blown war raging on the border between South West Africa and Angola in one of the foremost Cold War proxy wars of the era, one that few people were aware of at the time, and is almost forgotten today.

None of these issues occupied my mind at the time. I was too busy growing up.

Oudtshoorn's School of Infantry Programme was an elite training facility for commissioned and non-commissioned officers. The Junior Leadership Programme wasn't elite in the sense that it produced the toughest infantry commanders, rather it turned out the most replete and well-trained, thinking infantry soldiers, or junior leaders, or "JLs", affectionately known as Pongos. The term Pongo means large ape, or orang-utan, or in this case, horny young soldier who'd do anything to get a girl for the night.

The ordinary infantry soldier in other South African Infantry (SAI) units was given just three months of basic training, and the ill-treatment meted out to new recruits in these camps was legendary: conscripts were known to cave in from the abuse, deprivation, physical exertion and heat exhaustion. Infantry School was said to be less daunting than going to any other infantry unit. At Infantry School, I and my fellow officers-in-training could expect more than eight months of in-house advanced military training, including basics, after which we would be posted to South West Africa for up to two months, to practice the art of war. After border duty, a few weeks would be dedicated to preparations for the passing-out parade. I would have to grin and bear it for a whole year.

Even though the Officers' Course was supposed to be quite tough, it was considered worth it in the end. Mates who went from varsity to Infantry School trained and suffered for the first year, after which they were posted to cushy positions as commissioned officers and commanders for the remaining year of their service. All things considered, being treated more humanely than your run-of-the mill infantry recruit ranked high in dispelling my fear of the looming obligation. I had a fair idea of what to expect and I counted myself fortunate to be in this position of relative enlightenment.

Although the SADF was based on the British military model, it was overwhelmingly Afrikaans, especially the army. Most of the PF members were Afrikaans, and these career soldiers were the most reviled of all. They treated everybody like scum – especially conscripted national servicemen – and were generally a miserable lot.

Like many of my fellow English-speaking recruits, I regarded conscription as a downright pain, a necessary evil to bear before moving on to the more important things in life, like family and career. No one ever spoke about the possibility of dying, of your lifeless remains lying prone in a black plastic body bag under the nation's flag.

Back in the rising heat of that January morning in Oudtshoorn, well over a thousand new intakes were being split into companies by several dozen

Afrikaans NCOs. Individuals of every stripe had ended up at Oudtshoorn. Almost without exception, to be in Bravo or Foxtrot, you had to be a graduate. Those who had a tertiary education, whether completed or not, were placed in these two companies. Bravo Company was designated the teachers' company. The reason Bravo Company was established at Infantry School was that these graduates were expected to become involved in the Cadet Corps in schools. Teachers made up over eighty percent of Bravo Company, with just a smattering of other graduates making up the balance.

Alpha, Charlie and Delta Companies were comprised of younger school-leavers. Alpha, Bravo and Foxtrot were candidate officer companies, the rest were companies for candidate NCOs. Echo, Golf and Hotel Companies were July intakes for school-leavers. Whereas the other companies' average age was eighteen, Bravo's was twenty-two. The youngsters allocated to the other companies looked tense and wet behind the ears, but what they showed on the outside, we were all feeling on the inside.

To begin with, all the graduates – who numbered over six hundred – were massed together before being placed in either Bravo or Foxtrot. The two graduate companies were larger than usual company strength, and were further split up into smaller, more manageable platoons of about forty-five men each to *klaar* in. These platoons were temporary, however, and within the first two weeks we were split up again and reshuffled, causing some consternation as we were all just getting to know the faces around us. It was during this reshuffling period that I learned that Foxtrot Company was designated the sportsmen's company, although the brass would not openly admit it, and those with a talent for a particular sport, especially rugby, were assigned there. Although I was an avid cricketer and soccer player at high school, with certain athletics events thrown in for good measure, I never played rugby. Nor were we encouraged to play the game at school – most public English-medium schools in Pretoria were not geared to provide rugby as a school sport.

Members of Foxtrot generally received better treatment, being spared a lot of the rigorous training the rest of us had to go through. Many Bravo Company recruits – me included – endeavoured to get transferred to Foxtrot in the first week, trying to persuade their platoon commanders that they were proficient in some or other sport. In my case, I was informed in no uncertain terms that skydiving wasn't considered by Infantry School to be a sport. Perhaps Foxtrot was so named because of all the fancy footwork required to get into the company and stay there, thereby avoiding having to do any real soldiering.

Foxtrot would come to be the most detested of all the companies at Infantry School. After receiving rank, most of Foxtrot's new one-pip looties would be posted to undemanding billets in the Republic, while the rest of the men in other companies had to go to SAI camps or to the South West African Border as operational commissioned officers. It was patently clear that the army placed far more value on the services of sportsmen. The so-called sportsmen were soon furtively looked down upon and came to be resentfully referred to as the gyppo-*gats* or *balbakkers*, suggesting they were skiving off, or lying around idle while toasting their wedding tackle under the African sun.

After the reshuffle and once the two graduate companies had settled into their final make-up, my company, Bravo, was in the order of about 450 strong. When I was placed in Bravo Company it consisted of ten platoons, but each day was a war of attrition, and we were soon whittled down to seven platoons which remained fairly constant for most of the rest of the year. In the end, only six platoons departed for border duty.

Bravo, along with other Infantry School companies was structured as follows: The company commander was a major or PF captain, soon to become a major, a PF captain or a two-pip PF lieutenant who was soon to become a captain. Each company had platoon commanders, who were two-pip looties, including a communications operations (comops) officer, an admin officer and an ops officer. These were all national servicemen looties. Each company had a company sergeant major who was a PF adjutant officer AO1 or AO2, or on rare occasions a PF staff sergeant who was about to be promoted. The second-in-command (2IC) of the company NCOs would also be a PF sergeant or a staff sergeant, depending on the rank above him. Each company had platoon NCOs. These were all national servicemen corporals. Bravo Company had two clerks because of our large size. Admin clerks started off being one-liners, or lance corporals, also known as one-stripers or "lance jacks", and by the end of the year would attain their two-stripes, becoming full corporals.

Each platoon was assigned a national service corporal, or two-striper, who was designated the platoon sergeant. Ours, evident from the name embroidered above his right shirt pocket, was Corporal Joubert. There was also a national service lance corporal, or one-striper, in our case, Corporal Potgieter. During that first day, the two corporals were with us all the time, breaking us in and preparing us to meet our platoon commander, Lieutenant

Pretorius. All three of our superiors would turn out to be dyed-in-the-wool Afrikaners, especially our two-pip lieutenant, who would come to be known by us English-speakers as "Lootie".

Along with several other Bravo Company platoons, my platoon was marched off by our corporals for a medical exam while others went off to the quartermaster's storehouse. We waited anxiously in long lines, still in our civvies and chatting quietly amongst ourselves. The wait seemed to take ages. Eventually we were each handed a comprehensive medical questionnaire and a pencil with which to complete it. I wondered why we completed the form in pencil. Was it because they expected us to make mistakes, or, more ominously, because the medics might want to change the results after the fact?

Forms completed, we were put through a battery of mental and physical tests. My turn finally arrived with a dozen or so others who had been waiting with me. First I was asked several general knowledge and personal questions, which I assumed were posed to test my mental capacity. Then my height and weight were measured and recorded on a little white card. My hearing was tested, then my eyesight, and then I was required to urinate on a little strip of litmus paper. I compared my strip of test paper with the recruit to my right, but couldn't identify any visible difference. Blood was drawn from some of us, some were given injections. Some guys fainted after their jabs, and I wondered how they would cope with training.

We were told to strip down to our underpants to receive two injections: one in the arm and one in the rump, administered by two young and attractive nurses. Then we were subjected to a test of a somewhat intimate nature which brought back memories from primary school, when a rather stern and elderly matron had told me to cough while examining my nuts with an instrument resembling a spoon. This time, the test was rather more pleasant, being carried out as it was by these young lovelies, but they were at pains to point out to us that they had seen thousands of new recruits in their jocks and we were not to think their treatment of us was in any way special or suggestive. This didn't stop us from ragging each other about this procedure which we found part embarrassing, part arousing.

I went through the battery of tests secretly hoping the medics would find some medical condition that might get me discharged from military duty altogether – something manageable and not life-threatening, but that would let me off the hook with my dignity intact. I had no desire to be returned to unit (RTU), though, which is what happened if one scored poor ratings but was not discharged. Being a pen pusher for two years in the army was no life for me.

Clothed once more, I was taken to see the dentist, and then the doctor, who gave me a brief examination and looked at the comprehensive medical questionnaire that had been filled in, before classifying me G1K1.

A G1K1 rating was regarded as a first-class mental and physical rating. Troops spitefully referred to the G1K1 recruit as cannon fodder. Depending on different assessed values for G and K, the worst case scenario was a G5-rating. This lowest rating meant that the recruit was considered seriously physically and/or mentally unfit for service and was disdainfully looked upon as an accident waiting to happen, inadequate for the purposes of military training, and discharged at once on medical grounds and sent home.

Several conscripts were called out and told to stand to one side. The NCOs joked about them being the "sick, lame and lazy" – these were the blokes who were unfit for any kind of duty following the tests carried out on them. I realized that, although they had failed their medical tests, they were more fortunate than I – they were going home. They were visibly relieved, and some admitted to hoping for a "dignified" way out of doing their national service.

Another group of conscripts were herded to another side. These were not G5s, but neither were they G1s. They were going to be RTU.

The first signs of attrition had set in: without fear or favour, those that were seen to be surplus to requirement were sent, or more accurately, kicked off the Junior Leadership Course.

After the medical examinations, those of us considered capable of staying the distance were hustled from the medical centre in rough platoon-formation and at more-or-less of a march in our civvies to the quartermaster's storehouse, where we lined up in single file to receive all sorts of military uniform and kit. This process took several hours.

A number of enlisted soldiers were supporting the career NCOs in the stores as they buried us under a small mountain of clothing, apparel and accessories. We received: Light-green underpants (referred to as Santa Marias), olive green socks, PT clothing consisting of two green running vests and two brown tee-shirts with a pair of black training shorts, brown *tekkies* or running shoes, two brown training overalls, two sets of "browns" which are long- and short-sleeved nutria shirts with matching combat trousers, two pairs of brown boots, an olive-green web belt with brass press-studs, a nutria *bosbaadjie* or bush jacket, chest webbing and a battle jacket. For the head, we were given a brown woollen balaclava, a nutria *boshoed* or bush hat, a nutria nylon-Kevlar battle helmet with cover, referred to as a *staaldak* or "steel roof", and a green beret. Other accessories included plastic upper arm epaulets and flashes and various insignia to be worn, the most notable of which was the famous infantry *bokkop* or springbok head, in silver, to be attached to the front of the beret, above the left eye.

Complaints that sleeves or trousers were too short or too long fell on deaf ears, and we resorted to swapping amongst ourselves or surreptitiously pilfering the correct sizes from the kit piled on a long counter in front of the quartermaster's storehouse.

Other accoutrement we were handed included a yellow plastic cup with handle, two two-litre and one pint-sized dark green water bottles, a metal fire-bucket or water bottle holder with folding metal handle which would double up as a mug, shaving cup and cooking pot. There was a white *tokkeltou*, or length of rope with an eye in one end and metal toggle on the other to be used in conjunction with one's webbing, a brown plastic raincoat and a brown "bivvy" or bivouac or poncho which was a sizeable brown square plastic sheet with an opening and a hood in the centre and number of eyeholes along the edges. Amongst the bedding provided was a brown waterproof groundsheet with a number of eyeholes along the edges, light brown sleeping bag and inner, a pillow, a grey blanket, and sheets which must once have been white but were now greying with age and use. Along with all of this, we were issued with a nutria *grootsak* or H-frame backpack, a large green metal *trommel* or lockable trunk, and a large light brown duffel bag called a *balsak*.

The staff ordered us to pack as much of this equipment into the *trommel* and *balsak* as possible. We were about to have our first lesson in how to handle pressure.

The distance from the quartermaster's storehouse to the lines was about 550 meters. We were ordered to collect our kit, form up in our platoons and keep in formation while carrying it all to the lines. The smart ones among us had jammed the *trommel* full of the lightest items, such as bedding, attached the stuffed *balsak* to one arm and the rucksack to the other. Others had draped the blankets and sheets over arms and necks, and still they were straining under the bulk. The not-so-clever ones had gear piled everywhere and were straining to juggle it all: on their heads, around their necks, on their backs, around their waists, and unfortunately even on top of an already heavy *trommel*. The objective was almost impossible, and even the largest and strongest guys barely managed. The road became littered with kit in no time, and whenever something fell, the whole platoon would be made to stop and wait for the hapless butterfingers to pick it up while the corporals ejected attention-grabbing expletives and abuse.

I tried to balance the duffel bag on one shoulder and the rucksack on the other while carrying the trunk by its two metal handles, a method which worked in short bursts, but the weight and awkward bulkiness forced me to stop and catch my breath every few meters, my arms and fingers aching from the strain.

Our corporals did not view this chaotic, bumbling spectacle with much sympathy. They gave us encouragement when we seemed to be making progress, but it sounded more like thinly-disguised threats. Exhausted, we stumbled along in something resembling a formation, up the long incline to the barracks. Pausing to catch our breath and regain composure somewhere around the halfway mark, our platoon sergeant, Corporal Joubert, with a glint in his eye, informed us that we would be given permission to return to the storehouse the following day to exchange those items that didn't fit.

Approaching the bungalows, we were ordered to do a right wheel into the company lines, which only resulted in the platoon descending into even more chaos. My platoon's bungalow was unfortunately all the way back at the end of the row, furthest from the company mustering area and the quartermaster's storehouse. Puffing, panting and wheezing, we stumbled through the length of Bravo Company's lines, which comprised prefabricated *kaserne* or bungalows, sometimes referred to as barracks, designated by the company symbol of an owl wearing a graduate cap and perched on an R4 rifle, painted on a signpost in front of the first bungalow. Bravo's barracks was a row of seven bungalows occupying the northwest corner of the main camp. Close by were two other rows of seven bungalows sometimes used by other companies, three of those bungalows which were now to be used to accommodate the excess Bravo recruits. Back then the bungalows had a well-maintained tar strip in front of the lines. Each bungalow had a silver-grey corrugated iron roof, concrete prefabricated wall panels and a lockable wooden double-door entrance painted grey sans security gate.

Coordinates: 33°34'35.14"S 22°11'10.69"E

My platoon's new quarters, bungalow number seven, were next to an open field to the north. Just inside the entrance to the left of the bungalow was a large ironing area. The front and centre of the bungalow held the showers, with the toilets and basins to the right. A long passage led away centrally to twelve rooms, six on either side. One extra large room at the end of the passage to the right was called the *vrye tyd bestuur kamer* (VTB) or leisure-time room, where we could watch TV or videos, and a smaller room at the head of the passage to the right was designated Room 12 and set aside as the platoon commander's admin room. All the other rooms were cramped, housing five steel cupboards and five black, steel-framed folding beds, each with a thin foam-rubber mattress about ten centimetres thick, wrapped in a pee-stained canvas covering of thin blue stripes on a white background which we called a *pisvel*, or foreskin. Beside each bed, neatly placed against the wall, was a concrete kerb stone, about thirty centimetres square and fifteen centimetres thick. Later, when we were bold enough to ask what these were and why they were there, Corporal Joubert would laugh at us and reply cryptically, "Those, my friends, are your marbles. You will become quite intimate with them, in time." I swallowed uncomfortably, assuming this to mean that the marbles would be used for punishment. I was right.

We were randomly allocated five to a room (I went into Room 1, the first room on the left, across from the platoon commander's admin room, Room 12) and given fifteen minutes to lock away all our kit and don our brown training overalls, the outfit that would be our standard attire for the year. The overalls were matched with a pair of olive green socks, an olive green web belt, a brown bush hat and one of the two pairs of new boots. As I pulled on my new boots, which were unyieldingly hard and leaden, I experienced a wave of confirmation settle around me uncomfortably: I was in the army now. The corporals stood by instructing us on how to wear the uniform: the seam of the bush hat was to face backwards, the green metal clasp of the web belt was to face forwards in the middle of one's waist. Woe betide any soldier caught flouting these directions.

We were instructed to write our force number, surname and initials on the inside of our bush hats using a permanent black marker. On the inside of our web belts we were to write our force number, surname and initials and our blood type. Later, before departing for the border, each recruit would receive two metal dog tags on a chain carrying the same information, with the addition of a statement of our religion. Receiving my dog tags presented me with the uncomfortable reality of what I was to face on the border. But that was in the future.

For now, dressed to specification, we were called into the passage by our platoon sergeant, Corporal Joubert, who I reckoned to be no more than nineteen or twenty years old. To me, his head appeared too large for his stocky body and average height, giving him an almost comical look. Joubert was quietly self-assured and seemed indifferent to the fact that we were all older than him. In a surprisingly pleasant way, he formally introduced himself and his side-kick, Lance Corporal Potgieter, who was also a youngster at barely nineteen. Of medium height, Potgieter was all hands, feet and head. Joubert explained to us that whenever our lieutenant, himself, or Corporal Potgieter came into the bungalow or our room, we were to stand to attention. He went on to give us a run-down of how and who we were expected to acknowledge, either by saluting or *strek*king. Anybody displaying a rank on their shoulders was to be saluted when we were wearing headgear or *strek*ked when we weren't. Anybody with rank designations on their upper arms (here, he tapped his own designation with two fingers) was to be *strek*ked. To *strek* was like coming to attention, with an upright posture and straight arms, fists clenched at one's sides. Of course, to begin with, us newbies, fresh off civvy street, got the acknowledging of rank wrong a lot, and we spent time doing extra PT as punishment, until we were either taught how to do it correctly or finally figured out what we were doing wrong. Joubert went on to inform us that we should address officers and NCOs by their rank and not "sir" as we might have expected.

Our platoon commander arrived, and Corporal Joubert introduced him to us. Lieutenant Pretorius was taller than average, just a few inches shorter than me. He was barely a year older than us, but with his light-coloured hair and blonde moustache he looked much older than that. His English left a lot to be desired. A national serviceman and a teacher like many of the graduates, Pretorius gave me the distinct impression he was a stickler for the rules: a real by-the-book, humourless, pain-in-the-ass type.

Lieutenant Pretorius briefed us in a terse, matter-of-fact way. After welcoming us in clipped tones, he told us we were expected to pull our weight and keep our noses clean. But it was his last words that got my attention.

"You okes, you better take my advice," he said, narrowing his eyes. "If you want to survive this year, you must learn to work together – I expects you to work together. And if you don't, I promise you," he repeated for emphasis, glaring from one to the next, "I promise you, I will make your life extremely difficult. *Verstaan ons mekaar?*" ("Do we understand each other?")

To which we all nodded and replied in unison, *"Ja, luitenant!"*

It occurred to me that these three men, these dyed-in-the-wool Afrikaners, were on a mission, that no matter what we did, whether right or wrong, these three would find an excuse to make our lives miserable. I was right.

By this stage it was lunch time, and after a curt goodbye from Pretorius, we were marched down to a large mess hall where we sat down at tables positioned in long, orderly rows to a surprisingly decent meal of cold meats, potato salad and piles of white and brown bread. The food was served on white army crockery embossed with the Infantry School emblem. Jugs of ice-cold milk and fruit juice quenched our thirsty palates. When lunch was over, we returned to Bravo Company's barracks for a short midday break. Most of the guys were quiet, caught up in their own thoughts. I lay on that pee-stained mattress, wondering what was to become of me here.

Too soon, our two corporals returned to show us how to prepare for inspections. We were told how to properly clean and polish the yellow-brown Marley tiles of the passage floor. First it had to be thoroughly washed and dried, and each tiny mark removed with Brasso and steel-wool, after which a thin layer of Cobra floor polish would be applied and spread over the floor before polishing and buffing. One way of polishing and buffing the passage floor was for two recruits to sit on top of pillows on a grey army-issue blanket, pulled from the corners by two others. By the end of the year, we had streamlined this process so that just one guy was needed to pull and one to be pulled. By then we knew all the tricks and inspections were less rigorous.

Cleaning the ablution facilities was equally painstaking. Every night, after 21h15, four of the five toilets in the bathroom would be out of bounds. Then began the unpleasant task of scrubbing and polishing all the toilets, washbasins and fittings until they gleamed. It was common to come across a recruit sitting with his legs wrapped around the base of a toilet, scouring away at the grime with an old toothbrush. After the ablutions were cleaned to sparkling, all but the last toilet were chained shut. This one toilet, dimly lit by an overhead light bulb, was left functioning until the next morning, when it was given a quick but thorough once-over.

Polishing the passage floor and cleaning the toilets was usually done last thing at night, after everyone had completed their ablutions and just before lights-out. If one of us had to go to the bathroom during the night, we had to wear "taxis", durable homemade cloth bags, large enough to accommodate boots, which were pulled closed and tied around the shins with strings or elastic. Anybody found traipsing about without taxis on after the floor had been polished was liable to receive a thump to the chest for dirtying the floor. Many of us only procured taxis after our first pass and so had to use other acceptable methods, such as an extra pair of large socks, pulled over feet or boots, to avoid a thumping.

Later we lined up in front of the barracks for company Roll Call, before being marched off to supper. My first army supper was savoured in the same large dining hall in which we had eaten lunch. Bravo Company was joined by Charlie and Delta, two NCO companies. At a later stage, Bravo would eat separately from the other companies. I took stock of Infantry School's culinary procedures: it certainly wasn't what I expected. There was no queuing for food to be dished up, but rather we were provided with a well-orchestrated catering experience. In orderly fashion, the new recruits filed in and stood behind their chairs while everyone found a seat at one of the long tables, which each seated twelve. After thanksgiving we were told by the NCO on duty to be seated, and whilst we quietly chatted amongst ourselves, large oval-shaped silver-plated casserole dishes with lids were brought out and placed at the head of each table by national servicemen working as cooks in the kitchen under the supervision of a permanent force senior NCO. Those seated at the head of each table served up fair portions for the rest and passed the plates down the line.

The food was surprisingly first-rate, and there were abundant quantities of it to nourish us all. On each table, slices of white and brown bread were piled high on silver-plated platters, with butter and jam nearby for spreading, and jugs were standing by filled with milk, orange and mango juice. The main meal consisted of cooked meat with two starches and veggies, and was followed by jelly and custard and tinned fruit for pudding. In the days and weeks to follow, as we became fitter and our hunger increased, there was always lots of food to sustain us. Lunch was usually processed cold meats, potato salad or variations of cold pasta dishes, and dinner a red or white meat with vegetables.

When the meal was finished, the plates and cutlery were neatly stacked by the same recruits who had served the meal. To begin with, the guys thought that being the table's server was an advantage – you'd always have first dibs to second-helpings, what with the serving dishes right at your side – but we soon learned that there was more than enough food available for all us to fill ourselves with our first helping anyway, and the role just became a chore.

Even being served three square meals a day, we did not have to wash a single plate, unlike some of the other SAI *plase*. At Infantry School, washing up was some other sucker's chore, probably with the assistance of the black and coloured day staff.

I knew that the servicemen at other SAI camps ate out of a *varkpan*, literally a "pig's pan", which was a rectangular aluminium dixie with fold-away handles. Their cutlery consisted of a *pikstel*, a metal spoon and fork that slotted into a knife for ease of use and storage. We had each been given a dixie and a *pikstel* with our kit, but we would only really start to use them during *Vasbyt*. During the conventional warfare phase of training and while on border duty in South West Africa, these items would become indispensable, and we learned quickly how to carefully wash our utensils in the cold water wash-drums. If you didn't vigilantly scrape the items clean and wash them thoroughly, you could find yourself the victim of gut-wrenching food poisoning. To avoid getting gyppo-guts, we learned to wrap the dixie in disposable plastic sandwich bags during the various phases out in the veld and on the Border.

Mealtimes at Infantry School were civilised affairs, and we were never expected to wolf down our food like at most other SAI camps, where the approach to meals was *"Eet nou, kou later!"* or "Eat now, chew later!"

Following our supper, Bravo Company was mustered outside the mess hall in our respective platoons and marched back to the mustering area in front of our lines where our company commander, or officer commanding (OC), Major Drost, and Company Sergeant Major (CSM) Lategaan addressed us. The sun was setting; its bright orb burned the edge of the earth with the last light of day, streaking the large expanse of sky with glowing orange as it slipped behind the Swartberg Mountain range, which stretched before us to the north.

We were told that the public telephones outside Bungalow 1 would be off-limits to us until after basics, and there was to be no snooping around anywhere in the camp until we were given permission to move around freely. When this permission was finally granted, they added, we would be expected to go around in pairs.

That evening in barracks at prefabricated Bungalow 7, I met the other newcomers in my platoon. Most of the guys were relatively trim and fit, with the exception of a few really scrawny men, one ultra-nerd and one oversized recruit. Afrikaners were in the majority, and inevitably, friendships were struck up between the few English-speakers that were there. That night, I met fellow English-speakers Kerry Pile, Miles Sowden and Ian Cameron, and before long we were comparing notes on our families, home-towns, education, thoughts and dreams. Our friendships had begun.

As alliances were made, the guys chopped and changed their rooms to share with those they felt they would get along best with. Ian, who was to be my roommate and best pal that year, joined me in Room 1. A short, upbeat guy, he told me that he had studied a commerce degree at Rhodes University in Grahamstown and spoke fondly of his girlfriend, who he affectionately referred to as *"Vlam"* because of her mop of red hair. Ian would come to be known as "Cammie", and I would soon discover that, although he was blessed with unsurpassed physical and mental toughness, he skived off whenever he could and, more infuriatingly, was hardly ever caught.

The historical Afrikaans-English antagonism, a perpetual undercurrent in the wider South African society, was particularly evident in the army. Us English-speakers called the Afrikaners "Dutchmen" – a common epithet used by English-speaking South Africans. In the army, though, we used a grading system to describe the whole spectrum of Dutchman-types. The term "tame Dutchman" was used to refer to those Afrikaners, typically from the Cape or Natal, who were more moderate or even liberal in their thoughts and behaviour. There were cliques in each platoon comprising what we called "heavy Dutchmen", who, with thick accents, an intolerance of English and abrasive personalities to match, wanted little to do with us English-speakers. For the purposes of our own prejudiced convenience, though, the English-speaking recruits often lumped the Afrikaners all together and referred to all of them as "Dutchmen".

Although the attitudes of even the heaviest Dutchmen amongst us changed as the year wore on, there was an undeniable antipathy present, bubbling just below the surface, between the English and Afrikaans *troepe*. Even a seemingly friendly jibe, like, "Hey, *soutpiel*, give me a hand to polish the floor," contained a barb that had its roots in times long past.

On many occasions in my youth, in the spiteful name-calling games that kids play, the English-speaking boys were tauntingly referred to as *"souties!"* or *"soutpiele!"* or *"rooinekke!"* by the Afrikaans boys. The English-speakers returned the favour by mockingly referring to the Afrikaners as "Dutchmen" or "rockspiders".

The term *"soutie"* or *"soutpiel"* (literally, "salty penis") was a reference to a caricature of the English-speaking South African, supposedly having one foot in the Republic and the other in England, so that his third appendage was marinated in the salty waters of the Atlantic Ocean. This term describes how the Afrikaners viewed the English-speakers as still holding allegiance to the British Crown. The implied length of the English-speaker's appendage, and the associated phallic prowess, went unnoticed by those who developed the label.

"*Rooinek*" was a throwback term, probably emerging from the First Anglo-Boer War, when the brainless British generals had their soldiers deployed in the African veld in full military colours – specifically the bright red tunics of the late nineteenth century British Army – making them highly visible targets and easy pickings for the *Boer* commandos. It also aptly describes the vivid red of the colonial necks burnt under the fierce African sun. Interestingly, the Afrikaans term "khaki" as used for English-speakers became common during the Second Anglo-Boer War, when the ill-fated red tunics of the British soldiers had been replaced by drab-coloured uniforms more appropriate to the South African landscape and facilitating the evasion of the wholesale shooting-gallery slaughter of British soldiers at the hands of the *Boer*s.

The corresponding term, "Dutchman", employed by the name-calling English-speaking boys of my youth and my fellow English-speakers in the army, referred to the Dutch heritage of the Afrikaner and draws on the historical contempt of the British for the Dutch, seen to be inferior in class and intellect to His Majesty's subjects. Think of the English terms, "going Dutch" and "Dutch courage", and even, more vulgarly, "Dutch oven". The term "rockspider" suggested that Afrikaners were loathsome like a spider, and likely to hide away under a rock when confronted and attack when least expected. A popular joke from that time was, "If English children go to a nursery, where do Afrikaans children go? To a rockery!"

We had more derogatory names for Afrikaners: hairy-backs, boneheads, clutch-plates, crunchies, wing-nuts and tappets. *"Kydaars!"* we would spit at the Afrikaans boys, mocking the phrase they would use ("Look there!") when pointing to someone or something, or "planks!", referring to the heavy Afrikaans accent that made a person sound "as thick as two short planks". A rhyming tune I remember from childhood went, "Afrikaner, Afrikaner, *vrot* banana!"

Of course, we seldom treated the Afrikaans girls with the same disrespect we showed their brothers. By the time I got to high school, the Afrikaans girls I saw hanging around outside their schools and at the bus stops were more attractive than ugly by a large percentage. In fact, it seemed to me that the Afrikaans girls I eyed surreptitiously as I passed them by had more sex appeal than most of their English-speaking counterparts – their *je ne sais quoi* most likely a result of their mixed French, Dutch and German heritage. But the inevitable cultural and language barriers ensured that they remained inaccessible – out of reach and mostly out of mind.

In the name-calling game between English and Afrikaans, the English, it seems, led the race in creating disparaging terms for the other. We were inclined, at the time, to view the Afrikaners as intolerant and narrow-minded, as unthinking conformists. But English-speaking South Africans needed to hold a mirror up to their own bigotry, instead of pointing out the shortfalls of the Afrikaners.

Corporal Joubert surprised us English-speakers on one occasion and took our side by suggesting that if an Afrikaner referred to us as a *soutpiel*, we were to retort with *"peperpoes"*, an expression too vulgar to think about.

South Africa's history is convoluted, and through its course, political machinations have made for strange bedfellows. Many Afrikaners have British-sounding surnames; English, Irish, and Welsh, but especially Scottish. This phenomenon can be traced back to the Anglo-Boer Wars, when many of the King's soldiers chose to remain in South Africa after the wars ended. The traditionalist and dour Calvinist Scots found resonance amongst the conservative and devout Dutch Reformed Afrikaners, not least due to the fact that their religious beliefs were practically carbon copies, and in time, descendants of the *Voortrekkers* came to bear names reminiscent of a faraway country up north.

At the end of my year at Oudtshoorn, the English-speaking guys accounted for only twelve percent of our platoon's total of thirty-four men.

Night fell on Bungalow 7 and my thoughts became bleaker. Falling asleep was hard. I missed Kimberly desperately.

Chapter 3

It was summer, late 1980. I was seventeen. She rode past me on her bicycle.

I was on my skateboard outside my parent's house, occupying myself in the late afternoon sunlight by practicing ollies on the pavement. I saw her approaching on her bicycle and stopped, catching the board mid-pop. "Hello," I said as she neared.

"Hello," she replied, flashing me a wondrous smile as she pedalled by. Stunned, I watched her round the corner at the top of the street and disappear from view. Too late! Why hadn't I stopped her?

A week later I was out on my silver Yamaha 175 DT Enduro when I saw her riding her bicycle again. I wasn't about to let this chance pass me by. I stopped the scrambler a short distance in front of her, flipped out the side-stand and leant on my left foot.

"Hey, stop!" I called to her. She stopped her bike and leant against it. "Can I ask you what your name is this time?" I gave her what I hoped was a roguish grin. She smiled that glorious smile again.

"I'm Kimberly," she said.

"What school are you at?" I asked. "Pretoria Girls."

"What standard?" I tried to draw the conversation out. "Standard seven," she said.

"You're at the wrong school, you know," I said. She cocked her head. "Why?" She asked.

"You should be at The Glen," I said. "Because I'm at The Glen." I was taken aback at my own boldness.

I got her number, and soon I was on her doorstep every afternoon. With my trusty steed parked on the pavement, I was the good knight come to visit his damsel.

Our first kiss took place on top of Alan's mother's washing machine in the laundry room of their Brooklyn home. We were attending a party there towards the end of the year. Kimberly was ravishing in her coral cat suit which exposed her figure beautifully. Getting that first passionate kiss took me a while, but by the time 1980 was over, Kimberly and I were intoxicated with each other. She convinced her parents to let her move to The Glen in the new school year.

We revelled in our first erotic encounter, and although we didn't actually progress to the real thing, we became more and more daring with our exploration of each other's bodies. I stroked her hair, ran my schoolboy hands over her body and breathed her in. From the furthest shadows of the garden, Pan watched our silhouettes with an impious gaze.

***

"Word wakker! Staan op! Staan op!" Bang-bang-bang. My second morning in Oudtshoorn started with a fright at 05h00, when the corporals woke us by bashing on the cupboards and shouting down the long passageway for us to wake up and get up. We got out of our beds, pulled on our browns and assembled in the mess hall for breakfast. The meal began with the choice of Weetbix or Jungle Oats with milk, followed by scrambled eggs and bacon. The tables were again laden with slices of white and brown bread, butter and jam, and jugs of milk. Coffee was provided to wash down the feast, and as soon as it was finished we were hustled in marching formation to the barbershop near the main parade ground.

Our attempts at marching in time were farcical. One of the two corporals would belt out, *"Links, regs, links, regs, LIIINKS …"* ("Left, right, left, right, LEEEFT …") and we would stutter and stumble along, losing our feet and feeling ungainly. I inadvertently caught the heel of the guy in front of me, causing him to lose stride, which caused the whole formation to hiccough and trip over their feet. The guys tittered.

Guys were peeled off in groups of six to have their hair cut while the rest of the men were drilled by the corporal. None of the new recruits had arrived at Infantry School with particularly long hair – in fact, everyone in our platoon had reasonably short hair. None of us were traumatised like so many ordinary SAI *troepies*, by the shearing of their lovingly cultivated locks.

I sank into the barber's chair and asked for a short-back-and-sides, but the barber had heard this one before. I guess he didn't appreciate my cheek, so I emerged with my hair shorn shorter than those who had refrained to comment. By the time we had all had our heads shaved to Infantry School standard – for most, this was a number four, for me a number two – it was lunchtime.

After another lunch of cold meat and potato salad and a brief siesta back at the bungalow, we went drilling again, now sporting military-issue hair cuts under our brown bush hats. We looked the part.

All the drilling instructions were delivered in Afrikaans and some of us English speakers struggled to pick them up. Although our brown training overalls were extremely practical, they were poorly-ventilated and hot in the oppressive heat of January. This combined with the rigours of the drilling manoeuvres forced us to wear our small pouched water bottles attached to our web belts, which were drained and refilled every half hour during smoke breaks, which passed for water breaks.

Drills continued until late afternoon, after which we enjoyed another good meal and retired to our bungalows. The guys chatted companionably again in the evening before turning in. When I lay under my grey blanket, I felt an unexpected melancholy well up inside me. I thought of Kimberly and felt alone. I rubbed off the sudden excess moisture which afflicted my eyes and was relieved that the lights were out.

Apart from the few hours we slept each night, Kimberly and I had spent the last few days before call-up together. She helped me prepare to go, and went with me to buy the list of necessities that had been sent with my final call-up papers. Friends who'd been to the army had advised me to add a couple of essentials to the shopping list, and so it was that Kimberly and I found ourselves shopping for several metres of a small-link, rust-proof metal chain with an accompanying combination lock for stringing through washing to prevent it from being stolen off the line, and a space blanket which was a thin heat-retaining fibre blanket, covered on one side by a durable silver foil and designed to keep one warm in icy conditions. We picked up a tin of spray-on starch for moulding and ironing clothing and – believe it or not – the corners of your bed! Also to be procured were three toothbrushes (one for cleaning teeth, one for cleaning my rifle and one for cleaning toilets), several large tins of dark-brown boot polish, shoe brushes and ladies nylon pantyhose for buffing boots (or perhaps as a last resort, for hanging oneself), methylated spirits for hardening my feet, washing powder, clothes pegs, Brasso, Cobra wax floor polish, Q20 all-purpose lubricant spray, a steam-iron, a flashlight and lots of stationery.

As I packed all these things and prepared to go, my mother presented me with a food parcel of cookies and fudge. Kimberly also gave me a parcel of high-energy candy and sweets. I nestled these loving gifts amongst the required paraphernalia and thought about how much I would miss home.

"Twenty-five thousand troops will be mobilised for national service by January," the news reader announced over footage from the previous year showing girlfriends and wives running alongside trains, waving goodbye to their departing loved-ones. The SADF carried out two intakes of troops each year, one in January and one in July. Now in early January, the newspapers were carrying similar pictures of recruits gathering at train stations country-wide to be transported to army, navy and air force camps. Even the radio stations broadcast special tributes to national servicemen, and Springbok Radio had an established weekend afternoon programme called "Forces Favourites", hosted by that grand dame of radio, the *Bosmoedertjie* Esmé Everard, which broadcast messages to the *troepe* – often from girlfriends – along with special requests and dedications. Much of the music was possibly the worst music ever, and patriotic enough to cause severe depression. Popular choices that year were *The Longest Day* by Paul Anka, Sonja Herholdt's evergreen *Ek Verlang Na Jou* ("I Miss You"), Rina Hugo's fairly recent *Troepie Doepie*, which sang longingly about a beloved away in the army, and the soon to be smash hit (but actually despised by army guys) 1986 song, *You're In The Army Now*, by Status Quo.

Barely two days into our national service, it became obvious that many new recruits were quitting. Quite aside from those who had been legitimately discharged following their medicals, some of the guys were taking leave on rather more dubious grounds, having discovered that they were simply not cut out for this form of human behavioural exploitation. Within a week a few of the guys had bailed out due to over-exertion and heat-stroke – especially one or two generously-proportioned blokes. Many a time we were ordered to carry a *troep*'s kit back to the quartermaster's stores after they had been whisked away unseen, never to be heard of again. Some possibly became instant G5s, or worse, were sent off to other SAI camps where their lives would become a nightmare far worse than Infantry School. Other strange geek-types who had studied rare varieties of physics or chemistry were spirited away – I surmised that their special type of qualifications had been identified by the army as useful to some dastardly scheme being developed in a dark laboratory in a secret location.

These personnel changes aside, our platoon soon settled into a fairly constant configuration and we became more comfortable with each other's company. Out of forty-five men, just five of us were English-speaking. Sticking together, perhaps out of a sense of self-preservation, it was an advantage that we did actually get on well. Kerry Pile could have been the face of the South African infantry soldier over which the chicks would have swooned: he had a thatch of white hair and golden-boy good looks. His fair complexion meant that the slightest heat or embarrassment caused his face to flush blood-red. It was Kerry who first introduced me to the music of Mike and The Mechanics. Miles Sowden was a nerd-deluxe who gave the impression of being a bit dozy. We all thought he'd be one of the first to leave Infantry School, but he turned out to be gutsier than most of us. He did not respond to the nickname "Oink".

Ian and I became quite friendly with some of the tame Dutchmen in our platoon, especially Eugene Gouws who hailed from Port Elizabeth and introduced us to much of the latest music that year and from the recent past: Brian Adams and Chris de Burgh, among others. Gouws gave the impression of being a *vaakseun*, or dozy boy, appearing as if he was fairly laid-back, but he was actually easily stressed.

Johan Zaayman was another tame Dutchman I got on well with. He was from the Cape and spoke excellent English with hardly an accent. His father had been an ambassador and Zaayman had lived some years overseas. Johan Strydom was a friendly guy who reminded me of my mate Adi Fourie in one of the other platoons. They looked so similar, I sometimes confused them.

A Dutchman tending towards tame who was to make quite an impression on all of us was Danie van Schalkwyk, or "Schalle" as he came to be known. A dozy boy who must have weighed over 120 kilograms when he arrived, Schalle was down to a hundred kilograms within six weeks, and by the end of the year he was fit and lean, becoming a default light machine gun carrier. Despised by many of the other Afrikaners because of his size, Schalle had guts, and his courage soon had all us English guys rooting for him.

Christiaan Hay was a Dutchman, bordering on tame Dutchman, despite his very Scottish-sounding surname. I found him to be intellectually shrewd and I enjoyed his conversation. Another tame Dutchman with a very Welsh-sounding surname was Deon Davis, whose almost effeminate lisp drew disapproving looks from the other Dutchmen.

Lourens Erasmus was the likeable, unassuming giant of the platoon, but he preferred to keep to himself. Stefanus Botha from Port Elizabeth was the platoon story-teller, recounting tales of the absurd in a thickly Afrikaans accent. Although I enjoyed listening to his yarns, I never quite felt that I could trust him. His big mate was Adriaan Graham, a heavy Dutchman despite his very English-sounding surname. He was lean and sinewy and would glare at one with a steely blue-eyed intensity.

Kevin Fourie and Johan Rossouw were firm friends. Both appeared to me to be slightly effeminate, Fourie was given to mood swings and Rossouw was the pretty-boy of the platoon. Rossouw would sometimes wear his army kit like women's clothes – donning a blonde wig and sporting red lipstick (why he had these accoutrements was anyone's guess), wearing nylon stockings and a black dustbin bag for a dress, and brandishing a pointer as a "naughty boy's cane", he would mince up and down the passageways to entertain us. But his antics were not always appreciated by some of the heavy Dutchmen, who regarded him as an embarrassment to the Afrikaner nation.

A couple of the Dutchmen were real *plaasjapies* (country bumpkins), like Johan Gouws, a quirky, unsophisticated chap, who reminded me of a clown but was harmless and goofy. Anton Maas, who I would get to know better after Infantry School, was another *plaasjapie* and had a thick Malmesbury brei that was hard for even the Afrikaners to understand.

A bunch of the Dutchmen seemed to us to be made for the army, like Wikus Gresse and his buddy Jaco Lourens.

Some guys I didn't really get along with and mostly tried to avoid, like Willem Loubser, who had a persistently forlorn expression, and Otto van der Spuy, who was dismissive and temperamental and only ever looked out for number one. Many other Afrikaners, all with their own peculiar mannerisms and interesting personalities, made up the rest of the platoon.

That first week was like existing in a flurried haze – a daze of confusion in organised chaos. I could barely keep track of the blur that beset me: get up early, shit, shave, shower and dress; lock your steel cupboard; *"TREE AAN!"* ("FALL IN!" – the command we heard more than any other that year); Muster in a platoon outside the bungalow; Muster as a company before the barracks; Roll Call; march; eat; Muster; hurry up and wait; undertake a task; drill instruction, smoke and drink water; eat again – quickly but not wolfing food down, in case one puked; short break; Muster; march; drill instruction, smoke and drink water; march here-there-and-everywhere; more drill instruction, smoke and drink water; clean up; Muster; Roll Call; march all over Infantry School; eat; chat to other recruits; prepare for inspection; sleep a while and get rudely woken once more ... only to begin all over again.

That first Sunday, while on parade, we were told where the gathering points for the assortment of religious groups were. Most groups were dotted around at various points next to the parade ground, some with tents. We were told to assemble in groups according to our religious persuasions and faiths. As they called out the *Nederduitse Gereformeerdes*, or Dutch Reformed, most of the Afrikaans recruits on parade kicked up dust as they hurried off to the large gathering of the official religion of the SADF, for the NGK service.

Another large bunch of recruits went off to the *Hervormdes*, the off-shoot of the more conservative Dutch Reformed Church, followed by the *Apostolies* or Apostolics. The senior NCO calling out the denominations and directing their followers then called out, "Church of the Antichrist or Roman Catholics!" following this up with, *"Moeder Maria roep; sy wag vir julle!"* or "Mother Mary's calling; she's waiting for you lot!" The Roman Catholics made their way off in the direction he pointed with glowering looks. Then the Anglicans were called.

Soon there were very few of us recruits left on the Parade Ground. I knew that the last few churches – including but not limited to the Baptists, Methodists and Presbyterians – were regarded as being part of the so-called "Free Churches" and were seen to be much the same thing. If there wasn't a formal service for the church you belonged to, you were expected to fall in with one of the others. I went off with the Methodists.

Anyone who claimed to be agnostic or atheist was given a tongue-lashing of note, while simultaneously being interrogated, perhaps to establish his mental state. These "heathens" were given another chance to "become" religious, and there wasn't a single recruit that didn't quickly take on some or other faith. No faith other than those that were regarded as Christian, whether wholly or marginally, were tolerated.

That morning, religious instruction in the larger Christian denominations was delivered in the camp by army chaplains. Smaller congregations or those churches not commonly represented received instruction from civilian pastors. On future Sundays, we were told, we would be expected to dress up smartly in our browns in order to leave the camp to attend services at churches in town.

After attending a dull and poorly-attended Methodist service in camp that first Sunday morning, I opted to attend future Anglican services held in town. This gave me the chance to leave camp for a while and be amongst a group of recruits I was becoming friendly with.

Once the Sabbath routine had settled, Sundays began to feel different to the other days of the week. Around 06h00, whoever was on platoon duty that day would go down to the mess hall kitchen to collect coffee, Milo and rusks for us all. Platoon duty was mostly done in pairs, the ones nominally in charge of a platoon or a bungalow on any given day were referred to as *Peleton Piele* or Bungalow Bills, usually being responsible for locking the bungalows, calling the other recruits to attention and making sure we were ready for inspection.

After helping ourselves to an early morning drink in our fire-buckets, we would all return to our beds for a bit of a Sunday morning lie-in and a chat. By 07h00 we were all up and dressed and ready for church parade. By the end of the second week we had the option to also attend evening services. Initially I attended both morning and evening services, for a brief respite from the claustrophobia of the base.

That first Sunday, our lunch was a delicious roast with rice, potatoes and veggies, followed by custard and tinned fruit for pudding, with the ever-present piles of bread and jugs of cold drinks cluttering the tables. Sunday lunches soon became something to look forward to, and with the prospect of a scrumptious meal at midday, the most arduous task of a Sunday was to attend church parade on time. Church parade over, the rest of the Sunday was time to ourselves, and even the ranks left us alone to do our washing and ironing and prepare our kit for the week at our leisure, neither hounded nor harassed.

On my return in the dark from that first Anglican evening service in town, I saw that the Infantryman was lit up from around its base by several red spotlights. It looked grotesque. For the life of me, I couldn't understand why Infantry School had chosen red? Was this perhaps for traffic control purposes? Surely white spotlights, normally used for illumination, would have been more appropriate? But red! One couldn't help thinking of blood. For all of 1986, this ominous statue and all it represented would preside over my fate, along with hundreds of others.

Even as I faced the start of my second week at Infantry School, I had been unable to shake the apprehension. Uneasiness and angst had become constant companions.

Chapter 4

It was in the name of God that the Afrikaners forged their identity. And it was in the name of God that the Afrikaner nation sought actualisation.

In the course of their history, the Afrikaners, or *Boers*, or *Voortrekkers*, have been subjected to prejudice, persecution, exclusion and elimination. Having escaped severe religious oppression from the Roman Catholic Church in the lands of their fathers, in their new land, the Afrikaners faced discrimination, subjugation and extermination at the hands of the British and the butchering of members of their tribe by black Africans on the frontiers.

The Enlightenment swept into the Cape with the British land administrators of the early 1800s, bringing with it an end to slavery. Espousing the language of Reason, the British stripped the *Boers* of their land, their slaves and their livelihood. New laws seemed designed to appease the Xhosa. English was increasingly used as the official language and the meddling missionaries were continually at odds with the *Boers*. The enforced liberal Enlightenment of the British seemed to the Afrikaners to be nothing short of a revolution against God; its proponents, nothing more than charlatans and fools. Angered by these ungodly invaders, the Afrikaners stubbornly resisted interference from outsiders.

In the face of such an onslaught, Afrikaners turned to their God for strength and guidance. *Voortrekkers*, literally "pioneers", made their way northwards and eastwards into Africa from the southern tip in search of material and spiritual independence. A burning desire for land and an insatiable urge for freedom lit their fire.

The going was not smooth. The *Voortrekkers* faced hostility from the Ndebeles, who massacred entire *trekker laagers*, sent large armies to battle the *Boers*, and stole their stock. They were double-crossed by the Zulu king, Dingane, and were repeatedly attacked by Bushmen. A mutual distrust between the Afrikaners and the black people inevitably arose. Surrounded by heathens who could not be trusted or understood, the *Voortrekkers* felt justified in their view of the black man as unteachable: dull-witted adolescents at best, animals in the shape of men at worst. There was a Biblical precedent for such an idea: Jesus himself had made the same judgments, once even calling a Gentile woman a "dog".

With the dreaded Colonialists and their godless ways at their backs, and the savage and unknown ahead, these brave and steadfast trailblazers conquered the wild and strange lands of Africa, overcoming the hostility of the native peoples, privation and disease along the way. A valiant struggle for the survival of the Afrikaner nation was underway. The *Voortrekkers* were indomitable and courageous against overwhelming odds.

The continued survival of this fledgling nation under extreme circumstances led them to believe that they were a people chosen by God, their informally articulated Reformed Theology seemingly affirming this status at every opportunity. As they saw God help and protect them in the course of their exodus, the Afrikaners' confidence soared. Their assurance in God's grace and their status as a chosen people became unshakable. For all their hardship and afflictions, the land affectionately called *Zuid-Afrika* by the Afrikaners was rightfully theirs for the taking, their Promised Land, a gift from God which they would turn into a land of milk and honey by the sweat of their brow and the strength of their inflexible convictions.

The Calvinism of the *Voortrekkers* promoted a nationalism based on their assumption of their separate, unique national identity as created by God. In believing that God had created them as a separate and chosen nation, the *Boer*s compared themselves to the Israelites. In Biblical times, a nation was defined not so much by its political status as by ethnic, geographical and linguistic factors. The Afrikaner nation was shaped by its own language, culture and lifestyle. Standing on the verses in the Bible which specifically forbade God's people to mix with those of other cultures and religions, the Afrikaners avoided the contamination of their people through assimilation and intermarriage. Maintaining their cultural and linguistic purity became a sacred duty. The Afrikaners took all the steps necessary to preserve themselves and their calling, even if it meant violence.

The *laager* of the Battle of Blood River, the circular formation of wagons which became the Afrikaner's means of survival in the face of the heathen and incomprehensible natives of the unexplored lands, was, in time, imitated in the *Voortrekkers'* psyche. The *laager*, or wagon fortress, became symbolic of *Boer* solidarity, and of their assurance that God would keep them safe against overwhelming odds, if only they would be faithful to Him and rally to the aid of one another. A "*laager* mentality" began to emerge amongst the Afrikaners, by which the Afrikaner nation closed ranks in crisis and protected their own unquestioningly.

Incited by religious fervour and fortified by God's support, the Afrikaner refused to be a victim, standing firm for what he believed in and risking his life to defend his people, all the while certain of the support and protection of his kin. The identity of the Afrikaner was threatened by outsiders, and the Afrikaner did not believe in showing mercy towards the enemy.

As the foundations of the Afrikaans Calvinist religion were consolidated and the tenets of what was to become the *Nederlandse Gereformeerde Kerk* (NGK) took hold, the *Boers* were at pains to distance themselves from the newly "enlightened" Dutch Reformed Church, which was seen to be corrupting the Biblical faith. The *Boers* were equally eager to set themselves apart from the Church in the Cape, which they viewed with a deep mistrust as an attempt by the British-led Cape Government to regain political control. The slogan which emerged to capture the spirit of the new church's standpoint is revealing: "Separation is Strength!"

Between the maturing *Boer* religion and the *laager* mentality of the *Voortrekkers*, "Separation is Strength" was first a psychological attitude and later a political imperative. As the *Boers* responded to their persecution and the danger they faced from every side, the foundations were laid for the establishment of Apartheid. The Afrikaners were doing what they always did, what anyone would do: the Afrikaners were defending their own. If a stranger came into your house and tried to kill your family, would you not defend your family with your life?

Chapter 5

In 1963, the year I was born, South Africa under the Nationalist Government was witnessing the unfolding of the Rivonia Trial. Nelson Mandela and his co-accused were before the court, defending their lives against various charges of terrorism and attempting to overthrow the government. The Afrikaner government was simultaneously and progressively stamping its authority on all facets of society to entrench its philosophies and aims.

It was the sixties, an era marked by vast political and social upheaval across the globe. The United States' war in Vietnam had dragged on for decades: the blood of two million Vietnamese civilians darkening the soil of the Southeast Asian land and tarnishing America's reputation globally. In Africa, no fewer than thirty-three of the continent's countries shrugged off the fetters of their European colonial masters and declared their independence.

In South Africa, it was the decade in which the South African government, under Hendrik Verwoerd, stepped up the laws enforcing segregation, his separate development approach of "good neighbourliness" being adopted in mapping out the principles by which nine ethnic groups of native South Africans would come to be classified and subsequently banished to Bantustans or "homelands".

On 21 March 1960, the PAC led a protest in which a large crowd of black civilians gave themselves up for arrest for not carrying their passbooks. The small contingent of white policemen, many barely out of boyhood, were petrified by the menacing and advancing crowd of over twenty thousand that had gathered, many throwing stones. The policemen opened fire on the protesters, killing sixty-nine and wounding almost two hundred people. The event came to be known as the Sharpeville Massacre and sparked outrage around the world. Waves of protests and riots followed the incident, leading to the government imposing a state of emergency and detaining thousands of people.

Undeterred by rising tensions, on 31 May 1961, South Africa severed its colonial ties with the Commonwealth and declared herself a Republic. Pardonable beliefs on the part of the Afrikaners based on their distant past had been replaced by a blind, subjective, nationalist faith. Any moral high ground the Afrikaners could have laid claim to from their pioneering *Voortrekker* days became tainted. The Afrikaners, led by their Nationalist Government, instituted Apartheid as a means to cement white minority rule. The seeds that would herald the beginning of the end of the Afrikaners' right to sovereignty were planted.

At the hands of God's chosen white African nation, persecution of black South Africans escalated. The Afrikaner government, supported by the National Party, claimed its actions to be taken in the name of God. With typical bully-mentality, the abuse the Afrikaners had endured became their excuse to abuse others.

On 16 June 1976, an estimated twenty thousand high school students gathered in Soweto to protest the institution of Afrikaans as the medium of instruction in their schools. Although the uprising addressed the symptom of Bantu education, it had at its heart the struggle for liberation. When stones were thrown from the protesters, police responded with teargas and live bullets, resulting in hundreds of deaths and injuries.

In 1977, when I was just thirteen and embarking on my high school career, the Nationalist Government extended compulsory national service for white South African males from one year to two. The upshot of a carefully devised pro-military marketing crusade, this development coincided with a well-orchestrated spin-doctoring of their obsequious lies and deception and the acceleration of their disinformation campaign against banned political organisations such as the ANC, AZAPO and the PAC. The war had just escalated.

In my adolescence I felt a mixture of political and apolitical ambivalence towards national service. I knew that English-speaking South Africans, whether right or wrong, viewed the Afrikaners as a white minority nation seeking to assert and maintain their nationalist power and privilege in the face of what they perceived to be threats to their sovereignty. They weren't going to let a bunch of terrorists, and communists to boot, take their hard-fought-for country away from them – no way! To hell with the fact that the world saw Apartheid as wrong. The liberal Western world's support for those so-called "freedom fighters" was totally misplaced. How could they be so stupid?

The SADF, by extension, was nothing short of the show of the Nationalists' military might.

For most *verligte* or moderate Afrikaners and many English-speaking white South Africans, national service was seen as something akin to a rite of passage into manhood, as well as a case of doing your bit for your country. But they weren't entirely convinced that conscription was right. I was inclined to agree with my fellow English South Africans that the conscription of all young white men into the SADF for the purposes of upholding the Afrikaans nationalist regime was a heavy-handed and bullying tactic.

Few Afrikaans men in my position suffered the same ambivalence towards conscription. Staunch Afrikaner families took pride in their every male child heeding the call and fulfilling his duty to his country. *Diensplig vir Volk en Vaderland* (service to the Nation and the Fatherland) was every boy's obligation and believed to make a man of you. The young men who bravely and willingly took up arms in defence of their people were revered, and this mindset ensured that they seldom tried to worm their way out of their patriotic duty. These young Afrikaner men and their families blindly believed the Nationalist Government's rhetoric which stressed the ever-looming threat of the *rooi gevaar*, communism, and the *swart gevaar*, Black Nationalism.

The ordinary Afrikaner was bombarded with government-sanctioned propaganda, much of it disseminated through their dominant conservative church, the *Nederduitse Gereformeerde Kerk* or NGK, and state-controlled media. In particular, the Bible was interpreted to serve the nationalists' own ends. Apartheid South Africa was governed with a potent blend of nationalism and theocracy.

But I saw a vein of truth coursing through much of the anti-communist rhetoric as purveyed by the Apartheid government. The world was in the thick of the Cold War, and barely a corner of the globe was untouched by the struggle between capitalism and communism. The Soviets – as well as to a lesser extent the Cubans, East Germans, North Koreans, any number of Eastern Bloc countries of the time, and Communist China – were peddling communism throughout many developing or politically destabilised countries around the world. Theirs was a brand of communism designed to meld with most socialist or nationalist ideals, but in reality, merely a means to an end for the Russian super-power. The purpose of their meddling in these vulnerable countries was to create areas of strategic military superiority and get their collectivist hands on valuable natural resources in the hopes of gaining an upper hand over the West.

Africa was a well-positioned collection of susceptible countries, a potentially valuable pawn in Russia's Cold War manoeuvrings. Most African states were either trying to come to grips with the withdrawal of their colonial masters or ruled by tin-pot dictators and megalomaniac criminals, where the powerful lived in extreme opulence at the expense of the impoverished masses – a fact that remains true even today. Because of the inherent instability in almost every African state, along with the ever-present cronyism, nepotism, corruption, greed, factional fighting, politically-motivated murders and genocides that plagued the continent, Africa was riper than ever for the communist plucking.

But, despite all this, the South African Nationalist Government could not escape the fact that their own fabrications and disinformation strategies were packaged to ultimately support minority white rule at the expense of political and economic freedom of the majority. South Africa was a police state with all arms of the state being used to quash resistance.

In reality, a white male school-leaver had only three options open to him. First, he could report for national service on completing school, when he was seventeen or eighteen years old, and after two years he could return to his life to begin his studies or begin working.

Second, he could enrol at a tertiary institution, effectively delaying call-up until he had qualified, but two years of national service would still have to be completed.

Third, he could apply for an exemption from national service on medical or religious grounds. Exemptions were granted for genuine medical conditions, but exemptions on religious grounds seldom were. Religious objectors were still "conscripted' and given menial non-combative tasks. Those objectors who refused to support the military even in this way could be given several years of community service, or if they were less fortunate, sent to military prison.

I suppose there were other options. One could always fake insanity or homosexual tendencies. One could indulge in self-mutilation or even attempt suicide – taking care that one failed in the attempt, of course, if one wasn't to defeat the purpose of the act. I could have done any of these things to escape national service, but the benefit didn't seem equal to the sacrifice.

A real fourth option did, in fact, exist for school-leavers and graduates facing conscription. Some lily-livered cowards simply sneaked out of the country. I can only assume that these were rich kids from affluent and well-connected families. Skipping the country wasn't really an option for most of us, even if we weren't comfortable with the idea of being in the army. The draft-dodgers were despised by those who accepted their fate. I know I despised them.

During my time in the army, it was believed by many of my contemporaries that the members of the End Conscription Campaign worked underground to smuggle these draft-dodgers out of the country. Perhaps that is why many strident supporters of national service harboured resentment towards campaign-members, even years after they had completed their national service. I find it interesting that, to this day, the "liberators" of South Africa have never recognised a single End Conscription Campaign member that refused to do their national service on the grounds that it was unjust to comply with the SADF against their fellow countrymen.

But escape the country or go underground were the only options for those who genuinely objected to defending Apartheid. The penalties borne by captured objectors were harsh: incarceration, possible torture, "accidental" death while imprisoned. Politically-motivated murders were often passed off as accidental deaths or suicides. Those who refused to submit to national service on political grounds were sentenced to as much as three years of hard labour within the military penal system. Extreme cases saw objectors subjected to up to six years of incarceration with hard labour.

Objectors in military prison were forced to wear bright prison overalls and red helmets. Singled out and lit up like Christmas trees in their garish uniforms, they became an open target for mental and physical abuse at the hands of government-sanctioned psychopaths in military boots with IQs equal to their boot size. That thought was far more frightening than the stories the *oumanne* used to tell.

Objectors were depicted as traitors, adherents to causes such as the End Conscription Campaign were branded as communists. The government propaganda machine was effective.

On receiving our call-up papers, most of us had little idea of what to expect. All I knew was that I had to report for duty.

I was in a dilemma, as I had been for most of my life. Us English-speaking South Africans had a reputation for being more liberal than the Afrikaners – at least on the surface. Let's be honest, we were content to benefit from Apartheid as much as any white person in the country at the time. But I came from a relatively conservative background. Having grown up in *verkrampte* Pretoria, matriculating from an English-medium school that was nevertheless as steadfastly traditionalist as any South African government school of the era, I went into one of the most liberal tertiary education institutions in the country. I was trying to work out what I supported and what I abhorred. I certainly didn't espouse the ideologies of the Afrikaner-led

Nationalist Government. But I hardly advocated the possibility of communism or Black Nationalism either. A truly multi-racial, democratically elected future government seemed to me a far-fetched ideal. I knew that a "one man, one vote" democracy would threaten whites who, at the time, were outnumbered in the country at a rate of about seven to one. A true Westminster- or American-styled democracy could only marginalise white people entirely. Visions sprang to mind of Zimbabwe's 1980 elections and the inauguration of the brutal "freedom fighter", Robert Mugabe, as president.

In the early eighties, I was sitting in the waiting area of my local barbershop, flicking through a *Scope* magazine. Between the pages of topless beauties sporting stars on their nipples was an article describing the chaos leading up to and following Zimbabwean independence. Included in the story was a description of the slaughter of over twenty thousand Ndebele civilians in Matabeleland at the hands of the Mugabe government's North Korean-trained Fifth Brigade. Innocent men and women had their genitals, lips, ears cut off; babies had been disembowelled alive. Photos of two passenger planes shot down by terrorists – one, two years, one, one year prior to elections – showed dead white passengers, innocent men, women and children, strewn everywhere. Crash survivors, the report detailed, were brutally and heartlessly executed.

Was South Africa doomed to go the same way?

I saw Britain and America as the biggest sell-outs of the disaster that was Zimbabwe. Britain was Rhodesia's colonial master, America was the avaricious Western super-power bully. Other Western countries – Canada, Denmark, Ireland, Norway, Sweden, there were many – seemed to suffer from the same bleeding-heart liberal, save-the-world-and-the-black-man-from-those-evil-whites syndrome, offering exile, refuge, funding and support to the banned freedom fighters. They despised the Afrikaners and the other whites who propped up Apartheid in South Africa. How dare those whites display such insolence, snubbing their noses at the liberal Western world?

In the background the predatory and rapacious communists were yapping: providing weapons and support to those terrorists who cared so little about human life.

The possibility of the Nationalist Government's capitulation to the ANC was inconceivable to most white South Africans as the eighties reached their midpoint. It was beyond their powers of imagination to envisage that control should literally be handed over to the ANC like the passing of a baton in a relay-race. Those whites, so safely ensconced in their Apartheid ivory towers, could not have known that things would come to a head and the country would face the possibility of a full-blown civil war. They could not have known that the powers-that-be would come to realise that the potential for a bloody street-pitched conflict should be avoided at all costs.

As I contemplated my looming national service, I could never have guessed that Nelson Mandela would be released from prison in 1990, slowing the increase of violent mass action countrywide and putting an end to increasingly punitive sanctions. I could not have known that the rapidly imploding Soviet Union at the turn of the decade would lead to the demise of its brand of communism worldwide and bring an end to the Cold War in 1991. In the space of half a decade, the country and the world were to undergo seismic shifts that resulted in what would amount to an entirely new political landscape, and I, like most of my fellow white South Africans, did not have the power to foresee any of it.

In 1992, following the realisation that the government's Total Strategy campaign had come to nought and given that the Soviet threat was dead, white South Africans voted by a vast majority in support of negotiated reforms initiated by FW de Klerk's cabinet. This was the beginning of the dismantling of Apartheid, and the events that would lead to the pariah nation of South Africa being welcomed back from the political wilderness onto the international political stage.

Had I been gifted with the ability to foresee the future somehow, I would have seen South Africans – both black and white – embracing the possibility of genuine reconciliation and meaningful change with quiet optimism in the early nineties. I also would have seen this hopeful anticipation scuppered when the negotiated settlement led to the installing of an ersatz constitutional democracy in 1994. Looking further into the murky depths of the future, I would have encountered the symptoms of an ever-worsening economic war in which the autocratic ruling party – the erstwhile "freedom fighters" of the ANC – would, with a cavalier disposition borne out of a "lie and deny" attitude, bleed the "haves" through a myriad of laws and taxes, supposedly to support the "have-nots", but in reality accomplishing nothing but their own self-enrichment. Who could have believed that the "new" South Africa would descend into large-scale and rampant crime and violence, much of it resulting from the year-on-year increase in unemployment?

Almost two decades later, the oft-touted "Rainbow Nation" of the new South Africa would seldom be spoken of anymore. The euphoria and goodwill that accompanied the country's metamorphosis would have all but evaporated, replaced by an ever-widening chasm of mistrust and self-imposed separation between her citizens. The government's antagonism towards its own people will have made many white folk feel like exiles in their own land, while the vast majority of the black population would remain languishing in grinding poverty, economically and politically marginalised.

I wonder now what my thoughts would have been as I gazed into the future. Would my thoughts have turned to the age-old philosophy that suggests that people who take a rebel as their king will reap their just desserts? Would I have been able to draw the correspondence between power and privilege running amok and the inevitable chaos, cronyism, nepotism, corruption, greed, incompetence, politically-motivated murders and the like that follows? Would I conclude that the country got the government it deserved?

But I get ahead of myself. None of this could have occurred to me as I contemplated my upcoming national service.

Even if I had truly believed in the potential for some semblance of democracy in the country, if I had chosen to actively engage in support of such a pending democracy, evading conscription would have required of me that I disappear underground or run away overseas. I was born and raised in South Africa. I loved my country. My life was blooming here in the soil of the land, and I couldn't imagine letting everything that meant so much to me go for half a life as a ghost underground or a whole new life as an exile in a foreign land. I suppose my choice finally boiled down to self-interest: Which course of action would secure my own well-being, benefit my own future, best? Which of the options open to me did I consider the least of all possible evils? My decision came to me clearly: I would do my two years of national service. Some would argue that self-preservation is the coward's way out.

Chapter 6

I heard it so many times: "You're in the army now!" Basic training, commonly referred to as "basics", was said to be the worst part of any recruit's national service, sarcastically described by those who'd done it as "The best part of your life you don't want to relive." The SADF's philosophy of basics was to break the recruit down so that they could rebuild him to their requirements.

In all other SAI camps, basic training was seen as nothing but an extended *rondfok* and *uitkak*, mindless physical and mental abuse during which recruits were purposely roughed up and tormented. Luckily for me, Infantry School's approach to basics was marginally gentler and a little more respectful than elsewhere in the army.

Don't get me wrong, Infantry School was in no way more tolerant of non-compliance than elsewhere in the SADF. Like SAI camps everywhere, anyone who dared to challenge the system was singled out for punishment. The establishment was itching for a recruit to give them a reason to victimise him, and staying under the radar was your best strategy for avoiding being picked on – at the very least it ensured that the ranks would be hard-pressed for any real reason to have it in for you – but it was still no guarantee that you could avoid their unwanted attention.

At Infantry School, we were better informed about our training than our counterparts at SAI camps elsewhere. Once basics started, we could be sure that by the end of the week, we mostly knew the programme for the following week: the type of training, what it would entail, how long it would take and what kind of evaluation to expect. Towards the end of each training phase, we were briefed on the next phase. But, frustratingly, we were kept in the dark as to when passes would be given.

Upcoming passes were used as leverage to sharpen us up and improve our standard of conduct, but in time we knew that Bravo was not as petty as many of the other companies at Infantry School, and certainly not as most other SAI camps, where a pass might well have been cancelled had the guys not shaped up. Threats about cancelled passes were mostly empty, and Bravo's ranks actually had a policy of giving extra time off added to a pass when an individual performed particularly well.

In the first few weeks, mostly late January and early February, many Bravo recruits had to write supplementary exams at their colleges or varsities if they had only just failed their previous year's exam. This policy was allowed by Infantry School, as they would generally not tolerate candidate officers on the course who had not or would not be graduating academically. Many who failed their supplementary exams or who were found to have failed their exams without being able to do any "supp" were sent away from Infantry School to other SAI camps around the country.

I don't know what the criteria was for keeping on a recruit who was not a graduate, but it appeared that if he made it through the Junior Leaders course, he would stay a one-pipper or one-star second-lieutenant throughout his two-year national service. These supplementary writers were envied, because they would be away for several days, which counted as a pass among the rest of us.

Music has always been such an integral part of my life. In my adolescent years, I had a taste for the underground sounds of Bad Company, Golden Earring, Led Zeppelin and Nazareth – music less accepted by the more conservative English-speakers and mostly detested by Afrikaners and my parents. The music I listened to then is like a soundtrack to my youth, and just a few bars of Robert Plant's distinctive vocals over the driving guitar of *Whole Lotta Love* has the ability to conjure up intense memories of the time. Although my musical preferences lent towards the less conventional, such as Foghat and Jo Jo Zep & The Falcons, and the more mainstream sounds of Dire Straits, Foreigner, Men At Work, Queen and their ilk were also part of my playlists growing up, and are equally wrapped into my memory bank, woven into the five-threaded tapestry of remembrance side-by-side with other senses: the smell of Everysun after-sun lotion, the way flip-flops feel between the toes, the musky flavour of Chappies.

My memories of the year at Infantry School are set to the soundtrack of Bryan Adams' 1984 album *Reckless*, which became something of a theme for the guys in my platoon. Eugene Gouws had introduced us to the album, and *She's Only Happy When She's Dancin'*, *Run To You* and *Summer Of '69* were often heard echoing around Bungalow 7 on a Sunday afternoon as we ironed our browns or while we polished the passage floor with vigour in the evenings. Like young men everywhere, we sang along as Bryan Adams belted out *Kids Wanna Rock*, and paused in buffing the floor to play air guitar solos with enthusiasm. I particularly loved the spirited track *Run To You*, which made me think of Kimberly, and the ballad *Heaven*, which was haunting and emotional and made me long to hold her in my arms.

It was a common SAI practice, and we were not spared: our 05h00 start to the morning became progressively earlier as each week passed. Things were moving up a gear. Corporals Joubert and Potgieter would give us a rude awakening by entering the barracks and bashing their open hands against the grey steel cupboards, bellowing, *"STAAN OP, rowers!"* meaning *"GET UP, recruits!"* Slow risers had their beds lifted up and dropped with force. From time to time they threatened to upend beds to leave the occupants sprawled on the floor. On rare occasions they blew whistles.

Within forty-five minutes we had to be shaved, showered and dressed in our brown training overalls and boots. If you didn't race to the ablutions fast enough, you had to wait in line, and being at the back of the queue meant you'd have a cold shave and shower. We soon worked out our own time-saving tactics, but this didn't prevent some guys having cold showers each day.

Our weekdays mostly looked like this:

05h00 - 05h45 Reveille, wash and shave
05h45 - 06h15 Breakfast
06h15 - 06h45 Prepare for Platoon Inspection
06h45 - 07h15 Platoon Inspection
07h15 - 07h45 Platoon Administration and Sick-report
07h45 - 08h00 Prayer Parade
08h00 - 10h00 Drilling Instruction
10h00 - 10h20 Tea
10h20 - 12h00 Lectures / Lessons
12h00 - 12h45 Lunch
12h45 - 16h00 Lectures / Lessons
16h00 - 16h45 Physical Training
16h45 - 17h00 Post Parade
17h00 - 18h00 Supper
18h00 - 21h00 Free Time, sometimes Night Training / Manoeuvres or Lectures / Lessons
21h00 - 21h15 Muster / Call-over
21h15 - 22h00 Free Time, mostly spent preparing for the following day's activities
22h00 - 22h15 Quiet Time
22h15 - 05h00 Lights Out

Inspections could be superficial or detailed. Outside our bungalow before breakfast, the corporals would carry out a cursory inspection to assess how we appeared as a group. We had to all look the same, regardless of the weather, so if most of the guys had their sleeves rolled up, we all had to do the same. Sometimes the corporals decided on how uniform we should be. Similarly, before Bravo assembled on the parade ground, there was frantic coordinating amongst us to decide what to wear and how to wear it. Sometimes, as a form of punishment, if one person was wearing a bush jacket, we were all made to wear bush jackets, or if one person was wearing a sweater, then everyone had to.

After breakfast, we would prepare for the more rigorous inspection, which checked our personal appearance, the state of our kit and rooms, and finally the inside and outside of the bungalow. We spent half an hour doing the last of the cleaning and polishing and making sure everything was in order before the corporals arrived promptly at 06h45 for platoon inspection. Joubert would shout, *"Maak gereed vir inspeksie! Staan by jou bed!"* ("Prepare for inspection! Stand at your bed!") and we would bustle to finish preparations and take our positions. *"AAANDAG!"* would follow to call the platoon to attention as the loot entered. Even after the loot had entered the bungalow, we would scurry about, hearts pumping, to attend to the last details we hoped could be the difference between passing the inspection and getting an *oppie*.

An *opfok*, sometimes called an *oppie* or an *afkak parade* by the corporals, was the meting out of physical punishment in response to a contravention of procedure or any other offence committed by a *troep*. In the case of inspections, it usually lasted the duration of the inspection, and sometimes beyond.

As time went on, the inspections became more exacting. The degree to which we were expected to conform to an endless inventory of seemingly mindless minutiae of precision and neatness was extraordinary. There's a saying in the army: "If it moves, salute it, if it doesn't, polish it." Everything had to be just-so and uniform.

The sheets and grey blankets covering our mattresses had to be made perfectly flat, a feat which could be hard to achieve because the steel lattice of the bed frames sagged with age and the mattresses sank forlornly in the middle. As punishment for a recruit's "boat-bed", he would be made to get into it and "row" before being served with an *opfok*.

To overcome the beds' sagging middles, we initially kicked the metal slats of the bed frames' undersides back into place before making the beds, but this robbed us of time to complete the crucial finishing touches to our kit and the rest of the bungalow. We eventually discovered that we could prop the mattress up where it was too low by putting clothes pegs between it and the bed frame.

Not once did we have to "shave" our beds, a method I had heard recruits at other SAI camps were expected to employ, which involved the use of shaving cream to achieve the near-flawless square edges and corners of the made-up bed. This practice was strictly forbidden at Infantry School, but square edges were expected nonetheless.

With so much attention being placed on the neatness of our beds, it took us an age to prepare them every morning. Those recruits that were slower or less risk-averse took to preparing their beds the night before and sleeping on the floor, but this was also forbidden, and the corporals carried out spot raids in the dead of night to catch the floor-sleepers in the act. The punishment for gyppoing the bed-making routine took on various forms, not all of which were exacted immediately. Eventually, some of us rose half an hour earlier to put our beds together by the light of shielded torch beams, because switching the lights on early was also not allowed.

I took to sleeping on any extra bed that became available in my room, and there were a couple as recruits dropped out, but this good fortune didn't last for long as our bungalow was periodically rearranged to prevent the use of open beds. Towards the end of basics, when Lieutenant Pretorius said he wasn't going to use his admin room anymore, Ian and I jumped at the chance to move in there. It could only accommodate two recruits.

Part of army life at Infantry School was having black and coloured "servants" to launder our bed sheets weekly, and every Thursday we would go down to the quartermaster's storehouse to exchange our soiled bed linen for fresh sheets. On laundry day and when we went on pass we made up *swart* beds, "black" beds, by neatly covering our mattresses with just a blanket.

Each recruit's *kas* stood against the wall opposite his bed. The *kas* was a grey metal cupboard with two swing doors which opened from the centre to reveal shelves on the left and hanger space on the right. For the purposes of inspections, each shelf had to contain certain items in order, a system referred to as *inspeksiekas*. In the centre of the top shelf we had to display one *pakkie*, or pack, of browns – summer shirt on top, winter shirt in the middle and brown combat pants below. The shirts were to be folded precisely so that the exposed edge was flat and exactly the width of a button, with the second button appearing in the middle, successfully achieved by using starch and an iron. The shelf below contained a brown PT vest, a brown PT tee-shirt, black

PT shorts, underpants and socks. On the third shelf was placed our dixie and cup, shaving gear, toothbrush and toothpaste, and the bottom shelf contained boot polish, buffer and cleaning cloths. In the right-hand section of the *kas*, the extra training overall, bush jacket and other nutria clothing all had to hang at a slight angle, spaced equally apart on coat hangers, facing the same direction, with sleeves all turned to one side, and our clean PT *tekkies* and extra boots filled the space below. Both pairs of boots had to be shined to a mirror finish, only achieved by carefully applying dark brown polish and spit to the leather, buffing gently in small circles using a fine cloth or old nylon stockings, and finally ironing!

Once our rifles had been issued, these would be kept in the *kas* below the hanging space. For inspection, it would be removed and placed across the bed, near the foot.

To find shortcuts around this gruelling regimen, many of us became ingenious at cutting corners; by necessity gyypoing wherever we could get away with it. All our nutria clothing, such as training overalls and browns, were to be ironed for each inspection, but the recruits quickly learned to use only one set, leaving the duplicates in the *kas* for inspections, temporarily avoiding the added task of preparing them for inspection every night. Browns were only worn on special occasions during basics, anyway, like going to church parade in town. The rest of the time we only wore training overalls. We thought we were very clever when we bought spare clothing so that one set could be permanently set out for inspection, but this worked for only a short while until NCOs got wind of the ploy.

For *uitpakinspeksie*, "unpacked inspection", we had to place our green beret on top of our puffed out pillows, and below, propped against the edge of the pillow, our information card. Next to that, on the large portion of folded-over sheet, was our *pikstel*, uncoupled and with knife, spoon and fork placed in order, vertically and slightly apart, polished until you could see your own reflection.

The recruit's *trommel* stood at the foot of his bed and had to be open at inspection time. It contained the *balsak*, folded and squared-off to make a rectangular box-shape that fitted perfectly into a quarter or third of the space in the *trommel*, usually to the left. To achieve the required squareness to this heavy canvas bag, we used shaving cream and starch, which dried to make it somewhat firm and the edges stand up stiff and straight. On the opposite side to the *balsak* was the extra brown bath towel, covering the rest of the extra clothing and equipment, such as rifle magazines. What few personal items we had were neatly packed into the *balsak* and hidden from view under the towel. On top of this was placed the rifle's *sluitstuk* or firing pin and breech piece mechanism. For security reasons, the firing pin with its breech piece mechanism, or "block", had to be kept separate from the rest of the rifle, which was stored in the *kas*. Both the rifle and breech piece mechanism had separate serial numbers.

We had to be present at all inspections, and if we were suddenly ordered to depart the bungalow, we had to lock our *trommels* and cupboards immediately, secure both rifle and the firing pin with its breech piece. Failure to secure your rifle and especially its key parts could get a recruit kicked off the course. Early on, a number of us were once caught out for not locking our cupboard and *trommels*, leaving our rifles and firing pins with their breech piece mechanisms unsecured. That afternoon after PT we were given our first experience of *gang PT*, or passage PT. Passage PT entailed running up and down the passageway to the shrill call of a whistle, stop-starting in response to the corporal's blows. It was a physically taxing punishment, loud and debilitating in that confined space. And it messed up the floors so that they had to be cleaned extra hard that evening. We learned the hard way that everything must be locked away, and I promised myself that I wouldn't make the same mistake again, but one must be careful when making such vows...

Inspections were individually or collectively failed almost every day with surprising consistency. The words from the corporal were standard: *"So, julle wil nie saamwerk nie ...?"* ("So, you don't want to cooperate ...?") he would say, as he poured the last remnants of water from our water-bottles all over our inspection items, one of the corporals' all-time favourite practices in the beginning. Other hot favourites for tightening the screws on us while we were still raw was checking for dust in the recesses of our cupboards and checking the squareness of our *balsakke*. The potentials for forcing a failure were endless.

Transgression identified, the working-over began. This is how inspections continued for the next couple of months. We would do our best and they would trash our efforts. After each inspection, which was usually not up to standard, we would get the traditional *oppie*.

Somewhere around our third week at Infantry School, Ian was caught out in an inspection. Ian wasn't terribly neat and tried to cut corners wherever he could, and this time they had him fair and square. Corporal Potgieter was delighted to make an example of him. He started by giving Ian push-ups. "How many should I do, corporal?" Ian asked innocently. For a failed inspection, we were usually told to do between thirty and fifty really good ones, depending on the nature of the transgression and the corporal's mood at the time. The corporal delivering the *oppie* would count as the offender performed each push-up, counting slower and slower in order to exert maximum physical stress. If he was in a particularly vindictive mood, or if the recruit was really slacking off, the corporal would intentionally fluff the tallying, repeating numbers two, three or even four times, so that by the time he reached the specified thirty, the sweating recruit had performed fifty or more push-ups.

Corporal Potgieter was not accustomed to brazenness such as Ian's.

"Okay, wise guy, let's see how many you can do!" he said, probably expecting Ian to fold at about seventy or so. Little did he know that Ian had a sublime talent for making PT look effortless. By the time Ian reached a hundred, himself counting each push-up slowly, Corporal Potgieter was looking flummoxed. The recruits standing by began to snicker.

"*Bly stil!*" he shouted at us, and Ian kept on. He had reached number 125 and was still going strong when Lieutenant Pretorius lost patience. He clicked his tongue.

"Let's move it along, corporal!" he shouted at Potgieter. "We're already late for admin and Sick Report." Us *troepe* loved it! English-speakers: 1, platoon-leaders: 0.

Because my platoon's bungalow was closest to the grassed area northwest of the camp, our NCOs devised a means of punishment that was a symphony of movement in two parts. If one of the recruits had transgressed in some way, the rank would say, "*Sien jy daardie boom? Bring my 'n blaar!*" ("Do you see that tree? Bring me a leaf!"). Most often, the returning *troep* would be told, "*Nie daardie blaar nie, die ander een!*" ("Not that leaf, the other one!"), and the out-of-breath recruit would have to turn around and repeat the journey. Several times, when the whole platoon had transgressed, we all had to fetch leaves.

Once, when Ian returned from his leaf-fetching excursion and the corporal – as usual – told him, "*Nie daardie blaar nie, die ander een!*" Ian grinned. "Don't worry, corporal," he opened his other hand to reveal another leaf. "I brought that leaf too!" The NCOs laughed at Ian's joke, but he had to run to the tree twice more as penance. As we all watched Ian run effortlessly to the shrubbed boundary and back, I realised that Ian knew he would be made to pay for his insolence, and this was his way of buying the rest of us a little time to recover. He had outsmarted them again! English-speakers: 2; platoon-leaders: 0.

The second part came later. By this stage we all knew the routine well, and the command was abbreviated to, *"Sien julle daardie boom? Is julle al terug?"* ("Do you lot see that tree? Are you back yet?"), an instruction for us to go and run around whichever tree had been pointed out. No sooner had the last stragglers returned from running around the tree – some of us grabbing a handful of leaves, just in case – than we'd be made to repeat the exercise.

The scrawny trees and shrubs on the camp's boundary began to lose what little foliage they had. As the trees in the area near the last barracks became barer, the NCOs reverted to *"Vat 'n boompie toer!"* ("Take a tree-tour!"), no leaves required. Eventually the NCOs would just say, *"Raak die draad!"* or "Touch the wire!", on which instruction we'd run to the camp's northerly fence, touch it and run back while the corporals leaned against the nearest barracks, nonchalantly picking their finger nails clean with pocket knives.

The NCOs carried little black books, in which they tallied the number of transgressions and failures a recruit racked up. Three strikes and you were reported to the loot, who then gave the corporals permission for a bigger *oppie* and instructions for its implementation. These *opfok* sessions were usually reserved for afternoon PT, and were wryly called "personal coaching" by the NCOs. We realised early on that, regardless of how hard we worked for an inspection, there would always be an *oppie*, for the whole platoon or just a few of us depending on the lootie's or the corporals' mood.

We were soon told about "pinks" – pink forms that were filled in by the loot and placed on a recruit's personal file, detailing his worst transgressions. None of us wanted to get one of these, but it was inevitable that after three minor transgressions or a serious transgression, a recruit would be notified that he was about to receive a pink. No doubt there were many occasions when no pink was actually written up, but the threat was enough to get our full compliance.

We were terrified by the prospect of the monthly inspections from Bravo's company commander, overseen by Sergeant Major Lategaan. Rumour had it that he carried around a Michael Jackson-type white glove for running along the tops of cupboards, along window frames and under bed frames, looking for the smallest specks of dust and booking one and all for a serious company *oppie* when they were discovered.

To begin with, the inspection *oppies* drove everyone to push themselves individually, when the clever thing would have been to act as a team. This only led to more *oppies*, sometimes marked with bouts of puking, until we grudgingly learnt the value of *samewerking*, or teamwork. Slowing down to cover for our sluggish and weaker mates had the added benefit of conserving energy. All *oppie* counter-measure strategies worked for a short while, until they were exposed. The NCOs and looties knew all the tricks, anyway. They'd seen it all before.

It occurred to me that *oppies* were more of a matter of head-games than strength and stamina. Graduate recruits would only allow themselves to be pushed up to a point, and the establishment sought to explore the increment leading to that point, to push the limit. But I think that everyone really knew where the limit was, even if it was an unwritten law of the graduate officers' training programme, and the ranks wouldn't have overstepped the line. To do so would have been counter-productive.

One of Bravo corporals' favourite threats in those first weeks was that they would send us running to the flagpole on Buttkop, a steep, flat-topped kopje behind the shooting range. It was little more than two kilometres from our lines, and looked imposing as it squatted on the landscape. When this threat was delivered, we usually complied with whatever order was given, especially as the run was suggested whenever we were about to go down to the mess hall for a meal.

Only once in that year did I hear of a platoon who had been sent on that run to the top of Buttkop. We encountered the guys on their return, and they were dead-beat, arriving halfway through supper. This got our attention and ensured our obedience in the short-term, but we soon learned the art of distinguishing whether we could push things or if it was time to back off.

Drills and lectures occupied most mornings for the first few months. Corporal Joubert was a fine drill instructor. I cannot recall him making a mistake. Most of us were familiar with drilling from doing cadets at school a few of the guys had even been drill sergeants – but I struggled with the commands which were now delivered almost exclusively in Afrikaans. Under our platoon sergeant's instruction, our school cadet-standard of drilling was taken to a much higher level.

Drilling, the foundation of military discipline everywhere, is the essential feature of army training. Without it, no conventional army would function effectively. When drilling is performed with skill, all limbs and booted feet working in perfect unison, the effect is thrilling.

Joubert's unique style of drilling somehow coaxed a little more out of us. Audibly different to the other drill instructors, he would sound-off like, *'Lik, ak, lik, ak, lik, ak, UUUS!"* which seemed to have the effect of stiffening our bearing just a little more. Corporal Potgieter, on the other hand, lacked passion, commitment or precision in his drilling and snapped at us when we cocked up his ambiguous commands.

My least favourite drilling command was, *"Makeerie … Pas …"* or "Mark … Time …" when we had to stop and march on the spot, an exercise which was often used to cruelly extend the action following this command for inordinate lengths of time. I couldn't wait for, *"Voorwaarts … MARS!"* ("Forward… MARCH!"). Another much-hated command was, *"Loopas … mars!"* ("On the double, quick, MARCH!"). This double-time custom required much effort and endurance.

The drilling sessions at Infantry School reminded me of cadet practice the standard nine and ten boys used to do in high school. Cadets was basically preparing us for life in the army – it was all about drilling, and those who wanted to could take part in shooting practice. I was never crazy about the idea, but every Thursday morning for an hour we were marched up and down between the buildings and on the fields by designated cadet leaders. The cadet squad leaders were enthusiastic about their roles, even wearing brown shirts and shorts for drills. We each had turns to drill the squad, too, but most of us jested more than we drilled, provoking the "brown shorts" to squeal on us and drawing ire from the male teachers and principal. Stefan and I used the opportunity to look out for the hottest chicks in school and see if they were watching us from the balconies. That's when I first spotted Carolyn and suggested to Stefan that he make a move on her.

We also did bomb, fire and gunfire drills at school. The bell would ring in a certain way to indicate that a drill had begun and which procedure was to be carried out. Bomb and fire drill procedures were much the same, in that each class had to evacuate their classroom and congregate on the sports fields for Roll Call, the only difference between the two being that in the bomb drill, we left our suitcases behind in the classrooms, in case one contained a mini-limpet mine or something. Many of us lost our lunchboxes to the school's resident reprobates and pilferers while our bags were unattended.

In the case of a gunfire drill, we all had to drop to the floor and crouch under our desks, a rehearsal the boys loved, as the girls inadvertently showed a little thigh, or sometimes even panties, getting into that awkward position. Nubile young teachers weren't exempt from our lascivious looks either. From floor height, us guys would gawk up at them, sitting or crouching at their desks in front of the class, their short skirts and skimpy blouses giving us tantalising glimpses of what lay beneath. I often wondered if they exposed themselves intentionally to tease us.

At Infantry School, the corporals would dismiss us to drink water and smoke after each drill session on the parade ground and around the network of roads around the base. Smoking was officially frowned upon, but the water break was really just another name for a smoke break, and eventually the corporals didn't give a toss and would say, *"Rook en drink water."* The short break would be ended with the order, *"Tree aan in drie geledere, BEWEEG!"* ("Fall in, in three ranks, MOVE!"), eventually shortened to *"TREE AAN!"*

At some point in the year, after Bravo Company had practiced drilling endlessly and we'd become more proficient at it, we participated in an inter-company drilling competition. The corporals mocked our efforts at drilling, saying the school-leavers in the other companies would do better than us in the competition, but they were wrong. Soon we were proficient enough to take part in the main battalion parade which was held every Thursday between 08h00 and 10h00 on the main parade ground.

We arrived for the first battalion parade in our browns, as we hadn't received our fancy step-outs yet. Although a loudhailer was used, those stuck at the far back of the ensemble of companies couldn't easily hear the commands, and we sort of shuffled about in a muddle while the commandant, the regimental sergeant major and all the company commanders did much inspecting, saluting and marching up and down. Hoping to improve matters, a massive megaphone-type loudhailer was employed the following week. After a while, none of us could hear the commands … we were all temporarily deafened! The fiasco continued until someone found the volume dial on the amplifier.

The battalion parades improved dramatically thereafter, except for standing at attention – or even at ease – for long periods of time. In the searing heat of the scorching Oudtshoorn sun we all dehydrated quickly. Every now and again there'd be an audible *thud!* as a recruit keeled over in a faint from the heat. On several occasions, they would just be left lying where they fell until the end of the parade.

Many of those throat-parching days were spent in the vain hope of receiving a particular stand-down order. I would keep an eye on the flagpole at the head of the parade ground, hoping to see the mythical flag that was believed to be raised there on days too hot for drilling or training, which would lead to us being banished to our bungalows. Of course, this never happened. My one-pint water-bottle attached to my web belt was lugged around everywhere I went and became quite the life-saver under those conditions. We were relieved to be given ice-cold mango juice and milk in place of tea and coffee at tea times on those unbearably hot days.

Contrary to official policy, the SADF was not bilingual. The official language of the SADF was Afrikaans: commands, conventions, names, paperwork ... everything was in Afrikaans, and lectures were no different. When some of us English-speakers expressed resentment at the widespread use of Afrikaans and suggested we were being discriminated against, we were informed that the plan was to alternate between Afrikaans and English on a monthly basis, but they never did revert to English. I believe they did try speaking only English on the base for a day, but even that was evidently too much for them.

Fortunately, we were allowed to write the tests that were given every second or third week in English.

Lectures were delivered in a large theatre-like hall with uncomfortable folding chairs of slatted wood. We would try to keep our eyes open in that awful morning heat in that stuffy hall, while various officers droned on and on about whichever topic was at hand. Once I was jerked awake by hearing a comops officer saying, *"Engels is die taal van die vyand!"* ("English is the language of the enemy!"). I must have misheard him, I thought, rubbing my eyes to make myself more alert. I looked at Ian next to me, and he gave me a look of outrage. The officer continued, *"Engels is die taal van die antichris!"* ("English is the language of the antichrist!"). I sat up a bit straighter, began composing a retort in my head, but Ian put a hand on my arm and shook his head at me.

"Engels," the officer went on, oblivious to the rage he had triggered amongst the English-speaking recruits, *"is die rooitaal."* ("English is the red language", meaning the language of the communists). Rage seething inside me, I was entirely deaf to the rest of the officer's point, and even now I regret not finding the courage to stand up to him. Like the rest of the English guys at the lecture, I allowed my fear of being kicked off the course, or sent to some other God-forsaken unit of the SADF, prevent me from challenging the bigoted officer.

As part of our training, we were occasionally expected to write out *Die Stem*, the South African anthem. My ire was raised by the fact that we were expected to write it out in Afrikaans. Once, probably in response to complaints from the *rooinekke*, we were told to write the anthem out in

English, and, of course, the English guys did better than the Afrikaners. We knew the anthem in both languages, but the Afrikaans guys, whose grasp of the English language left a lot to be desired, were entirely unable to recall the English version.

Our R4 assault rifles were issued in our second week at Infantry School. This was a big moment. We were excited as they rounded us up and marched us down to the armoury at the quartermaster's storehouse. The rifles were stacked up on the long counter in the storehouse. Sergeant Major Lategaan was standing by to explain the rifle's specifications.

"This R4 is the standard South African Infantry assault weapon," he said to us in Afrikaans as he held an R4 up in front of him. "This is a rifle, not a gun." He grasped his crotch and said in English, "This is the gun you use for fun!" which caused chuckles and sniggers amongst the conscripts assembled. Lategaan continued.

"The R4 is gas-operated. It has a mass of 4.3 kilograms when empty, and 5.1 kilograms with a full 35-round magazine. The sharp-point round has a 5.56 by 45 mm bullet, which travels at a speed of 988 metres per second. The bullet usually tumbles after point-of-impact, making a really nasty mess." The sergeant major grinned as we took in the implication of a tumbling bullet. "The R4," he went on, "has a rate of fire of 650 rounds per minute, and its maximum effective range is almost five hundred metres. Some of you may not know this, but the R4 is based upon the Israeli Galil, which was inspired by the AK47." A murmur rose up from those who knew weapons. I would get a chance to handle a Galil later that year on the firing range. Lategaan smiled, "Those Israelis are smart, hey?"

"Do you know," he went on. "The AK47 is the most prolific and effective assault rifle ever manufactured? You can leave an AK47 in the mud and water for ages, fetch it later, and it will still fire! Guerrilla armies love this weapon, because they are notorious for not maintaining their firearms. But!" Here Lategaan let the weapon fall to his side, and he raised a finger in our direction. "In this army," he said pointedly, "we do maintenance, because we never want to be left guessing when crunch-time comes. Do you understand me?" We nodded and okayed, and I felt a little uncomfortable at the thought of what crunch-time might be. "Your rifle," said Lategaan, cradling the weapon in both hands once again, "is your wife, your girlfriend. Handle her with care and she will take care of you … just when you need her the most!"

I later learnt that the R4 assault rifle's development started after the Arab-Israeli war of 1967, with design and prototype production initiated in the early 1970s. The South African military armaments research and production institution, known as the Armaments Corporation, or more commonly called Armscor, began large-scale manufacture of the weapon in the late 1970s. The R4 entered service in the SADF in the early 1980s, replacing the reliable but much heavier R1 assault rifle.

Lecture over, we were each issued with an R4, 35-round standard steel magazines, one 50-round assault steel magazine, an olive-green carry-strap and a cleaning kit. Each rifle's serial number was carefully noted in a large green ordnance book, and we were instructed to memorise our weapon's serial number.

In the weeks and months to follow, the fact that us recruits were now in possession of our rifles opened up a whole new avenue of *rondfok* to our corporals. There was the dreaded rifle PT, in which we were made to stand holding the rifle at its extremities with our arms extended in front of us. Then there was *knie lig*, or "knee lifts", which entailed holding the rifle above your head with one hand on the barrel and one hand on the butt and running on the spot for ages. There were endless permutations of drills possible with a rifle, and our corporals ensured that we got to know them all well.

Every day we would be told, *"Vir inspeksie, hou geweer!"* ("For inspection, bear your weapon!"), whereupon our rifles were inspected not only for dust or rust, but all manner of creatures and other obscure objects supposedly and impossibly hidden within. The exaggerations presented as to what could be found in our weapons were so ludicrous that it was hard to keep from sniggering at the corporals' assertions – the punishment for such a response would have been unthinkable.

We all looked forward to firing our weapons, and soon after receiving our R4s we were driven out northwards into the veld several kilometres from the main camp. Company Sergeant Major Lategaan brought us into the undulating and rough terrain, platoon by platoon and ordered us to jump down into a large donga.

"I am now going to do something that you all need to get used to," he bellowed, before firing a burst from his R4 over our heads. The sound of automatic rifle fire cracking above us was glorious and terrifying.

We met Captain Barrie for the first time on our second excursion to the firing range. A PF and proud of it, he was of average height, lean and neatly turned-out. He had an air of pretension and liked to stroke his fair moustache with self-importance. He had a vast knowledge of weapons which would impress us during the conventional warfare phase of our training, and he had recently been to France to learn about their latest weaponry.

Saturday mornings were usually set aside for route marches. We started off doing short marches with relatively light packs. The marches steadily became longer and the packs heavier as we became accustomed to the exertion. Marching long distances is not difficult in itself, but we had to complete them in a predetermined time, and this could be hard going. Daylight marches were interspersed with night marches, and being more of a night owl, I found these much more bearable. The night time air was cooler, and the darkness gave me space for my own thoughts. The fact that the others couldn't see my suffering helped, too.

Once, we lined up and moved out on a march just as the day's light was fading. The marching order was full kit, which meant that we were lugging our *grootsakke* with marble, chest webbing, R4 and water. In the last few minutes before darkness, I caught sight of one of Bravo's other platoons moving out in total silence, silhouetted figures passing across the fading crimson and orange of the twilight sky, the light like streaks of paint spread across a canvas. It was a brief moment of awe.

These route marches were progressively preparing us for the next major hurdle we were to face at Infantry School: *Vasbyt*, the five-day route march that would follow the end of basic training.

If there was any maintenance to be done on base, we did it on Saturday mornings or sports parade day. We weren't expected to mow lawns – the black and coloured staff did that. But we were expected to spend our Saturdays taking care of the large grassed areas around the base, trimming their edges and ridding the green expanse of weeds. I hated squatting in the grass with nothing but my *pikstel* to dig up lousy weeds.

The NCOs loved getting us to do the "chicken parade". The whole platoon would be made to form a straight line and move across the designated area picking up every tiny bit of litter and *stompie* encountered, advancing at a slow pace and bending to pick at the ground like a brood of chickens at mealtime.

I was never a smoker, but I had to learn to tolerate those who were. Some of the most awful *oppies* I experienced involved the entire platoon being sent out to find the *stompies* strewn around the backdoor of our bungalow. It angered me that the non-smokers amongst us had to pick up the smokers' old and smelly fag ends. Behind each bungalow was a long and high earthen embankment. It was as long as the lines and clad in large round boulders and succulent flowering plants which acted as a retaining wall of sorts. Each platoon at one point or another would have to manoeuvre, lever or even remove each of these stones one by one to clean them and remove the *stompies* from between them.

The standard and expected reply to all commands was an enthusiastic *"Ja, korporaal!"* or "Yes, corporal!" and our early days were spent getting this response to be a habit.

Like all SAI camps, "hurry up and wait" was to become the norm. Recruits would run everywhere, unless we were drilling. Even so, during most of our drilling we still ended up running for any mistakes made on drill commands. We had to Muster each day if we were to go anywhere in the camp. Wherever we went, we went in platoon formation, marching to the regimented voices of our two corporals. The tempo was quickening each day, with a sense of foreboding that something dramatic was going to take place soon.

One persistent Army myth that had been going on for years was the use of *blou vitriol,* or blue stone (copper sulphate), alleged to have been surreptitiously placed in coffee or similar beverages, to suppress the horniness of virile young men. Either it was a complete myth or their copper sulphate wasn't working! Horny dreams involving the fairer sex still resulted in early morning salutes!

Every bungalow in the lines had a leisure time room or *vrye tyd bestuur kamer* or *VTB kamer*. The VTB room, at the end of the bungalow passage, was slightly larger than the other rooms and contained a TV and enough cheap government-style cloth chairs to accommodate about three quarters of the platoon at once. We were expected to decorate one designated wall during the course of the year, probably to show our enthusiasm for being there or something to that effect. Courtesy of some fairly talented recruits, walls were adorned with wonderful desert, lunar and sunset landscapes. All designs had to be approved by the comops officer, though, to ensure nothing subversive or lurid was painted there.

Every Wednesday, Thursday and Friday night that we were in base we were allowed to watch a video sanctioned by the *dominee*. Once or twice we caught a glimpse of a female nipple or thigh on some B-rate movie, a scene neglected by the *dominee* in his censorship role, but soon enough, he would get wind of the slip and the video would mysteriously disappear. We wondered if he kept those for his private collection.

We hardly had time to watch any videos during basics, despite the five rand being deducted off our pay each month to pay for the privilege. By the end of the year, we realised that the guys operating the regimental fund were really coining it.

We were expected to write at least one letter a week, which was handed to the lootie in an unsealed envelope. Any sensitive information of a military nature contained in the letters was censored before they were mailed. Within the first two weeks, letters and parcels started arriving from home for the recruits. *Posparade,* or post parade, was just before supper, and anyone fortunate enough to receive a letter was told, *"Voorste posisie af!"* or *"Voorsteun posisie af!"*, meaning, "Front support position!", which was face down on the ground in preparation for push-ups, and made to do ten push-ups for every letter received. Later, this was shortened to *"Sak vir tien",* or "Drop for ten". Letters emitting the faintest whiff of perfume or suspected to come from girlfriends required substantially more push-ups than those apparently from parents. Parcels extracted twenty push-ups from the receiver, and the contents were voluntarily shared out with instructors at the risk of being dubbed the company or platoon pet.

Recruits with girlfriends all feared the dreaded *Dear Johnny* letter arriving. It was not uncommon for a *troep* to be unceremoniously dumped by letter, often for another guy back home. The poor rejected lover, far away in the army, could do little about it. I had no worries, though. Kimberly and I were as tight as ever. Weren't we?

After Bravo Company had endured the humiliation of earning our mail by push-ups a few times at the hands of our corporals, Sergeant Major Lategaan got wind of the practice and caught them at it. Pulling rank, which was not his to pull, he "forced" the looties to take over the task of handing out correspondence and food packages, but this didn't stop the looties from occasionally performing the old *"Sak vir twintig"* routine.

My turn to *sak vir twintig* came around quickly. Kimberly's first letter arrived during my second week at Infantry School and brought with it an unexpected longing for home and her easy company. The non-descript light blue envelope certainly wasn't scented with perfume, but her neat, girlish hand gave away the fact that this letter wasn't from a mother or granny, and the corporals ragged me gently about it. I didn't care. I was so excited to hear from her, I wanted to rip the letter open right there and read it, but I restrained myself and slipped it into my pocket, saving it to be savoured over later in my room during our free time.

Her casual words updating me about what was happening at home, how she was enjoying varsity, the latest *skinder* from our circle of friends brought with them a reminder of the world out there, the memory of normality, which nourished me like a plate of home-cooked stew. The letter ended too soon, and I replied immediately. Her letters during that year would become a source of inspiration and sustenance to me, and, because I had asked my mother to keep her letters to important family news only, the only regular connection to my world aside from the occasional *kospakkie* filled with my favourite things from my mom.

Ranking as one of my worst (and best) experiences in basics started one day after drilling on the main parade ground, about four weeks into training. The guys were messing around as we marched in three lines off the parade ground back to barracks, jinking at the last moment to try and get the guy behind to trip on the small creosote-painted wooden poles that marked the north western exit. I was not concentrating and didn't see the pole in front of me until it was too late. I did my best to dodge it, but failed, scraping the front of my left shin on a pole, right through my overalls. It stung sharply, and back at the bungalow I washed the wound with water, but I thought it was trivial and forgot about it.

Getting ready for supper the next evening, I had a hard time pulling my left boot on, but finally managed and set off for the mess hall. It was a hot summer evening, so I decided to change into my PT shorts to go with Ian to the tuck shop after supper, and again, I had great difficulty getting my boot off and my *tekkie* on. Inspecting my foot more closely, I discovered it had started to swell, and as I hesitantly poked and prodded at my ballooning limb, pain shot through my foot and up my leg. In the next half hour, as Ian made a trip to the tuck shop alone, my foot distended at an alarming rate, and when I tried to put weight on it I just crumpled.

"Hey, Ian," I said when he returned. "I can't walk on this foot!" I lifted my leg to show him the swollen foot at the end. Ian clicked his tongue.

"Don't be a sissy, man!" he said, and my mouth fell open in disbelief. "It's nothing. You'll be fine!" Seeing my stunned expression, he laughed. "Just a joke, bud!" he said. "It's the size of a football! Come, let me help you get to sickbay."

It was always a pain to report sick. First you had to report at the company office just after breakfast in your browns, not your overall. There you would stand outside, waiting for consent to go to the sickbay. Each rank that passed would have to be *strek*ked or saluted, while they in turn would demand to know what was wrong, inevitably providing their own diagnosis that you were just another "sick, lame and lazy" who was gyppoing.

Eventually you were taken to the sickbay, where you had to fill in a form from the nurses while you waited for the doctor. He would also look at you with a suspicious eye while you explained what the problem was, before examining you to diagnose the ailment. The less serious cases received a pill or were put on light duty, more serious cases were exempted from physical exertion for a day or two, while those with critical ailments were hospitalised at the sick bay to recuperate.

Going to the sickbay after hours was a different matter. I hobbled along leaning on Ian for support. As the nurse on duty interrogated me about what happened, it dawned on me that I must have blood poisoning. Admitted to sickbay and given a bed, the doctor came and supervised as two nurses pumped me full of penicillin from an IV. I soon dozed off into a heavy slumber.

I awoke some hours later, itching all over. I called the nurse on duty, and when she put the light on I saw that I was covered from head to toe in water blisters. The left arm in which the drip was inserted was most afflicted. Realising I must be allergic to penicillin, a condition I wasn't aware of, she called another nurse and together they changed the intravenous bag for a sulphate antibiotic solution.

The next morning I was heaps better, with hardly a sign of those water blisters. A medic sent my folks a telegram to inform them of my plight. News of my suffering travelled fast, and Kimberly's Uncle Alan and his wife, who lived in Oudtshoorn and strangers to me, arrived to visit, bearing a parcel of treats.

My mother phoned, greatly concerned and ready to come down to Oudtshoorn with my dad to tend to me, but after some reassurance from me that I was already on the mend and she needn't worry, she calmed down to a panic. I spent the better part of a week in sickbay, lying in bed, reading a book and eating the treats Kimberly's relatives had brought me – pure bliss! Ian and some of the others came by to visit, and their faces were a picture of envy that I was having a chance to rest away from the lunacy that was our training.

At the end of basics, we faced the worst inspection to date: the dreaded commandant's inspection. Preparation for this inspection was long, hard and frenzied. We even went so far as to scratch the muck out from the grooves in the narrow gaps in the Marley tiles covering the floor of our bungalow and washing and wiping down in the nooks and crannies behind and below the toilet cisterns, until they gleamed. The commandant arrived on the big day in the company of the regimental sergeant major, with Major Drost and Sergeant Major Lategaan trailing in their wake. The regimental sergeant major searched high and low, scratching and wiping everywhere, knowing precisely where we might have gypped. The insides of several cupboards were dismantled, the back of insignia checked, light bulbs fingered for dust – the regimental sergeant major looked in more places than we had ever even thought of cleaning or gyppoing! There was a collective sigh of relief when they finally left – it was the toughest inspection we had ever faced.

When basics came to an end, we were finally given permission to make and receive phone calls from the call boxes outside Bungalow 1. The unwritten code was that at peak times, when calls were expected or about to be made, no one could spend more than ten minutes on the phone. I looked forward to Kimberly's phone calls, but I sometimes missed her because of the time it took for someone to get from Bungalow 1 all the way to Bungalow 7 to call me. Guys waiting to make a call were reluctant to lose their spot in the queue to summon others getting incoming calls, so they would send someone passing by to the far bungalows to call us. Later, as the company was whittled down and we got to know the guys from other platoons, the lads would make an effort to call someone to the phone, regardless.

I looked at my watch. We'd been on the phone for almost six minutes already. Kimberly and I had exchanged pleasantries and given each other updates about our respective lives, but time was running out.

"Michael?" Kimberly said. "Are you okay?" I must have gone quiet.

"Ja," I said. "Ja, I'm okay. Listen, I'm gonna get booted off this phone soon. Kimberly ..."

"Yes?"

I paused, searching for the words. "Kimberly," I started. "You know I miss you, right?"

Kimberly's voice was hushed and tender. "Of course, Michael. I miss you, too."

"I know, I know." I fiddled with the misshapen black cord that was all that connected us over the vast distance. "I just ..." I closed my eyes. "Just ... Kimberly, just wait for me, okay?"

"Of course, Michael!"

"I'll see you soon, but ... you know ... two years is a long time." "Hey, Michael! It's okay. Don't worry about me!"

"I don't worry about you, Kimberly. I worry about us." The guy behind me rapped his knuckles on the side of the blue call box and pointed at his watch. "Listen, I've got to go. I love you."

"I love you, too, babe. Hang in there."

I replaced the receiver with a heavy heart. There was something that needed to be said, but I hadn't been able to put it into words.

By the end of basics, I felt utterly alienated from my old life. I had lived away from home while studying, but while I was in Johannesburg, I could opt to go home to Pretoria at any time. Here I felt imprisoned. I would look upon the landscape around me, populated with alien *fynbos* that stretched kilometre upon kilometre all the way to the Swartberg Mountains, and long for home and familiarity. Even in the oppressive heat of Oudtshoorn in late summer, depression and loneliness drizzled down on me like a thin and persistent winter rain.

Chapter 7

The sweet-smelling sea breeze brushed my flushed cheeks and ruffled my hair as I lay on my back on the sand, a dry flotsam log under my head. I had the whole stretch of beach to myself. I'd had a tiff with Kimberly, and skulked off alone to the seashore to cool down. I'd felt quite sorry for myself as I took up this reclining position at the water's edge, but who could remain bad-tempered in this paradise? I took a swig of my beer and wondered if anyone had noticed my absence.

Early in December 1985, Kimberly and I left Pretoria to spend the Christmas holidays on the Eastern Cape coast with a crowd of our friends, a vacation that had been planned and looked forward to for months. Sixteen of us travelled in several vehicles, with motorbike trailers and scramblers hooked up behind, down to Transkei, stopping off at Mpande Bay, Coffee Bay with its renowned Hole-In-The-Wall, and Mazeppa Bay in turn.

At each bay we pitched tents in the camping grounds and spent our days exploring the pristine rocky alcoves and sandy beaches that were guarded by almost impenetrable sub-tropical vegetation. From higher-up, the slopes of a myriad of hills, sporadically dissected by deeply incised gorges and interspersed with a mix of cattle-trodden sloping fields and lush grasslands, looked down on us silently.

Transkei was an independent homeland, created in 1976 by the Nationalist Government for the Xhosa people. One of the cornerstones of Apartheid was to separate black reserves or homelands from white South Africa, through labyrinthine Apartheid laws. Ironically, the rural landscape of coastal Transkei was an unspoilt Garden of Eden, a treasure trove that fed the wild and carefree feelings of our youth. It was an elixir for the soul.

In the mornings, the guys would leave their girlfriends still wrapped in the misty residue of sleep and set off on our bikes. Making our way across the estuary at Mpande Bay, we would ride up into the hills and sometimes as far as Coffee Bay, following the small paths and animal trails that crisscrossed the terrain, forging our own trails where there were none. We'd pop wheelies and ramp up and over every dune we found. We looked for mud patches on wet hillsides, to see who was first to sink their back wheel and open the throttle to spray the others with sludge.

Returning to the campsite midmorning, we'd make a huge breakfast to share, having a *braaivleis* on the open fire or rustling up a fried meal on the Cadac gas cooker. Stefan's preferred breakfast was a sample of the hair of the dog that bit him the night before – usually about three beers.

The music we listened to then consumed us, body and soul. We followed the Top 100 for 1985 on the various local radio stations. To circumvent control by the "thought police", independent station Capital Radio 604 broadcast uncensored music and news to keen listeners in South Africa from transmitters located in the Transkei. We also listened to Radio 702 and Radio 5, slightly more restrained broadcasters, but also independent. We seldom listened to the State-controlled Springbok Radio, although the English broadcast wasn't bad.

The days were spent inventing our own entertainment and enjoying the company of good friends. We rode bare-backed the Xhosa ponies that grazed near our tents at Mpande Bay, and wandered inland to bathe in fresh-water streams. We "skied" on the wet seashore behind the motorbikes in our flip-flops. The girls, including Diane, Michelle and Kimberly, took turns on the smallest scrambler, learning to ride through the veld. Harald's girlfriend, Caroline, got brave and had a go on one of the larger bikes, but took a tumble that ripped her thumb open. With no hospital for miles, the locals directed us to an inland mission station where some nuns under the instruction of a medical orderly stitched the digit up with precision and Caroline suffered no infection.

At each stop, we were adopted by gillies, local teenage boys who would take "ownership" of us and our possessions, protecting, assisting and guiding us in exchange for a small wage negotiated in money, food and a ride on our bikes daily. Allan, laughingly watched by Thomas, Dave and Jiri, would engage the gillies in horseplay, tackling them to the ground for a wrestle, but with three of the youngsters ganging up on him, he didn't stand a chance.

We bought succulent langoustines and crayfish from the locals to braai for our suppers, cheap at the price of a Rand each, and delicious swathed in garlic, hot off the open fire. Later we discovered that the salesmen kept their wares fresh by dangling them in string bags in the camp's long-drops!

I was thinking fondly of these fresh memories in the late afternoon sun as I lay sprawled in my reclining position on the beach when two young women, fair skins tanned to perfection and walking barefoot, their nubile bodies wrapped in bright sarongs, appeared out of the foliage and came close to where I was. Whispering to each other and giggling coyly, they proceeded to remove their cloth coverings and prance naked into the waves, right in front of me. I was stunned and couldn't tear my eyes from their beauty as they laughed and frolicked in the shallows.

To add to my nervous excitement, the girls looked at me over their shoulders, one winking invitingly, the other beckoning me with a curled finger to join them. I knew I shouldn't move, nor could I! Blushing, I tried to be nonchalant and took another swig from my beer, only to discover the bottle was empty, which brought about more giggling from the sea nymphs. The experience was like an erotic waking dream, and I wondered if I was suffering from some lasting effect of marijuana.

Like many – albeit more liberal – souls before us, we didn't pass up on the opportunity to smoke a spliff of *dagga* while we were there. The area is world-renowned for the cultivation of a powerful strain of the illegal herb, and us guys bravely volunteered to sample the wares, just in case there were any unintended consequences, before we would allow the girls to try.

The effects of the drug were varied: some of us retreated into sullen silences, while others gabbed away excitedly. For me, the beautiful vegetation melted into a psychedelic painting as a pink-clouded sunset gave way to the opulent celestial display of the country night sky. Time seemed to freeze and Roxy Music's *Avalon* echoed in my mind for an age. When the high subsided, I was overcome by a powerful hunger. We convinced the girls that smoking weed wasn't a good idea.

Our time in that tropical utopia wasn't entirely free from reminders of the real world that awaited us beyond the fantasy world of the Wild Coast. At Mpande one night, Pierre's car was broken into, the rear windshield expertly excised and Pierre's and his brother Wimpie's clothes stolen. We secured the camp better after that, and took care to guard our green stores tent for the remainder of our time there.

Once, while us guys were messing around on our bikes on the long dirt road which was the only route in and out of Mpande Bay, a huge bus came flying past us, kicking up dust. As it went by, some of its local passengers leant out of the rear windows, giving us the finger and the raised fist of the Black Consciousness salute while shouting "Fuck off, *Boere!*" aggressively. We didn't feel much welcomed and it put a damper on the day, but we decided not to dwell on their animosity or take offence. We knew we weren't *Boere*.

At Coffee Bay we camped at the Hole-In-The-Wall. We stood on the colossal cliffs overlooking the Hole, an opening in a detached cliff, carved over centuries by the waves of the majestic Indian Ocean. The azure water stretched beyond and I was hypnotised by the beauty of the scene. Anthony swam the treacherous stretch all the way to the ledge at the Hole. Later, at the Coffee Bay Hotel, some locals told us that they'd caught massive man-eating sharks there.

We held our Christmas party on reed mats on the beach at Hole-In-The-Wall, a picnic feast accompanied by champagne. We held games of dare, the losers being made to down their drinks and run stark naked around a massive beached tree trunk.

We made our way to the magnificent and remote resort of Mazeppa Bay just before New Year, where my optometrist-in-training mate from res, Stephen, travelled from his hometown of East London nearby, and Simon rode the thousand-odd kilometres from Pretoria on his Honda XR 500R scrambler, to join us. We camped right on the edge of the camping ground, where the rocks drop off to the waters below. Here, the grassy terrain was open and flat, sloping gently down to the surging sea, and the girls had the freedom to ride around on the smaller scramblers, revelling in their new-found skill.

The resort held a contest between the cottagers, the caravaners and the tent dwellers, us being the latter. Beach sports included athletics and touch-rugby, three-legged, egg-and-spoon and sack races, and tug-o-war. We won most of the contests, taking overall honours. Several of us entered the Mr and Miss Mazeppa Bay competition for a laugh. I made it all the way to the semi-finals, but scuppered my chances by wearing a fedora and feigning a thick Afrikaans accent, whereupon the judges were drained of all sense of humour. The girls fared better, with three of them making it to the semi-finals.

As light faded on New Year's Day, Diane received the devastating news that her father had been killed in a motor accident. She flew home immediately and the rest of us packed up camp and left for Pretoria the next day, sombre in the realisation that life was short and often unexpectedly ended.

But that was still to come as I watched the desirable pair of naked strangers cavort on that Wild Coast beach. In time, they emerged from the water, glistening and breathless, and proceeded to dry themselves off provocatively – so close to me that drops of salt water flecked my skin from their dripping hair. With smiles in my direction, they left to return to their campsite, and for a while I lay where I was, my heart pounding from the excitement of it all.

When I got back to camp, I relayed my story to the others, but they didn't believe a word of my tale of the two sea nymphs, least of all Kimberly, who simply told me to lay off the beers. These were the best days of our lives – these were halcyon days.

Chapter 8

There isn't a word for *vasbyt* in the English language. Directly translated, it means "bite unyieldingly" (*vas*: fast, firm, fixed; *byt*: bite), but the Afrikaans idiom *vasbyt* means "hang in there", "persevere" or "grit your teeth and bare it". To me, "guts it out" describes the term most accurately.

"*Vasbyt, min dae*" ("Hang in there, not long to go") was a common encouragement to troops during national service.

At Infantry School, the word *vasbyt* was endowed with a whole new meaning. *Vasbyt* was the name given to five days of intense, non-stop route marching under full kit and weapons on gravel, mountainous roads.

The five days of *Vasbyt* was the culmination of basic training. But I saw it as a separate round of elimination, weeding out those who wouldn't make it at Infantry School. *Vasbyt* would prove who was physically and mentally fit, so that time and effort would not be wasted on unworthy recruits.

We already knew *Vasbyt* was looming when the lootie asked us who wanted to be the platoon photographer, starting with documenting *Vasbyt*. Ian, enthusiastic as ever, said "*Ek sal, luitenant!*" He liked to volunteer for those missions he knew would have some real advantage to them. With that, Ian became our photographer, and I have piles of photos from that time.

The order to prepare for *Vasbyt* came on a Sunday evening in March. The directions were clear. All of Bravo Company was to be ready to depart before daybreak. We were to dress in training overalls and boots. From our web belt must be suspended the pint-sized water bottle, held by its metal fire bucket, in its pouch, with its strap. This fire bucket was soon to double up as a handy mug, shaving mirror and cooking pot while we were away. In addition, we were to wear our battle gear: the nylon-Kevlar battle helmet, or *staaldak*, with its cover and Velcro nylon chest webbing for our magazines.

The remainder of our kit was to be packed into our *grootsakke*, the army-issue H-frame backpacks in which all this paraphernalia would be hauled. This included: four pairs each of underpants and socks (which would prove to be the most important items to take along), PT clothing, bush hat, *tekkies*, our spare pair of boots and spare overalls, plastic raincoat, two 2-litre water bottles, our *tokkeltou*, plastic bivvy, waterproof groundsheet, sleeping bag and inner.

That night, Ian and I messed around. Ian and I wrote out a placard:
Noël vir Vasbyt
On the way to Timbuktu
Wys Cairo 'n Noël
From the Nutty Inmates of Room 12
In army slang, a *"Noël"*, according to Eugene who had joined us while we were writing our placard, is to give someone the middle finger. "Give *Vasbyt* the finger!" our poster said, "We might be on the way to the middle of nowhere, a hell of a long way to go ("from Cape to Cairo" as the old saying went), but we aren't afraid!" Dressed in civvies, the three of us sat on a *trommel* together, our arms draped over each other's shoulders with the placard pinned to Ian's shirt. We pulled tough and resolute faces while Kerry took our photo.

Early Monday morning saw us all packed-up and labouring under the weight of our *grootsakke*. As the sky lightened, we clambered onto several SAMIL 50 trucks, which headed out of the main gate, past the airbase outside Oudtshoorn, in a westerly direction on the R62 to Calitzdorp. We then turned due south off the R62, towards the Outeniqua Mountain range.

We passed through a small farming area green with vineyards called Volmoed, or "full of courage", its presence broadcast from a large blue and white municipal signpost. I took this as a good omen. Shortly after, however, another sign pronounced our arrival in Armoed. Now, there is no such word as *armoed* in Afrikaans. The word *armoede* means poverty. Perhaps Armoed (without the final "e"), taken in conjunction with the recently passed Volmoed, could be taken to mean "poor of courage". We hoped this wasn't a sign of things to come!

Coordinates: 33°41'22.58"S 22°04'37.77"E

Just south of Armoed, the vehicles came to a stop at a junction with a gravel road running in a northwesterly direction. Here we were ordered to alight. The great trek was on!

We milled around the trucks while our corporals handed out various platoon weapons and ordnance. Besides our kit, either worn or in our rucksack, we were handed first-line ammunition for our R4s. Each section carried an *LMG* (FN MAG or light machine gun), handed to the biggest and strongest guy. The second strongest and fittest man in the section was designated the MAG's ammo carrier and feeder. Shared among the rest of the section was the other ammo we had to carry: Claymore mines, rifle grenades and illumination and colour flares. The Claymore mine and two rifle grenades I was handed to carry made my backpack heavier, and for the first hour or so, I was concerned they might go off. But I soon forgot about them, only to be reminded of their presence at the end of the day when I rummaged around in my rucksack for something else. I needn't have worried – they couldn't just explode through being bumped or dropped – but I wasn't fully aware of this at the time … nor was I quite convinced.

Ration packs or "rat-packs", containing our food for the duration, were distributed. Initially the novelty and variety of these rat-packs made for exciting eating, but this soon wore off. These small cardboard boxes wrapped in tough, clear plastic, contained a packet of matches each and several Esbit fuel tablets for cooking tins of meat, such as steak and onions or spaghetti and meat balls or corned beef and hash, or God-forbid, curried fish, and tins of vegetables, such as diced carrots or peas. In each rat-pack was a packet of "dog biscuits", those infamous hard biscuits which were wonderfully versatile: dunked into coffee or used for bartering, a roll of processed cheese, a couple of rolls of Super C energy sweets, bland chewing gum, energy bars and fruit bars or fruit rolls. A packet of ProNutro cereal, sachets of salt, sugar, coffee, tea and creamer, condensed milk, energy drinks or milkshake formula powders with small clear plastic bags for mixing and one or two other barely edible extras completed the various rat-pack menu inventories.

Our full H-frame rucksacks now weighed well over forty kilograms each.

Our platoon, a little more than forty-strong by this time, was split into three squads or "sticks", more correctly termed "sections". A section is the smallest fighting unit in a platoon, usually comprising eleven men. We were about fourteen recruits to a section. Our platoon commander, Lieutenant Pretorius, our platoon sergeant, Corporal Joubert, and Corporal Potgieter each took a section. Corporal Pottie, as he had become known, was put in charge of my section. Before each leg, one of the section members would be put in charge of the group as section leader.

Earlier in the year I had seen hanging on the wall in one of the lecture rooms pictures of recruits on *Vasbyt* a decade or more before us. In one picture, two guys were carrying between them a *trommel* filled with marbles, those awful concrete blocks. In another, a huge truck tyre was carried between two *troepe*, balanced on wooden poles. Fortunately, we were not encumbered with *trommels* and tyres, as those poor souls in the seventies were. Plus, we were lucky to wear the latest nylon and Velcro lightweight webbing, not the old, heavy and ill-fitting green canvas-style webbing they wore. But we were weighed down all the same.

We quickly realised that we needed to help one another to heave our substantial and now heavily-laden backpacks onto our shoulders. Distinctly absent during all of this activity was the usual volley of loud commands accompanied by taunts and threats from our corporals. The silence was like an ominous prelude, signalling dark days to come.

The load thus distributed amongst us, the long march began. We set off as separate Bravo Company sections, a section heading out whenever it was ready. The leading men of each syndicate wore bright red-orange hazard sashes, the rear man had a bright red cloth spread over the top of his rucksack as a hazard warning. The leading syndicate carried the Bravo Company banner and the National Flag. I was reminded of descriptions of the legions of infantrymen of the Roman Empire, marching in full military regalia, standards and banners held aloft.

Our route began down a straight stretch of picturesque gravel road, travelling in a roughly northwesterly direction. A long column of men, we lurched and tottered, hauling our enormous loads, our bodies casting elongated shadows before us, shaped by the watery early morning sun.

The road turned south and then eased into a southwesterly direction. We marched along a fertile, pretty valley, with a little stream passing through vineyards. It looked so charming that I wondered whether the stories I had heard about *Vasbyt* had been exaggerated. We weren't aware of the route or the actual distances involved, but within a day or two, we realised we were marching past the Gamkaberg Nature Reserve and on towards the Gourits Eco-trail, which essentially consists of a large mountain, part of the Outeniqua Mountain Range, around which we were to walk. We were told we had to cover thirty kilometres a day, and if we didn't, we would have to make it up the next day. This notion gnawed at us throughout the first days of trudging torture.

The instructors mostly left us alone to get on with the march, each walking alongside his section. I suspect they found the going a little tough themselves, although they carried no kit; they wore only their browns, boots and bush-hats. They probably remembered keenly their *Vasbyt* a year ago.

We had to keep pace in order to keep up with the sections ahead of us. One boot-step after another, one mile after another, we trudged on, enjoying the open air and chatting quietly among ourselves. An air of positive expectation permeated the ranks of men. That first day's march was tough, but not as bad as we expected.

By the time we got to our temporary base somewhere in the veld that afternoon, our feet and shoulders ached. Our clothing was starting to show signs of salty-white sweat stains. We were instructed to place our kit and rucksacks in such a way that each section individually formed a small, roughly circular encampment. We aired our feet and counted our blisters. We also replenished our empty water bottles from the mobile water car. We then began to massage our tired feet.

Tired as we were, we mustered for company Roll Call and Sick Report. A couple of guys had aches and pains to report. Then we prepared to sleep under the stars in our sleeping bags. Our makeshift beds ready, supper was rustled together from our rat-packs. I randomly chose a tin each of meat and veggies, and prised the tins open with the edge of the handle of my *pikstel* knife, cooking the tins of food together in my fire-bucket over an Esbit fuel tablet or two. Sitting together with some mates and chatting, with little groups of diners dotted around the area, I ate from my fire-bucket with the fork from my *pikstel*. Dinner was hardly a feast, but I was glad to eat – it wasn't bad tasting either! Following my tinned dinner, I dipped into my packet of "dog biscuits", dunking them into a freshly boiled brew of tea made in my rinsed-out fire-bucket. My slap-up meal was rounded off with a roll of Super Cs. It may not have been my preferred choice of meal, but I felt my hunger had been sated. For those of us who found supper insufficient, a mobile tuck shop had been brought in, and we were able to buy sweets from it. The chocolate Bar Ones and Texes were magnificent! Like many of the others, I took the opportunity to write home before the light faded.

We thought the NCOs and officers had it cushy, as they had a mobile canteen all to themselves. They also had green canvas army tents with beds. I resented them, until I realised that they had already been through what we were doing, a year before.

The camps were furnished with portable, chemically-treated field toilets, like Portaloos, and we jokingly referred to them as "rockets", suggesting they might be catapulted into space if the exhaust gases were powerful enough.

Several individuals didn't make it to camp that first day. Their feet bore massive open blisters and they stopped walking. They simply buckled under the strain and opted out. The field ambulances were accompanying us constantly, and if any of us complained about sore feet or blisters, we were taken to an ambulance and our feet were soaked with Merthiolate, an antiseptic ointment which stings like the devil as it dries out the raw flesh and skin. About fifteen minutes later the patient had to be back on the road walking, otherwise he was RTU and kicked off the course.

I felt sympathy for the victims of bad feet, socks or boots who were RTU that first day. Having made it through the gruelling first six weeks of Infantry School, they were now unceremoniously on their way out, and they must have been disappointed. As a special honour to the guys whose feet failed them, the ambulances would drive them back at the end of day one with the bay doors open so that they could bid their comrades goodbye. In many respects we envied them.

The bad news of the day was that we'd apparently only covered twenty-five of the allotted thirty kilometres for the first day. We were told by both Officer Commanding Major Drost and Company Sergeant Major Lategaan that we would have to double our efforts on day two to catch up those lost kilometres. Our minds went numb. What we should have realised was that we had walked into an already prepared temporary field base, which housed several essential vehicles, with the NCOs and officers tents already erected.

Considering how we were feeling after just one day, and how many of us had already bailed, I wondered if we were going to manage a whole week of *Vasbyt*. We were already taking strain. I remembered the pictures of the old boys in the lecture hall. *Are we softer than those tough nuts who'd soldiered before us?* I wondered. Then I remembered being told by one of the fitter platoon sergeants that being rugged and super-fit was less important than the ability to fight. The army wanted men who could stay the distance in any contact situation: stand and fight, first and foremost. His key advice to successful hiking was good-fitting, durable boots and fresh socks to keep one's feet dry.

The night was cool, and autumn was upon us. We all slept fairly well as our bodies were tired, despite the few aches and pains in our shoulders and feet and the odd stone poking us through our sleeping bags. My left shoulder was bruised and tender to the touch.

At 05h00 on day two we were woken and we grabbed some coffee and rusks from the mobile canteen. We assembled for Roll Call, and at 06h00 those sections that were ready started to trudge out of camp. We helped one another lift our heavy loads and began to move, signalling the start to our second day on the road. The gravel road meandered in front of us; the gently rising and falling gradients lay ahead. My feet were numb from the cold night and the previous day's walking and it took a little while to get into a decent stride.

Within half an hour my shoulders felt as if I had not taken the backpack off at the end of the first day! My *staaldak* weighed down on my head like a ton of bricks. But we were in good spirits as we marched along in our respective sections. A few of the heartier members of my section chatted quietly, but I wasn't up to much small talk, especially as the day wore on. Even though the early mornings were crisp, by 10h00 the sun baked down on us. From time to time, we walked alongside or crossed over some pretty streams and even a sizable river, muttering and mumbling to one another about wanting to jump into that cool refreshing water. But these thoughts were fleeting, as we knew it was forbidden to break formation, unless ordered to do so. We all started to take in more water. We stopped for half an hour at midday to eat and rest our weary feet and shoulders. Then on with the backpack again, to start the afternoon stint. As the daylight hours wore on, there were audible grunts of discomfort and the odd curse; talking was now at a premium. Once again the field ambulances accompanied us. And once again a number of guys gave up.

Another aspect started to creep in. It wasn't the pain of the feet or ankles or knees or even hips. Nor was it a sore back and aching shoulders. Like a thief in the night, an inner voice whispered to me: *"What are you doing this for? It's torture. Why don't you bail now?"* The psychological component had settled in. Several guys started to complain, some bitterly: *"korporaal, ek kannie meer nie!"* When questioned whether it was their feet they said no; they had buckled under the mental strain of lugging all that kit, for kilometre upon endless kilometre. They felt that they had reached the end of their endurance and didn't have the energy and will-power to go on. Only reasoned and encouraging coaxing by their NCOs and officers, saw them grit their teeth and continue.

That second day was a lot tougher than the first day. By the time we got to our temporary base that afternoon, our feet and shoulders were throbbing. Our clothing was hard and glazed in patches from the salty-white sweat stains, leaving our skin red and chafed. Again, we had to make small circular encampments designating each section's area. We carefully rinsed our feet with water from our water bottles. There was little amusement to be gained from counting our blisters now. We replenished our empty water bottles from a water car. We tried massaging our tired and blistered feet, which were now excruciatingly sore.

After company Roll Call and individual sick reports that evening, of which there were now quite a few, we spoke quietly among ourselves and got ready for the second night of camping. We ate dinner from our rat-packs again. Some wrote letters.

Several more blokes didn't make it that day – not just because of feet problems, but because they had cracked. They were immediately removed from the rest of us – I suppose so that their defeat wouldn't infect our already fragile spirits. The good news was that we'd apparently reached our allotted thirty kilometres for the second day, but the bad news was that we hadn't caught up the lost kilometres from the first day! But by now we thought, *"Stuff off OC and CSM, we don't give a toss about the lost kilometres."* Not even the odd stone poking me through my sleeping bag could prevent me from sleeping soundly.

Again, we arose at the same time and left the camp at 06h00 to start our third day on the march. The harsh gravel road disappeared into the distance; steep hills and incised valleys loomed ahead. My feet were numb. It took an age to get into a semblance of a decent stride. Almost immediately my shoulders were sore and ached for the rest of the day – by now my left shoulder throbbed continuously. Hardly anyone spoke, but when they did it was a half-hearted attempt to add a few words of encouragement to others who were faltering; words that they used to motivate their own flagging spirits.

I had to dig deeply into myself to find the mental strength to keep going. I steeled my mind against the pain and the monotony I endured for those ten hours. I caught myself asking: *How powerful is my inner strength? How resilient is my mind?*

Day three was the most difficult day of the march. I switched off from the fatigue and discomfort. I went into autopilot, speaking little and trying not to think. I believe humans have two basic instincts – survival and procreation. When you are eighteen or twenty-two years old, you think the last is the most important. I now know: the first is the primary of the two. During the latter stages of the march my mind began to play tricks. While plodding along I visualised a juicy Big Al's burger accompanied by chips and a large Coca-Cola, with Kimberly beaming across a restaurant table at me. I had made the decision to keep going.

Vaguely I recalled that our direction began to change from southwest to a northwesterly direction – hope that this was the turning point, the furthest point from the start of *Vasbyt*, brought about a state of considerable elation within me. But within a short while, my spirits sagged, as the monotony and pain overpowered me again. Each breath seemed to rasp and rattle in my burning lungs. Every fibre of my being was screaming for me to stop this excruciating lunacy. My water was quickly finished. My calves cramped. I sucked on Super Cs, which seemed to help, but I was anxious to break at midday – more to rest my weary and aching feet and shoulders than to eat. Not a soul spoke, and I assumed everyone was fixating on the midday rest like I was. We were each immersed in our singular thought of survival.

When we finally got our break, I scrounged some bandaging from a medic and wrapped the left strap of my rucksack with it, creating more of a padding that wouldn't cut into my shoulder so much.

When the time came to move again, I heard groans and swearing as the heavy backpacks were lifted clumsily. I too, swore. Some, like me, needed pulling up onto their feet. The afternoon stint had begun. The terrain was becoming more difficult with each agonising step. I felt pulverised by pain and utter discomfort. The field ambulances now felt like a pack of hyenas waiting for a vulnerable moment of weakness to attack, a constant reminder of our physical frailty. Once again, a number of men capitulated.

With absolute relief we entered our temporary base – they had chosen it well, knowing our condition – a beautiful grassed valley with a clear spring mountain stream running through it, water tinkling over grey and black stones and white quartz pebbles made smooth from years of tumbling against one another. What a wondrous and most welcome sight. Our feet and shoulders were toast and our clothing was stiff with white salt stains. Several guys removed boots and socks and simply walked into the water, with full kit and *staaldak* still in place.

The beauty of our surroundings lifted our wilting spirits. Again, we had to make small circular encampments roughly designating our section's area. I carefully peeled my socks off, looking at how the pattern of the socks had embedded itself in my heels and soles; how the skin, now a ruptured blister, peeled away along with the sock. Tenderly we washed our feet, gently hobbling in that wonderfully cool and refreshing stream, avoiding the pebbles as best we could. A few stripped down to their underpants and simply lay in the water, not able to bear the stones beneath their mangled feet. Blisters that had ruptured exposed the next layer of red and raw skin, liquid oozed from the unopened but broken ones.

We replenished our water bottles in that clear mountain stream, and tried to rinse three days of smelly and ooze-stained socks. We hung the wrung-out socks on bushes, hoping for them to drip dry. My tired and blistered feet were too sore and raw to massage. I lay down on my open sleeping bag with my legs stretched out and air-dried my mutilated appendages.

After company Roll Call and Sick Report we prepared for our evening meal. I saw a few mates and we had a brief chat: there was Ross, Dave Allpass, Adi Fourie, Shaun, Walmsley and a few other *Engelsmanne* I enjoyed keeping company with.

The NCOs and officers almost showed sympathy at times. Several more blokes had bailed, but it now looked as though we had crossed over that mental and physical halfway mark. No mention was made again of the lost kilometres – it was probably just a ruse to test our mental strength. Some wrote letters, but no sooner had the sun set than most recruits were fast asleep. As I lay in my makeshift bed, I could feel a large blister on my left shoulder.

On awakening on day four we could hardly move. We didn't want to get up and out of our sleeping bags. The NCOs came around and encouraged us, knowing that they wouldn't get anywhere by threatening us with an *oppie* – they were appealing to our intellect and logic. We had to make the decision to carry on, not them. The coffee and rusks did little to motivate us. Roll Call was short as we shifted weight from foot to foot. We didn't even have our backpacks on yet! That morning, we only got going around 06h30.

Half-heartedly I wincingly faltered out of that beautiful camp site. I hated the dead weight of my backpack. The endless gravel road snaked away in the distance; impossible mountainous terrain was all around, closing in on us. The sections now stretched out in a very long and haphazard formation, staggering up those hills and slopes, only to stumble down the other side. I had no semblance of any stride at all. I kept shifting my rucksack to alleviate the searing pain in my shoulders, but nothing worked. I felt all the jagged edges of pain that day.

This, the second last day of *Vasbyt*, was the day I came closest to bailing. Reaching inside to draw on my inner strength, I decided to grit my teeth and dig in. I was propelled by the strength of mental fortitude. Just as well, because physically, I was a wreck.

I overcame my repulsion for the task at hand by looking down at my boots as I walked. Corporal Pottie warned me that this form of myopic boot-watching would backfire on me, but I couldn't bear to look up to see one rise in the road after another – it was too banal and too painful to dwell on. Each step was agonising, as the sun bore down relentlessly. To make matters worse, the afternoon session of day four was my turn with the MAG. Hanging from my neck, the weapon felt like a noose. The guys tried to help me out. A stronger walker walked ahead of me, his *tokkeltou* around his waist and linked to my *tokkeltou* which I wore around my waist. But I couldn't tolerate the dragging sensation on my web belt, so the guys took it in turns to push me from behind up some steep hills. Ian did a fair amount of pushing – and he was only half my size! Without a word, Ian intermittently took the MAG from us supposedly bigger guys and made us look pathetic, what with his sheer guts and determination. Even Corporal Pottie was urging me on.

My relief on entering the temporary base at sunset brought me close to tears I suspect the others felt the same. The evening was a blur to me, filled with the usual routine and the unshakeable urge to retch at every movement. My feet were nothing but ruptured blisters and raw skin. I could see that other guys were faring even worse. With moist eyes and a gritty determination, we all set about quietly doing our chores, barely looking at one another for fear of seeing our own weakness in someone else's eyes. On my shoulder, the massive blister had broken open and it ached and burned incessantly. I placed a dry gauze patch from the medic over the wound, struggling even to lift my arms.

That evening I lay back in my sleeping bag and passed out immediately, dead to the world, not even knowing I had slept until that awful reveille at 05h00 woke me. The final day had dawned. I suppose that's when those of us still left on *Vasbyt* realised that it was only another ten hours, only another thirty-odd kilometres, until this torture would be over. I had sensed the day before that we had rounded the end of that section of the Outeniqua Mountain range and were heading in a northeasterly direction. We were headed back towards Oudtshoorn.

The start to day five seemed to me like a desolate road to nowhere, created by a God revelling in our anguish and suffering. I couldn't feel my feet anymore. I was in a complete daze. Corporal Pottie had to keep on urging us to get into formation. We were now so close to Oudtshoorn, we might be spotted by higher stars and bars or the general public. Frankly, we didn't give a flying banana. Eventually that miserable gravel road came to a Y-junction in a tarred road. I recognised it and relief came flooding back. It was the R62 from Oudtshoorn to Calitzdorp. Somewhere, unnoticed by me, we had changed direction from northeast to east. Without doubt, this was the home stretch.

Corporal Pottie indicated to us that we were to cross the tar road. As I approached the centre of the road, an unexpected oncoming vehicle jarred a couple of us into running towards the other side, but the signal from my brain to my legs and feet was on the blink! I was numb from my knees down, and my attempt at running approached more of a hobble. I couldn't even find the energy to walk quickly to the other side. A thought of defeat passed through my mind: *Oh well, I almost made it* ...

The driver, realising our dilemma, braked hard. As he slowly passed us, he stared in disbelief at the sorry sight of our rabble of a squad.

We were told to keep off the tar, not least because one of us might have stumbled and would be in danger of being run over, but also because our booted feet pounding on the hard surface of the road was agony on our mutilated feet. Corporal Pottie slowed us up for the last kilometre, ordering us to get into a decent formation and hold our heads up high. We sensed the honour in this and mustered what little dignity we had left. We walked into camp with pride. Our pride was reflected in the faces of the military and civilian staff as they beheld the long column of marching men entering the camp.

With the other men of my platoon, I hobbled to the barracks and crashed onto my bed. The soft mattress beneath me filled me with sheer pleasure and delight. I must have lain there for over an hour before I even tried to move. When I finally roused myself to deal with the aftermath of *Vasbyt*, it was with the slow and hesitant movements of an old man. There wasn't a single recruit who didn't have some Merthiolate treatment on their wounds that week at sick parade. Our platoon had lost at least five souls on that mission.

During the week following *Vasbyt* we took it easy in camp, wearing our PT clothes and *tekkies* and doing basic lectures with a lot of time off for recreation. We later received a *Vasbyt* certificate and learned that we had covered 125 kilometres of a roughly U-shaped circuit around that mountain. We all argued that it must have surely been closer to 135 or even 140 kilometres, but could not quite have been 150 kilometres — but who really cared! We'd done it and made the grade.

Vasbyt taught me that I could push my body and mind much further than I ever thought possible. Achieving what had seemed impossible helped to boost my self-confidence, which in turn instilled in me the lasting knowledge, gained through that experience, of what I was capable of.

Vasbyt was about discipline and persistence, a test of character and endurance that is not for the faint-hearted. I bear the physical scars: the start of Iliotibial Band Syndrome or ITBS in both knees and a scar on my left shoulder that is still a badge of honour to this day.

Chapter 9

We were granted our first pass a week after *Vasbyt*. I was excited to be going home – I couldn't wait to see Kimberly – and relieved to leave the relentless pace of Infantry School for a while. Adi, who was from Port Elizabeth, had never visited Pretoria, so he joined me for the few days I would be home.

The morning of that first day of pass, we were up and already dressed at 04h00 to catch the bus back to the good ol' Transvaal. Dressed in our browns for the first time aside from Sunday church parade and sports parade, we were drilled to the parade ground where a short lecture was delivered about how we were expected to behave like the pride of the infantry. I overheard some of the young NCO companies being warned not to go AWOL. Springbok Atlas buses were parked on the parade ground, ready to ferry recruits to Cape Town, Durban, Joburg, Port Elizabeth and Pretoria. By far, the majority of us were returning to the Transvaal. We always travelled home from Oudtshoorn in Springbok Atlas buses – the bus company must have done a roaring trade with the SADF.

The long-awaited *"Uit … TREE!"* finally came, and in an orderly fashion, without clamour, we briskly clambered aboard the buses and took our seats. We were off!

We travelled on the N12 through De Rust and then north through the handsome Meiringspoort where the *Grootrivier*, or Great River, has eroded a deep cleft more than twenty-five kilometres through the seemingly impenetrable Swartberg Mountain Range. The N12 road, which winds along the floor of the gorge, crosses the great waterway over twenty times, but because it wasn't yet light, we could barely make out the soaring cliffs and spectacular rock formations on either side of us in the moonlight. At times, it seemed the winding road was floating above the river as we crossed it to and fro.

Past the turnoff to Prince Albert we turned onto the N1 in a northwesterly direction, the sun now rising in the east, and from that point on, town after monotonous *platteland* town scrolled past the window: Beaufort West, Richmond, Hanover, Colesberg, Springfontein, Trompsburg, Edenburg, the legislative capital Bloemfontein, Kroonstad. Finally, we passed through Joburg and arrived at the Pretoria railway station, where my parents collected Adi and me just after 16h00.

It was good to be home, and the break was pleasant. For a couple of days, my feet were still sore and numb from *Vasbyt*, but I felt good that the ordeal was over and I had survived. Now I could discuss the experience with the *oumanne* as an equal, and not just listen to their stories. It was nice to eat my mom's homemade food and sleep in my soft and comfy bed. And there were no inspections!

I introduced Adi to a few of my mates, and we frequented pubs to restore ourselves with plenty of beer and wine. We hung around nightclubs and enjoyed a *braaivleis* or two. Kimberly was at varsity during the weekdays and I didn't want to hang around Joburg waiting for her lectures to end each day, so the two of us had very little private time together.

The pass was over all too soon and we had to return to Infantry School. Leaving Pretoria from Church Square that last morning at 06h00 wasn't easy, especially knowing what we would face on our return to Oudtshoorn. I choked up saying goodbye to Kimberly, who had come to see us off, regretting that I hadn't been able to bask in her company more, hold her close and listen to the sweet sound of her voice as she told me of everything I had missed while I was away. Suddenly I wished that I had hung around her campus like a love-sick teenager, waiting for her and taking advantage of every five minutes I could have held her hand. But now it was time to part, and I didn't know when I would see her again. I kissed her gently on the mouth, then stepped back and took both her hands in mine.

"Goodbye so soon …" I said, trying to smile reassuringly at her.

"I know …" Kimberly's eyes were sad. "I hardly got to see you," she said quietly.

"I know, my brown-eyed girl," I said, brushing her hair from her cheek and avoiding her eyes. I swallowed hard. "I'll be back … hopefully soon." Kimberly nodded, pressed her lips together. "Hey," I tried to make my voice light. "You be good, now, you hear?" Kimberly reddened, both of us thinking of her past infidelities.

"Oh, come on. You know I will." She became bustling, official. "Come," she said, clucking like a mother hen. "You have to get going. I'll see you soon." She said a warm goodbye to Adi, then turning to me, she smiled and hugged me awkwardly.

Our embrace was interrupted by the bus driver shouting that it was time to go. Reluctantly pulling myself from Kimberly's arms, I clambered on board the bus with Adi and we grabbed two seats near the back of the bus. As the bus departed, my parting words to Kimberly from the open window were: "I never did get to eat that Al's burger with you ..." She gave me a puzzled look as the bus pulled away under the watchful gaze of *Oom* Paul Kruger's statue.

I felt sorry for myself on the bus, my butt going numb from the hard back and vinyl seats. I rested my forehead against the cold glass of the bus window and tried to daydream myself into a more pleasant place as the monotonous miles rolled by. But the closer we got to Oudtshoorn, the more my mood sank until, as we rounded the bloodied-lit infantryman statue and passed through the main gate at twilight, I reached an all-time low.

"Okay, *manne*," the first words from Corporal Joubert on our return were. *"Die party is oor. Nou gaan ons regtig begin werk!"* The party, he told us, was over. We were going to really work now.

We had more than six weeks of basics, a week of *Vasbyt* and our first pass behind us. Up to eight weeks of platoon weapons training lay ahead. We were facing a tough time. The platoon weapons phase of our training would demand physical guts and staying power. As tough as *Vasbyt* had been, this would require a different but no less demanding type of endurance. Platoon weapons would leave me glassy-eyed with exhaustion.

During platoon weapons phase, we became familiar with the various platoon weapons, how to use them and, in due course, how to teach others to use them. Instruction began with lectures in wooden huts or gazebos enclosed on two sides with wooden panels. We endured the lessons in much discomfort: dressed in our webbing, weighed down by our helmets, our rifles at hand, trying desperately to stay awake in the still and pressing morning heat. Lectures were followed by exams which were written most Saturdays in the mess hall. And along with trying to sharpen our minds, we continued to get our bodies into top condition and became supremely fit and ragingly hungry.

We were up every morning at 04h00 to drill for an hour and a half before breakfast, after which we would droop into our seats for lectures or practical demonstrations. It was a struggle just to stay awake.

Soon, the theory we were taught was put into practice, and we began our practical weapons training. Before we could fire live ammunition, we went through rigorous dry drill exercises, each platoon being trained by their own platoon sergeants. For example, a wooden dummy mortar bomb would be loaded into an actual Patmor mortar pipe by the Patmor operator, having been handed the mortar bomb by his support man – Ian and I were partners in most of these platoon weapons practices, undertaken on the open expanse of grass immediately in front of Bungalow 7. It was all about our understanding of the rigorous procedures allied to firing any of the required platoon weapons.

Once the dry drills had been perfected we were taken in SAMILs to two expanses of open ground that were designated live weapons training areas, one to the north, one to the west, both several kilometres out. Here we fired the real stuff.

I found learning to be a grenadier a thrilling experience, and bonded with the American-made M79 Grenade Launcher, or *snotneus* ("snot-nose"). We weren't supposed to call the M79 a *snotneus*, to do so was grounds for a little extra PT, but we mostly did amongst ourselves. The M79 is light and versatile, and I could quickly aim it at any target between 150 and 350 metres and hit it easily. But she could give you a mean punch in the shoulder if she wasn't held correctly, and the forty-millimetre cartridge yielded a spectacular explosion.

The Israeli-made 60 mm patrol mortar or "Patmor" packed an even bigger punch than the *snotneus*, and even the dumbest of soldiers could use it. I relished the *wa-whoomp* the mortar bomb made when it detonated. When firing with the lowest or zero charge, we could actually see the mortar bomb leaving the pipe and track it until it hit the target, which was only a short distance away, no more than a hundred metres.

Apart from the *snotneus* and Patmor, we were also shown how to use the Belgian-made FN MAG or Light Machine Gun, which is a belt-fed suppression weapon, and the South African manufactured Milkor Multiple Grenade Launcher (MGL), known as the "Meerkat". The Meerkat was originally developed with the intention of replacing the *snotneus*, and served with the SADF during the Border War under the designation Y2, in other words, in secret.

We trained with Claymore mines and various grenades, such as the hand tossed M26 Fragmentation Hand Grenade, concussion hand grenade and smoke grenade. We also trained with the 75 mm Rifle Grenade with HE and FRAG for the R4.

I enjoyed the intrigue of activating the anti-personnel Claymore mines: coupling the detonation leads to the convex green plastic casing. Command-detonated and directional, these mines were used primarily to ambush the enemy, but also as booby traps for retreating infantrymen outnumbered or outweaponed by the enemy. The mine itself has little metal spikes that act as anchor feet, and the convex body is aimed towards the enemy. Thousands of metal balls explode outwards into the kill zone, maiming or killing the enemy. I placed many of these mines for the lootie, initially thinking it was a privilege. *He must have identified a talent in me that he's grooming*, I thought. Until it occurred to me that he was giving me this responsibility because he felt I was expendable.

Grenade-tossing was utterly nerve-wracking, but the terror was coupled with an incredible adrenaline rush. After pulling the pin, you throw the grenade as accurately as possible towards your intended target, timing the explosion precisely. We usually threw the grenades from behind a concrete protective barrier, but sometimes we would throw from behind an earthen berm, which is really nothing more than a bank of earth providing some rather inadequate protection.

I loved firing the rifle grenades. They can quickly be added to an infantryman's arsenal with no extra launch weapon required — just the R4. The soldier merely has to carry the grenades and a few 5.56 mm blanks.

Through platoon weapons training, we came to know thoroughly every weapon an infantry platoon could use – from the small firearms to the mighty MAG – and could strip each one down to its smallest part. We understood how each was designed and how it was used, enabling us to both operate it effectively and teach others how to use it.

The most intimate weapon we had to be proficient in was the R4 assault rifle, our personal weapon which was carried with us every day, wherever we went. We learnt how to strip the R4 down and then reassemble it, and then we were timed as we did it. I became so good at disassembling and reassembling my R4 that I could do it blindfolded in less than thirty seconds. We practiced this exercise blindfolded so that we could do it in the pitch dark of night. It was preached to us that this drill would save our lives.

We were all enthusiastic about the weapons training, treating the exercises like advanced amusement park games. We knew the various weapons intimately and down to their last detail, and we could fervently argue the benefits of one over the other in theoretical situations. But it certainly never occurred to me that the equipment I was handling like toys was in fact designed to tear into a person's flesh and rip them apart. I guess I had no foresight. In retrospect, it wasn't inconceivable that a few amongst us harboured malicious thoughts of actually taking a life on the border with one of these killing machines.

One day I was cleaning my rifle's *sluitstuk* when the two corporals rushed in and shouted for us to *"TREE AAN!"* immediately. We knew that if they discovered a rifle or a rifle's firing pin with its breech piece unsecured, they would make a note of the serial number. If it was your rifle or block, you owned up and hoped to God you would be spared the consequences. In my rush to respond to the corporals' command, I left my firing pin with breech piece lying in the unlocked cupboard, right next to my rifle, having already locked my *trommel*. I had just committed the cardinal sin. Corporal Potgieter held up the rifle and called out the rifle number. For a brief moment, I didn't realise that it was my rifle number, then I recognised the digits and went cold.

When I confessed to being the guilty party, Corporal Potgieter showed me both the breech piece and rifle with a self-satisfied grin. I realised the seriousness of the offence and knew that, not only was I in line for the *oppie* of my life, but my error could get me kicked off the course. My rifle was handed back to me, but the corporal kept the breech piece to show Lieutenant Pretorius. I was desperate to persuade the corporals and Pretorius that my slip-up shouldn't lead to me being sent away. In the rush to assemble outside, I told them, I had inadvertently let this happen. I went on to tell them that I understood how crucial it was to secure my rifle and its parts, that I understood the severity of my mistake and would never dream of doing it again. After my earnest plea, possibly coming across as a string of excuses, I felt I was rather convincing, and somehow, by good fortune perhaps, all three were convinced. I was saved.

I didn't even get an *oppie* for that mistake. However, Lieutenant Pretorius recorded my transgression in his little black book, threatening to give me a pink. I began to fear that the three were aiming to systematically target me: looking out for any demerits to log and waiting to catch me out for a biggie.

There was a recruit in one of the other platoons whom the instructors took to calling *"Sluitstuk"*, because he repeatedly left his *trommel* open. To make matters worse, the first few times he was caught out, he didn't even know what his rifle or breech piece numbers were – almost as bad as actually leaving the parts lying around. He was subjected to several personal coaching sessions with his corporals. Eventually it dawned on him that he'd better learn his lesson – which he finally did.

Our rifles had to be constantly maintained and cleaned. After we had fired our weapons on the range, we would take them into the shower with us to give them a hot rub-down and clean them of most of the burnt gunpowder and dirt and dust acquired from the shooting range. All water had to be dried off carefully to prevent rusting. For the finer art of cleaning, we would sit on our beds on our grey blankets, sometimes cross-legged, chatting to one another, listening to the latest Top 20 hits of '86 or the most popular songs of the '80s or to Gouws' tape-deck blaring, and tend to our rifles and all their parts. When the small plastic vials of oil supplied in our cleaning kits came to an end, we reverted to spraying the parts with Q20 and then wiping them down with a soft mutton cloth – every nook and cranny. We would thread a pull-through cleaning rope with brass ends through the barrel. One end would have a small barrel-sized wire brush screwed on to take most of the larger dirt particles. Once this was done a few times, we would pull a small piece of white cotton cloth called a "two by four" through the barrel, attached to a slotted brass end on the pull-through. Fine steel wool came in very handy for any rusty parts.

We learned things such as military discipline and first aid during the platoon weapons phase. We did more advanced *veldkuns*, or fieldcraft, than during basics, including map work and compass for navigation training, which was used to fill gaps between weapons training or lectures. Navigation involved day and night exercises, either as a squad or as a platoon, and we learnt how to orient yourself in the field and transpose gathered information to a map, from which you could calculate your position or bearing and distance to and from anything represented on the map. I enjoyed navigation, mostly because it meant having a break to sit on my haunches while I studied the map. We used 1:10 000 scale maps of Oudtshoorn, the smallest scale maps available and probably the most ideal for an infantryman, as they provided quite fine terrain detail for any defined area. For longer route marches involving navigation, we also used 1:50 000 scale maps, but this was rare and the crucial detail that we needed was absent at that scale. We had to learn to calculate coordinates and degrees. We would also use a compass and heading settings. We had to be able to navigate by day or night, and also learnt how to navigate using star constellations. Once we had mastered the art of interpreting the landscape according to a map and vice versa, we were made to do it on the move. We were tested on map interpretation, and had to rattle off certain bearings and coordinates on command. If a recruit was unable to give the correct answer to a question within a minute, he was taken off for a quick "orientation" – of course, an *oppie*.

Night exercises could be hazardous, as you march in single file or in a silent V-formation, moving across an unfamiliar landscape. Often I'd hear a loud swearing as some poor bloke tripped over a rock or stepped into an aardvark hole. Once, our section leader simply disappeared in front of us, only to be discovered languishing in a donga almost three metres deep! Fortunately he survived unhurt.

On another occasion, I was given charge of a section of the platoon. The loot had concealed himself in the bush to the northeast of the base, and we had to find him. I navigated well, and came to his hideout within the required half hour, but as we ended the exercise, I forgot to give the others the command to make their weapons safe.

"Warren!" the loot shouted, and I jumped. "Come here!" I stood to attention in front of him. He looked at me coldly, and when he finally spoke, his thickly accented English was heavy with sarcasm. "And, tell me, Warren." He sucked at his teeth with a sound of irritation, flicked his eyes up at me with an eyebrow raised. "What are you supposed to do before coming into a base? Hey? Even if it's a temporary base?" The realisation of my error dawned on me, and my heart sank.

"You must secure your weapon, lieutenant!" I tried not to let my anxiety sound in my voice.

The loot was a man of few words.

He gave me a meaningful look before insisting, "Give me your magazine!" I obeyed and handed the magazine over. I have never seen a rifle magazine travel so far in the air before. It took Ian, Kerry and me over ten minutes of searching high and low through the dense bushes littering the veld before my magazine was retrieved.

By this stage I had reached a level of fitness I'd never thought possible. Training had bruised and injured, strained and honed my body, so that my muscles rippled. Wherever we went, we went at a march or a run. But even at these levels of fitness, the worst part of the day for most of us recruits – except perhaps for Ian and one or two other already super-fit guys – was PT, usually the last part of formal training for the day. Just the thought of PT unnerved me, and my stomach always turned over as I dressed for the session, thinking of the potential for it to turn into an *opfok* session. In reality, it wasn't often that a platoon commander decided that his platoon would stay on for extra PT. Invariably, we realised that it came down from higher up than the platoon commanders, that someone had issued an order: "*Hulle disipliene is uiters swak* (their discipline is really poor), you'd better punish these recruits during PT."

We were made to do numerous push-ups, endless sit-ups. Pull-ups were done on bars between poles in a designated area for this type of training. We were matched up with a buddy about the same weight and height as ourselves to do the training in pairs. To begin with, we were allowed to give a little assistance, but later he would have to stand below and watch, calling out the count as our partners went.

We ran the 2.4 kilometre on the service road that exited the base at the North Gate and ran alongside the camp to the northeast. The surface was mixed gravel and sand. At school I was pretty average at cross-country running, especially the 2.4. My best time was about eight and a half minutes in running shorts, vest and running shoes. But here we ran in training overalls.

In the first few weeks of basics we ran in *tekkies*, shorts and our brown army T-shirt. Now we ran in overalls and boots. A week into platoon weapons phase, we were made to run in overalls and boots, while carrying our R4s. By the time we neared the end of platoon weapons, we would be running in overalls, boots, R4s with *staaldak*, chest webbing with all magazines and a full two-litre water bottle.

I surprised myself by running a personal best of nine minutes twenty seconds with all this kit on.

Times were recorded and kept and we were not allowed to get a time more than thirty seconds slower than our previous, or we'd be made to repeat the run the following day. If you didn't get consistently good times, you would be reprimanded for holding up the squad, and then everyone would get a lower average time thanks to your miserable efforts. Guys who were consistently at the back of the pack and didn't improve their times were booted off the course. It was harsh.

There were longer and sweatier runs of between five and ten kilometres, but the odd twenty kilometre run carrying long creosote poles like telephone poles between you and your designated buddy, and weighing at least forty or more kilograms, was no joke, regardless of how strong and fit you were.

For the first few months, I became very apprehensive every time we were driven out into the field or to the shooting range. I was afraid that we were about to be given a *bosbus*. Early on in our shooting range practices, when coming back from Swartberg shooting range, we were twice made to jump off the trucks and make our way back to base in formation at double-quick pace. Trying to keep up with the SAMIL with all your kit and rifle is no joke, especially with the dust from the truck's rear wheels being spewed all over us and into our eyes and mouths. This was known as a *bosbus*, which was not the bus in the bush that its name implies, but an *opfok* in the bush behind a

SAMIL. In retrospect I see that this was totally unwarranted, but it was part of Infantry School's own brand of psychological warfare against its troops to keep us guessing.

Disembarking from a moving SAMIL 50 truck was an art – fun for some, but nasty and painful for others. Before jumping, you would have to judge the speed at which the truck was travelling. Choosing your moment carefully, you would leap off and try and synchronise your opposing velocity with that of the truck. Being the last rifleman to jump helped – then you had enough room to run from the back of the truck and accurately match the truck's speed. The idea was to jump off and touch down with both feet without falling. Unfortunately for the first few jumpers, they couldn't time their speed correctly, and they would end up in a somersault or in a heap on the road. Fortunately, no one was badly injured. The drivers were extremely careful. They were national servicemen, our mates, not PF instructors as was the case in some other bases.

I remember one particularly awful rifle PT when my staying power was sorely tested. We were made to run through the veld and had been going at it for nearly twenty minutes when we were given the order to leopard crawl. The dust made me choke and gag as I made my way through the grass on my knees and elbows. Soon, another order was issued, and we all got to our knees to crawl. Another order, and we all lifted our rifles above our heads. We were made to run around this bush, then that one, then go belly down and leopard crawl again. Breathless, parched and aching, I wished for some sort of cover to slip behind: a thick bush or a big rock or even a large anthill, somewhere to hide and catch my breath before falling into ragged formation as the platoon stuttered past again. It was nothing but wishful thinking, I just had to suck it up and keep going.

During PT, we weren't ever taken apart to the point of being hospitalised, but we still suffered. Pole and rifle PT were tolerable but the worst PT was training with our marbles; that dreaded concrete block. Each marble weighed about twenty kilograms. It was unbearable.

Buddy PT involved pairing up with someone of similar build and height and taking turns carrying one another: *skaap dra* (carrying the sheep), commonly known as the fireman's lift, or *baba dra* (carrying the baby), which is self-explanatory, except I've never heard of a ninety-kilogram baby in full battle gear. The idea of this was to be able to support one another as a team, and perhaps more importantly, to be able to carry your mate if he was wounded in battle. But it was pure agony, staggering under the weight of your buddy, and much cursing accompanied these forays, leading to us having to repeat the exercise several times until we were knackered. We would come to understand the reasoning behind buddy PT when we did the first aid course.

Water PT was a punishment reserved for special occasions. Once we were corporately disciplined with water PT. With whistles blowing, we were made to run around the bungalow with our two-litre water bottles, the corporals timing us. This time, some of the guys didn't make it in the specified time, so we would all have to run again. The next time, others would run too fast and leave their mates behind, and we would all have to run again. Twenty-five minutes of running in the sweltering Oudtshoorn heat, consuming litres of water to keep from dehydrating, and it wasn't long before guys started vomiting. Water bottles cascaded around the bungalow as guys scrambled to make it in the allotted time ... it was not a pretty sight.

One especially demanding PT session was *hindernes oorsteek* across an obstacle course made up of tyres and ropes and various wooden structures. It was punishment for faring badly in a test we had written. Personally, I had done well in this particular test, but we were made to suffer in unison. About a quarter of us hadn't failed the test miserably, and we were made to complete the course twice within a certain time limit after which we would be spared further pain and exhaustion. The rest had to do the course twice more again because they hadn't done well in the test. Then another bunch who had not only fared poorly in the test, but had also failed their inspections or had been caught out for not locking their kit away, did the course twice more again.

The corporals bellowed at us as we hustled through the course, *"Beweeg! Hardloop!"* ("Move! Run!"). Poor van Schalkwyk looked as though he was going to drop out from exhaustion halfway through his second lap through the obstacle course. Those of us that were close by propped him up on the runs and helped him over the difficult parts where we could. It appeared the concept of helping your buddy was starting to take root. Schalle wheezed and panted, eventually lying on the ground turning alarmingly red, purple, white and green in turn. I wondered if he might be having a heart attack. With time, he arose, ashen-faced and half-dead, and valiantly pulled himself through. He'd made it! And we all celebrated for him. Even the lootie raised an eyebrow in amazement and approval.

There were a few other *vaakseuns* like Schalle. All of them were nice guys and almost all of them eventually made it through Infantry School in the end. But they certainly had a hard time of it to begin with.

We were beginning to look out for each other, discovering that it wasn't all about each man for himself anymore, and that was what the whole "buddy system" the army was trying to instil in us was all about. All the challenges the PT sessions made us face were aimed at teaching us to work as a team. Often, the corporals would shout, *"Julle maatjies wil nie saamwerk nie!"* ("Your buddies don't want to work together!"), and we would know that we weren't giving the exercise everything we had and we were in danger of facing another round. They were trying to encourage unity, but it felt as if they were forcing teamwork down our throats. I, like many of the others, railed against this. Perhaps because we were older, had more life experience, it was hard for us to learn this lesson, but we did eventually realise that we would have to work together if we were to survive the training.

Even though it felt as if the PT sessions were designed to finish us off, they did always keep an eye out for us. There was always a field ambulance with attendant medic on call, just a few minutes away from where we were being taken apart.

During the first few months there were some occasions that I felt we were really being pushed during PT. Once, Sergeant Major Lategaan, being a typical PF member, told the NCOs what to do, suggesting to the platoon commanders that they should go along to keep an eye on their troops. In a roundabout way, he was telling the platoon commanders that, as a PF, he was calling the shots. I didn't feel that Lategaan was a particularly unfair CSM, but I recognised that these PF NCOs faced a problem in dealing with the national serviceman looties – particularly those who were both ranked and degreed, and who weren't likely to take nonsense from a senior PF NCO. The average one-pip platoon commander was a young whippersnapper, often scared of his company sergeant major who was more mature and commanding than him. For a lot of us in Bravo, though, our staff sergeant was barely two or three years older than us, and we weren't likely to put up with crap from him. We were likely to be less tolerant once we had rank.

An NCO with a chip on his shoulder had a hard time telling an indignant officer-to-be how to behave. In some companies, where NCOs straight out of school might have been more compliant, this problem was probably rare, but our guys weren't like that. Corporal Pottie wasn't straight out of school he'd been at Oudtshoorn the previous year and tried to act more maturely and he generally knew how to read us, but often he would have to be reminded of who he was dealing with by Lieutenant Pretorius. Pottie would be taken aside by the loot for a confidential word, but we would overhear.

"*Luister, korporaal,*" Pretorius would say. "*Jy moet passop! Hierdie ouens is slimmer en ouer as jy. Dink eers voordat jy iets deur hulle koppe probeer kry.*" ("Listen, corporal – watch out. These guys are brighter than you. Think before you try and tell them something"). This reprimand pleased us guys no end when we overheard it.

It was sometimes hard to remember, but the intention of Infantry School training was to produce infantry officers and NCOs – not just to bully us gratuitously! We knew that some of us would be kept behind at Infantry School to run the scene the following year and many of the guys worked hard to prove themselves, thinking it would be the best students who would be asked to stay. But it was clear to me that the authorities were more likely to keep those recruits who were most yielding to Infantry School's ways, rather than those who were particularly good at what they did.

Some of the English-speaking guys liked to think they were being tough by resisting the Dutchmen training them. I was one of them. We weren't. In fact, we were working against our own best interests. I think the lootie and the corporals saw that I was a bit *hardegat,* "hard-arsed", and I suppose they were always planning their moment of revenge against me.

I guess I didn't recognise that cooperation with the instructors was damned hard work, and accepting the training and seeing it through showed mental and physical strength. The instructors were only doing what they had to do, and a soldier's chance of cracking was greater when he resisted the process not necessarily because they made it worse for you, but because you came off second-best when you resisted. In any case, we who were resistant knew there were limits beyond which not even the physical training instructors would go. So being resistant wasn't nearly as brave or as dangerous as it was made to look. Their training to achieve cooperation amongst the troops was a gradual process which we never really noticed. It was subtle conditioning on a physical and mental level. Basics, followed by *Vasbyt,* followed by platoon weapons training certainly toughened me up. Permanently.

As officers-in-training, we were subjected to careful monitoring to assess our mental state. The army wanted to be sure that we were suitable officer material, and not only did we have to be strong mentally, but we had to have the "right" political orientation, too. We visited the Military Psychological Institute professionals, or *koptiffies,* three times that year. During the first two visits, psychometric testing was carried out. The last visit merely confirmed whether the *koptiffie* had assessed us correctly. Some guys were kicked off the course, whilst the majority stayed. Proportionately more English-speaking guys than Afrikaners disappeared. Ian had suggested that to avoid being singled out and perhaps being kicked off the course, we should play it cool and show a certain level of disinterest in the country's politics. His strategy must have been right. We stayed. We grudgingly acknowledged that the head-doctors had a role to play and didn't put up too much opposition, although we mischievously set them up for a brain teaser or two. The NCOs and some officers would mockingly say of the army psychologists, *"Hier kom die manne met die dik brille en wit jasse!"* ("Here come the men with the thick glasses and white coats!").

In late April, I was given leave to attend *gradeplegtigheid* – my graduation ceremony at Wits. There were a lot of us from Bravo who would be allowed to go home for four or five days to attend our graduations, those who hadn't yet formally received our degrees and the teachers who mostly followed their degrees with a Higher Diploma in Education. For those of us who stayed far away, the army even paid for our flights home.

I left camp mid-morning on Friday in my step-outs, beret and brown army shoes and rode a transport truck with several other recruits to the airport at George to catch a plane to Johannesburg where Kimberly would be waiting to pick me up. It was such a relief to escape.

At home, I stepped on the scale. I had gone from a scrawny, weakling, bag-o-bones weighing seventy-six kilograms in my 1.92 metre frame to eighty-seven kilograms in just a few weeks of platoon weapons training. The excellent food served at Infantry School had to take some credit, and I had often had second and even third helpings of a meal, but it was muscle that I had packed on and not an ounce of fat. I had developed abs I never had before, and my physique had toughened up. I was very pleased with my bulkier frame!

Saturday morning was spent in downtown Pretoria organising a gown and cap to be hired. My parents and Kimberly attended the ceremony at Wits Great Hall. Tuesday 22 April, the day of my graduation ceremony, was also my father's fifty-first birthday, so we had two wonderful occasions to celebrate. But the next day I was back on the plane to George to return to my life of drudgery, and within a day of getting back there, it was as if I hadn't left at all.

Chapter 10

In 1981, my last year of school, I only considered two universities: the University of Cape Town, UCT, and the University of the Witwatersrand, commonly known as Wits. UCT and Wits were both English-medium universities. At that time, the University of Pretoria, or Tukkies, was perceived by many to be a bastion of repressive intellectual Afrikanerdom. In the end, I chose to go to Wits. When Kimberly finished school two years later, she also enrolled at Wits, mostly because I was there.

Wits was a breeding ground for leftist politics. If a student wasn't swept up by the anti-government rhetoric, at the very least they became more politically aware and had their existing beliefs challenged. Both Wits and UCT spawned generations of radicals amongst their white students, and many young men were galvanised to join the End Conscription Campaign from these campuses.

I was apolitical. Finances dictated my position to a large degree: I was at varsity on a bank loan my parents had helped me to secure, and I felt a responsibility to remain focussed on getting my qualification. I tried not to allow sideshows to disrupt my studies, but politics seemed to creep into every facet of one's personal and family life.

One afternoon in 1984, while I was in the laboratory on the third floor of the Biochemistry Building, the SAP raided the Wits campus. This was not unusual. Wits was a repeat target for the Apartheid government, who resented the vocal dissent of the young leftist students there. But the police's forays into university grounds were becoming increasingly frequent and brutal. From my elevated viewpoint, I watched as students of every kind – most of which had been quietly sitting dotted about the lawns were beaten with batons and attacked by dogs. Arcs of teargas spewed into the air from canisters flung from members of the SAP. I looked on aghast, relieved to be ensconced in the relative safety of the lab.

If the government aimed to win white people over, specifically English-speaking white people, they were not going to achieve it this way. Student opinions were polarised by this event, and it provided fuel to the fire for the politically active students on campus.

This kind of harassment of Wits students continued throughout my last year of varsity, and increased later after I had finished my degree and joined the army.

It was during my last year at varsity that I found myself having a heated conversation with several of my buddies from Pretoria. We were visiting Alan at his house in Brooklyn, and the subject had turned to whether South Africa could immediately and effectively be governed by blacks, were they to rise to power legitimately through the ballot. Without a single dissent, my friends were of the opinion that blacks would be incapable of ruling the land successfully.

I played true to what was expected of a liberal Witsie.

"Of course they could!" I stated emphatically. "There's no reason, if black people were given power tomorrow, they shouldn't govern the country effectively ... They'd probably do a better job than the Nats!" I declared. If I'm honest, I must confess that part of me only wanted to play devil's advocate, to test my friends' political leanings and cast doubt on their beliefs. The retort was roundly condemned by all. I pursued my line of argument: "If blacks were given the same educational opportunities provided to whites," I said, "this country wouldn't be in the unfortunate state it's in today." Some of the guys objected loudly, while others just shook their heads.

"What are you saying, Mike?" Alan asked indignantly. "The Bantu Education system is just as good as ours!"

"Crap!" I retorted, but Thomas piped up before I could defend my position.

"The problem isn't the education system," he said. "If the blacks would just apply themselves to their education, instead of boycotting and burning their schools down, they would be better off. So would the whole country!"

These young men didn't see that Apartheid was a bad system. How could they? How could I? We were living in an era in which white South Africa was systematically being fed disinformation by the government. We were the products of the Apartheid government's insidious and sophisticated propaganda machine.

***

The SADF's strategic communication initiatives, known as communications operations, or comops, were a key component of their strategy for the dissemination of the party-line. The primary – if unspoken – aim of comops at Infantry School was to neutralise in schools the effect of the negative press against the Apartheid government and promote positive attitudes, behaviours and ideologies in support of the State.

The teachers of Bravo Company were at the frontline of this programme, expected, as they were, to be responsible for the cadet companies at government high schools across the nation. The teachers were given extra training in the line of urban coinops, or urban counter-insurgency training, because they were more likely to encounter resistance in the urban environment. This included a week-long course in how to train cadets at a school, another day of *skoolbeveiliging*, or safeguarding a school, and visits to schools in Oudtshoorn to observe school cadet corps in operation and to practice protecting a school from terrorist attacks. Those of us who weren't teachers had a relatively relaxed time while they were out doing extra coinops, given time to write letters or chat in the barracks.

Because of the extra responsibility placed on the teachers emerging from Infantry School, we were subjected to extra comops training. During basics, we were lectured weekly on the justifications for the Apartheid government's resistance to what they called the "Total Onslaught", or the challenges faced from every facet of society, both internal and external to the country, in combating the threat of communism and countering the rise of radical black nationalists. The lectures on the SADF's philosophy and role in the "Total Strategy" adopted by the government to counter the Total Onslaught were delivered by visiting PF officers from the comops division or our designated company comops officer.

Early on, these sessions included encouraging us to write letters home, and gently probing us to establish our mental state. We were asked some fairly inane things, like, "How's the training going?" or "Have you adjusted to the routine here?" Sometimes, with feigned concern, we were asked, "Are you all in good spirits?" Eventually, the question that was intended all along would come: "Do any of you have problems you want to talk about?" The officer would look at us with great feeling, pretending to care. "You can trust us," he would say meaningfully. "Anything you say will be kept confidential." I knew this wasn't true.

These regular indoctrination sessions were just the precursor to the comops training we were about to receive. The ordinary SAI *plaas* rifleman did not receive this level of comops training. Our week of comops arrived towards the end of the Junior Leadership phase of training, following the basics and platoon weapons phases. We were told that comops would give us an understanding of the necessity of all our training; that we would then understand the importance of protecting our country which was under siege.

I had found enduring an hour of comops every week bad enough. The thought of suffering a whole week of it was horrendous.

We knew comops week was looming when several Bravo platoons were recruited to leave the Infantry School base to go and set up the comops camp. When the day finally arrived, we were herded into those lumbering SAMILs and driven off northwards to a pretty *kloof* at the southern foot of the Swartberg Mountains.

Coordinates: 33°28'37.64"S 22°08'45.08"E

A large rectangle of levelled, grassed land was set amongst the scrub of the surrounding veld, on which was pitched a large, straight-sided *kraal* of green canvas army tents large enough to accommodate a company of several hundred recruits. In the centre of the *kraal* stood a large tent made up of the roofs of four smaller tents. This was the lecture "hall". Close by was a volleyball court. Several indigenous trees dotted the area. There were permanent water towers at the outside edge of the camp, and various temporary structures for kitchens, medics, signals, a tuck shop and ablutions enclosed the encampment. The southern service road which led back to the main base would be used for our afternoon PT.

On our arrival, we were divided up into groups – the platoons being deliberately mixed up to encourage interaction with other recruits – and each group assigned to a tent. The tents were given names of various *Voortrekker* leaders, Boer War heroes and Afrikaner politicians and statesmen. There were, among others, tents called Sarel Cilliers, Piet Uys, Hans van Rensburg, Piet Retief, Andries Hendrik Potgieter, Gerrit Maritz, Andries Pretorius, *Generaal* de Wet, *Generaal* de la Rey, Louis Botha and Paul Kruger.

I decided to throw caution to the wind and stir up the pot.

"Korporaal," I spoke with exaggerated politeness to a Bravo corporal called de Wet, who shared his last name with a *Boer* general after which one of our comops tents was named. "Why is there no Tent Jan Smuts?" Jan Christiaan Smuts was an Afrikaner known as one of the greatest intellectuals South Africa has ever produced. He was the first student in the history of Cambridge University to achieve a double cum laude in law, and went on to become a great war hero, leading *Boer* commandos for the Transvaal in the Second Boer War, leading armies of South Africa against Germany in World War I and commanding the British Army in East Africa. He served as Prime

Minister of the South African Union from 1919 to 1924 and from 1939 to 1948. Although he believed in the segregation of races, he vocally subscribed to the view that blacks were potentially whites' equals – on the proviso, of course, that they embrace the culture and morals of European society – and openly opposed the deepening of racial segregation as perpetrated by the Apartheid government. This philosophy hardly endeared Smuts to the powers-that-be in the SADF.

The corporal sucked at his front teeth with irritation and looked away from me.

"*Vat jou kak êrens anders!*" he said, "Take your crap somewhere else!" and I stifled a laugh.

We English-speaking guys soon referred to the comops guys as "brainwashers", not without some disdain. Brainwashers are not to be confused with the thick-lensed *koptiffies*, the military psychologists who stood around at the edges of the groups observing us quietly. The brainwashers resembled surfer-dudes, with haircuts that were deliberately non-military. These guys were meant to convey the image of relaxed and friendly blokes, people we might have been friends with in civvy life. But I saw through them. I could see they had cushy jobs, applying their covert head-games on us, playing with our minds as if we were clay – soft in the head and pliable in their hands.

All the rules were entirely relaxed during comops week. We wore casual clothes: tee-shirts, shorts and *plakkies*. Our firearms remained locked up back at the base. The only time we saw our company commanders and company NCOs was when they came for PT, and that wasn't even every day. They were obviously kicking back, at the base. We were sent off on runs alone some afternoons, which led to several interesting discussions among a few of us. We were allowed to visit the refrigerated SAMIL 50 which acted as a *snoepie* to buy soft drinks and chocolates. It was an undemanding time, and they kept us comfortable so that we were open to accepting as much of their information as possible.

Brainwashing is a hotly contentious issue, and the experts are still undecided about whether it is ever truly successful. For effective mind-control to take place, subjects need to be in a completely isolated environment so that behaviours, attitudes and beliefs can be influenced. The *kopsmokkeling*, or head-smuggling, of my time at Infantry School was dismal and barely made an impact on the English-speakers. We sat daydreaming through talks describing the Total Onslaught the country was facing. We were lectured on revolutionary warfare and counter-revolutionary warfare. We were given a thorough run-down of the psychological propaganda that accompanied warfare. But what it all boiled down to was the SADF prescribing to us how we should view our circumstances, and how we were expected to respond to them, or, in a nutshell, the Nationalist Government was morally right, their actions justified, and we had no choice but to accept and comply with their philosophies. I saw that most of the Afrikaans guys loved comops week, and decided it was because they were so easily persuaded, but more so because comops was an affirmation of their identity and purpose, whereas the English guys weren't as much a part of the prevailing ideologies, and were even sidelined and exploited by the system.

We'd all been to *veldskool* during our school years. Comops week felt like *veldskool*. *Veldskool* was a yearly week-long excursion into the bush sponsored by the Transvaal Education Department. During the last two years of primary school and several years of high school, the boys and girls would be sent off separately to remote campsites somewhere near the border, to allow us to break free from the perils of the suburbs. The girls' *veldskool* was more like a school holiday camp, while the boys' had more of a military slant, with the intention of preparing young boys for the compulsory army duty they would be subjected to on completing school.

On *veldskool*, our days would be filled with activities such as hoisting the South African flag in the mornings and lowering it in the evenings while we all sang *Die Stem*. We marched, we did cadet formations, we did PT. We would be made to do night marches and simulated night ambushes. We were made to try and creep up as close as possible to an instructor protecting a hurricane lantern out in the veld, in the dead of night, without being heard or seen by him – nigh impossible! We were given instruction on how to read spoor and maps. We were frozen in lukewarm showers in late autumn. It was like a week of being in the army. But it wasn't all bad, to my memory. I found some of the camps fairly enjoyable, and we got to visit some interesting places, like Pilgrim's Rest. The worst *veldskool* experiences were those held at Gravelotte or Thabazimbi.

The most memorable *veldskool* I experienced was in standard eight, when we were taken to Amsterdam, not far from Ermelo in the Eastern Transvaal, right on the border with Swaziland. The location comprised a series of existing school buildings which were exclusively used to train youngsters in the art of *veldskool* activities. I remember listening to lectures about terrorists who were sent from their bases in Swaziland to bomb targets in South Africa, and being warned that we should be extra cautious during our stay there, as terrorists might well cross over the mountains right near the school. The food was barely edible: greasy fried eggs that could have bounced like tennis balls and sago pudding that we referred to as "frogs' eggs" – I hated it! The food was so bad that an adventurous school mate by the name of Ian Willis actually caught a night adder, killed it with a pocket knife, skinned it, and cooked it on an open fire. He offered me a piece. It tasted a bit like chicken.

These were the memories that revisited me during the comops week as I listened to a pseudo-religious *koptiffie* attempt to use the Bible to justify the Nationalist Government's actions. I had been raised in a household that attended the Methodist Church, and although I hadn't been to church for many years, my jaw dropped at the tall stories emerging from this officer's mouth. He was so clearly quoting the Bible out of context. We had been encouraged to participate in this discussion, but I declined, concluding that it wasn't worth the effort of reasoning with this man.

One of the other English-speaking guys, Roy Mansfield, was braver. He raised a hand, and when the comops officer nodded to him, he stood up, saying, "Has it occurred to anyone that we're fighting a conflict which we call noble, while the poor sod at the receiving end of our bullets believes as much in his cause as we believe in ours?" There was a moment of stunned silence before a chorus of outraged Afrikaners began talking all at once. Amongst the refrains of "What?!" and "You don't know what you're talking about!" came the accusation from an ardent Dutchman: *"Kafferboetie!"*

The comops facilitator seemed to come to Mansfield's aid. "Wait a minute, wait a minute," he said, waving his hands to quiet the cacophony of the riled noisemakers. "We must consider his point." A semblance of calm descended, and the guys each had a chance to speak.

"Well," one Afrikaner addressed Mansfield. "What are you doing here if you feel that way?"

I was impressed by Mansfield's control as he answered. "I'm merely proposing a point-of-view," he said. "I'm not advocating a position for or against." But his words fell on deaf ears. It was impossible for these indoctrinated Afrikaners to consider his point without feeling it necessary to defend their position. Mansfield was merely shouted down and sidelined.

I was reminded of my Granddad's seventieth birthday celebration in 1983. Kimberly and I went along to my uncle's house in Johannesburg where there was a clan-gathering of note. We were all happily seated in the large lounge of my uncle's thatched house when my uncle voiced his opinion that all whites, even private homeowners, were exploiting the blacks: blacks, he said, were receiving a pittance for domestic and gardening work. After a few seconds of deathly silence, a heated discussion ensued, with most putting forward the counter-argument that there were just too many of "them". "They" were breeding like flies, the gathered clan-members agreed, and the small white population that was being steadily outnumbered could not be expected to support so many blacks and their extended families, especially since "they" seemed to have no concept of decency, restraint or morals. I felt sorry for my uncle then, as I felt sorry for Roy Mansfield during comops; that a legitimate concern could so easily be quashed by the overriding view that held fast to a standard white South African argument.

Some of the more moderate Afrikaners we had befriended at Infantry School chatted to us about the incident a bit later, saying they saw Mansfield's point. I thought it was a pity they hadn't had the guts to support him in the earlier argument. I realised that it had been prudent to keep my politics to myself thus far, and that I should continue to do so. I was determined to lie low and enjoy the easy time that was comops week. I found myself dozing through the lectures. Some of the guys thought that the position of comops officer was a desirable one, the comops officers seemed to have such comfortable jobs, but it was nothing that I ever had designs on doing.

Later, some of us asked a few careful questions of our looties from which I learned that the brainwashers who had led the course worked undercover for one of the surreptitious military units affiliated to the SADF, designed to infiltrate the civilian population to propagate and disseminate information that would lead to the general compliance of a nation with their government when convinced that they were facing a Total Onslaught.

It was cunning on the part of the authorities to schedule comops week just before we were to go on our next pass. We were in a more relaxed mood.

*****

I believe a key motivator persuading me going ahead with national service was the vivid flashbacks of the horrendous Church Street bombing of 1983.

It was the afternoon of Friday 20 May. I had returned to Pretoria from res and was visiting Kimberly at her parents' house. We were chatting cosily in the kitchen when a tremor stopped the conversation. I had often felt earth tremors in Pretoria from the far away gold mines around Johannesburg's

West and East Rands, but somehow I knew this was different. Seconds later we heard a booming sound, and we looked at each other in confusion.

It was soon all over the radio stations that a bomb had ripped through the Pretoria city main street, and the SABC TV news that evening confirmed the reports with stark images of my hometown in chaos.

The grisly details of the incident were laid bare in the following morning's Pretoria News, and even the relatively independent newspapers vividly described the bombing's horrific aftermath. The black and white photographs and the detailed reports they accompanied are seared into my memory forever. Flying glass had amputated the limbs of passers-by. A young blonde-haired girl had been decapitated by a sheet of glass. A news photographer had slipped on what turned out to be the bloodied scalp of a black man. More than a dozen people were killed that day and almost two hundred injured. The bomb was detonated at the height of rush hour, and most of the victims were innocent civilians.

I later learned that the ANC's most senior figure and its world-recognised figurehead, Nelson Mandela, although he was imprisoned at the time and Oliver Tambo was the acting president of the organisation, had sanctioned this monstrous act, a fact which was confirmed by Mandela himself in his autobiography when it was published twelve years later.

The bombing is not often spoken of and is at odds with the idea of Mandela as a universal icon of peace. To this day, Mandela has never denounced the use of violence as a tool of resistance, although he advocates passive resistance. I guess he regarded the use of such violence as the last resort, the earlier peaceful protests having failed to bring about any change.

A succession of hand grenade attacks, limpet mine, landmine and car bomb attacks were carried out against the civilians of South Africa following the Church Street bombing and continuing right up to my final call up in 1985, finally convincing me that doing my national service was a lesser evil than that being perpetrated by the ANC and other banned organisations. The armed liberation struggle had escalated, and targeting the Apartheid state was no longer a case of destroying military targets, but had moved into a full-blown terror campaign against innocent civilians.

In the name of resistance to Apartheid, bomb attacks were carried out on banks, a dry cleaner, a bakery, several department stores, a girls' school in Durban. A nightclub at a hotel was bombed, injuring several kids in residence there. A landmine on a farm near Messina was detonated by a vehicle, killing five and injuring five others – three of the dead were very young children. An

Amanzimtoti shopping centre was devastated by a blast that killed five and injured scores more. The list goes on. How could attacks directed at civilians be justified? As with the Nationalists, the perpetrators of these crimes are still to face their day of reckoning…

The axiom holds true: one man's freedom fighter is another man's terrorist.

Chapter 11

Adi had invited me to go to Port Elizabeth with him during the pass following platoon weapons, but I yearned for Kimberly. I had to see her. I had so enjoyed the flight back home from George for graduation, I decided to blow my small army salary on a ticket home. In those days, we just arrived at the airport to catch a flight – no forewarning was given to civilian organisations, most probably for fear of attacks on SADF members. Somehow, a seat was always available.

I went straight to Kimberly at her residence at the Johannesburg College of Education. She seemed quite thrilled to see me. We greeted and hugged one another warmly. I wanted to see my old res mate Harald, so we both popped in at his res to greet him. The three of us chatted like old times.

Over the weekend, Kimberly and I travelled to Pretoria to spend time with our families. Kimberly and I treated ourselves to special outings during my passes: We went to the movies at Menlyn Park Shopping Centre near our homes or Sterland Mall on the corner of Beatrix and Pretorius Streets. We went to Sunnyside and did window shopping at Sunnypark Shopping Centre in Esselen Street. We ate out at restaurants, pizza at Pizza Hut, lunch at Billy's Baked Potato or Red Eagle Spur, dinner at the Waterfall Restaurant in the Nedbank Plaza on the corner of Church and Beatrix Streets. We sampled the best pea and ham soup in Pretoria – no, in the country – at the Gourmet 2 000 in the Arcadia Centre. We were unconcerned by the fact that these places did not allow blacks, coloureds or Indians to dine there – although black waiters served the tables in many of these establishments. I savoured these special times with Kimberly, when life felt normal again.

On occasion, over a glass of wine, our sweet nothings would give way to reflections on our privileged life as whites in South Africa. Conversation would turn to the restrictions placed on non-whites, especially blacks, in our country, and how it might feel to be at the receiving end of such treatment. Kimberly and I were in agreement that such prejudice was wrong, and expressed hope that the situation might change at some point in the future.

Once, when I was in my first year of varsity, I tried to discuss the Northern Ireland situation with Kimberly's mom. She was a devout Roman Catholic, so I had little doubt where her sentiments lay. I got nowhere by asking her a few sharp questions about the religious differences between the Roman Catholics and Protestants (the latter of which I nominally was), or why the British Army was involved in the conflict. She merely rebuffed me out of hand, citing some or other book I should read to save me from my ignorance.

I began to see that Kimberly's mom had quite a liberal political streak. Whereas Kimberly's eldest sister, Kara, who was already married, was not as feisty and opinionated as her mother, the second eldest daughter of the family, Roberta, who was a few years older than me and a budding writer and journalist for the local Pretoria rag, had liberal leanings similar to those of her mother. Kimberly wasn't an out-and-out liberal like her mother or second eldest sister, she was more moderate in her outlook. The youngest of the four girls, Laura, was about six or seven years younger than Kimberly. Kimberly's poor father was a well-read and thoughtful fellow, but rather hen-pecked by his wife and four daughters.

It had been so long since I had been with Kimberly, and her womanly charms captivated me just as they had years ago. Our passions flared and my insides seemed to collide as I kissed her long and furiously, bruising her lips ever so slightly against my stubble. I explored every part of her, every contour and curve, her slender limbs and silky body, until her body responded to mine with the same grinding urgency and rhythm, until we reached a giddy near-oblivion. This brief pleasure would have to last me for many months to come.

The aspect of conventional warfare that our training focussed on was trench warfare. If you know anything about being in trenches, whether in battle or in training, you'll know There's nothing conventional about it. I had heard stories of soldiers in World War I who had to put up with appalling conditions while fighting from the trenches. Cold and wet, the rain would fill the dugouts and turn the soil into slimy mud. The troops stayed in the trenches for ten days to two weeks at a time, moving about in wet boots for days and often succumbing to unimaginable fungal infections. Aside from death by infection, many were killed in the constant barrage of shelling and hail of bullets they faced. Those that survived had to live alongside the half-submerged corpses of their mates, the carcasses infested with maggots and eaten by rats. Lice swarmed in the soldiers' hair and bred in the seams of their clothing, the relentless itch driving many to near-insanity. Toilets were nothing more than buckets and the men were unable to wash. The smell of filth, excrement, death and decaying flesh hung in the air. Always on guard against surprise attacks, the troops slept very little and sported the angry, red eyes of the grossly insomniac. Rations were scarce. Many went without food for days and thousands suffered from malnutrition.

As uncomfortable as the trenches were for us at Infantry School, I had to admit that we were better off than the trench soldiers of the Great War. We didn't face a real enemy, for one thing. And we got to sleep a little more.

The course was to last almost seven weeks. The first two weeks would be spent learning the theory and doing basic preparations at the base and in the veld. The last week would be spent back in the base writing exams on all we had learned. This left a month in between, which was to be spent out in the field, braving the elements and testing the limits of our own determination.

Winter in the southern Cape is cold and wet with regular snowfall. The order to pack our rucksacks and prepare to depart the base at 04h00 the next morning came on a Sunday evening in the middle of June. Having heard about the ruthless cold that could seize this part of the world, some of us had organised ourselves *grootjasse*, or great coats, and I packed mine in my *grootsak* along with the required items which included my spare pair of boots, bush jacket, bivvy and groundsheet.

We marched out in the dark. The route led us into the veld, west of camp, a few kilometres past the shooting range. The stretch of land we occupied – somewhere between a spot called "rock", and another called "hard place" – was wryly called the *Kanzas Vlaktes*, or Kansas Plains, a cynical reference to the great American plains we'd seen in Westerns and on TV. Officially, it was called Prince Alfred's Gate, or PAG for short. We would spend a lot of time out on the *Kanzas Vlaktes*.

Coordinates: 33°35'01.84"S 22°09'45.56"E

On arrival at the designated site, we breakfasted in the dark. The morning was cool and crisp without a sign of rain. Dawn finally broke some hours after we had left the relative comfort of the base, and we received our first field lecture on the philosophy of conventional warfare.

We had heard it all before back in the base, but they were trying to really drum it into our heads. At the time, the SADF was primarily involved in conflicts – both internal and external to the country – that amounted to unconventional warfare, so the chance that we would be required to undertake the tactics of conventional warfare on the battlefields were slim. We were learning trench warfare, they told us, to prepare us for the unlikely possibility that the revolutionary warfare of the enemy would develop into conventional warfare. This was not entirely unthinkable, especially as the guerrillas were getting more and more support from hard-line communist countries, which were already providing these so-called freedom fighters with the resources to change their approach and mobilise differently. The Angola-South West Africa theatre of war was proof of this. An infantryman had to be trained and prepared to operate in both types of combat.

We were expected to sleep in trenches – or what passed for trenches, considering we often started to dig late in the afternoon. To begin with, we simply dug a deep hole in the ground, like a foxhole, that a man could stand upright in, but the corporals wanted proper trenches, so we had to dig our trenches again so that they were long enough to accommodate a prone body and about waist-deep – a trench that could act as a defence against enemy fire, whether from rifle, mortar or cannon. A groundsheet was placed at the bottom of the trench and a bivvy over the top. With the prospect of winter's icy grip about to take hold of Oudtshoorn, we could expect all sorts of weather ... most of it bad. Sleeping in a trench is uncomfortable enough, but waking in the morning to find your helmet covered in ice is worse! I hated having to shave in this weather, especially with ice-cold water.

My first and "permanent" trench was within Bravo Company's lines. We would inhabit one or two trenches for the four weeks out on *Kanzas Vlaktes*, except when occupying other trenches for the night during certain drills. We were also sometimes made to dig interconnecting trenches, to be shared with our mates, a practice which formed a network of defensive positions.

Within a few days the rain began to fall. Like the others, I had made clever little ridges around my trench that acted as gutters to take the water away, and secured my bivvy with a series of small rocks along the perimeter. The hole in the centre of the bivvy had to be securely tied to prevent water from running in and soaking the trench's occupant below. I secured the hood of my bivvy to the end of a nearby branch on one side of my trench, propping up the middle and creating a raised plastic roof to drain water away more efficiently. Many a time, halfway through a miserable night, a sudden rush of water followed by *"Ag, fok!"* would be heard as someone's bivvy collapsed and the sleeping soldier was drenched in the cold water that had pooled in the covering. I grimaced each time, knowing I could be next.

Nights in our trenches were never-ending nightmares of wet and bone-chilling cold. It rained most of the time. My feet were always cold and my nose ran constantly. I shivered uncontrollably. We had to always be prepared for anything, so we wore our boots and overalls all the time: while training during the day or at night while we slept. I learnt how to wriggle my way with some difficulty into my sleeping bag inner with the space blanket wrapped over the outside to try and achieve maximum warmth. I tried to keep my kit as dry as possible – especially my sleeping bag – but at some point everyone's clothing and sleeping bags would get soaked. We realised that the best way to overcome this problem was to wait until the sun had started to rise, open the bivvy up, and then snooze a while atop it, hoping that the weak rays of sunlight would come to some effect. That is, of course, if it wasn't raining. In the mornings, wet inners, sleeping bags and clothes would be hung out to dry on the nearest bushes, and if they didn't dry, someone would have to spend a night or two sleeping with just a space blanket. A rusty rifle ensured an *opfok*, so we were all careful to try and keep our R4s dry.

All this meant that we got very little sleep.

The weeks were spent out in our trenches. We would leave base on Monday afternoon and return only on Saturday afternoon. During the time we were on base, we would shower and clean our kit, attend church parade on Sunday morning, and then pack up all over again on Sunday night to be ready to go out to the trenches before daybreak on Monday. And so another horrendous week would begin.

Some guys bailed after only a week. Many more would do the same over the coming weeks as trench warfare was found to be more unbearable than *Vasbyt*. Soldiers complained to their corporals, who had no sympathy for them. And why should they? These corporals had done it all and stuck it out the year before. Our platoon's Corporal Potgieter was no different. "Come on!" He said with irritation to Dewald Kruger, who confided in Corporal Potgieter after just three days that he didn't feel he could continue under these conditions for another three and a half weeks. "It's not as bad as that! Pull yourself together, man!" I was surprised that Dewald was struggling with this phase of training: he was a fairly strapping-looking young Dutchman, with the confident swagger of a natural soldier. But the trenches had defeated him.

Kruger continued to have misgivings, and two days later, he bypassed Corporal Potgieter and went straight to the platoon sergeant, Corporal Joubert. Joubert was marginally more sympathetic, telling him, "I'll go to the platoon commander and tell him of your troubles. Just hang in there," he said with a rough kindness. "You still look alright to me."

A day passed, then two, and poor Dewald heard nothing from Corporal

Joubert. In the weak morning sun after church parade on Sunday, he approached the platoon sergeant.

"Corporal," he said cautiously. "Have you spoken to the platoon commander yet?"

"Ja, ja," came the response. "I discussed your worries with Lieutenant Pretorius. I don't know why he hasn't come back to me about it yet."

"Can I speak to him?" the recruit asked. The platoon sergeant obliged and took him to see the lieutenant, who was rather surprised to see him. "What's wrong?" he asked Kruger, who proceeded to tell the whole story again. "Okay," said Lieutenant Pretorius. "I'll speak to the company commander about how you feel. But just hang in there," he added. "You're doing well!"

Again Dewald heard nothing for a day, and then another. Cornering the platoon commander, Dewald asked him whether he had had a chance to speak to the company commander yet. "No, no, not yet," Lieutenant Pretorius replied. "I must first speak to the company 2IC."

In the middle of the second week, the lootie came to Dewald to tell him that he could make an appointment with the company commander. After three days of anxious waiting, Dewald was told he could go to the company commander when there were orders the following week.

Eventually, he actually landed an interview with the company commander. After listening patiently to Dewald's account, he told him he would consider his request and sent him back to his platoon. Next thing, Dewald was called out to be taken to see the *dominee*.

"What's wrong?" The *dominee* enquired with concern, eliciting another recount of Dewald's whole story, after which the *dominee* sent him back to training with the parting words, "Stay strong, son. Trust in God."

By now rifleman Kruger believed his case would be taken forward. Two days later, he was called out and sent back to the main base to "go and have a chat." After a shower and a change into fresh clothing, he was sent to see a psychologist. Once again, the whole story was retold, and Kruger finished off by saying, "There's nothing wrong with me, exactly, it's just ... I don't think I can do it, you see. I'm not coping. I'm not going to commit suicide or anything like that. You don't need to worry about me. I just feel like I can't go on ..."

Dewald was sent back to the veld, expecting his case to be finalised quickly. Two days later he was told to return to the base, this time to see a social worker. "Is everything okay at home?" the social worker asked after listening to yet another repeat of the story. "Do you want to make a call to your parents?"

Dewald shook his head, feeling exasperated. "No, no, everything's fine at home ..."

"Do you have a girlfriend?" the social worker asked. "A wife? Is everything alright between the two of you?"

"Ja, ja," Dewald insisted. "It's not that," he said. "It's what's happening here. I can't handle it anymore. I want out!"

Again, old Dewald was sent back to the veld. After two days, the company commander came to check up on him.

"How are you doing?" He asked. "Are you all right?"

By this time, Dewald realised that he was in a deliberate holding pattern and nothing would get him off the course. There was no point in complaining, and he capitulated, replying, "I'm fine, thank you very much, major."

"Your case is being reviewed," the major said. "Don't do anything foolish, now, you hear?"

The end of trench warfare training was nearing, and there was only a week left of this agony before we returned to base for evaluations. This would be followed by a few weeks of preparations before we would be sent to the border. Dewald began to think, *Hang on ... It might be worth my while to stick this out, what with these pricks taking so long.*

This is how they dragged it out and strung a recruit along, playing for time so that disgruntled recruits eventually gave up on the whole process of requesting to leave Infantry School. The diversionary process they designed gave Dewald something to hate more than the trench warfare training itself, if that was possible.

Several guys would report sick just to get out of the veld for a while. When the NCOs asked, "Any sick reports?" hands would go up. *"Wat is verkeerd met jou?"* each one was asked, "What is wrong with you?", to which the reply was, *"Nee, korporaal, my enkel is seer"* or *"My kop is seer"* or *"My keel is seer"* or whichever body part was sore that day.

"Have you been to the medic?" The NCO would ask.

"Yes, I've been to the medic," the recruit would reply, "and he has given me a note."

"Right," they were told. "You can report sick back at the base."

The supposedly genuine sick reports would travel into base, have a shower, and get taken to the base's sickbay to see the doctor on duty. By mid-morning or lunch time they would be back in the field again.

Those of us who stuck it out in the trenches frowned on this behaviour. There was no honour in trying to cheat while your buddies suffered and would have to pick up the slack in your absence. Ian, the clever blighter, would ask Lieutenant Pretorius if he couldn't run back to the base to fetch anything for him. The lootie knew this was a gyppo, but humoured Ian once or twice and sent him off on an errand. Ian, it seemed to me, was the only *Engelsman* the lootie actually liked. Ian would take our cupboard or *trommel* keys, organise the key for our bungalow, take down our requests for *pakkies*, items of clothing, or whatever else we needed and return with these in an hour or two. What a mate!

My knees were bad ever since basics, the badly-fitting army boots didn't suit my pronation, and I did report sick once or twice to the medic in the veld. But I chose never to go back to the base.

Mental and physical tenacity is a variable asset, and some recruits totally cracked. Those guys that couldn't stomach the misery of the trenches – to the degree that they might shoot one of the other recruits or themselves – were considered risky to have around, and they were quickly loaded up and taken back to base for immediate transfer out of Infantry School. I always wondered what happened to some of the guys I had come to know. Ian and I would do a recall and count after each phase of training, tallying up how many had been removed and who they were. We didn't begrudge them, knowing that at any stage we might ourselves crack or have something happen to us to get us kicked off the course.

PF Captain Barrie arrived one day during our second week out on *Kanzas Vlaktes*. The recruits bristled with dislike for him as he stroked his moustache in his self-important way. Despite our aversion to this *snor*-stroking man, we were impressed by the lecture he gave us, in both Afrikaans and fluent English, on the cannon-fired Sabot, an anti-tank warhead developed by the United States. The Sabot doesn't contain any explosives itself, but relies on its mass and velocity to pierce the target. The shell, when fired, releases a heavy and hard chunk of metal as the fin-stabilised casing is discarded in-flight. The metal projectile pierces the heavy armour of a tank and ricochets, often in fragmented chunks, around the interior. As he described the action of the Sabot, Captain Barrie smiled widely and menacingly underneath his silly moustache.

"If you like blood and gore," he said, "I can tell you some very interesting stories about what this weapon does to the tank itself ... and especially to the enemy inside." The relish he took in the notion sickened me to my stomach. I looked away.

The more he droned on, the more our attitude towards him changed. We went from being impressed by his knowledge, to thinking he was a right moron. He boasted about having been on course in France – apparently "undercover", so we weren't supposed to have been told – and clearly thought himself a big shot. We weren't impressed with his conceit and arrogance, and being only a few years older than most of us, we showed him respect for his rank only. We had no time for his patronising ways.

Captain Barrie took us through the drill of "taking the high ground". This involved fire and movement through the veld from our trenches, starting in a leopard crawl before moving into our staggered pattern of forward-firing movement. Having taken the high ground, we had to be dug-in before the next morning to be ready to repel the enemy. In practice, this meant that the platoon would be ready to take the next high ground the following night.

The exercise was backbreaking. If we didn't perform to Captain Barrie's satisfaction, he would make us do it all over again. After one poor performance, Captain Barrie threatened to make us do the drill every single day, all day, until we carried it out properly.

The veld was covered in *rygies*, little flowering succulents, interspersed with grass and thorn scrub. In patches, the ground was infested with *dubbeltjies*, tiny irritating thorns that hooked themselves into our hands and clothes wherever contact was made with the ground. Following our leopard crawl, our clothes would be soaked with the sap of the *rygies*. We sweated like proverbial pigs and after a few days of this we stank to high heaven.

We took up our positions that first night, digging our trenches where Barrie indicated they should be. He went through Bravo's lines, platoon after platoon, marking where he wanted us to dig our trenches with broken twigs and branches. The soil was sandy and loose enough that you could dig a shallow hole quickly. But below that lay *kalksteen*, a calcium carbonate deposit, alternating with hard white rock. Spades and picks were destroyed trying to break through that stuff. A few paces back and to either side of where we were instructed to dig were some old but deeper half-dug trenches which some poor bastards before us must have really sweated over.

It didn't take us long to realise that all we had to do was to clear the rubble out of those old half-dug trenches and they would suffice. Under cover of darkness, everybody crept silently, moving backwards or sideways, remembering to carry along Barrie's little sticks which marked our arcs of fire and our relative positions, and scrambled into those old trenches.

That evening was spent lighting matches and coaxing failing flashlights to illuminate fingers, hands, elbows, knees and legs in order to dig out the infuriating little devils that had taken up residence there during our leopard crawl.

The following morning, Captain Barrie almost had a coronary.

"You sneaky little runts!" he blustered, growing red in the face. "That bush was five paces away. I measured it before you guys even got here. Did you think you could outsmart me?" He insisted that that night we should take up the positions as he had originally demarcated. But this time he used the bushes as markers.

It was a case of self-preservation: instead of filling up the old trenches, we filled the shallow holes we had first dug with loose stones. The bushes Barrie had used as markers were yanked loose and repositioned accordingly. When he looked on the fruit of our labours the following morning he remarked, "Not quite the standard I expect, but I suppose it will have to do."

Of course, had he returned to our position a day or two later, he would have seen those harvested bushes wilting. Our platoon sergeants knew about this, but they didn't say anything. National servicemen were brothers and didn't like to squeal on each other. Besides, they had probably done the same thing themselves the year before.

Not everything about conventional warfare training was doom and gloom. *Loopgraaf opruiming*, or "trench-clearing", was exciting. It was the stuff of movies. At a specified area consisting of a network of interconnected trenches, three men would proceed down a cleared trench, weapons held at the ready, moving quietly and using only hand signals to indicate actions to be taken. When the designated leader came to an interconnecting trench and spotted an opening that signified a protected "enemy" bunker, he would point it out. From a secure position at right angles to the bunker, he would give the signal, and the other two would stand with their backs to the walls of the trench, either side of the opening to the bunker, their weapons held in front of their bodies, pointing skywards. The leader would motion, and the first in line would pull the pin of the grenade and throw the grenade around the corner, into the bunker, yelling, "Grenade!" The yelling of "Grenade!" was mostly as a warning to galvanise his two buddies and other allies in the immediate area.

The moment the grenade exploded, the second in line would leap forward and fire into the dust-filled bunker, while the third would cover him. A car tyre inside the bunker was there to aim at, and it was preferable for the grenade to go through the hole in the middle.

This exercise really got the adrenaline pumping.

In the movies, you see grenades that take ages to detonate: the hero falls onto the rolling grenade, then picks it up and throws it back at the enemy where it goes off spectacularly. This is pure fiction. Our grenades were set to detonate at two and a half seconds. The grenades we used for training only had a detonator in the grenade-shaped metal casing that had holes drilled through it to allow for the discharged air and blasted parts of the exploded detonator to be expelled. If one of these practice grenades went off in your hand, the detonator could still potentially blow your fingers or hand off, but it was reasonably safe to train with in that it couldn't severely maim or kill like a high explosive grenade could.

There were some funny moments. Once, three recruits thought to be particularly good at trench-clearing were nominated to give us a demonstration. The demonstration was going along swimmingly when one guy threw a grenade which hit the tyre inside the bunker and rebounded – right out of the bunker entrance – to land at their feet. With desperate yells of *"Fokfokfok!"* the three scrambled to get out of the trench before the grenade exploded, but there wasn't time and *blam!* it went off as they crouched there with their fingers in their ears and their backs towards it. The officers, NCOs and troops all roared with laughter, but if the grenade hadn't been a practice model, the incident could have turned out very differently.

During the nights we had to stand guard duty. A roster was drawn up, and each of us was allocated an hour to stand guard. After staying awake for an hour acting as sentry, we had to make sure that the next guy was properly awake to start his hour of watch. We used passwords which only we, our NCO and our lootie knew. When we heard someone approaching, we would ask, *"Wie gaan daar?"* ("Who goes there?") and then ask for the password.

God help the poor soul on duty if the NCOs came around during the night and he was caught napping. He'd be given a severe *oppie* the next morning after platoon inspection and Roll Call. Many a time the wrong guy got an *oppie* because his guard duty replacement would deny ever having been woken up to take over. This wasn't malicious; it was a reflection of our state of minds and lack of sleep that we would respond to the guy waking us up, and then promptly drift back off to sleep, so that in the end a whole chain of recruits had failed to stay awake for their shifts.

This problem of sleep-deprived sentries was solved in one of three ways. The proper way of "standing" guard duty was to use a thin rope tied to each recruit's arm in turn. A short, sharp tug on the rope was supposed to ensure that the next recruit would be awake to do guard duty, while lying in his trench. This didn't quite work out while we were in the trenches, what with the rope snagging on those dense little bushes or other equipment, making a noise when tugged, and mostly failing to wake the next sentry (or he would wake and then promptly fall asleep again). When the rope method failed, the NCOs made us get out of our trenches and sit upright for guard duty. The recruits still managed to fall asleep while sitting, though, and subsequently failed to wake their buddies. The final method of combating the sleeping-guard syndrome was for each of us to lie awake for another ten minutes or so after handing over duty, and then softly but purposefully call out our buddy's name. When no response was forthcoming, you knew he was sleeping again, and you would have to get out of your sleeping bag to crawl over to the offender's trench. Dropping the butt of your R4 into his stomach was usually sufficient to wake him, and keep him awake.

One night during our last week in the veld, I slept fitfully. I sensed that something had changed: gone was the constant splatter of the rain and sleet on our plastic bivvies and the environment was filled with an eerie silence. Surfacing sometime after midnight, I poked my head out of my trench to look around. What I beheld was a heart-stoppingly beautiful alien landscape: about half an inch of snow had fallen on the veld, and the moon threw an eerie glow over the white-dusted land.

The snow fell softly throughout the night, coming to a halt by mid-morning when the snow on the ground began to melt rapidly. I was grateful that the arrival of the snow had caused the rain to dissipate, but the rest of that week was bitterly cold and windy.

Getting back to base after the misery of the trenches was an unbelievable relief. Our last week of conventional warfare training was also the instructors' evaluations. They had been grilled on their style of presentation and it had to be right.

The quality of our training in this phase was good, and no expense was spared. We all had the opportunity to operate the weapons in platoon weapons phase, and now we could use them in trench-clearing operations. Like most of the guys, I had a preference for the *snotneus*.

We shot off countless practice rounds from that weapon over our two years of national service. I knew what the effect was of shooting it high or low at targets, at targets to the left or right, or lobbing it in a trajectory to get a specific longer or shorter ground shot.

During the conventional warfare phase of training, before even starting the trench-clearing training, we each threw several grenades from the protection of a concrete structure. We even fired off the Russian-made RPG-7 rocket-propelled grenade launchers.

Those in command made sure that we knew the applications and limitations of all these types of weapons in an operational setting, and we studied all that we had learned for the final exam, but it had been repeated so often to us that we all knew the work backwards and coasted through the written exam.

Although the standard of training during conventional warfare was good, I didn't always find it relevant. I guessed it was as much about toughening us up as about training us. Personally, I suffered more physically than psychologically during this phase of training, but there were bad days when I found myself dwelling on my thoughts and I had to make an effort to snap out of it.

Due to the steady and systematic loss of Bravo recruits in all platoons after this phase and the previous phases, our platoon, along with others was reconstituted. Now as Platoon 3, we moved bungalows accordingly.

We were granted another pass after conventional warfare. I refused Adi's second invitation to travel with him to Port Elizabeth to meet his friends and family. I missed Kimberly too much, and opted to go home and see her instead. I think Adi gave up trying to persuade me to join him on pass. Once again, I spent my money on a South African Airways (SAA) air ticket home.

When we boarded the 04h00 bus to the airport at George, it was announced that there was too much fog for planes to fly from there, and we had to drive all the way to Port Elizabeth instead. Perhaps there was fog, perhaps there wasn't. Perhaps the authorities had got wind of some other potential danger. All I remember was that for most of the 360-odd kilometres to Port Elizabeth, I had to hold my bladder until my eyes watered. That Springbok Atlas bus didn't stop for anything!

My weekend in Pretoria was as precious as any time off was for us servicemen. Kimberly was at res, so I was forced to visit her there. I began to detect a new dynamic at play in our relationship. Something was off between Kimberly and me, but I couldn't put my finger on it. I wondered if our brief times together during my passes and the long wait for me while I was in Oudtshoorn were taking their toll on Kimberly, and tried to take it easy on her. In an effort to bridge the gap between us, I attempted to impress on her my looming border duty, even going so far as to suggest I may not return. An exaggeration on my part, perhaps, but the possibility did seem to evoke tenderness on her part, and she became more attentive and loving.

On the return flight to George, I did nothing but stare blankly out the window. A wave of yearning for Kimberly welled up in me, and I was devastated to be leaving her again for who-knew-how-long. If love is the most powerful emotion there is, longing must be a close second. My veil of depression was deepened by the dread that I wouldn't make it through the border phase, and I was paralysed with a brief but intense melancholy.

Chapter 12

We weren't called "riflemen" for nothing. Shooting was a huge part of our training at Infantry School, and we were all required to master it. Our first shooting lesson was held within two weeks of getting our R4s during basics. Several platoons were marched off to the range together, taking along our groundsheets, battle helmets, battle jackets and R4s with 35-round magazines.

The target area lay southwest of Bravo's lines, a stone's throw from the western boundary fence of the camp. With thirty-six target areas, it was just shorter than five hundred metres long and about two hundred metres wide, with hundred-metre stretches demarcated by distance markers, metal boards with painted numerals, placed along the sides of the range. Below the targets at the far end was a sunken area, like a baseball dugout, which was called the *skietgat* or shooting hole, in which recruits wearing their helmets and battle jackets would man two manual targets. These were hoisted on the shouted command *"Teiken OP!"* ("Target UP!") and lowered on the command *"Teiken AF!"* ("Target DOWN!"). The *skietwal*, or shooting wall, was a massive raised earthen embankment a short distance from the *skietgat*, against which the rounds would harmlessly collide. The target was the standard NATO paper image of an attacking infantryman, whom Ian and I lost no time in nicknaming "Joe". Joe was attached to a thin wooden backing board, suspended between two long upright wooden poles. A red flag at either end of the two sections indicated that the section of the range was active. Behind the targets, right at the front of the range above the *skietwal*, another red flag raised high above the shooting range for all to see signalled that the range was in use.

Early on during shooting practice, the recruits in the *skietgat* would have to point out where the shooter had pierced the target by using a long pointer that could be seen from a distance. Spotting a 5.56-millimetre hole in a target above your head was difficult at the best of times, and the helmeted pointer would often just guess where the last bullet had penetrated. This practice probably contributed to the rather average shooters on course that year.

We were taught to load a magazine using a thumb-pressing technique that enabled one to load the rounds quickly. We did the drill for weapon safe, weapon on safety and also for a jam, or *storing*.

We learnt how to hold the weapon while lying stomach to the ground on our groundsheets: If you shot right-handed, the feet were stretched out behind, slightly apart and marginally to the left. The left elbow was on the ground, with the left hand lightly holding the rifle on the hand grip in front of the trigger. We found that the best way to hold the R4 was to rest the base of the rifle grip on the left hand, without gripping, so that one could relax on each shot. The right elbow was on the ground at the back of the butt, the right thumb slightly over the top of the butt, with the index finger through the trigger guard and on the trigger. The intent was always to squeeze the trigger, and not to pull or jerk it.

Some of us shot with either the left or right eye closed, but the better shooters kept both eyes open, the dominant eye peering through the rear sight to line up the front sight to the centre of the rear, framing the target.

Two to three recruits were grouped to a target, meaning a maximum of seventy-two shooters at once, with up to 144 recruits in the *skietgat* manning the targets. For our first shoot, we used little round paper targets, shooting to ascertain the degree to which the weapons were out. We only fired a few rounds that day, and I loved it.

When I received my little round paper target from the blokes in the *skietgat*, I was pleased to see that most of my rounds had hit the target tightly together at the bottom left. Adjustments were made to the sights of our R4s by the staff sergeants, platoon sergeants and corporals, and we left the range confident that we could at least shoot in more or less the right direction. We were to find that with the sights adjusted, shooting a grouping on a target was not too difficult. Of course, this was the easy kind of shooting: lying down and firing at leisure at a static target between fifty and a hundred metres away. Soon we would have to take a step up and aim for ol'Joe.

Before leaving the shooting range, we had to pick up all the *doppies*, or empty shells, that were lying around. Woe betide us if any stray *doppies* were found! The corporals scouted very carefully for overlooked shells, even old tarnished ones, hoping to catch us out for an *oppie* after shooting practice. I'm convinced they used to drop a few deliberately, just so that they would not be denied the opportunity to chase us around for a bit. Empty shells and remaining live rounds were thrown into ammo crates, and we would be made to declare: *"Ek verklaar, geen skerppunt ammunisie, leë doppies of enige dele daarvan in my besit nie, korporaal!"* ("I declare, no sharp-point ammunition, empty shells or any parts thereof in my possession, corporal!"), although many times during that year, 5.56 millimetre live rounds and empty shells would find their way off the shooting range.

After practice, we would be told, *"Vir inspeksie, hou geweer!"* and we would hold out our rifles, cocked, with the breech mechanism held back and open for the inspecting NCO.

We shot once or twice more during basics, learning to hit target images. During platoon weapons, we visited the shooting range several times, learning to shoot more accurately and consistently from different positions and distances. The first week of conventional warfare comprised lectures alternated with sessions at the shooting range learning to shoot more skilfully. During this period, we would master two shooting drills or what they called *Tabel 1 en Tabel 2* (Table 1 and Table 2). The first was shooting from a static position at a target one hundred metres away, and the second involved shooting from a static kneeling or prone position at a target two hundred metres away and then running to the one hundred metre marker to fire from a standing position.

By the end of the conventional warfare phase, we were shooting *Tabel 3* (Table 3) from the 300-metre marker, beginning from a static prone position, running to the 200-metre marker to shoot from a kneeling position and then running to the 100-metre marker to fire from a standing position. We practiced this combination during the rural coin-ops phase of training which was to follow conventional warfare, and undertook the *Tabel 3* drill competitively in a shooting contest just before going to the border.

Various barrelled, hand-held weapons were fired at the range over the months, even the mighty FN MAG, which we could hear being fired from the range occasionally as we went about our business on the base. Only once were we given a demonstration of the MAG firing on the range – it was an awesome sight to behold from about four hundred metres out! Other, louder explosions could be heard from further afield where other ordnance was being exploded.

There was always a designated range safety officer on hand while we practiced, who was either a senior CO or senior NCO.

The second time we went to the range, Captain Barrie arrived to observe our first "real" shooting lesson at the NATO targets. We were given very specific instructions to face forward and towards the NATO infantryman, and never to look around or turn our rifles away from pointing at the targets. We had been given little yellow Styrofoam earplugs which were manipulated to squeeze into the ear hole, which made it difficult to hear commands properly.

In the confusion of firing noise and inaudible commands, I turned slightly, pulling one plug from my ear, and asked, "Staff Sergeant, what if ...?" *Thwack!*

I received a boot to the back of my helmet which knocked the front into the dirt. Several other recruits were given the same treatment.

One poor recruit stood up and started to turn around to indicate that his rifle had jammed with a round stuck in the breech. The drill in such cases was to *"Stamp, span, rig, vuur!"*, "Hit (the magazine), cock (the weapon), aim, fire!" It was crucial that you remained faced towards the target to avoid any mishaps and potential tragedy. After receiving a skull crushing slap on the front of his helmet by a PF staff sergeant, the offender was given an *oppie*. We learnt quickly to remain facing forward.

Later on we would be allowed to wear our bush hats while shooting, but we always had to wear our helmets in the *skietgat* to avoid possible impact from ricochets or flying shrapnel. Or the odd slap around the ear hole we might receive from an irate corporal.

Colonel Hennie Schultz, in that typical PF mould, was disliked and feared by all at Infantry School. Whenever his white Toyota Corolla appeared on the firing range, a jolt of anxiety would pass through the instructing staff, and they would start acting more *paraat* than usual, shouting and screaming and trying to impress him with their vigour. I had never dealt with Colonel Schultz personally, but I shared the aversion to him for the fear he instilled in his subordinates.

Colonel Schultz loved to insist, *"Maak elke skoot tel!"*, "Make every shot count!" If we didn't, we got to know the rifle range very well. Colonel Schultz's favourite *oppie* was playing *Nommer Asseblief* (Number Please), the title taken from a popular Afrikaans TV series of the time. He would get the instructors to pick a number from those on the numbered poles above the *skietwal*, and then make Bravo Company run up the wall behind the shooting range, around the corresponding number and back down again. This was repeated over and over until we were hammered.

From time to time we would be taken out to the Swartberg shooting range, just more than six kilometres north of base camp. We were transported there in SAMIL 50s so that we weren't tired for shooting practice. Twice we were given the infamous *bosbus* on the return journey, and other times there were no SAMILs to fetch us, so we would run the six-plus kilometres back. I wasn't a particularly strong runner, what with my bad knees, and I hated it. I had some difficulty keeping up with the squad. A few times Bravo and Foxtrot companies practiced together. We would hardly have started running when a few SAMIL 50s would come charging up to collect the rugby players and other sportsmen to take them off to practice. As their SAMILs passed us by, returning to base, they would laugh and cheerily show us the middle finger. We would fume. Few, if any, of the Foxtrot officers ever ended up in operational units on the border during my time in the army. The rest of us were expected to run around the bush fighting a war, while they slept at home, warm and safe.

Our final shooting competition just before we went off to the border determined who would earn their *skietbalkies*, or shooting badges. In the shooting sessions we had during the latter half of the year when we were practicing for the final competition, the guys became quite cocky and pilfered extra rounds out of the 5.56 mm ammo box to fill up their magazines. These would sometimes be shot off childishly at the metal range signs, flagpoles and flags at the back of the target area, or at their buddy's cast-iron *valplate*, or fall plates. The fall plates were the last targets we would shoot at from a hundred or fifty metres. There were usually five of them, and they were tricky to strike dead-centre to cause them to fall as they were so heavy.

Many of the extra rounds the guys snuck out were used to get higher scores in the final competition.

Another trick involved the little round black, blue, green, red or yellow stickers which we used to close up the latest holes and to freshen the target for the next round or the next shooter – simply peeling off a few of these while counting your mates' score made it look as if the most recent shooter had actually shot them.

And yet another trick to bolster scores in the competition was to get your *skietgat* buddy to jab extra holes into the infantryman target with a ballpoint pen. A *skietbalkie* earned in this way was referred to as a "Bic badge".

Chapter 13

Conventional warfare training was followed by rural counter-insurgency, or rural "coinops". Many of the Bravo Company members would be doing this kind of work the following year, so a lot of attention was devoted to this instruction.

We were made to do section and platoon attacks over and over until we could have done them in our sleep. We had already practiced these formations during the trench warfare training when taking higher ground, but now the exercises were honed to a fine art. While we were doing section attacks, Major Drost would walk behind us with a loud-hailer, coaching us through each stage.

We walked almost abreast, in standard patrol formation, the centre leading in a slight V-formation with two scouts out front. The scouts had rifle grenades on their R4s, and action was initiated by the firing of grenades in the direction of the supposed enemy, whilst the V-formation rapidly closed up the line with the two scouts out in front. Simultaneously, the MAG element moved out to high ground, usually to the left of the section, where they would set up and give covering fire from the flank, keeping a safe distance of 11 mills (military parlance for degrees) between our troops and the arc of fire of the MAG. This distance was judged by the spreading of five fingers of a hand and holding them up between the arc of fire of the MAG and the soldiers leading the advance on the enemy.

Following heavy fire directed at the imagined enemy for about a minute, fire and movement would begin. This action requires a cool head, and you have to look out for your buddies while you proceed. We would become adept at this drill. Half the attacking force would usually stand or kneel, or occasionally lie down, to fire while the rest would rapidly move forward and between them. Having moved ahead for a few metres, the advancing section would go down to fire, while the others would get up and make their short advance. This interweaving action would continue until the section had passed through the enemy position, and a section could move with surprising speed in this manner. One recruit losing his concentration or carrying out the drill incorrectly could be very dangerous, but fortunately, this never happened to us.

Once we had pretty much got the hang of the exercise, the lootie gave everyone a chance to be section leader. I got my turn soon enough, and took up the section leader's position to the rear of the section. I was never very good at Afrikaans, but I delivered the command to attack as best I could, saying, *"Staan op, stap!"* ("Stand up, walk!"). The Afrikaans guys started to snicker, probably due to my poor elocution and English accent. Even the lootie had a chuckle at my expense. Composing himself, the lootie brought things to a halt and went through the instructions with me very slowly, all the time extolling the virtues of Afrikaans as an "action-driven language".

Round two, and I gave the command, *"Staan op, stap!"* and the recruits did as they were ordered. Then my mind went blank. I couldn't remember a single command! I stammered, "Uhm ... uhm ... uhm ..." as I tried to recall what the lootie had just told me, but nothing came.

Meanwhile, the section was fast disappearing over the horizon. The guys knew they shouldn't be continuing, but they were obeying orders nonetheless, enjoying my predicament enormously.

"Stop! Stop! Kom terug!" ("Stop! Stop! Come back!") the lootie shouted to the guys before turning to me. "Warren?" He was dumbfounded. *"Wat die donner doen jy? Weet jy nie wat om te doen nie?"* ("What in the blazes are you doing? Don't you know what to do?")

I had to confess, *"Ek dink nie so nie, luitenant."* ("I don't think so, lieutenant.")

The loot was irritated. *"Doen weer!"* He ordered gruffly for me to do it again. I felt like a total idiot.

I began again for the third time. This time the guys helped me out, even if I wasn't quite getting the Afrikaans right. After they were brought to a halt at the end of the exercise, the lootie turned to me. *"Nou sien jy, hoe maklik was dit?"* ("You see now, how easy was that?") I had been so scared of stuffing up that I caused myself to blunder. I resolved then to concentrate more on what the Afrikaans orders were and how they were used.

Ian and I laughed about the whole episode later, but it stung me and the memory of the incident lingered for a long time. I think the lootie thought I was full of crap and somehow playing him for a fool. He was getting more than a little tired of this *Engelsman*.

We were coming to the end of rural coinops, but Lieutenant Pretorius was not letting up on his *kak* ways. During one fire and movement drill through the veld, he decided we were all stuffing around and proceeded to give us an *oppie*. He marched us all to a secluded rocky depression a few kilometres northwest of camp where he made us do rifle PT and star-jumps. Star-jumps had recently been banned at Infantry School and throughout the SADF because of their likelihood to cause shin splints. I was suffering from inflammation of the iliotibial band in both knees as a result of my pronation problem which was aggravated by those awful army boots and the four weeks of trench warfare training in the cold and wet. As a result, I was experiencing severe pain in my knees. As Pretorius's *oppie* progressed, I got slower and slower and couldn't keep up with the rest of the platoon. I tried to indicate to the lieutenant that my knees were excruciatingly sore, but he thought he knew better and I was gypping. He decided to give me a personal *oppie*.

Telling Corporals Joubert and Potgieter to continue with stuffing up the rest of the platoon, Lieutenant Pretorius called me over. He told me to pick up one of the many large stones lying on the ground. I bent down and picked one up, but he booted it out of my hands.

"Not that one, Warren!" he barked. "A bigger one!" The stone I chose felt as heavy as my marble back at base, but it was more difficult to carry because it had round edges which were hard to grasp. My fingers kept slipping. Pretorius indicated two very large rocks several metres apart and told me to run around them carrying my stone. I circled the rocks until I couldn't carry the stone any longer and I dropped it. As a result, I was made to do quite a number of push ups "for failing to hold onto your new marble," he said. Push ups complete, I had to pick up my "new marble" and run around the rocks again. This punishment went on until I was an utter wreck. Dismissing me with distaste, the lieutenant called Ian over to help me.

When I had recovered some and managed to walk agonisingly back to the base, I went straight to the sickbay, with the lootie's permission. That night I was hospitalised for the second time that year. I was given cortisone injections to both knees and kept in the sickbay for two days. Ian and Adi and some of the others stopped by to visit me while I was there, but not once did any of my platoon's rank come to visit. I guess they weren't allowed to show that level of concern for a *troep*. And why would they? I was just a *rooinek* to them.

Later, an informal contest was held by Bravo Company, the guys nominating various individuals or platoons for such things as "neatest in the company" and "most improved". I cherished my nomination as "most persistent and hang-in-there recruit". Following my numerous *oppies* and two stays in hospital, the guys reckoned I was one tenacious son-of-a-gun, and I took their votes for me to be a real honour, even if it wasn't an officially recognised award. Even the lootie seemed to approve of the nomination.

The day of our final shooting competition arrived, and we were each given thirty rounds for our 35-round magazine, with a potential maximum of 150 points to be scored. The allocation of rounds was carefully monitored to prevent cheating, but we all snuck in an extra round or two while the corporals weren't looking. I had two extra rounds, while Ian had five, which took him to the maximum a 35-round magazine could handle. The more rounds you stuffed into that magazine, the weaker the spring became and the more likely the magazine was to jam.

The whole of Bravo Company was present and hopeful to get their shooting badges. I lined up a short distance behind the 300-metre marker with the first thirty-six guys, eyeing my Joe and trying to focus on the task at hand. A score of five points each was given for a shot to the heart or head of the target, the other parts giving scores of lower values. After a short pause, the staff sergeant blew his whistle and we went forward, quickly walking to the 300-metre mark in unison and then down onto our bellies. I settled into position quickly and took aim through the R4's sights at the NATO target so far off in the distance. The first shot went off, *blam!*, and I flinched slightly. This was it! The competition was on. Slowly and steadily, I squeezed the trigger, holding my breath on each shot as we'd been taught, trying not to hyperventilate. My pulse was pounding in my neck, my heart racing from the adrenaline rush. *Bang!* Two second pause. *Bang!* Two second pause. *Bang!* Two second pause. I kept going until I had shot the tenth round just as the whistle blew, signalling us to stop and secure our rifles on safety. The whistle blew again, and we were up and running to the 200-metre marker. Running a hundred metres under those conditions can be exhilarating. All thirty-six of us arrived almost simultaneously, breathless with the excitement and tension. We hardly had enough time to settle into a secure kneeling position when the whistle blew again for us to start firing. I kept myself steady, knelt, aimed the weapon, then squeezed of another ten rounds at the infantryman target. Those thirty seconds went by in a flash.

The whistle blew, and we secured our weapons. The whistle blew, and we got to our feet to scamper to the 100-metre mark. Standing, I shot five rounds at ol'Joe, then another five at the *valplate* to knock them over, all in the space of thirty seconds. I nailed all five fall plates before the order was issued for us to make our weapons safe and stand at ease while the scores were calculated. When the instructor had finished working out the scores, we were given permission to go to the *skietgat* to see how we'd done. I hurried over to Ian in the dugout.

I leaned over the edge and looked down. "How'd I do?" I asked.

Ian stared up at me incredulously before hoisting the target for me to see. "You got all but three rounds in ol'Joe's head or heart!" he said.

"You're joking!" I said. "Did you jab extra holes into Joe or remove any stickers?"

"No ways!" Ian replied. "The corporals were watching us like hawks here! I didn't dare!" He lowered his voice some more and asked, "Did you shoot your extra rounds?"

Grinning, I opened my cupped right hand to show him the two unused rounds.

I hadn't wanted to gyppo the competition. I wanted to really see what I was capable of. In the end, I scored 135 out of 150. I became the talking point among my buds and between Pretorius, Joubert and Pottie. I was one of only two from the whole of Bravo Company to receive a silver *skietbalkie* that day. And, I might add, I achieved it legitimately. Many of the others got their bronze badges having used their extra rounds.

We knew that the border phase was just around the corner. The tension and excitement had been building in the base for a while, and now there was a tangible buzz amongst the guys.

Corporal Joubert informed us at this time that he would be leaving us to go on a course – he was joining the PF ranks. His replacement was to be a Corporal Coetzee, who would be going to South West Africa with us. We wished Joubert well, and he expressed good wishes in return for our upcoming phase on the border.

One day near the end of the last week before we departed for the border, the whole of Bravo Company was ordered to take their kit and lay it out on our groundsheets on the open field north of Bungalow 7. The brass came to check that we were properly prepared and had everything we would need for our tour of duty. Wearing our bush hats and bush jackets over our overalls, we lugged our *balsakke* crammed with kit, our R4s, and all our magazines to the grass and dumped it out on the groundsheets. We stood in an orderly fashion in designated rows of platoons, and under the watchful gaze of senior NCOs, Corporals Joubert and Potgieter walked by the men of Platoon 3 to inspect our goods. If we were short something, Lieutenant Pretorius gave us permission to acquire the item from the quartermaster's stores, but only after a believable explanation as to why the item was missing had been given. In many instances, the recruit would have to pay for the replacement item himself. Those who had passed border kit inspection could take all their kit back to their bungalows and lay low until the process was complete. In dribs and drabs, the men left the field, and as I left, I couldn't help but feel sorry for those that had one or other issue with their kit and were kept standing for hours in the Oudtshoorn heat.

That afternoon, we sat for a platoon photo session. White candidate officer tabs for the shoulders and white plastic bands with Velcro attachments to place around the boots were handed out to us, and we proudly donned these for the photo shoot. Photograph taken, we were expected to remove our tabs and boot bands and put them away – we would only be allowed to wear them again once we had officially received them, which would probably be some time after we returned from the border. We carried them with us, though, even to the border. I guess this was a kind of psychological prompt on the part of the ranks: we were close to achieving the goal we were aiming for, completing JLs successfully and becoming one-pip looties. They wanted to keep us on track and motivated during the difficult times ahead.

For the photograph, we wore our berets, green Infantry School cravats, our browns with the white candidate officer tabs at our shoulders and boot bands wrapped around the top of our boots. We were specifically instructed not to smile. Maybe this was to show that we meant business, that border phase was not meant to be a *jollie patrollie* ("jolly patrol"). The border was something far more serious. I wondered if the group photo was taken that afternoon because of the very real possibility that not all the men would return from the border.

Chapter 14

The sun-scorched bushveld shimmered in the midday glare.

"Hey, *Engelsman*," the deeply-tanned and battle-scarred staff sergeant asked brusquely as he leaned back against the massive wheel of the Ratel armoured vehicle. His browns had been bleached to the colour of sand by continual exposure to the unrelenting sun. "Do you know what the word *'Boer'* means?" His grin was patronising. He stroked his considerable moustache.

"Sure," I responded with confidence. "'*Boer*' is the Afrikaans word for 'farmer', someone who lives and works on the land."

"Really, *Engelsman?*" The old man's tone was sarcastic. "Is that what you think?"

I suspected the crafty old staff sergeant was leading me into a verbal ambush, but I was determined to see where this was going. "Well," I replied with some caution. "The label has come to symbolise a white Afrikaans-speaking South African, much like you."

The staff sergeant gazed indifferently at me with his piercing, steely-blue eyes.

"Actually, my friend," he paused theatrically. "It means much more than that." He sneered. "To us true, traditional Afrikaners, the label of *'Boer'* is about freedom – the freedom of our people to determine our own future, in our own land. We believe that's a cause worth fighting for, even dying for. Don't you?" He stared at me, searching my face for a reaction. His short fingers dug about in his shirt pocket, and withdrew clasping a pocket knife. "Hey," he said with a grunt. "Surely you've heard us called "the white tribe of Africa"?" He narrowed his eyes at me as he opened the knife, flicked it closed.

"But, Staff Sergeant," I spoke carefully. "Don't the blacks feel the same way about their own people? Aren't they entitled to the same rights; the same freedoms?"

The staff sergeant grimaced, collected his thoughts before replying. "Of course," he said as the knife snapped closed again. "It is simply foolish to resist change forever." He raised an eyebrow at me, "But the time is not right," he said. "Now, the meddling communists are manipulating the ANC, propping up SWAPO," he clicked his tongue. "Bloody freedom fighters!" he said almost under his breath. The knife clicked closed again. "With the communists interfering, we'll only end up with chaos." The soldier narrowed his eyes, pointed the blade of the knife in my direction. "We need to find our own solution," he said emphatically. "We need an African solution to this impasse." He clicked his tongue again, flicked the blade in the direction of the veld beyond the Ratel's nose. "To hell with what the rest of the world thinks." For a minute, the whistling of the cicadas and the quiet "click" of the knife blade was all that could be heard.

The staff sergeant sucked at his teeth and addressed me again.

"So, *Engelsman*," he said, looking at me from beneath his expressive eyebrows. "You thought you knew what a *Boer* was ..." he half shrugged a shoulder. "You don't quite have the insight." The knife closed with a click. "But let me ask you this: Do you know anything about the Bush War?"

"Yes," I responded warily. "I know it started on 28 August 1966 in South West Africa. It's been going on unabated for almost twenty years, with no end in sight. It's one of Africa's longest conflicts."

"Hmmm," the staff sergeant said. "So you do know something!" I thought I saw the shadow of a smile under his moustache. "Did you know," he went on, "the Bush War was started when South Africa sent a force of just more than a hundred SAP under the command of ten SADF paratroopers into a secret SWAPO base at Ongulumbashe in Owamboland in South West Africa?" He raised a forefinger and wagged it in rhythm with his speech. "The South Africans exchanged fire with SWAPO forces," he said. "Two SWAPO guerrillas were killed and nine taken prisoner. Fewer than fifty were eventually caught. But," he flicked his knife closed again, returned it to his pocket. "There were no South African losses." He rearranged himself against the wheel of the Ratel, put his hands in his trouser pockets.

"Do you know what events caused the 1966 clash?" the crafty old *Boer* asked me next.

I was eager to impress him. I cleared my throat. "South West Africa – or Namibia, to the inhabitants – became part of the Union of South Africa in 1910," I said. The staff sergeant put his head to one side, motioned for me to continue. "The communist forces – essentially the Soviet Union – started the Border War when they supposedly fought for Namibia's independence, a war that was closely associated with and following on from the Angolan Civil War. In the context of the Cold War, both the Soviet Union and the United States have been trying to influence the outcome of the Angolan Civil War."

I paused to take a breath, the staff sergeant grunted. "South Africa had been responsible for the administration of Namibia since the end of World War I," I continued. "The intention had been for Namibia to become a United Nations Trust Territory following World War II. But, when the League of Nations folded in the aftermath of the Second World War, the UN General Assembly passed a resolution terminating the mandate. South Africa no longer had the right to administer South West Africa." The old man was nodding. I took it to mean I should continue.

"The South African government, though," I went on, "was not willing to relinquish South West Africa, and applied instead to formally incorporate it into South Africa. This application was denied by the International Court of Justice in the fifties, because, they said, the indigenous peoples hadn't been properly consulted. Wanting total control of Namibia without the UN's interference, South Africa refused to supervise South West Africa under a trusteeship system with the UN, and refused to recognise any of the UN's officials. We have been preventing South West Africa from gaining independence ever since. We have effectively been running the country as a fifth province, despite the fact that it was never actually incorporated into South Africa."

"Yes," the staff sergeant interjected. "South Africans have a history of stubborn resistance against all odds." He gave a wheezy chuckle, and then looked at me with those eyes. *"Engelsman,"* he said. "Do you know why we insisted on controlling Namibia?"

"I think so," I responded. "South Africa is opposed to communism. We want to preserve Christianity and Western democracy, and communism threatens these ideals. South Africa wants to rid the continent of communism and its power. To the South African government, continuing the war is a means to buy time in order to create the conditions under which SWAPO will lose the South West African-Namibian election.

"Plus," I went on, "South Africa is frustrated by the way our role in the fight at Ongulumbashe is being denied in public, and we don't like the menial task of preventing the uprising of a few blacks our police have been given."

"That may be true," the staff sergeant said. "But, *Engelsman*, do you know this? If the National Union for the Total Independence of Angola – UNITA – and South Africa together controlled southern Angola, it would be difficult for SWAPO to fight for Namibian independence from bases in Angola. South Africa originally wanted the UN to control the regions bordering South West Africa to prevent SWAPO from launching attacks from within the Angolan border. And, of course, SWAPO get Angolan support because of the current set-up."

"I didn't know that, Staff Sergeant," I replied. "It seems very logical. I know UNITA has been supporting South Africa in its fight against the Angolan government, SWAPO and their communist allies."

"*Engelsman,*" the wily old fox said, lifting a finger to point in my direction again. "Is SWAPO powerful enough to be seen as a threat?" He asked. He rubbed his chin thoughtfully, waiting for my reply.

"Well," I said. "SWAPO is a Marxist terror group in South West Africa. They object to the Apartheid policies South Africa has imposed on Namibia. This is the reason many black Namibians support SWAPO. I know that sometime in the sixties or seventies, hundreds of Namibians, including women, were made to undress before being whipped in public. They were beaten on the buttocks with a long palm-tree cane. Anyone who tried to go against the dictatorial South African government received electric shock treatment and was imprisoned without trial for months ... even years. The prisons in Owamboland were full to overflowing." The staff sergeant was nodding in agreement, although I could see he flinched uncomfortably at the mention of our dictatorial government.

"PLAN," I went on, unperturbed by his patriotic allegiances, "The People's Liberation Army of Namibia, is the military wing of SWAPO, and it was formed in response to this treatment of the locals by the authoritarian South African government," I rubbed it in a little more. "PLAN promised the people the realisation of communist ideals, such as eradicating racism and uniting all Namibian people. It claims it will guard Namibia's independence and build a classless, non-exploitative society. Because they have been oppressed for so long, the locals thought this was exactly what they needed. In the seventies, SWAPO started spreading stories that the South African Security Forces were maltreating the local population in Namibia. The churches and international human rights organisations acted strongly against the Security Forces because of this. Newspapers regularly published reports about murders, assaults, rape and the like – some true, many fallacious."

The staff sergeant interrupted, "So, *Engelsman,*" he said, leaning towards me. "Is SWAPO really fighting for the people's rights? Or are their promises to the Namibians just a facade to get into power?"

"Of that, I am not sure, Staff Sergeant," I replied, realising the gaps in my knowledge.

"Well, let me tell you," he said. "SWAPO isn't much better than our own bunch of... what's the word you used? Oh yes, "dictatorial" nationalist politicians," The old man was now playing me at my own game. "All SWAPO's members are from the tribe of Owambo. They regard themselves as being ethnically superior to the rest of the population. The Owambos don't want to share power with any other tribe, especially knowing that many of those from the other tribes are better educated. SWAPO's leadership supports suppressing those other tribes, and especially any educated people. It's the nature of the beast: communism keeps people controlled and suppressed in this way." He paused, seeming to reflect on what he had just said. After a minute, he continued. "SWAPO," he said, "tries to control the Namibian people through fear, panic and terror. It is using landmines, sabotage and murders in this war. And it is murdering local chiefs and black officials who are serving the South African administration. It wants to show the locals that it will not tolerate traitors to its cause, and that they would benefit from supporting SWAPO. In fact, most other tribal chiefs support South Africa. It's really only the Owambos who despise us South Africans being in South West Africa."

The staff sergeant sucked at his teeth, then spat into the dust at his feet. "Even while this is going on," he continued. "SWAPO gets support and campaigning from the Council of Churches of Namibia. Church leaders have been bribed without knowing what will happen if SWAPO's one-party government wins the elections." He raised a single eyebrow to indicate the irony of his statement.

"That really is bad news," I said, coming to terms with the implications of what he said. "If SWAPO is manipulating the Namibians this way, has it been manipulating the war as well?" I asked.

"Of course!" the staff sergeant was emphatic. "It's been breaking its agreements and promises to the global community, and violating treaties. This war has just been a tool for SWAPO to make the world give in to its agenda."

"Staff Sergeant," I began. "Do you know if South Africa has been able to control the civil war in Namibia?"

"Well," he responded. "The police couldn't cope with South Africa's internal violence as well as the SWAPO revolt. That's why we brought in the military in the seventies. This happened just before the Portuguese government was defeated and the new government announced that it would pull out of the African countries it controlled. When the new Portuguese government announced a ceasefire making way for free elections in Angola, a power vacuum was created that was the perfect opportunity for South Africa. Angola was in a state of chaos. Three freedom movements were fighting each other for control of the country: MPLA, FNLA and the pro-Western, South Africa- and United States- supported UNITA.

"The SADF lacked combat experience, but it was better placed to do the job of containing the expanding SWAPO presence than the police were. It had more personnel and weapons, and had already started training some of its soldiers in counter-insurgency operations in the sixties. Some of the senior SADF officers had thought a lot on how to fight a counter-insurgency war. But by the seventies, the SADF's weapons were outdated and it couldn't acquire new weaponry because of the international sanctions against South Africa.

"Also," the staff sergeant was really hitting his stride now, enjoying giving me this lecture in military history. "The SADF at the time was not bush-savvy. It was made up of boys who had just finished school, been given a gun and three months training, and sent into an environment they knew nothing about. This meant that the SADF often failed to find the SWAPO terrorists they were supposed to be countering, and SWAPO's militants had better tactics than the SADF. They were skilled at using anti-tracking methods and managed to conceal themselves from their opponent. These guys were trained by the Cubans, hey," he rubbed his forehead with the back of his hand. "They had good physical endurance, and they were wily!

"The poor SADF soldiers had little idea of what their task involved. In those days, the SADF tended to act before strategising, as if the brass didn't need to understand what it was going to do or how it was going to do it. And this," his finger went up for emphasis again, "this is why the SADF made so many mistakes early in the war.

"You know," the staff sergeant went on. "South Africa has been trying to win the hearts of the Namibian people to help us win the war. They could help us to cut off shelter and information to SWAPO. But the culture differences are a big problem. We don't understand the ways of the tribal people in Namibia. The SADF knows very little about its enemy ... and the locals aren't helping us. But know this, *Engelsman*," he said. "South Africa has had a lot of success in the war. To date, it has made many cross-border raids targeting SWAPO and their PLAN base-camps in Angola and Zambia. Sophisticated and expensive military aid from the Soviet Union, fifty thousand Cuban troops and thousands of international military advisors from various communist countries, not just the USSR, did not prevent our success in the raids. And the kill ratio is clearly in our favour at ten to one.

"We cleared Caprivi of all terrorist incursions during the late seventies. We are busy getting rid of all terrorists in Kavangoland. SWAPO bases are still continually being pushed north. These terrorists have to travel three hundred kilometres south by foot to be able to access Namibia.

"We are destroying SWAPO's stronghold in Owamboland – you know, Owamboland holds almost fifty percent of the Namibian population. Most of SWAPO's leaders are Owambos, so Owamboland is the area where SWAPO have the most support. SWAPO's move to Caprivi was good for South Africa's control of the battle."

"Okay," I said, interrupting the staff sergeant's soliloquy. "But after the Portuguese left Angola, we couldn't depend on it to prevent SWAPO from getting to Namibia through Angola. Owamboland remains the heartland of SWAPO support. Not so, Staff Sergeant?"

"You're right," he said. "You see, in the seventies, the MPLA took control of Luanda and made itself the government of Angola. The MPLA declared independence, even while the civil war was going on, and Portugal recognised them. And," he went on, "SWAPO has been allowed to act as a legitimate political party, anyway. Another South African official explained to me that this was to "keep it out in the open, and keep the faint-hearted from going to Angola".

"The US and other countries have withdrawn their support for South Africa and UNITA, but the Organisation of African Unity is supporting the MPLA. UNITA has been essential for our strategy, because it prevented SWAPO from getting to Okavango and the western Caprivi. This was important to control the insurgency into Owamboland."

"So," I said. "This is why South Africa decided to end the war in South West Africa and Angola by negotiation in 1976: because of this Western betrayal, international sanctions and domestic strikes, communist aggression, and a prolonged war."

"That's right, *Engelsman*," the staff sergeant agreed. "But you don't have all the facts. The Angolans and Cuba claimed that they had driven the SADF out of Angola. The truth is that the small SADF taskforce advanced a distance of three thousand kilometres into Angola in just thirty-three days. Actually, it was never supposed to take the whole of the country. And it would have been impossible to control such a large territory under the circumstances. The SADF won all its battles. The only exception to this was its temporary retreat at the Battle of Ebo, which is what the Cubans and

Angolans base their claims on. The MPLA may have declared independence, but neither the FNLA nor UNITA recognised it. SWAPO has been trying to attack us in spite of the negotiations. So the civil war went on."

"Staff Sergeant," I asked. "Has SWAPO become stronger? And what is happening with Angola?"

"At one stage, yes, SWAPO was strengthening," the old *Boer* replied. "Thousands of young Namibians went across the border to join SWAPO, and their armed wing went from about four hundred trained guerrillas to approximately two thousand in just two years. But the situation in Angola has become problematic for SWAPO since the mid-seventies. Since the early eighties, SWAPO's power has been reducing. In one year, sixty-four percent of the population gave information to the Security Forces about SWAPO's movements." The staff sergeant gave me a meaningful look. "A SWAPO soldier is only in Owamboland for about six days before the Security Forces know where he is." He opened his hands and said, "So the number of SWAPO soldiers in Owamboland has decreased. Most of SWAPO's members were employed in administration and logistics at base camps and headquarters. That left only 1 500 available for the war in Namibia. Plus," his forefinger went up again, "SWAPO had to pay heavily for the MPLA's hospitality. SWAPO was forced to furnish two infantry brigades for the war against UNITA.

"And that's not all," he went on. "Now the Soviet Union realises that the communist system is failing. The financial and military aid flowing to Angola and Namibia is steadily being reduced. And the Soviets are cash-strapped. They are involved in a number of conflicts worldwide, and there are whisperings that suggest that all is not well with communism globally." "I see," I said, taking in the possibility of a world without the threat of communism. "But, staff," I asked. "With all this going on, who do you think will win the Namibian elections?"

"You know, *Engelsman*," the staff sergeant said. "The Namibians are starting to see SWAPO's true colours. They will realise soon enough that South Africa had been defending their interests all along. They'll realise that we are the right choice." The staff sergeant's hands returned to their pockets and he rocked slightly on his heels.

"I hope so, staff," I replied. "Thanks for the insight." I turned to go, then looked back at the staff sergeant to say, "In an ironic kind of way, it seems that South Africa is helping another nation by fighting this war."

I walked away realising that perhaps the SADF wasn't focussed solely on the interests of South Africa after all. Could it be that it really was involved in the preservation of another country's well-being? Was the SADF the good guy in the story after all? In all that is strange, it appeared to be the case.

I opened my eyes in the darkness. Was it just a dream? It seemed so real. Perhaps it was…

***

I sat bolt-upright in bed. Droning beasts of burden were low overhead, their massively powerful turboprops roaring towards the military airbase southwest of town. We had heard and seen them time and again over the months – some wearing white, silver and orange livery, others in camouflage – making their way to or from the landing strip a little more than two kilometres from Infantry School. At night the aircrafts' landing lights could be seen from our barracks as they thundered towards the landing strip from the north. This time, the planes were flying in to pick us up and ferry us out. This was it. Border-time!

The news had been broken to us the previous day by Lieutenant Pretorius. I got that all-too-familiar hollow feeling in the pit of my stomach. The pay phones had been on double-duty all evening as the guys queued up to say goodbye to their loved ones. In my bungalow, the members of my platoon were busily polishing the floors with great gusto, pushing along a *trommel* and blanket, bashing and bumping and shouting and generally making a racket. The sound of an electric polisher drifted over from the bungalow next door. Ian and I toasted our successful deployment and safe return with coffee out of pale yellow plastic army mugs with a couple of our mates in our room.

I wished the time away, wanting to board those craft and fly. The wait was excruciating.

Roll Call at 21h45 was followed by quiet time and then lights out. They expected us to sleep? Judging by the levels of nervous excitement in our bungalow, I knew sleep would be difficult for all of us. I must have eventually drifted off to dream about the staff sergeant – making sense of what was looming, I suppose. Now I lay in the darkness listening to our vessels preparing for our departure and thinking about how I would have to get used to being away again, just as I had become accustomed to being at Infantry School. In just a few hours, I would be awoken to a different reality.

The war on the border reached mythical status in the minds of white boys in South Africa in the seventies and eighties. How could it be otherwise? The virtual media blackout of the Bush War reduced official references to the operational area to the occasional subdued announcement by SABC news anchors of a soldier's death in the line of duty. In such a climate of secrecy, the war stories of returning soldiers – already embellished and subjective – created a mental patchwork from which arose an image that was part *veldskool*, part Vietnam. Certainly, the civilian population were of the opinion that the soldiers were heroes – fighting the Commies, sometimes dying in service to their country. The only thing I knew for sure was that the border was a place from which the boys returned as men.

"*Staan op!*" Bang bang bang. "*Staan op, troepe! Maak gou!*" It was the din of the corporals banging on our metal cupboards and shouting that woke me, so I must have drifted back to sleep at some point. Now it was 04h00, and I felt as though I hadn't got any rest at all. "*Opskud! Opskud!*" This was it. The border would be the culmination of all the training I had endured: basics, *Vasbyt*, the platoon weapons and conventional warfare phases, section leading. I was still on the course and we were heading out to play our part in the Bush War. I was not really scared. Not yet.

As my bare feet touched the floor I became aware of the wave of excitement that surged throughout Bravo's lines – in fact, the whole of Infantry School was abuzz.

We wanted to leave our brown training overalls behind, but no such luck. With all our gear packed, we marched to the waiting SAMIL 50 trucks in our berets, bush jackets and browns carrying full kit and wearing our dog tags for the first time. A short two kilometre ride to the Oudtshoorn airbase later, we beheld those monstrous planes, the interplay of monolithic images and shadows from the bright loading spotlights creating an otherworldly sight on the concrete concourse.

The American-made Lockheed-Martin four-engine C-130 Hercules, or "Flossie" in SADF parlance, is a real workhorse. A heavy troop carrier with low airspeed flying ability, short landing distance and minimum run take-off, the Flossie is immensely powerful and capable of carrying many tons of cargo, equipment or personnel. Several Flossies stood ready for boarding, scattered about the rudimentary airfield, a couple in their SAFAIR colours, a few more in camouflage green and brown – a real armada of planes.

Platoons boarded the craft and took off for Grootfontein in separate batches, several hours apart, and the sun rose over the runway as we were subjected to the "hurry up and wait" philosophy of air travel so typical of the army.

My platoon boarded the last of the Flossies when the sun was high. Our kit was packed in two piles on large wooden pallets at the centre of the plane, *staaldakke* attached to the top of our rucksacks piled upright and against each other, *balsakke* laid one on top of the other, and all of it strapped down to nullify the effects of turbulence. We held our rifles between our knees. The engines howled as the revs picked up and the plane taxied to the start of the runway, engines at almost full throttle. The brakes were released and we rapidly picked up speed. In a moment we were airborne. Without a window to look out of, I imagined our vessel rising above the Swartberg Mountains, aiming north-northwest towards South West Africa and Grootfontein over 1 600 kilometres away.

It was an uncomfortable flight. The seats along both sides of the length of the fuselage were made out of red, latticed nylon webbing straps which sagged like old hammocks and made my back ache. There were no toilets and we were not allowed to take a standing break. With only a few dim internal running lights on and no windows, the only way to tell whether you were ascending or descending was by the changing tone of the droning engines. I looked around – a mix of excitement and apprehension clouded the faces of my comrades. The din of the engines was so awful that I could hardly hear Ian next to me trying to speak. We tried anyway.

"This is it, Mike. Are you gee'd up for it?" yelled Ian. "Yeah, I think so. And you?" I shouted back.

"Sure, why not? It's bound to be a gas!" I wasn't so sure – I was left with my own thoughts.

Chatting proved too difficult, and we soon reverted to silence, trying to doze or reading paperbacks, as the Flossie groaned onwards to Grootfontein.

Eventually we touched down at Grootfontein close to midday, just over three hours after takeoff. The cargo doors opened and we were confronted with an intense heat radiating off the runway, which forced us to quickly shed our bush jackets. Our kit was ejected onto the tarmac while the propellers were still turning, ground crew scurrying about doing quick checks and a limited refuel of the plane. As the last arriving company members exited the plane, sunburnt troops returning to "The States' clambered on board. The rear cargo ramp lifted, and a minute later the plane rolled forward towards the runway. The aircraft couldn't have been on the ground for more than fifteen minutes.

It was a mission to sort out all our kit lying on the airstrip. When I found my rucksack and *balsak*, I joined the others boarding *wit olifante* (white elephants), the large open-bed, mine resistant SAMIL trucks that were to drive us to Oshivelo. The *wit olifante* followed a dirt road up to Tsumeb, where we joined a main tar road to Oshivelo, approximately 220 kilometres to the northwest.

On arrival at Oshivelo Base, there was a cacophony of noise. What a welcome to the operational area! Atlas Aircraft Corporation SA 330 Puma and Alouette III helicopter gunships were circling overhead while MK II Impala jet fighters – armed to the teeth with missiles – were waiting for takeoff at the start of the runway.

Oshivelo Gate is right on the northeastern border of the Etosha Park Game Reserve. The Oshivelo Base was a standing base with a proper security fence. Permanent force members stationed here were housed on the base with their families, the kids attending school on the base, probably run by teachers employed by the SADF. 61 Mechanised Brigade was billeted slightly further up the road less than twenty kilometres away at Omuthiya, another base consisting of permanent concrete and brick structures with proper security fences.

For the time that we would be here, the soldiers of Infantry School were to be deployed in a temporary base on the perimeter of Oshivelo. With no permanent infrastructure at all, we set-to immediately, pitching tents and digging trenches. We dug trenches for stand to; trenches for *pislelies*, long brown funnels for peeing into which direct the pee deep into the soil; trenches for our go-carts, pit latrines over which brown fibreglass and plastic bases moulded in the shape of toilets were placed. The go-carts were treated chemically, but that didn't take away the stench or the *brommers* (blowflies). They were called go-carts because if we all went to the ablutions at the same time – which was mostly the case as we were kept on a strict timetable – it looked like we were all sitting on go-carts, about to race.

We slept in tents with a groundsheet under our sleeping bags. There were no such luxuries as mattresses, beds or field stretchers.

Temporary base set up, no time was lost getting us training. Although we were all very fit by the time we got there, the orientation training at Oshivelo was hard. We did all the normal Infantry training: foot patrols, vehicle movement, night marches, ambushes and so on. Discipline eased up a bit while we were there. We still had to stand for inspection, but it was really just to ensure that things appeared orderly, not the detailed inspections we had at Infantry School. Our weapons were still checked minutely, though.

Vehicle movement drills were introduced immediately and we spent the first three days doing them in the bush with Company Sergeant Major Lategaan. These drills were carried out with a Buffel, a mine-protected armoured personnel carrier developed by the SADF specifically for the Border War and introduced in the late seventies. Weighing a staggering six tonnes, the Buffel has a large metal side flap or gate either side which can be let down to allow ten troopers access in and out of the vehicle – but not with any ease. In the drill, two men, usually the strongest and tallest (I did this often, being tall), would wait for the other members of the squad to clamber up into position – seated but at the ready – before hoisting the heavy hinged metal gates up after them. Once these were secured, the two remaining men would clamber up the sides on short fixed metal-rung ladders and jump in. We all laughed at Ian one day, the shortest in our platoon, when he was ordered to close one gate and couldn't get it closed, even with his arms outstretched above his head, holding the gate up, going nowhere fast. He laughed too, as he knew he had been set up for the ragging.

Dismounting the vehicle was easier: the bolted flaps were released from inside the vehicle and the flaps kicked open to release the troops. First, two guys would jump the almost three metre high sides of the vehicle to act as first-line defence. From the ground, they would sometimes stupidly attempt to hold the panels as they swung open, trying to prevent them from dropping freely, but the panels were heavy and this part of the drill often got us into trouble, resulting in us having to perform the drill several times over as punishment. The drill was fast and intense. The flaps were almost impossible to hold onto. They would fall open with an almighty clang. I suspected that in the heat of battle, in the act of dismounting the Buffel, the panels would inevitably be left to fall, what with bullets and rockets whizzing past and grenades going off.

Having dismounted the vehicle, the troops would take up *rondomverdediging*, or defensive positions, around the Buffel and hold them briefly before being ordered back into the troop compartment. Before returning to our places on the back of the Buffel, we had to perform the drill of clearing our rifles and making sure they were safe. An accidental shot fired off – even if safely – could be sufficient grounds for a soldier to be RTU, especially if he already had a string of infractions behind him. When travelling in the Buffel, we strapped ourselves in. Riding through the bush was extremely bumpy, and the straps would also serve to keep one in the vehicle should it encounter a mine.

We performed this drill over and over until we were *gatvol*: climb up into position, ride around a bit, then jump out, go to ground around the Buffel in a defensive pattern, hold the defensive pattern while the troops jumped in quickly, close metal flaps, jump in, ride on a short bit ...

When we encountered a dirt road which had to be crossed, there was a whole drill involving sweeping for buried mines in the portion of the road the Buffel was to traverse. Roads were crossed at ninety degrees, and if a sapper (army engineer) was with us, they would go forward into the dirt road with a mine detector, supported by one or two armed men, to scan the crossing point for mines.

We never travelled with any sappers, though, so two *troepe*, supported by one or two armed buddies, would be designated mine sweepers. We learnt how to look for mines by poking around in the sand with a *soeksteekstok* (literally, a "search-prod-rod") in a particular way in search of dummy mines buried in the sand by NCOs. It was a bizarre version of treasure hunt, and the NCOs would raise our levels of stress a bit by insisting that they hadn't buried a bogus mine where our *soeksteekstok* had just encountered a solid object in the sand. Out in the bush with the Buffel, where the odds of encountering the real thing were higher, the sand on the roads was soft and almost entirely without stones or rocks. Any hard object detected beneath the sandy surface would bring on instant anxiety. Fortunately, we never encountered any real mines – only tubers and bulbs.

I hated the vehicle movement drills. My knees and shins took strain from the climbing and jumping under *staaldak*, webbing with magazines and my R4, and from the kneeling and lying on the ground.

Vehicle movement training with Major Lategaan on the Friday included two live attacks on a mock target. During the first attack, the Buffel I was in drew fire and our young driver nearly overturned the Buffel trying to get us into the correct position. There was no shortage of firepower. It was not uncommon to fire off two hundred rounds from our R4s in just a few minutes, which we did with relish. On Saturday night, we staged an attack from our base. By the end of Saturday, the men were exhausted, but the training continued relentlessly.

With all the shooting we were doing in our training, we went through many cases of 5.56 mm rounds. We shot so many that most of us managed to acquire an empty case. Before long, just about everyone had an ammo case or two beneath their sleeping areas, placed in holes that had been dug in the ground, covered with wooden laths retrieved from ordnance crates and hidden from view by a camouflage scattering of dirt. These were useful for storing the extra kit we didn't need to carry every day and as an underground pantry for stowing away our *kospakkies* from home.

Just before dusk we would do PT. We did a daily 2.4 kilometre run, or further if we had transgressed, on the *Groot Wit Pad*, the great white road that ran almost parallel to the tar road between Oshivelo and 61 Mechanised Battalion at Omuthiya. Vehicles passing by would churn up a fine white dust which would settle on us and mingle with our sweat so that a shower was imperative on our return to base. Showers were taken in mobile SAMIL shower trucks. As many guys as could fit into the vehicle at once would line up and the water would be switched on for a minute. With the water off, we would all soap ourselves up, then the water would be turned on again for another minute and we'd wash it all off. Showering that quickly took some getting used to, and to begin with I predictably got soap in my eyes.

I watched as a taxi came in from the southeast, hovering briefly over our temporary base before landing in a large open area close to the intersection of the camp entrance with the *Groot Wit Pad*. In border slang, a "taxi" is a Puma helicopter, a bit smaller than the Super Frelon helicopters we saw now and again, which we called "Putcos", a reference to the bus company that ferried black commuters between the townships and the centres of Johannesburg and Pretoria. The smaller Alouettes were called "minis". The taxi was *fwp-fwp*ing through the air towards this make-shift landing pad at the entrance to the camp.

"Anyone want to take a flip in a Puma?" Lieutenant Pretorius turned to us and shouted the question. Ian and I were close to him. One excited look at each other and we both leapt forward.

"Yes, sir!"

"Me, sir!" we both yelled in unison over the racket of the rotor-blades. "Cameron, *maak gou!*" Pretorius beckoned ("be quick!"). I stepped forward with Ian, and Pretorius shook his head. "Not you, Warren. There are *troepe* from the other platoons who should be allowed the chance." I was disappointed. I stood by and watched as Ian and several other guys boarded the helicopter. As the bird took to the air I realised that I wasn't particularly favoured by that Dutchman lootie, but Ian was. It would dawn on me in time that the lootie was grooming Ian to stay on at Infantry School. I wonder how many of the others that took that ride on the Puma that day also stayed behind at Oudtshoorn the following year?

As we were in officer training, a fair amount of time was spent practicing the working out and giving of orders. We would draw up orders for actions as if we were platoon commanders, planning movements and assigning roles and responsibilities. In working out an ambush, for example, we would make use of sand models to chart out the action. Using small objects from the veld – like stones and twigs – we would create a model of the surroundings, scratching lines and arrows in the sand to denote positions and expected movement. It wasn't much fun – we would work out orders again and again, and if you got it wrong, you'd get Lieutenant Pretorius's boot through your sand model and you'd have to start all over again.

With the sand model built, Pretorius would say to one of us, "You do the warning order." Before the poor soldier had finished giving the warning order, Pretorius would switch to the next guy's warning order. He was testing principles with us.

"You've forgotten to give the warning order to your company quartermaster that you needed that item," he would say. It was that sort of detail that was drilled into us. Finally, Lieutenant Pretorius would give his orders, which were, of course, the correct ones, and we would all have to make corrections to our own orders.

Once we had perfected the orders, we would be taken out a few kilometres from base to put the model into practice. These drills emphasised for me how important good orders are to the success of an operation. Good orders are the result of careful and logical planning, and vital to the role of an officer.

Our first live ambush was done with Staff Sergeant Smuts, a PF who, with his receding hairline and neat moustache, resembled his namesake immortalised in Parliament Square more than he might have wished. Ambushes are almost always done at night, and part of ambush training was learning *verberging en vermoming*, "camouflage and disguise". The art of concealment in South West Africa involved the liberal use of what we called "Black is Beautiful" – the army-issue black cammo cream which was applied to the face and other exposed skin. We were taught how the enemy would "read" the bush instinctively from left to right, like reading a book, so the most effective pattern to use in applying the cream was to smear it with splayed fingers from top right to bottom left. Some of the guys just smeared their faces and arms completely. The cammo cream got into everything and went everywhere. The stuff was amazing – just a fingertip of it could cover a large area of exposed skin, and still have enough over for a buddy! The rest of our camouflage involved the addition of foliage, so that our webbing and bodies sprouted grass, leaves and branches and we ended up looking like autumn with legs. When we showed up in costume to *Tree Aan!* we were *kak*ked out for our piss-poor attempts.

We moved out for the ambush at 16h30 and set up our positions at dusk. The ambush was initiated with a whistle at 20h00. For a platoon-sized ambush, our training required a standard set-up: three MAGs, several Claymore mines, quite a few trip-flares, three 60 mm Patmors with a dozen or more illumination and high-explosive mortar bombs and a whole lot of riflemen shooting like crazy. The attack lasted about a minute, and by the end I had emptied all my magazines – about ninety rounds. What a rush!

There was no hot water when we got back to base, and soon the ablutions were covered in black smears with dirty black pools of water everywhere. A little of that cammo cream certainly went a long way, so it was important to be sure to wash all the stuff off your body, clothing and equipment. Those who forgot to wash the strap of their *staaldakke* were instantly camouflaged when next they donned their helmets!

The time we spent doing temporary bases (TBs) just outside the tented area of our base was the training I found most restful and pleasant. The days of TB training, or when we had chaplain's period, or when we had *kopsmokkeling* comops lectures, were the days we all slept better, and I would find myself wishing for these peaceful interludes in the midst of the unrelenting training we were subjected to in South West Africa.

Every three weeks or so, barbers would come to our temporary bases to cut our hair.

I spent a lot of time writing letters while I was in the base. Some months after returning from the border, I read a letter I had sent Kimberly from Oshivelo. I could hardly see what I had written – there were more black permanent-marker cross-outs than my own visible writing, and I'd hardly mentioned any place or activity in any detail at all. Letters written from the base were handed to Lieutenant Pretorius in open addressed envelopes for censoring by a security unit designated specifically for this purpose before being posted to their recipients.

Our post from home found its way to us up there in South West Africa, including *kospakkies*. The *kospakkies* were welcome, seeing as we were down to just two meals a day. Kimberly used to buy standard postal boxes made from corrugated cardboard, and fill them with treats to send to me. My mom used to do the same in old two-litre ice-cream tubs. Kimberly and my mom both always included several rolls of Super Cs. I used to pack these away into any available battle pockets, knowing that at some stage they would come in handy. By the time I was on the border, I was pretty *gatvol* of Super Cs! Once, I got two *pakkies* delivered to me at once, one from each of them. I remember thinking, *What am I going to do with all this stuff?* The only place I could store things while on the move so much was in my pack. I decided not to let any of the stuff go to waste, so, with several of my mates, I sat down to finish everything in those *kospakkies* in one sitting. We did our best, but there was just too much to eat at once – even for four of us.

The *Dankie Tannies* visited us from time to time, making their way up to our base from Grootfontein or Tsumeb for the day. *Dankie tannie* is Afrikaans for "thank you, auntie", and the women who came to be known by this moniker were from various organisations that provided comfort and support for the men on the border and their families back home. They would hand out their *pakkies*, bulging with disposable razors, pens and writing paper, a pocket knife cum nail clipper, a pack of cigarettes for those who smoked, some sweets, as well as a letter from Mrs Botha, all in an embossed fake leather folder.

Of all the training up on the border, I enjoyed the map-work the most. We each had an opportunity to act as the platoon orderly while walking patrol, a task which involved tracking the distance covered by counting paces. 1 600 paces with a pack on one's back was equivalent to a kilometre. At any stage, Lieutenant Pretorius would ask, *"Hoe ver is jy nou?"* ("How far are you now?"), and platoon orderly would have to mentally convert the number of paces into metres walked on that particular bearing. We did so much of this that we would find ourselves habitually counting off paces as we walked and being able to convert to metres without really knowing where we were in that sequence. I could have done it in my sleep.

We did quite a few long after-hour patrols. We had been told that the possibility of us encountering terrorists was less likely here than it was up north, but we had to be careful all the same. We were above the so-called red line and getting danger pay. We would return to our temporary base to sleep. I wasn't scared, but I was feeling the physical effects of all the training and patrolling. My body was sore and I had blisters.

One night we did a route march of about six clicks. We started out at dusk and did okay to begin with, but as it got dark we had to do battle with *haakdoring* (hook-thorn) bushes, those vicious shrubs that infested the terrain. With their inward-curling thorns and nasty personality, they grab you just as you think you've made it past them. *"Bliksem!"* You'd hear the poor victim whisper, *"Haai, julle ouens, help my!"* Try as you might to disentangle the poor bastard, the thorns would fight back and he'd find himself caught up deeper in the barbs. There were few of us who never experienced that painful embrace at one stage or another.

I had been on the border for about two weeks when, after all the standing orders training, we were to be evaluated. Officers and NCOs from bases all over the vicinity came to assess us. Platoons were selected for whichever evaluation from the proverbial hat – in fact, it was a *staaldak* we used. Even though it was right towards the end of our year, guys were still being thrown off the course at that stage. A handful of recruits were thrown off when they were already receiving their candidate officers' pay.

After evaluations, we received orders to move out of Oshivelo and redeploy to Omuthiya (not to be confused with Amuteya, which is approximately 140 kilometres northwest of Oshivelo). In our new home next door to 61 Mechanised Battalion we would begin the next phase of training, which was to comprise a lot of fire and movement section attacks and night ambushes, as well as deployment in the training area. At Omuthiya we stayed in a semi-permanent tent base. It was expected that we would be here for a few weeks of training before moving up closer to the actual border, and action!

Arriving at Omuthiya, we skirted left of the gate to 61 Mech's main base. As we passed 61 Mech, I could see a multitude of vehicles and equipment – plenty of Ratels: 20s, 60s and 90s, Ratel ZT3s, Olifant Mk 1A tanks and SAMILs of all descriptions, such as the Kwevoel mine-resistant SAMIL 100s, ambulances, and G5 cannon.

Behind 61 Mechanised Brigade's camp were a number of tents formed into rows either side of a clearly defined gravel path, along with a couple of thatched huts built in a compound formation. Several trees were scattered about the camp. I reckoned that this base must have been in use by our infantry divisions for some time.

One unforgettable feature of the landscape around Omuthiya was the flies. The Mopani flies infested the area by their thousands. Tiny and incessantly irritating little black flies that they were, they would bother us endlessly when we lay still. The only way of easing their torment of us was to keep moving, although there were always a couple that persisted in orbiting your head, emitting that irritating buzz and coming at you like a mosquito when you're too tired to put on the light and dispense with its miserable existence. Waving them off with a hand was useless. They would just come back at you.

While we were there, only two platoons out of six slept in the base at any one time, the rest out in the veld. Our platoon was one of the first to sleep in the base.

Ian and I joined several of our mates in the very first tent. We slept on a groundsheet on soft sandy earth, heads towards the walls and feet to the centre of the tent. Because we had extra kit and didn't have the luxury of an ammo case like we had at Oshivelo, almost everyone very soon buried their *kospakkies* from home, away and out of sight beneath and behind their rucksacks, which were against the tent walls.

I was scratching through one of my mom's plastic two-litre ice cream containers when Ian sounded the alarm.

"Whoa! Inspection!" His whisper was urgent. "Pottie's coming!" He dropped the tent's flap and hurried to his kit. The other guys scrambled to their sleeping positions to pack up their sleeping gear and their kits. Inspection was usually later. This one was sprung on us, a test to see how we were doing, to keep us on our toes.

I had woken up with a hunger that demanded to be satisfied. Between the intensity of the physical training up there and the fact that our meals had been reduced to just two a day, my appetite was raging. The early morning coffee and rusks had barely touched sides and breakfast was still an interminable three hours away. Thank goodness I had a *kospakkie* each from my mom and Kimberly, both filled to bursting with all kinds of delectable treats that brought with them the luxurious smells and tastes of home and freedom. I thought a cereal bar or a little biltong would keep me going, but I was interrupted in my hunt for food by Ian's signal.

Hurrying, I dug into the soft soil alongside the tent wall with two hands to make a hole in which to bury the *kospakkies*. Lieutenant Potgieter hadn't yet arrived at our tent, so I guessed he had started with the line of tents on the opposite side of the pathway. That gave me just a few more minutes to try and plant the contraband out of sight. Throwing the closed containers into the hole, I began shovelling the dirt back with two open hands, realising too late that a little mound of earth would give away the hidden treasure in a single glance. I was too late. I would have to leave it and hope for the best.

"Chips! Mike! Here he comes!" Ian called from the entrance. I moved my rucksack to cover the mound, placing my R4 on its bipod next to the rucksack pointing outwards towards the walls of the tent as was required, then dusting my hands off on my thighs. I saw the rucksack leaning ever so slightly to one side as Ian called us all to attention at the entrance to the tent.

Potgieter entered the tent in silence. He took his time checking each kit and rifle in turn, grunting now and then as he did so. As he came to my kit, I caught my breath and looked at the canvas ceiling of the tent, willing him to be blind to the little mound between the bottom of the rucksack and the tent wall. He gave another short grunt and bent down. Moving my rucksack aside, he scratched at the soil where my *kospakkies* were hidden. They weren't well concealed. It took him no time to discover my transgression. He opened the corner of the ice-cream tub, revealing its innards of shining plastic and foil wrappers. He stood up and sighed.

"Warren!" He barked.

"Corporal!" I looked with dismay at the exposed pantry.

"Secure your kit and bring your weapon!" Potgieter's voice boomed through the two rows of tents. I knew every platoon-member could hear. "Wait for me outside!"

"Yes, corporal." He turned on his heel and exited the tent. It felt like he took all the oxygen with him.

I knew I was in for an *opfok*. Holding my R4, a magazine in each pouch of my chest webbing, I stood at attention outside the tent. I watched as Potgieter inspected the remaining tents on our side of the path. Time passed excruciatingly slowly. I wondered if he deliberately slowed down, heightening the tension and expectation that was mounting in my chest. I heard whispers up and down the lines of tents. Guys were looking my way, some with pity, others with grim satisfaction. After the longest ten minutes, Potgieter swept past me with a brusk "Warren!" indicating that I should follow him. As I turned to hand my rifle to Ian for safe-keeping, Pottie looked back and said "Nah-uh. Bring it with you."

About a hundred metres from our tents was an earth-walled dam – not very big, probably no more than two hundred metres in circumference – with an almost rectangular shape. We approached the dam and I saw, to the side of the bank, a number of sandbags packed one on top of another. Lounging against the heap of sandbags was a medic, the sight of whom caused me alarm. *Why is there a medic here already?* I thought. *Was Potgieter gunning for me all along?* I couldn't help but wonder.

Pottie turned to me, his youthful, round face breaking into a grin.

"Grab yourself a sandbag," he said, inclining his head slightly towards the pile. I slung my rifle over my shoulder and twisted it onto my back. I took what looked to be the lightest sandbag, knowing that they were probably all much the same. Hefting the bag onto my shoulders, I turned to Potgieter, awaiting the next instruction. All traces of his smile had vanished. "Warren," he said in a calm and quiet voice. "I've had enough of your *kak*." Pausing dramatically, he planted his feet apart, putting his hands behind his back. He stretched his neck so that it clicked audibly. When he spoke again, he raised his voice and enunciated his words, as if speaking to an imbecile.

"I am going to teach you a lesson, *troep!*" He loaded the last word with spite, rolling the "r" and discharging the plosive like a weapon. "I am going to break you!" In that moment, looking into Potgieter's narrowed eyes, I resolved not to give him the satisfaction.

For nearly two hours, Potgieter took me apart on that dam wall with a whistle: blowing when I was to run and then blowing again to stop for about ten seconds of rest. I ran in an anti-clockwise direction around and on top of that dam wall, staggering and stumbling as the exertion took its toll. I kicked up little puffs of dust as I pitched and weaved. Below the dam on the training ground, the others had started a fire and movement dry drill exercise. From their position they could see my progress as I stopped and started, lumbered and lurched to the metronomic trill of the corporal's whistle. I had the distinct impression he was sending the troops a message, making an example of me.

After almost half an hour, I had a stitch which begged me to stop. I ignored it and kept moving. The morning sun grew hotter and I sweated profusely. I craved a long, cold drink of water. My shoulders seized up under the weight of the sandbag, then my head began to throb as if it was going to explode. *You can do this, Mike,* I kept an internal monologue going, talking myself into staying on my feet. *You are stronger than him, Mike. Just keep putting one foot in front of the other. You can do this ...*

I must have been circling that dam for over an hour and a half when I stumbled and fell for the first time. Landing on my hands and knees, the sandbag on the dam wall in front of me, I watched as my bush hat flew off my head and landed on the surface of the water, turning slightly as it landed before it came to rest in the still heat of the semi-desert morning. I was drenched, panting, my heart pounding in my ears. A shadow fell over me and I looked up to see Corporal Potgieter standing over me, legs astride and hands on hips. He had a mean and twisted grin on his face.

"Have you had enough, Warren?" he barked at me. Leaning down towards my face, he raised his voice a notch. "Well? Have you?!" A droplet of flying spittle landed on my cheek.

My reply was hoarse but emphatic. "No, corporal." Potgieter grimaced as if sucking on a lemon and pulled himself upright, not taking his eyes from me. With every ounce of strength I had, I pulled myself to my feet and hefted the sandbag into my arms. I didn't have the strength to lift it to my shoulders, so I cradled it in my arms like a baby. For a second or two, I looked Potgieter in the eye. Then he stepped aside and blew his whistle. I staggered forward, tottering and swaying, but determinedly on my feet. My hamstrings burned, my calf muscles trembled. I persisted, breathing with some effort through my dry mouth. My tongue was swollen and felt like a cloth gag in my mouth. I was uncomfortable, but single-minded: I was not going to let Pottie break me.

Seeing me suffering, Corporal Potgieter gave in to cruelty, blowing the whistle at shorter intervals. The stop-start interfered with my flow, and I stumbled again, landing with some force on my knees. I couldn't believe Potgieter's mean-spiritedness. I heard him chuckle at my misfortune.

"How about now, Warren?" I looked up to see him leaning on one knee, peering down at me. His tone was mocking. "Had enough now?" I shook my head, unable to find the strength to speak.

Digging really deep into myself, I found the fortitude to return to my feet, tottering and swaying. I raised the sandbag to my chest.

I had almost made it a full circuit around the dam when my legs gave in beneath me. This time, I fell onto the sandbag, and for a few seconds I just lay there in relief at being off my feet. From behind me I heard Pottie shouting again.

"Well, Warren?" He nudged my lifeless foot with his boot. "Are you breaking yet?" I rolled over and looked into his face, squinting from the sun. When I spoke, there was barely a whisper.

"You won't break me, corporal!" Potgieter's eyes bulged with anger and frustration, and the scowl that settled on his face brought me profound satisfaction. I dragged myself onto my feet and with shaking arms lifted the sandbag again. Potgieter blew the whistle and I stumbled forward.

The next time I fell, after Potgieter had demanded whether I was ready to quit and I had refused, he called the medic over to have a look at me. The medic gripped my jaw and looked into my eyes. I felt his coarse hand on my swollen lips.

"He's dehydrated," he said to the corporal. To me, he said, "You must have some water." I tried to swallow, but my tongue stuck to the roof of my mouth. I shook my head.

"No," I gasped, and moved to get up.

"Just admit it, Warren." Potgieter was impatient. "You're done." I was on my feet.

"No," I said again, and pulled the sandbag into my arms. It felt like lead. I encircled it with my arms, supporting the base with one hand and letting the top fall over the opposite arm. Potgieter blew his whistle and I made my way forward falteringly. I could feel my overall sticking to my back, under my arms. The rifle kept poking uncomfortably into the small of my back. But I kept going. I was moving – slowly by now, but moving – and Potgieter walked behind me, shouting.

"Haven't you had enough yet?" he was demanding, but I kept moving. *Frreep.* I stopped. *Frreep.* I moved. "Warren! Quit, you punk." I was smiling through my dry lips now, knowing I was getting to him. *Frreep.* I stopped. *Frreep.* I moved. "Just give in, now, Warren. You know you're done." I shook my head and kept moving, the sandbag heavier than ever, the coarse fabric cutting into my clasping fingers, slipping out of the grasp of my sweat-soaked fingers. *Frreep.* I stopped. *Frreep.* I moved. Potgieter asked me again if I was ready to quit. Then again. And again. A pleading note had crept into his voice, which only served to firm my resolve. "Just quit, Warren!" Pottie demanded through clenched teeth. "Quit!" The satisfaction of showing him up gave me the strength to keep going. Pottie had finally met his match.

"Ag, go join the others," he waved his hand dismissively in my direction and stormed off towards the camp looking thoroughly cheesed off. I dropped the sandbag and mentally chuckled to myself. I had trumped him! Him and his cohorts, the platoon sergeant and Lieutenant Pretorius. The *Engelsman* had shown them up! I felt like I deserved a trophy. I walked unsteadily over to the lieutenant and pronounced myself present and available to train. Concern and admiration mingled in his face as he looked at me. He nodded once, saying, "Go have a drink, Warren, and rest for a bit. Then you can join us." I was grateful, and limped over to a shady bush, the flies for once easy to ignore. Looking over to the others, I saw them sneaking compassionate and supportive looks my way. Ian gave me a huge grin and the slightest suggestion of a thumbs-up. I grinned back.

Half an hour later, still trembling but feeling somewhat restored, I slowly got to my feet and joined the platoon on the training ground. A single section was lining up to carry out a drill while the rest of the guys looked on.

"Welcome back, Warren," the lieutenant said with grudging admiration as I approached. "Why don't you take over as commander?" I knew he was doing this as a sign of respect. I had no great strength left, but I was honoured to take the section through their paces.

That evening the boys clamoured around me to hear my story. I had gained a whole new level of respect for taking Pottie on at his own game and beating him. Corporal Potgieter was forced to accept that I was no pushover, and I think he came to respect me just a little more after that. The English-speaking lads were over the moon at the doggedness I had shown. English-speakers: 3; platoon-leaders: 0.

Chapter 15

It had been an interminable weekend at home from res without Kimberly, but now, a week later, we were to be reunited. I couldn't wait to see her. I practically ran to her house. I stepped through the front door, and walked into a wall of ice. I knew immediately that something was different and I was alarmed.

"Kimberly?" I called.

She walked towards me from the dining room with her arms crossed at the waist. A small smile on her lips looked more like a swallowed grimace. "Hi." I had expected her to run into my arms, but she seemed pointedly casual. She pecked me quickly and looked away. "Coffee?"

I followed her to the kitchen, trying to suppress the anxiety that overwhelmed me.

"Ja, thanks." I feigned enthusiasm, "Hey! Kimmie!" I said, using her mom's pet name for her in a lame attempt to lighten the mood. "Tell me about the tour." She had spent a week in the Eastern Transvaal, a school trip with her classmates. I stood behind her, tried to stroke her shoulders affectionately, but she slipped out of my grasp.

"It was okay." She scratched her neck, fiddled with the kettle, took mugs from the cupboard.

"Well ...? Tell me about it! What did you do?" Spooning coffee and sugar into the mugs, she half shrugged a shoulder. She abandoned the coffee, walked towards the sun room where her dad was reading the paper in his favourite chair. My alarm was growing. "Kimberly! What's going on?" I followed her. She had never been this way before.

"What do you mean?" she said. "Nothing's going on." She doubled back, returned to the kettle.

"So?" I said. "Why are you avoiding me?" She rolled her eyes.

"I'm not!" She poured water from the kettle.

"You are!" I couldn't stop my voice from becoming strained. Kimberly brushed past me and moved towards the lounge, picked up a pile of books and walked towards the bookshelf on the one side, where she started to replace them in some kind of order.

"It was fine, okay? What do you want?" Her voice was pitched high, she was getting defensive. I followed her through the lounge, past the sun room and back to the kitchen. She was carrying half the pile of books with her.

"I just want you to tell me about it!" This was weird. I was panicking. I didn't want to believe what I suspected.

Kimberly's mom peered around the doorway from the dining room. "Mike!" She sounded quite brisk. "That's enough. Stop badgering her! Can't you see she's had a trying week?" With that, I knew. Kimberly's mom had never defended her like that. My heart raced and it felt as though my world was starting to crumble. In a flash, I grasped what had happened.

I couldn't accuse her on the basis of a suspicion. I tried to talk more quietly, but now all too earnestly.

"Kimberly, did something happen?" She put the books down in the sun room, rubbed her forehead.

"What do you mean? Of course nothing happened. It was a stupid school tour." She was making her way back to the kitchen. She seemed to be trying to escape me.

I might have been more abrasive than I meant to be: "Why are you avoiding answering me? Why are you avoiding me?"

"I'm not. Why are you pestering me?" I tried to catch her by the elbow as she passed me.

"Hey. Stop. Look at me." She shrugged me off and kept walking. Her father dropped a corner of the *Saturday Star.*

"Quit it, Mike," he said.

I followed Kimberly, called to her, "Kimberly! What's going on?" She turned to me, took a breath to speak. She seemed to change her mind, walked back to the abandoned coffee. I was agitated, I might have been a bit loud, "Kimberly ... has something happened?" She turned away from me, dug through a drawer. "Kimberly – talk to me!"

Her father entered the kitchen, still clutching the morning paper, glaring at me over the top of his spectacles.

"Mike," he said, "take it easy." I couldn't believe he was talking to me like this, as if I was the ogre in this situation. He raised a finger to make his point. "Take it easy, or I'll have to ask you to leave".

Still looking at her father, I clutched Kimberly's arm. Dropping my voice, I spoke through a clenched jaw.

"Let's talk," I said. I guided her out of the back door of the kitchen, past the courtyard and into the garden. Outside, I turned her to face me. "Okay. What happened?" She became petulant, whiney like a child.

"Nothing happened, Michael. Why are you quizzing me like this?" "Because, I can tell. Something has changed," I was trying to keep my voice level and reasonable. "Something has changed and I want you to tell me what it is." I folded my arms to keep from shaking. I didn't unclench my fists.

She put the heel of her hand against her brow. I could feel my fingernails biting into the palms of my hands. I snapped, "Tell me!" She shuddered at my angry demand. More softly I pleaded, "Please tell me..." Her shoulders drooped and she encircled her waist with her fragile-looking arms.

"Oh, Michael. It was nothing ..." She looked away. I felt the rage swelling in my already tightened chest. I was right! I was right! Something had happened!

I dropped my hands to my sides. "Ian," I said, defeated.

More than once, Kimberly had dropped casually into conversation how much she enjoyed her "friend" Ian's company – he was such a nice guy, she had said, and so good looking, and always understanding. I never pressed her on this, never doubted the strength of our relationship. But now ... now it was all different. I was crushed with disappointment. I sank onto the wooden bench beside the path, put my head in my hands. With that, Kimberly's attitude changed. She sat beside me and put her arm around my shoulders.

"It was nothing, babe. A mistake," she sounded as if she were pleading with me. With her other hand she tried to turn my head towards her. Her voice was soft, verging on tearful, "Michael?" I couldn't look at her. I couldn't get my head around the idea. "Please believe me." She knelt on the grass in front of me, her hands on my knees. Through my fingers I could see her tears begin to fall. I didn't believe it. I didn't believe her. I was hurting so much, I wanted to hurt her in return. I said nothing while she begged. "Michael?" I watched as it dawned on her that she might have ruined the relationship irreparably. With more urgency, "Michael?" I stayed quiet. "Michael!" She shook me by the knees. "Michael! Say something!"

I rubbed my eyes with open hands, ran my fingers through my hair. I rested my chin on my hands and looked at her. I said nothing. She continued to plead with me.

"It was nothing, Michael." She sat back on her heels, "I made a mistake. It was just a kiss." She leant forward earnestly, the tears flowing now. "You have to believe me. It was just a kiss." I stayed silent, I couldn't speak. "It was the last night of the tour. A couple of us snuck out to the pool. We were having fun ..." She was looking away from me now. I looked at her in disbelief, to which she hurriedly responded, "We just kissed, Michael.

165

Nothing more. It didn't mean a thing".

There was so much going through my mind. I was mad at Kimberly for betraying me. Mad at her folks for defending her, as if she was innocent. Kimberly kept talking, kept trying to convince me that what she had done was nothing.

"I ... I don't know why I did it ..." I wondered if her tears showed true remorse, or if she was merely sorry she had been caught out. "... Please, Michael, you must believe me." I watched her, my first true love, crying and pleading with me. I wanted desperately to believe this really was nothing. I couldn't think of ending my relationship over a small indiscretion. I couldn't imagine my life without Kimberly.

Through all the hurt and anger, I reached out to her. I touched her hair with the palm of my shaking hand. I clasped the back of her head and drew her into my shoulder. She sobbed, wrapped her arms around my waist. Into her hair I whispered, "It's okay. It's okay. Don't worry." I held her small body against mine and wanted desperately to believe the words I spoke to her. "We'll be okay."

It didn't occur to me until much later that she never said the words, "I'm sorry."

***

By the time Bravo Company was posted to Omuthiya, we were down to six platoons of between thirty-four and thirty-six men each. During drills, the extra members of our platoons were assigned supporting roles, performing the functions of intelligence, trackers and mortar men. Each of us had turns taking on these support duties, meaning there were men in position for the drills and we all got to know what these roles entailed.

We did a lot of intensive live *vuur en beweging* section attacks at Omuthiya, using ammo like there was no tomorrow. RPG-7s, M79 *snotneus* grenade launchers and 75 mm rifle grenades were fired in the plenty; the 60 mm Patmor, the MAG, smoke grenades, the list went on. And, of course, our R4s. In one day of live section attack drills, I shot off all my rounds from four 35-round magazines. R4s are notoriously prone to jamming when the steel-bodied magazine is loaded with more than thirty to thirty-two rounds, so we never fully loaded them up, but still, that amounts to over 120 rounds shot!

When I got to the border, everyone was calling the M79 a *snotneus*. Even the platoon commander – who had been trying to enforce the discipline down in Oudtshoorn – called it ol' *snottie*. I took it that the dispensing of some of the formalities and rigidity of discipline at Infantry School was a nod to the fact that we were now facing a real situation. The games were over. This was war.

The SADF put on various demonstrations for us. 61 Mechanised Brigade brought along swift and highly mobile Ratels and Olifant tanks. The tanks impressed us with their huge, menacing presence and high and effective fire-power. They were fast and unstoppable, and we were told that they were able to resist and easily outgun and destroy all Soviet-made tanks of the time.

For one demonstration, the shell of an old kombi was placed in the centre of a practice ground, and the SAAF brought in various aircraft to take aim at it. First, a couple of impressive Dassault Mirage F1AZs and F1CZs were brought in at supersonic speed, likely in excess of Mach 1. Fire was called in from roughly two kilometres away, and they let rip with their air-to-ground rockets. The area the rockets hit was completely destroyed, and I expected the kombi to be blown apart, but the dust cleared and there it still stood. Of course, from where we were, it was impossible to see the shrapnel damage, but I still found the result to be a bit disappointing.

Some Impala MK IIs, flying at subsonic speed, were brought in next, using only their cannons, strafing and peppering the kombi with holes. Finally, an Aérospatiale Alouette III Gunship with a 20 mm Ga1 cannon mounted across the back was brought in. The gunner was behind the cannon, its barrel pointing out the side door. As the gunner fired, we could see the chopper spinning around on its own axis. Fire had to be taken in short bursts, allowing the chopper to return to the target after recoil. The Ga1 obliterated that kombi, and we all thought *Yeah! We'll take the Allouette any time!* The air force demonstrations reassured us that we had access to effective air support if it was required on the front line, and we were at least convinced that we would be safe from friendly fire if we called it in accurately.

It was in the course of the demonstrations put on for us that we were introduced to the infamous 32 Battalion. This "Buffalo Battalion", sometimes called *Os Terríveis* ("The Terrible Ones" in Portuguese), was a highly controversial unit of the SADF, made up of black Angolan soldiers and turned terrorists under white SADF officers and NCOs. A specialised infantry force that used small mobile armour, 32 Battalion almost always travelled by Casspirs, with the troops perched on top. Later I peeked inside one of their Casspirs, and saw it was quite bare, stripped down to absolute utility. They carried R1s rather than R4s, which were meant to be the better firearm for the kind of work they were doing. Several of them walked around with AK47s. They were tasked with demonstrating for us how, when caught in an ambush, they took the offensive. We watched as they stopped their vehicles, the soldiers jumping off to form up in a fire and movement configuration, their mobile MAGs going out on a flank to apply cross-fire to the enemy, their 60 mm mortar group firing from near the vehicles, over their own men. The drill was enacted much as we'd been taught, but the members of 32 Battalion were far more aggressive, more daring, than us. It was clear to me that these guys had little fear of dying, and I had no doubt that the exercise would have been carried out with the same precision in the real situation. I was awe struck by their agility, systematic movement and accuracy of firing.

We had a healthy respect for the guys of 32 Battalion. These men were battle-hardened, physically and mentally tough. Their unconventional uniforms were the expression of their unconventional attitude: these guys saluted nobody.

Nights were spent doing *swerf wag*, or roving sentry. It was after sunset that the wildness of our surroundings really came alive for me. I would walk the camp's perimeter, listening to the grunts of lions, knowing they were just there, just beyond the next line of bushes. Jackals and hyenas would appear to laugh at us as we stood guard, and elephants were known to roam the area. We encountered snakes, lizards, bats and small antelope, and even the insect life was particularly wild here: centipedes the size of sausages, beetles as big as golf balls. Piss moths were large dappled brown moths which emitted a caustic liquid which would cause serious blisters on contact with skin. Guys would pull on their overalls not knowing a piss moth had crept into them, and some very serious sores resulted. There were numerous African Ground squirrels, who, showing serious tree-climbing agility, would often suck at our water-bags hung in the trees. We would soon come across massive anthills, or termite mounds, easily twice the height of an average man. Often the base of these anthills would be broken open, either by foraging pangolins or by wandering locals who would use them to sleep or cook in. Once, some guys in my platoon used picks to open the base of one of these mounds after hearing mewls of distress from within, to find a kitten abandoned there by its mother. From time to time, we would incorporate these structures into our temporary bases, *troepe* using them as shelter from the sun, or resting against them as they sunbathed. Sunbathing was a waste of time for all us *troepe*, though, as the anti-malarial Darachlor tablets we took each week inhibited tanning.

Many nights were spent doing mock night ambush exercises. The ambush training had to be the most tense and nerve-wracking training we received. The dry exercises finally came to an end when we were informed that one of Bravo's platoons would be randomly selected to go and do the live exercise for internal evaluation purposes. Not knowing which platoon would be chosen from Bravo, we had to be sure that we were all a hundred percent ready to perform if called upon.

The chosen platoon would sometimes be given the opportunity to select their own platoon commander for the drill. When that happened, we would select one of the best guys for the job – usually the man who had been the orderly and knew a lot about all the roles. Sometimes, we would be dropped in the dwang when the evaluator identified who should carry out which role for the exercise. For this reason, we each had to be familiar with all the roles in the exercise. This was a useful technique for teaching us how to cope with any sudden change in an ambush situation.

For Bravo's internal evaluation, Company Sergeant Major Lategaan was to be the evaluator. One member of a platoon would be chosen to act as platoon commander that night, and the real platoon commander, Lieutenant Pretorius, would shadow him to observe our movements. Later, one or more of Bravo's platoons would be evaluated externally by staff members from other units and sectors.

It just so happened that Platoon 3 was chosen for the internal evaluation. Reconnaissance was carried out earlier in the day by those guys who were nominated as platoon commander, 2IC, and section leaders. The section leaders numbered three. Reconnoitring is undertaken in order to identify a suitable killing zone from which the ambush will be carried out. While they were doing their recce, the rest of us prepared for the night's ambush.

Some time after sunset, under cover of darkness, Platoon 3 moved into the killing ground to set up the killing group. An ambush is laid based on intelligence, and so the enemy would be expected from a specific direction. The nominated platoon commander channels his three sections into one large, central killing group and two smaller early warning and stopper groups. The roles of the early warning group and the stopper group are interchangeable, as the enemy may come from the opposite direction than expected.

The platoon enters the killing zone or killing ground in single file, making a loop and returning to their original tracks, so that if the enemy is following their tracks, he is still caught in the killing zone. Having ensured that they are not being followed, the men go down in a line, everyone connected by rope. The ropes were used as a means of communication: one tug means this, two tugs means that. Orders were given in this way.

The early warning and stopper groups have just R4s and rifle grenades. The rest of the ordnance is concentrated on the killing ground: Patmors and three MAGs. We used Claymore mines, and all of those had to be set up with *pooitjievakkels*, ground-based trip-flares – another *troep* and I were tasked to set these up. Arcs of fire were set up. This entailed the nominated platoon commander, under the watchful eye of Lieutenant Pretorius, standing over each man – at this point lying on his belly – and tapping him on the shoulder to warn him that he must observe and comply. The platoon commander places two sticks on the ground in front of the man, either side of his R4, to indicate his arc of fire.

Except for the guys with the rifle grenades, everyone's rifle is on rapid fire. We actually put a strip of plaster over the selector lever so that it wouldn't make a clicking noise in the quiet of the night. It is the job of the nominated platoon commander to go and place every rifle onto "fire", so that he knows that everyone's rifle is at the ready. In the early warning and stopper groups, the section leaders nominated as the NCOs carry out the switching of the rifles' selector levers to "fire" position before taking up their positions.

Before receiving the order to begin, we would carry out a test to check that communications were working. Communications between our three groups took place over radio, but voice-overs on radios couldn't be used in case of interception. What we would do, is send static pulses through by clicking the handset. Two clicks in quick succession, followed by a pause, and another two clicks, a pause and another two clicks meant one of the groups had picked up the enemy. Having received this warning over the radio, we would then listen as the early warning group sent information as to how many enemy soldiers were entering the kill zone. A click for every soldier told us he was entering the zone, and once the whole group was in the killing ground, the ambush would be initiated.

In ambush training, we would lie in position for four or five hours, just waiting for the order to be given. With Company Sergeant Major Lategaan standing behind us – if he heard any noise, then it was big points off our evaluation. He was within metres of the killing group.

Should a member of the platoon lying in ambush accidentally fire off too early, the entire platoon's position is compromised, and everyone must fire. The only way to get out of a compromised position is to fight your way out, and hope that you get the enemy. Holding our positions for such long periods also had the desired effect of testing whether we would fire off accidentally – and it did happen! When a guy pulled off a shot like that, the first thing that would go through your mind would be, *Is he going to be RTU?* Whether or not he was kicked off the course depended on his history on the course and his character. It was a pretty serious offence, certainly more serious than forgetting to carry out your weapon's safety drill when dismounting a Buffel. One guy accidentally fired off too early while I was on the border, but he wasn't kicked off the course. He got a massive sandbag *oppie* just like I'd received from Potgieter.

The nominated platoon commander is positioned directly behind the central MAG operator and his belt feeder, and the ambush is initiated when the platoon commander kicks the boots of the MAG operator, who fires off simultaneously with the central mortar guy. The first round out of the mortars is an illumination round. Thereafter, live rounds are fired.

The stopper group and the cut off group fire their rifle grenades to the left and right of the killing ground and all three mortars give covering fire behind the killing ground. All other fire is deployed in the killing ground.

At a certain stage, a signal is given, and the platoon executes fire and movement through the killing ground.

Following the end of the ambush, we were required to go through all the drills that follow, such as casevac, or casualty evacuation (usually by air), casualty reports, and so on.

To heighten the suspense and really keep us on our toes, the sergeant major kept it until the last minute before announcing who was to be evaluated.

During days, we were kept extremely busy out in the veld doing live patrol attacks. We would be up at 04h00 to be on the SAMILs by 06h00. Our kit was heavy and reminded me so much of *Vasbyt*, what with all the extra equipment: rat-packs, platoon weapons and ordnance.

During drills, each one of us had a turn to act as section leader, and after several turns, my throat was hoarse from all the shouting. By this stage we were very short on water – each of us had about seven or eight litres of water a day, which was to be used for drinking, cooking, bathing, everything. I was thirsty all the time. We generally didn't bath. When we did, it was done by digging a hole in the ground, tying a bivvy in a watertight fashion and spreading it across the depression. The bather would then strip down and splash around in a few litres of water, probably more for the cathartic psychological effects than for any real purposes of cleanliness.

Some *ouman* had told me about the kudu – a marvellous, life-saving piece of equipment which I had brought along with me to the border. The kudu is a type of canvas water bag, a bit like a Spanish wineskin, which carries about five litres of water. Once soaked, the kudu seals itself and keeps the water inside extremely cool and sweet-tasting. The army-issue two-litre plastic water bottles emitted tepid water that didn't really quench your thirst. The canvas-covered one litre water bottle could be kept wet to keep the contents cool, but nothing compared to the water from my kudu. The guys used to beg me for a drink from the kudu – man, can one item make you popular! I would strap the kudu to my rucksack as we walked, within easy reach.

Once, when out of base at Omuthiya, we settled into a TB for the night. First, point men or recce men enter into the chosen area to ensure that it is secure. The rest follow through the centre of the TB and out to their positions on the perimeter. The three *LMG* carriers are last into the camp. This is all undertaken in silence, communicating with hand signals. The final encampment is shaped like a triangle, with the lootie safely in the middle. Each side is more than twenty metres long, eleven or more men to a side at about two metre intervals. I thought I was clever to nab a position near a little bush, next to an acacia tree with overhanging branches, close to a mound of earth. The branches above created the perfect spot to secure cover and hang my canvas water bag on, within arm's reach so that I could easily have a swig of delicious water in the night.

We dug our trenches in the soft sand, put out our sleeping bags and quietly prepared food before it got dark, all the while looking outwards from the TB, keeping watch, until guard duty had formally been instituted for each of the three sides of the base for the night. Once night fell, we were forbidden to talk or whisper. There was to be no noise and no light. While out in a TB, we slept in our overalls with boots on.

The soft sand was an accommodating bed, and I slept quite peacefully there, until my slumber was disturbed by a soft *plop* on my sleeping bag. I peered, somewhat *deur die kak*, into the darkness, but in my semi-awake state I could discern nothing and reasoned that it must have been a twig or a leaf falling from above.

I was just drifting back to sleep when I was startled by an intense and burning pain on the skin of my belly. I smothered a yelp. It was so sharp and so sore that I was convinced I had been bitten by a snake. I groped about for my torch. In a few seconds, the pain had spread all over my stomach and chest. My panicked mind imagined an entire colony of scorpions invading my bed and launching an attack on my vulnerable abdomen. Finding my torch, I slid myself down into my sleeping bag, pulling the zip shut over my head, and used one hand to partially obscure the beam as I switched it on. I was afraid of waking the lootie and rousing his ire for using the light, but I was more afraid of what I might encounter in the depths of my sleeping bag. As the pale yellow beam of the flashlight flooded the bag's interior, I drew in a sharp breath. There were scores of them, deep red and black with big pincers: vicious, biting ants, too many to pick off. My attempts at brushing them off just flung them deeper into the sleeping bag. In my haste to exit I fumbled with the zip, eventually getting it open to shoot out doing a rubber-legged jig and swiping at my torso to try and get the ants out from under my clothes. During all this time, I didn't let out a scream or a shout, knowing I would be up for a massive *oppie* if I let on what was happening, but I probably whimpered a little as I tried to rid myself of the little pests. When I seemed to have removed the last ant from my skin, I knelt down next to my sleeping bag to try and deal with the remainders.

Finally rid of those dastardly creatures, I looked around. Where had they come from? And in such vast numbers! I looked closely at the mound near my position, thinking it might house a nest of ants, but it showed no evidence of tenants. I risked a minute trace of a beam through my fist over the immediate area. Nothing. All the guys were fast asleep, including those who were supposed to be on guard duty. Flicking a beam upwards and over the branches above my sleeping bag, I passed over the canvas water bag when something caught my eye. I returned the light to the bag hanging in the tree. Glistening in the faint beam of my torch, I noticed the bag seemed to writhe, and, on closer inspection, I discovered a squirming glob of ants swarming at the base of the bag, hanging from where the water had condensed. As I watched, ants fell off the bag directly onto where I had been sleeping below. I removed the water bag and dropped it far from my position. I gingerly crept back into my sleeping bag – half expecting another attack – and tried to sleep. My dreams were none too pleasant after that!

After five weeks at Omuthiya, following our evaluations there, we got word that we were to deploy closer to the border. I was relieved. The training was really getting to me, and the change would be welcome.

Dressed in our browns, we travelled again in the now-familiar Buffels, making our way northwest from Omuthiya past the swaying golden grasses of the Etosha Pan Game Reserve. I had never seen such an expanse of savannah before. The long golden grass stretched all the way to the horizon, and where it ended, the very bluest sky began: a vision of surreal beauty that I knew I may never have had the opportunity to witness were it not for my national service.

The sea of grass was but a prelude to the Etosha Pan itself, and we soon passed the great lunar landscape of the salt pan, its dusty surface sparkling silver through the shimmering waves of rising heat.

Coordinates: 17°56'24.32"S 16°01'58.70"E

Our convoy of Buffels travelled slowly. With every third or fourth armoured vehicle pulling a water car behind, the whole company slowed to a crawling pace just before Ondangwa, having travelled a road that was impossibly long and straight. I watched as the silhouette of a tall and slender Owambo woman standing on the side of the road drew near. Facing the road, her head was turned towards our convoy, and as we got closer, I saw her eyes were narrowed as she watched our passage. She was young – perhaps in her late twenties – and looked haggard and dishevelled and inebriated. Perhaps she had been lying in the long grass at the side of the road. As we passed her by, she lifted the skirt of her dress. One hand clenched in a black power fisted salute, the other pulled back at her privates as she emitted a stream of pee in our direction, aiming the stream back and forth as if she was firing an automatic weapon. She shouted something unintelligible at the passing vehicles.

Near the towns dotted along our route, we would slow down and look for the local children to do a little comops with them. When we came across a group of kids, we would throw out sweets – usually Super Cs – from our *kospakkies*, or from the extra rat-packs we were given for the purpose. News would travel fast, and in no time, we would be surrounded by a swarm of clamouring youngsters and teenagers. At one point in our journey, when we debussed for a pee break, a group of expectant youngsters emerged out of nowhere to surround us, and we obligingly passed out the anticipated treats. We were never approached by the adults.

We were trying to win over the hearts and minds of the people, but I couldn't help thinking that handing out sweets didn't really earn us the right to be in their country.

Our journey from Omuthiya took us through Ondangwa, past the airbase, to Oshakati, a distance of approximately 130 kilometres. Just outside Oshakati, we turned off the tar road roughly southwest towards Ongandjera and Okahao onto a dusty, potholed gravel road. The last small settlement on the way to our destination, Onesi, was on a turn off from Okahao, roughly in a northwest direction. From Oshakati to Onesi was another 130 kilometres.

The road was not without its hazards. We had to keep a constant lookout for stray animals. Reckless drivers in clapped-out Ford pickups sped along those roads with a complete disregard for traffic rules. We quickly learnt to pull over to the side of the road when they came along, rather than face the consequences of taking these cowboys on. The number of wrecks we had passed along the road told the tale of destruction wrought by these crazy local drivers.

The tail-end of winter had left the landscape dry and brown, the short grasses of the veld broken intermittently by shrubs and denuded pans. Now and then a dust devil was wound up from a pan as the wind stirred up its expectant contents. Trees were scarce, but here and there an acacia added a splash of brave green foliage to the otherwise monochrome vista. I grew tired of the taste of winter in my mouth as our convoy bundled onwards in the dust. The hypnotic effect of the rocking vehicle had brought all conversation to an end, and we watched in silence as the roadside slid by. The continuous bumping and swaying in the Buffel was quite unpleasant, not unlike a small boat travelling over the sea.

And then we saw them. Coming from the northwest, a cloud of dust signalled their approach. Two Casspirs travelled towards us, white, black and coloured men sitting atop. They were unshaven, wearing shorts and vests and non-standard combat flak jackets. Some had bandanas on their heads, one wore a skull cap. They looked like a band of modern-day pirates. Rough, tough and hardened, their AK47s dangled coolly from handmade leather and canvas straps and slings, homemade bandoliers chock-full of ammunition strung from a shoulder or two. *Koevoet.*

The Casspirs travelled steadily towards us, only slowing down near Tsandi to turn towards Oshakati, as they came close. As the *Koevoet* vehicles passed us by, we were roundly ignored, not given the faintest glance, by all the men atop ... all but one, a black Owambo – probably a terr they had turned after capturing him – who gave us a cold and expressionless look of disdain. A necklace of human ears hacked off the corpses of the men he had killed hung about his neck. Perhaps acknowledging our presence there would have been like according us a measure of status, some honour we were not yet worthy of.

Koevoet is the Afrikaans word for crowbar, and aptly describes the unit which was tasked with rooting out and capturing or eliminating suspected terrorists from the local population in South West Africa. Officially, their title was the South West Africa Police Counter-Insurgency Unit. I knew there was a *Koevoet* base in Onesi, in the direction from which the Casspirs had come, in an old German fortress opposite the Mission Station, and I suspected they were travelling from there to some military compound at Oshakati. As their silhouette faded from view down the gravel road, the dust settling behind them, I thought about *Koevoet* and all I had heard about them. We knew who they were and their reputation as the most effective, most feared and most brutal unit engaged within South West Africa against SWAPO was well established amongst us troops on the border, reinforced by rumours and legends repeated and embellished by conscripts in wide-eyed wonder. I once heard of a brutal and bloody brawl in a bar in which it had taken a dozen other guys to subdue just two *Koevoet* combatants. Seeing these hardened fighters on the road to Onesi confirmed for me their aura of fearlessness and aggression.

SADF personnel on the border were carefully kept away from *Koevoet* – whether this was because the authorities disapproved of their methods and didn't want to be seen to be collaborating, or because they wanted to give the "bandits' room to carry out their operations without interference, I don't know. Certainly, it was made clear that if *Koevoet* were known to be operating in an area, we were to bail out immediately and not be seen to be operating in conjunction with them.

Based on the stories I was told about *Koevoet*, it seemed that they operated with impunity. Chasing down their targets, they would charge through villages with complete disregard, flattening the locals' mahango fields and ripping up fences as they went. Livestock were crushed under the wheels of their Casspirs, and sometimes even the mark they were chasing down would be carelessly killed in this way. It seemed to me that much of the good work the regular troops were doing there to try and keep the local population neutral was being undone by these thugs, who left a trail of destruction in their wake.

As we neared Onesi, small groups of Buffels started peeling off one-by-one to take up areas of responsibility along the route, dividing the region up into sectors. My platoon was one of only two which finally passed through Onesi, the others having already reached their destinations. Intelligence suggested that Onesi was supposed to be the village of SWAPO leader Sam Nujoma's grandmother, and that she lived there still. Ongulumbashe, the place at which the Bush War started, is just south of Onesi. Approximately twenty-five kilometres northwest of Onesi, just before the road intersected the main north-south road C35, our four Buffels turned off towards our final stop.

Coordinates: 17°32'45.51"S 14°29'00.24"E

We found ourselves somewhere about five clicks south of present-day Olifa. To our northwest was the headquarters of 51 Battalion at Ruacana Town base. Just east of 51 Battalion was Hurricane Air Force Base, the largest air force base in the western part of the operational area, which housed all types of military personnel. The area here was flat and sandy, sparsely vegetated with various grasses. Vegetation was denser around little oases, where a pool or natural pan could be found, or a little village was built. The landscape featured Omarambas, large flat areas with a hint of a depression, running more or less in an east-west direction, which were dry when we were there, but would fill with water in the rainy season. Beautiful leafy trees cast welcome shade across the ground and dotted the horizon like sentinels. I would come to love that landscape for its harsh beauty, but it was unpleasant to tread upon day after day. I was struck immediately by the absence of birdsong from the environment.

We were now just that much closer to the actual border between South West Africa and Angola than we had been before.

***

"Hey, Mike!" Trevor was pulling his cap onto his head, car keys in his hand. "*Boet*, let's go to Glenfair for some charcoal and beer. We need to get that braai going."

"Sure." I kissed Kimberly and disentangled myself from her arms. "Need anything?" I asked her.

She shook her head, "Come back soon!" she said, and playfully pushed me. Before I reached the door she was already laughing with the girls.

Trevor thrust the passenger door of his mom's clapped-out old green

Datsun open for me, and I dropped myself into the seat. The shopping centre was just a few blocks from my folks' house where we were braaing, but the drive there was strangely quiet. I tried to fill the silence with small talk, but Trevor seemed preoccupied. We pulled into the parking lot and exited the car.

Trevor adjusted his cap with two hands and avoided my eyes.

"Hey, bud. Something's been bugging me." He shoved both hands into his pockets. We were approaching the entrance.

"Ja? Tell me." I looked into shop windows as we walked. I expected to have a heart-to-heart or an appeal for advice about some or other girl he'd met. The silence seemed strangely long. I took a sidelong glance at Trevor. He was looking straight ahead, scratching absently at his cheek.

"It's something Di told me ..." Diane was his sister, a friend of Kimberly's. "She told me some time ago, but I didn't know how to tell you ..." My carefree feeling started to evaporate.

"Trev, spit it out, bud! What are you talking about?"

We were nearing the liquor store, its brash lights glinting off the rows of bottles, the familiar smell of stale booze hanging around the air.

"It's Kimberly." He spoke so quietly, I barely heard him. "Kimberly?" I repeated.

"Ja." He stopped then, put his hand on my arm, peered earnestly at me. My heart beat a little faster.

"What? What is it, man?" I guess I sort of knew already.

"Di told me Kimberly cheated on you." He must have seen the confusion in my face. "Some guy at varsity, apparently."

I had a moment of denial.

"Crap!" I said. "She wouldn't." But I didn't believe my own words. "I'm there, man. We practically spend all our time together, except when we have lectures."

Trevor continued. "It was a couple of months ago, Mike. During her orientation week." I wracked my brain, trying to figure out when it could have happened. "Orientation weekend, Di said."

I remembered that weekend in January 1984 – it was the culmination of her varsity orientation week. I picked Kimberly up from her res Friday evening and the two of us rode my silver Yamaha scrambler down the oak-lined university avenues to the Sports Club at the bottom of Wits Main Campus. The late twilight air was heavy with summer and I almost didn't want to get to the party – I could have kept riding slowly all night with

Kimberly's arms loosely around my waist, her body gently pressed against my back.

We had a real blast that evening. The party was a ripper! I dropped her off in the early hours of Saturday morning, and following a late and lazy lie-in, I returned to her to say goodbye. She was going to spend the weekend at her new res, I was going home to spend some time with Stefan before he went off to varsity. We parted like two lovers should – a warm embrace and a long, passionate kiss.

Trevor and I finished the shopping in silence. I was tortured by the memories of that weekend. I waited until we were back in the car, two six packs and a bag of charcoal in the boot, before I grilled Trevor.

"What did Diane say?" I asked. "Did she say who?"

"A guy called Barry. Diane said he's about my height, a bit of a sportsman and he has brown curly hair. Apparently, he always wears a denim jacket, black or blue. You must have seen him at your res?"

"Ja, I know him. Dammit!" I felt sick to my stomach. "When?"

"There was a party that Saturday night – apparently it happened there." "What did she do?"

"I dunno, Mike. Diane just said Kimberly told her she had a fling." We were close to the house now. Trevor slowed the car down to a crawl. "She's bad news, man. She's no good for you."

"Trevor, I've been with Kimberly for nearly four years now. I owe it to her to find out what happened before I jump to conclusions."

"Mike, it's not the first time."

"I know, I know, but still ..." It dawned on me that Trevor couldn't have known about Kimberly's tryst with Ian two years before. "Wait, what do you mean?"

We were outside the gate now. Trevor let the car idle, rested an elbow on the window. He turned his head away from me as he spoke.

"Damon. Something happened with Damon." I swallowed hard.

"*What?!*" Damon was my mate! "What happened with Damon?!"

"I dunno, bud," Trevor seemed almost apologetic. "I only heard a rumour."

I had the same feeling as before, the feeling that my world was crumbling. I couldn't believe this was happening again. I had to speak to Kimberly. "Let's go, Trev, let's get back inside." He put the car in gear, drove through the gate.

"What are you going to do?" he asked.

"Talk to her." I spoke through a clenched jaw.

When we entered my folks' place, Kimberly was where I had left her, with her mates. I paused at the door to the patio and watched her laughing, her brown hair dancing on her shoulders as she tilted her head in a full-bellied guffaw. For a moment, her laugh of a brazen temptress repulsed me. I saw her for the first time through the lens of new-found knowledge. I was a mess inside: anger, sadness and my deep love for Kimberly all jostled for space. I walked over to her, rested a hand on the back of her chair.

"Hey," I said. She looked up at me and smiled her devastating smile. "Come, let's talk," I spoke quietly. Her smile faded and I saw anxiety cross her face.

"What is it?" she said. "Is everything okay?" I half turned towards the garden, put my hands in my pockets.

"Let's talk," I said.

In the garden she was breathless.

"Michael, what is it?"

I found it hard not to shout. "You cheated on me again?" It was more of a question than an accusation, but she was immediately defensive.

"What? No I didn't! What are you talking about?" "You and Barry, orientation weekend."

She went pale, stammered, "How ... who ..."

"Trevor told me. He said you told Diane about it." Her face reddened, filling with regret and I was conflicted again: did she regret doing it, or did she regret being found out? "Well?" I asked. "Did you?" She looked at me, but didn't answer. I raised my voice. "Did you?" Still no response. I took hold of her elbow. "Kimberly! Did you cheat on me again?" She flinched. "Okay. Okay. Yes." She shrugged off my hand. "I did, okay? I kissed him." She must have seen the disbelief in my face. "But that was all. I only kissed him."

I was disgusted and disappointed. I stepped backwards, away from Kimberly. I narrowed my eyes and looked at her. There was nothing I could say. She panicked.

"Well," there was a defiant tone to her voice. "You're the one who left, Michael." I couldn't believe my ears, was she really blaming me?

"So you thought it was okay to kiss some other guy? Barry? *Because I left?*" I was spitting with rage. "What were you thinking, Kimberly?"

"I wasn't thinking, Michael. I'd had a bit too much to drink, you'd left, I was lonely ..."

"That's a stupid excuse, Kimberly. I can't believe you did this to me again." I decided against confronting her with the story about Damon. This was enough bad news for me for the day. "And that was all, was it? Just a kiss?" She blushed.

"Yes." Her eyes flicked upwards towards mine, then down again quickly. In my heart I didn't believe her.

***

Soon after we arrived at our new South West African home, we were briefed on our responsibilities while stationed here: primarily, we were there as the physical presence of the SADF in the region, but we were also to source whatever information we could about the area and its local population. When we were informed that we would be doing vehicle movements rather than foot patrols, we were all pretty chuffed: this would be cushy! But it soon emerged that, although we were assigned Buffels for vehicle movement, we would end up mostly on foot anyway.

The infamous Captain Barrie was in charge of several platoons in the area, but as my platoon was stationed almost thirty kilometres away to the west from his base near Onesi, we were fortunate to be spared his attentions. Lieutenant Pretorius was pretty much given free rein over us and had only to report by radio to Captain Barrie on a regular basis.

We were told that the SADF Intelligence Units had information from undercover Owambo sources in the immediate communities that there were a few regular north to south routes, from Angola down into South West Africa, where we were stationed, that the terrs were using through the various terr-friendly communities in the area. We were to carry out reconnaissance missions to local communities to observe them and report back on whether or not they were likely to be SADF-friendly. It must be said that the locals played it both ways most of the time – who could blame them?

Our routine soon took shape. Our almost forty-strong platoon would drive out in four Buffels to a point selected by Lieutenant Pretorius. Finding a relatively secure spot – like an easily protected palm grove – three Buffels would leave us with one vehicle, which was to be Pretorius's bush headquarters. The stationary Buffel was camouflaged, and there the lootie would sit in relative comfort while the three sections of the platoon carried out their duties. Foot patrols were sent out two at a time, while the third remained to safeguard Pretorius and the vehicle.

Patrolling sticks were tasked to move three to five kilometres away to recce the immediate area. We would confirm that a village indicated on the map was in fact there and observe the activity there. While patrolling, we were to be alert for possible contact, applying the fieldcraft we had learned by looking for human spoor, identifying possible points of ambush and so on. We were to keep off roads, paths and well-worn tracks.

An Owambo interpreter, or *tolk*, was allotted to each platoon. We had two *tolke* for our platoon, one each to accompany the two patrolling sticks, thereby assisting us to understand what was happening in and around the villages and to communicate with the *plaaslike bevolking* (local population), which we referred to as PBs. These *tolke* were recruited from the locals and were often members of the home guards, men who protected the local headmen who were loyal to the political system of the time. In the seventies, the homeguard had been armed with old .303 rifles or even Portuguese or Spanish G3 assault rifles, but now in the mid-eighties, these were replaced with SADF R1s. The *tolke's* clothing ranged from civilian clothes to various mismatched getups of brown SADF military uniforms, sometimes a ragtag combination of both. Having them on patrol was often a bit of a security headache, as one could never be sure whether they were loyal to the security forces or actually supplied the enemy with information. Our two *tolke* both had R1s, and tightly fitting brown uniforms, with bush hats a few sizes smaller than they should have been – they didn't look too unlike guerrillas, except for their engaging grins, which they wore most of the time!

Patrolling sections were required to report back to Lieutenant Pretorius on an hourly basis, giving him our position so that he could plot our progress on his map. Once the necessary information had been gathered from the relevant community, the section leader would radio Pretorius to inform him that the mission had been completed. More often than not, Pretorius would have the section return to his bush office at the camouflaged Buffel to supply him with the Intel we had collected and bolster or relieve his static security. Sometimes, he would give orders for the section to move several clicks in another direction to carry out further reconnaissance activities. We walked our butts off in that flat and thirsty landscape.

The information gathered from these excursions was carefully recorded by Lieutenant Pretorius onto a map he was drawing up of the area. As the days passed, Pretorius's map was slowly populated with a multitude of little red and black markings. I asked him what he was doing, although it looked pretty obvious to me.

"Well, Warren," he cleared his throat and took on a self-important tone. "I'm plotting a map of the region indicating the apparent loyalties of the PBs around here." He moved the map so that I could get a better look. "You see," he said, circling a stubby finger over the area he had just been working on. "I am indicating which communities are most likely pro-SWAPO-PLAN with red, and those who appear to be neutral or pro-SADF with black." Looking at the map, I could already discern clear-cut lines being drawn through those red crosses that seemed to indicate the terrain over which the expected terrs had been or were presently travelling, receiving assistance from the locals on those routes.

The *kraals* and villages we visited on patrol fascinated me because they were so far removed from my experience growing up in suburban Pretoria. Typically, a village was made up of connected *kraals*, the communal cooking and storage area separating the men's quarters on one side from the women's on the other. A hut was usually circular, with its walls made from straight poles and branches stripped of leaves. The roof was typically conical in shape and made of grasses or Makalani palm leaves, tied together at the top of the cone with wire. I suspected that in the rainy season they were quite waterproof. A fence of closely woven, relatively straight and long poles and branches surrounded the *kraals*, protecting the people, livestock and crops from wild animals and keeping the cattle from roaming.

Renegade SAP and SADF units in South West Africa had been known to barge into villages and create havoc, but we operated under strict protocol. The section members remained on the perimeter of a village in strategically secure positions to observe, while the section leader entered the village with just one other soldier and an interpreter. The two men engaged in discussion with the headman, requesting his permission to look around. In the meantime, we would do a bit of comops with the children, even in those villages we suspected were aiding and abetting the enemy.

Many of the villages we encountered seemed to be in the middle of nowhere – how did they survive? Some looked hopeful, aspirant, while others were extremely neglected. Some villages were vibrant, others deserted. Once or twice, on entering a village, my skin would crawl with a sense of anticipation, the atmosphere charged with ominous energy, as though terrs would come bursting through when we least expected them to. In those moments I sometimes remembered scenes from various 'nam films I'd seen. Could it be that I heard a story about SADF soldiers on the Border entering an almost deserted village and coming across the body of a dead baby which had been booby-trapped by being stuffed full of hand grenades? Nah, surely that must have been from a "Nam war movie? My imagination ran wild! One story I certainly can remember being told to me was one from the Rhodesian Bush War which told of police searching a bus, and a police woman discovering the body of a dead baby used to conceal high explosive grenades and camouflaged on the back of a woman on board. I had to shake these thoughts off when they came to me unbidden, and wondered if my fellow soldiers had the same reactions.

The attitude of the headman and his villagers and the general atmosphere we encountered usually told us all we needed to know about the village's allegiance. The more we suspected something was amiss, the more thorough we were in going through each hut and corner of the village. We never picked up anything this way, perhaps fortunately, but we returned to the lootie with our impressions of the settlement for him to capture on his classified map.

"*Manne,*" Captain Barrie said. "Don't underestimate the value of what you are doing here." We were just returning to the lootie's day position after a day of patrolling, and Barrie was talking casually to us about our role here. "And I must emphasise that while you are positioned up here, you must always be alert. *Julle moet altyd op julle hoede wees.*" All around me, heads were nodding in agreement. *"Jy weet,"* he went on. "Once, I was leading a section ... it wasn't very long ago, and not far from here." Like many of the Afrikaner ranks I encountered, Captain Barrie had an ear for telling a story. We were packing up our kit in preparation for heading out to set up TB for the night. Hearing the approach of a good story, many of us paused to hear what Barrie was saying.

Captain Barrie had shifted into that space one occupies when reminiscing before an audience. His eyes focussed on a point somewhere above our heads, stroking his moustache, and I knew he was right back in the place he was recalling.

"We had just left a village," he said. "We had found no valuable information there, and we were making our way back to the TB. We hadn't gone three hundred metres when we crossed a little cattle path." The captain paused here, rubbing his chin. His eyes refocused and he looked at us guys watching him expectantly. "We were walking in silence, you see." His expression changed. I sensed he was about to deliver a climax. "All I could hear," he said, "was the foot falls of my men behind me. And then ... I'll never forget the sound ... a soldier stepped onto the sand of the path, and we all heard a hollow, tinny noise." Someone behind me whistled quietly through his teeth. *"Jinne!"* Barrie said, drawing out the "n". *"Ons het almal gekak!"* I would have crapped my pants, too, I suspect! The captain went on, "We all thought he had stepped on a mine. *Gelukkig was hy 'n skrander soldaat."* He tapped his temple with a finger ("Luckily he was a clever soldier."). "He froze. And we all froze, too." I wondered if the other guys' hearts were beating a little faster like mine was. I imagined how it must feel to step on a mine. You're dust. You're dust and you know it. What goes through your head in that instant? What would have gone through mine? Would I have thought of Kimberly? Of my parents? Of all the life I had yet to live? Would you even have time to think before you are obliterated? The *troepe* around me were all silent, all on tenterhooks to hear what happened next. Like all good story tellers, Barrie drew out this moment for its maximum effect.

Eventually Ian broke the silence. In a voice laden with wonder, he asked, "What happened?" Captain Barrie gave a deep-throated chuckle.

"Well, you can imagine, once we all got over the shock, we all piled in to scrape the sand away and see what we were dealing with. Three of us – me and two of my men – got down on our knees and gently, gently, with as much care as we could under the circumstances (you know, my hands were shaking terribly ... I bet the others' were, too!) we brushed the sand away." "But, sir," Botha interrupted the captain. "What could you do to save the guy? He was toast, right?"

"No, no," Barrie responded. "It would have been touch and go, *jy weet.* But help was just a radio away."

"What if the guy sneezed? Or farted?" Ian asked, with a supercilious grin on his face. A couple of nervous sniggers erupted around Captain Barrie's rapt listeners. The captain shrugged.

"We would all, then, have been "toast", as Botha here so eloquently put it." He smiled. *"Maar hier is ek, nê?* I lived to tell the story. So that didn't happen. I'll tell you what did happen." We all leant in a bit. "The poor young man, by now, was sweating dollops of fear. You can imagine! Eventually, we saw the surface of that object. I think the soldier was close to tears by then!" He gave a *harrumph.* "But I could see, it wasn't a mine at all! No, no. The soldier was very relieved, of course. He scrambled away from his position, and the whole section jumped in to clear the rest of the sand from the object ... and it wasn't buried very deep, I'll have you know ... when we finally got the sand clear, we found the guy had been standing – not on a mine – on a *trommel.* A dark-grey *trommel.* I knew immediately. Immediately." Now the captain was grinning. "It was weapons! We hauled the *trommel* out and opened it up, and it was chock-full of AK47s." A murmur went up in the audience. I hadn't realised that I had been holding my breath until I started breathing normally again. Barrie continued, "We did a quick search of the area. We found several more *trommels*. It was one of the biggest discoveries of an arms cache of the time. There was Russian writing on the sides and top of the boxes."

"But, sir," it was Ian again, "wasn't that kinda stupid?" He asked. "Of the terrorists, I mean. Burying the weapons right there. And on the path, too." "Well," Barrie responded. "Not really. It was quite clever of them, actually. You see, the terrs had probably reasoned, knowing that the SADF soldiers didn't use the paths or tracks, that to hide their weapons in the most obvious place possible was quite ingenious. They weren't far wrong, too. If that soldier had crossed the path just half a metre one side or the other, they would have been home clear and we would have been none the wiser." "Did you hand the stuff over, then, sir?" someone else asked.

"Yes, eventually," the captain said. "I radioed HQ to let them know what we had discovered. But before anyone came to take the cache away, we reburied what we found – and let me point out to you that we didn't initially find the whole batch. The extent of the weapons buried there was only established much later. But what we did is, we reburied the *trommels* we had found, and over the next couple of days, we staked the area out from a distance, carefully hidden, watching the comings and goings of the villagers. We had been watching for three days, and I was beginning to think nothing was happening. Plus, there were other villages we needed to visit in the area. But the villagers were just coming and going as always, nothing untoward happened at all. Then, at dusk, that third day, I saw the headman coming our way with two unarmed men – men we hadn't yet seen in the area, so we knew they were suspicious. The village wasn't that big, *jy weet*. We had already seen every face living there by then. Anyway, here the headman came with these men, and he walks over to the very spot my man had stepped on the *trommel*, and there the men start digging. We caught them red-handed!" By now, Captain Barrie's grin was enormous. "Red-handed!" he said again.

"So the men were questioned?" someone asked.

"Of course!" Barrie replied. "The men and the headman were taken into custody. Interrogation revealed a great deal of information about the routes being used by the terrs at the time. Information from those two captured terrs also led to other hidden weapons caches, also buried similarly under foot and cattle paths. Sappers were brought in to sweep the area, further stakeouts took place, but unfortunately, the bush telegraph works very well, and no further terrs were captured – they kept away. But we had uncovered a huge amount of their weapons. I'm sure it was a big blow to their cause!"

By the end of the first week, we had settled into the routine and I, for one, began feeling quite relaxed about being there. I don't suppose I felt invincible. The threat of encountering the enemy was always in my mind. But at least I was confident that we would be able to put up a pretty good fight if we found ourselves faced with hostility.

"Zero, Zero, this is Bravo One. Over." It was the middle of the afternoon and my section, under Corporal Potgieter, had just completed a recce mission to a village some distance southwest of Pretorius's bush office at the concealed Buffel. The lootie's voice, laden with static, returned to us over Pottie's radio.

"Bravo One, Zero. Go ahead. Over."

Pottie was radioing Pretorius to let him know that we were ready to return to his position. "Mission complete," he said, adding confidently, "Bravo One coming in. Over." But Pretorius had other ideas.

"Negative on that," Pretorius said. My heart sank. "New target," he gave us a set of coordinates. "Over." We couldn't believe Pretorius was going to send us on another mission so late in the day. Pottie tried to change the lootie's mind.

"It's late. We won't make it back before dark. We should come in. Over." Pretorius was having none of it.

"Orders from above, Bravo One," he came back. "Report back on completion. Out." Orders from Captain Barrie. I wasn't sure if I believed this to be true, but Pretorius's sign-off clearly said, no argument!

We scouted the village out and Potgieter radioed Pretorius to let him know that everything appeared normal.

"Moving out," he spoke into his handset after establishing contact with Zero. "Bravo One coming in. Over." I began to think with some concern that we would have to march half a dozen or so kilometres in the dark – you don't move fast under those circumstances, and worst of all, you're vulnerable to an ambush – but Pretorius was clear.

"Negative on that," he said. "Stay put until morning. Over." Pottie tried to reason with him.

"We are unprepared, sir, we have no food or kit. Plus, I'm not convinced the area is secure, over."

"I say again, stay put. Report to me in the AM. Out." Pretorius wasn't going to be persuaded. We were first stunned, then pissed off.

It was September. The spring days were extremely hot and dry, but at night the temperatures plummeted. Without bivvies or groundsheets, we had nothing to sleep under. On the assumption that we were walking out in the sweltering heat and returning at the end of the day, most of the section hadn't even packed bush jackets. I was one of the fortunate few who had, and even so, I was decidedly uncomfortable out in the freezing cold. Some of us had our battle jackets with us, others had their chest webbing. A battle jacket is webbing that mimics a type of military waistcoat and was the gear of choice in a combat situation as you could carry a lot in it, but still feel very mobile. Our H-frame rucksacks – with all our necessary equipment – were uselessly back in the Buffel, a good number of kilometres away, under the supervision of Lieutenant Pretorius. Wearing either a battle jacket or chest webbing was comfortable, but totally inadequate as a means to keep warm.

The night was unbearably cold. Even in my bush jacket, I was frozen to the bone. Some of the brave, manly-type guys couldn't bear it anymore and decided to buddy-up, snuggling up to each other and spooning to keep warm. Cold and hungry, none of us managed to get much sleep and we were all so pleased to see the sun the following morning.

We were never again caught unprepared. Perhaps Captain Barrie was just testing us out in the field, seeing how we'd cope in such a situation. We were careful, from that point on, to delay getting to the villages, ensuring that we completed our tasks just before dusk so that we could be sure to return to the Buffels and our necessary equipment for the night.

We soon discovered the cuca shops – little corrugated iron shacks out in the veld, many conveniently situated near telephone lines. Named after Cuca Beer, a Portuguese beer sold in Angola in the sixties and seventies, cuca shops are unlicensed liquor stores, places that would be called shebeens in South Africa. At one of the many quaintly-named establishments, one could buy mahango beer or Makalani Blitz, a type of moonshine liquor made from the fruit or nut of the ubiquitous makalani palm tree. But us troopers preferred to stick to the commercial alcoholic drinks that were available to buy, however limited in selection. Here you could also make telephone calls with cash paid up front before calling via a telephone hooked up to the nearby telephone pole.

Corporal Pottie didn't mind us going to these shops. He himself would buy a beer or two, Windhoek Lager usually being the only commercial beer available, sold in quarts or pints. The only wine available, and therefore the wine of choice amongst the *troepe*, was Tassenberg – or Tassies, as it was affectionately called – considered a real plonk of a red wine, which many preferred to mix with Coca Cola, it was that bad.

It was to the nearest cuca shop that we made our way on Thursday 25 September, the day I turned twenty-three. I phoned Kimberly from the cuca shop and had a bittersweet conversation with her – she couldn't believe I was phoning her from out in the bush, on the Border. That call got me into a spirited way and I bought the corporal and all the guys in my section drinks with my danger pay from the previous week. I loaded both my two-litre water bottles full of Tassies, and as we patrolled, we drank. By the time we got back to where we were setting up TB for the night I was *vrot* – so far gone that I did a leopard crawl routine for the guys. Exaggerating the technique we'd been taught at Infantry School, I crawled about fifty metres through the grass and criss-crossed over a gravel path, eliciting uncontained laughter to the point of tears from the others (who, it must be said, were almost as drunk as I was ... anything would have seemed funny to them). Of course, the following morning I woke up stiff, with the skin on my forearms and elbows scraped raw from the drunken antics of the previous day. In my state, I had forgotten to roll down my sleeves as we had been taught to do in the proper execution of the leopard crawl. In addition to my fragile limbs, I had the most interminable *babbelas* headache. The other guys were equally groggy, and I could see that even Corporal Pottie was not so *lekker* himself, but we still needed to go on patrol, so go on patrol we did.

Just half an hour into patrol, we begged Pottie not to go on because we were all suffering so badly. To begin with, he hesitated, but after a little more pleading on our part, and because he was feeling just as fragile as we were, he made us promise that we would never tell anyone – especially Lieutenant Pretorius – what he was about to do. Finding a small grove of sparse, straight trees, we lay down in what shade we could find to rest, slapping and shooing at the flies, while Pottie radioed in false coordinates every hour as if we were patrolling as planned. We were all so grateful to Pottie for his kindness. That was a turning point for me in my relationship with the corporal: I began to realise that he wasn't such a *doos* after all.

I watched as the point-men entered the proposed TB position. Even from a distance away, in the still of the South West African dusk, I could hear their boots fall and scrape in the dry grass of the savannah. When they had secured the area, they silently gave the hand signals which told us to move in. All three sections of the platoon had come together that afternoon, so the soldiers entering the TB numbered almost two score. We moved quickly and quietly through the centre of the TB and out to our positions on the perimeter. The three MAG men entered the base last, taking up their positions in the typical defensive triangular *laager* of men. I had already begun digging my trench in the soft sand when the lootie, the platoon sergeant and Pottie took up their positions, safely in the middle of the temporary encampment, acting as the platoon's HQ. The silence which routinely accompanied this procedure always heightened my sense of uneasiness.

We were in an area of Omarambas, so the bush had cleared into veld which was dotted with thorn scrub bushes and the odd small tree. No real shade or protection was offered by the sparse vegetation.

Our trenches dug and prepared for sleep, ablutions done, we set about preparing food and getting ready for night before darkness fell. From time to time, as I lifted my eyes outwards from the TB, I would place my right hand on my R4, resting on its bipod, reassuring myself that it was at the ready if it was needed before guard duty was formally instituted for each of the three sides of our base.

It was quite late when I climbed into my sleeping bag – browns, boots and all. I'm a light sleeper and I was next on guard duty, so I was programmed to wake soon. All the same, I was sleeping unusually peacefully when I was awoken by a yank of the cord around my wrist. Lying still in the darkness, peering towards the direction of the cord-puller, I heard only the howling and yapping of a jackal in the distance – a sound so much like the crying of a baby, it can be quite disconcerting in the middle of the night in the South West African veld. And then I heard it! A very strange sound, almost like the beating of a spoon on a tin pot. It was rhythmical but intermittent, and spine-chillingly unnatural. It was, to me, the confirmation that there was someone else out there, someone unauthorised and unknown, and possibly hostile, for I knew we had previously covered that eastern portion thoroughly on patrol, and there were no villages or any form of habitation out there, and certainly no friendly forces either.

I had heard that the enemy was very good at using a type of bush Morse code to communicate with one another over great distances, especially in the dead of night when the air is still and sound travels a long way. I also knew that the north-south power line close to Etunda on the border and moving down past Eunda was used by SWAPO to convey Intel between cadres in Angola and SWA. I guessed that the sound I was hearing was long-distance communication of some kind, and my mind raced with the possibilities. Was it insurgents requesting permission from a command group to initiate an attack against us? Was our position already being ranged in on? Was someone setting the coordinates to fire mortar bombs on us in just a minute or two?

I remembered a story I had heard about an infantry platoon in South West Africa a couple of years before. Having just entered their TB for the night, they were approached by two locals. The two men claimed to be stock herders, herding newly-purchased stock with another two tribesmen over some distance to their *kraals*. They were hungry and thirsty, they said, and begged the soldiers for food and water. The platoon commander got one of his troops to hand the men what they wanted, observing them closely and with some suspicion. He watched the two men walking away from the TB, recognising that something wasn't quite right and unable to put his finger on it, and as they disappeared over a small rise, it struck him: the two assumed PBs had walked in a straight line with a measured gait, as if counting their paces, back to where they had come from. Within seconds of them disappearing, he gave orders for his men to rapidly move out of the TB in silence. The platoon hadn't gone more than a few hundred metres when the first *wa-whoomp* was heard and enemy mortar fell directly in the centre of what had been their temporary base.

The strange tapping noise continued, and I yanked hard on Ian's cord to wake him. In whispers I told him what I had heard and he sat up to listen for the sound. Ian agreed that this was serious enough to warrant waking the platoon orderly, and I crawled over to where he was sleeping, disregarding our orders not to move from our positions. The orderly thought it best to wake the lootie, who came over to where I was. Lieutenant Pretorius crouched on his haunches and twisted his head one way and then the other, trying to locate the sound and determine its origin.

"Warren," he whispered to me. *"As jy regtig dink dis nou iets gevaarlik daar buite, begin vuur."* He had just given me discretion to begin firing. I lay down, clipped the sprung bipod back under the forestock, placed the safety lever in the single-fire position and silently pulled back on the lever to load a round into the chamber. I took aim at the general horizon which I knew to be out there somewhere, and began the tap-tap, tap-tap firing action we had been taught. The lootie was suddenly animated, moving up and down along the section, kicking the MAG man on his boots to start firing. The din was unbelievable as our flank began taking the bush apart. Some of the other guys jumped out of the opposite flank positions to see what the commotion was about.

After about thirty seconds, the lootie gave the order to stop firing. Acrid gunpowder smoke hung thickly in the air and empty shells littered the ground. We listened as best we could for the return of the tapping, but our ears had been deafened by the noise of the firing. The lootie didn't follow the required drill, which was to now vacate the TB, telling us only that we should all stay awake in our positions until dawn. All through the rest of that wakeful night, my ears were peeled for the hammering to return, but it never did. When dawn came, the whole platoon walked in an offensive line for more than a click down the firing front, but couldn't find a thing. I felt sheepish about my overreaction to the situation, but the lootie called me over and suggested that I had done the right thing.

"Rather safe than sorry," he said. The incident was reported to Captain Barrie, but nothing ever came of it.

It's easy to tire of the tedious contents of rat-packs. Some of the braver members of the platoon were fortunate to dine on fresh meat every week or two. It started when two platoons met up in the bush near a large village on patrol one afternoon. Riflemen Botha and Graham decided to haggle with the headman, eventually convincing him that he should sell them a goat from his herd. The poor beast was brought to camp on a tether, staring at us bug-eyed and pulling at his leash, bleating most horribly. I became convinced that the creature knew what was coming. These guys, the *manne*, were confident that they would be able to kill it, drain the blood, then skin it for braaing.

Botha, stripped to the waist, produced his knife. Graham was on stand-by, holding the beast in an arm-lock position. Some of the other guys pitched in to help, probably hoping for a share of the spoils. I told Ian that I wasn't interested in watching the slaughter, and moved off. I wondered whether I was soft – if I couldn't handle watching the slaughter of a goat for dinner, how would I react to seeing a human being targeted, possibly killed, whether it was a terr, a civilian or one of our own? I tried not to think about it further, and by the time I returned to the scene of the butchery, Botha was skinning the goat expertly. I guessed he must have had experience on a farm or a hunting expedition. He then hung the carcass on a nearby fence to drain it of its blood. Before long, a fire was going with some smaller pieces braaing above. Someone had found a long metal stake, and the rest of the carcass was prepared on a make-shift spit. A *potjie* emerged from somewhere – had someone brought it along, or had it been picked up in a cuca shop somewhere? – and a goat-meat *potjiekos* stew was set over coals.

When some of the meat was cooked, I was offered a piece to taste. To this day I prefer not to eat goat meat! The offering had a powerful odour and a strong taste, the likes of which I couldn't easily stomach, and from then on I mostly stuck to my boring ol' rat-pack tins of meat.

Another time a grid emerged from somewhere – had someone scavenged it off one of the many car wrecks along the roads? On enquiry, I found that the guys had used the grid off our lootie's Buffel, with permission granted on condition that the lootie received some of the braaied meat. Soon, *boerewors* brought in by the replenishment Buffels doing their rounds was sizzling over coals. With the success of bartering or purchasing, many of the guys would come back from patrol with a live fowl to slaughter and defeather for their evening meal, but it must be said these free range chickens were tough indeed!

"To the northeast, *manne!*" Pottie stopped us in our tracks. "Bravo Two has a terr – let's go check it out." A ripple of excitement coursed through the section. We rushed off in a half walking, half galloping gait. "They're just a few clicks from here," Pottie explained as we made our way. It was mid-afternoon and the sun was still high. When we got to the secured area, I saw a figure sitting in the veld, his arms around his knees. A soldier stood either side of him, R4s casually pointed towards the ground, ready to be used if the terr should decide to move.

We drew closer and I saw the captive: about thirty, he was terribly thin, his olive-green shirt and light green pants, drab and threadbare. On his feet was a pair of tennis shoes – once white – without laces; no socks. His lips were cracked and his filthy hair was matted. His downcast eyes were vacant. I doubted this prisoner was likely to try anything untoward. *Where are his comrades? Where is his weapon? Is this what we're fighting against?* I wondered to myself. He looked so forlorn and tattered, I found him pathetic.

Platoon Sergeant Coetzee was on the radio to the lootie. We were instructed to secure and guard the prisoner and wait for Pretorius to arrive in his Buffel. Having no rope with which to tie him up, someone cleverly opened their stash of bomb bandages and used these to tie his hands together in front of his chest. A bomb bandage was placed over his eyes and tied around his head as a blindfold. The prisoner was compliant. I thought he looked hopeless.

Through the interpreters, some of the guys were interrogating him. "Are you alone?"

"Where do you come from?" "Where are you going?"

The captive answered in broken Portuguese. One of the interpreters was getting over-excited. He began to shout, leant in with an arm raised as if to slap the prisoner. But Platoon Sergeant Coetzee caught him by the wrist. "Hey! What do you think you're doing?" Some heated words followed, as the Owambo insisted a little roughing up was the only way to get any information out of the creature. "Uh-uh," the corporal shook his head. "There will be no force here," he said. Looking around him, he raised his voice. "Did everyone hear me? No force, or you will answer to me! Now," he looked back at the interpreter, "let's see what he has to say for himself. Ask him why he's alone." The interpreter turned back to the prisoner, and they talked for a while in Portuguese. Slowly, the prisoner's story emerged.

He was a FAPLA soldier and had been on a reconnaissance mission with another combatant. They had crossed the border clandestinely near Etunda, and after a few days of roaming the South West African countryside, his partner had left him in search of food and water. Now lost and starving, the soldier decided to give himself up, walking directly up to the astonished ranks of Bravo Two. Kerry Pile interrupted the interrogation, asking Corporal Coetzee to untie the prisoner's hands.

"I want to give him some water," he explained. The corporal allowed the prisoner's hands to be untied, and Kerry knelt down next to the figure in the grass and offered him his water bottle. The prisoner closed his eyes and gulped at the bottle, dribbles of water running down his chin and neck.

The interrogators continued their questioning, asking the man where his weapon was. He explained that he had abandoned it somewhere in the veld – he had no bullets left and the weapon was useless to him.

One of the guys opened a tin of meat from his rat-pack and gave it to the prisoner. Digging into the tin with his fingers, the soldier gobbled up the food.

Lieutenant Pretorius arrived. Ordering for the prisoner's hands to be tied with rope, he had the guys load him onto his Buffel and rode off with an armed escort. I watched the Buffel disappear, listening to the conversations going on around me.

"Well, he was less than I expected!" someone said. "Is that the kind of guerrilla we're up against?"

"*Hy's nie veel van 'n* "terr" *nie,*" came a reply, suggesting the prisoner was hardly a vicious terrorist.

Someone else piped up, "Yeah? Well he's not SWAPO, he's FAPLA. There's a big difference!"

Personally, I felt a bit dejected. The soldier had seemed totally out of his depth in all respects. Yet here he was, fighting for a cause he must have believed in, regardless of the implications. I wondered what kind of sacrifices our enemy soldiers were making in pursuit of their cause. I knew that the SWAPO insurgents were probably the best trained and supplied of all these "liberation" groups.

My fellow soldiers and I would have no compunction in our minds that if we were attacked by them, we would fight back. But this encounter made me wonder whether we overestimated the might of our enemy. Sighing, I thought with relief about how well-equipped we were, the quality of our logistical support and our training. Plus there were plenty of us.

Just before returning to South Africa at the end of our stint up on the border, Ian and I were recounting the incident to some guys from one of the other platoons in our company that had operated under Captain Barrie near Onesi.

"Hey," this Dutchman said to us when we got to the end of our story. "That was towards the end of the second week up close to the border, wasn't it?" "Ja, about then," I said.

"You know, we also had an incident about that same time," he said.

"Ja, that's right," one of his mates chimed in. "We never actually saw any action up there," he added. "There was just this one incident. Smit," he elbowed his buddy next to him. "You remember, hey?" Smit nodded and the other guy looked back at us. "We hadn't been up there very long when we came across these two guys. We were following the drills, you know. Not a hundred percent, but at least we were trying."

Smit interrupted to explain, "Whenever we came across people away from the villages, like the odd male walking along by himself," he said, "we would stop them and ask them to show us some sort of identification, *jy weet?*"

"Right," the second guy continued. "So this one day, we come across two guys ..."

"Not together," someone interrupted him to point out. He sounded like an English-speaker, an inflection that suggested the Eastern Cape, maybe Port Elizabeth, or East London. "We found them at different times and in different places."

"But strange that we came across these two guys without IDs on the same day, right?" the first guy said.

"That's right," Smit said. "So anyway, we had these two Owambo *tolke* – we didn't have any intelligence guys with us, or anything like that – just these two Owambo guys ..."

The first soldier interrupted again. "They were quite a handful for us, actually," he said.

"Ja, man," Smit agreed, slapping his thigh. "They used to just make fires at night – open fires, to cook their rice and soup and whatnot on. *Ek bedoel*, we'd been told not to make fires at night, *jy weet?*" He looked at me for confirmation, and I nodded. "Or even show any light, *nê?* We used those Esbit fuel tablets they gave us, and that. You did it, too, right? Dig a hole for the Esbit," he was miming the procedure now with both hands, "and you put your *emmer* over it to heat anything ..."

"These guys just lighting a fire like that drove our lootie mad!" his mate added.

"That's right. He was trying to maintain discipline, or at least a show of it, *nê?* And these *tolke* just completely disregarded him. *Asof hy nooit gepraat het nie!*"

"And twice," someone interrupted, "they got into trouble for going off to the cuca shop and coming back pissed and compromising our security." They all laughed at the memory.

"But, on that day," Smit looked at us earnestly. "*Ek sê*, I was glad they were there, hey. When these guys were searched, *jy weet*, they found that the one guy had these chafe marks on his back."

"Chafe marks?" Ian asked.

"Ja," Smit said. "You see, what generally happened, if a guy had marks like that, it was from carrying something. So we assumed he was either a terr who carried a pack, or he'd been used by terrs to carry a pack."

"Okay," said another of the guys. "So he wasn't armed – neither of these guys were – but still, *jy weet?* There's still the chance that one or both of these guys are terrs."

"And they were not what I pictured a terrorist to look like, I can tell you that!" Smit said with some amusement. I chuckled with the guys, remembering the forlorn FAPLA soldier. Hardly the picture painted for us of the dreaded enemy. But we had been warned not to underestimate the enemy. Even an unarmed terrorist posed a threat. These were FAPLA guerrillas we were talking about. FAPLA combatants were known for being poorly trained and less passionately motivated than their SWAPO counterparts, and my platoon's experience with the hopeless soldier illustrated these points. But we had to remember that these guys had direct and indirect links to SWAPO and other communist allies. These seemingly innocuous characters could be spies or decoys, or part of a bigger plot against the SADF. We had to be on our guard. My wandering mind returned to the storyteller in front of me.

"So we had to figure out what their stories were, *jy weet?*" Smit said.

"And maybe get whatever intelligence we could from them," his buddy added.

"*Jinne*, I just wanted a go at them!" the Dutchman said. "Give me half an hour, and I would've nailed them, got any intel they might've had out of them!"

The Englishman spoke again, "Ag, you're talking out your arse, Nortje. You wouldn't have got jack." Nortje glowered at him.

"Stinking terrs," he growled. The English guy was about to speak again, when the first soldier interrupted him.

"Hold it, *julle!*" He held up a hand. To us he said, "So we secure these two guys, right, and we're waiting to get word as to what to do next."

"We'd radioed ahead to HQ," his mate said. "To find out what the next drill was: Was a chopper going to come and fetch them? Were we going to take them in by vehicle? You know."

Nortje butt in once more. "Our platoon commander," he said, "he was a bit of a wus! He was quite happy to tie the guys up and wait for somebody to come and take them away. Then they weren't his problem anymore." "Right, right," Smit said, adding, "but Barrie hears about this, right? And he gives our platoon commander instructions to use these two Owambos to try and extract some information from these guys. "Nothing physical," he says. "Just let them at these guys. They'll know what to do." So these *tolke* do a bit of their own interrogation."

"Man!" someone else said. "You shoulda seen what they did to these fellows! They make them assume the press-up position, okay. Not to do press-ups, just to stay in that position, you know?" He held his hands and arms in front, bent at the elbows, as if in the press-up position himself. Then he points at a spot just in front of his nose. "And they put down a cup of water in front of each of them, dribbling a little bit of water in the sand, right there, under their noses!" This drew a laugh from some of them. "And the *tolke* sit there with a little switch, a little stick, and whenever one of the guys moves his arms or wants to relax or something like that, they smack him on the back of his hands with the switch," he flicked his hand, making a snapping noise with his fingers. "No, no!" they say. "You mustn't move now." After about three hours of this, the guys just had dollops of sweat pouring off them!"

"And were the *tolke* questioning them all this time?" Ian asked.

"To begin with, yes," Smit replied. "The basic stuff you know, "Who are you?" and "Where do you come from?" and "What were you doing?" You know. Stuff like that. They didn't get much from them, though."

"After a while," the English-speaker chimed in, "they were asking, like,

"How did you get these marks on your back?" The guy kept insisting that he was a miner, from a mine in Angola, but they didn't believe him, so they kept repeating the question. They got louder and louder. They would swat at the ground right next to the poor guy's hand, shout the question at him, really threatening, you know? Eventually, they stopped asking any questions, and just let the guys stew in silence for a bit." The speaker looked as though he felt sorry for the guys, but some of the others were chortling at the memory.

"Man, they were breaking!" someone said, laughing.

"The one guy was almost in tears!" said another. I was appalled by how much some of these guys seemed to have enjoyed the episode. I was as keen as the next guy to do my duty and prevent terrorists from endangering lives, do my bit to stem the flow of the communist influence. But it seemed to me that some of these soldiers had forgotten they were dealing with human beings here.

"They could barely hold themselves up," the Englishman said. "They were shaking, their noses almost in the ground, almost in the water the *tolke* spilt there." He clicked his tongue with irritation. "If they were going to give up any information, they would've already."

"So," Smit picked up the story again. "They're just trying to keep themselves in that position, right? And we see the headman from the nearby village coming over our way. He's half running, *jy weet?* And waving a hand, like he wants to say something to us. A little kid is running alongside him. He comes up to us and talks quickly, waving his hands about, like he's agitated." Smit was waving his hands in demonstration. "And it turns out, he's telling the *tolke* that this guy – the one without the chafe marks, *né?* – this guy is a cattle thief, and he'd been in the village prison and escaped." "Have you seen one of those prisons?" the English guy asked us, interrupting Smit. We shook our heads. "They're like little corrugated-iron structures," he said. "Like a long-drop, you know? Sitting out in the baking sun."

"Anyway," Smit continued. "The headman identifies this guy as a thief, and says he's quite happy to take him, thank you very much."

"But we weren't about to hand the guy over to him," someone else added. "We made it clear to the headman that we would hand him over to SWAPOLTIN," This was the South West Africa Police Counter-Insurgency Unit. "They were fifteen kilometres away, and they could sort it out."

"So did the *tolke* get any intel from the incident?" I asked. They all shook their heads.

"Nah," said Smit. "A van came to pick them both up, and off they went." "Nothing ever came of that incident," the English guy explained. "It was later verified that the guy with the chafe marks was a miner from Angola." He was shaking his head at the pointlessness of it all.

Kerry Pile – wise young man and well-prepared soldier that he was – brought along to the border a Sony Walkman and a number of cassette tapes of the latest music releases. The Walkman was a comparatively new device in South Africa, and was not yet forbidden on patrol, but Kerry usually only listened to music over the headphones at night in the relatively safe and secure surrounds of the TB. Two weeks into patrol, I begged him to loan me his Walkman for a bit. It took some convincing, but eventually he agreed, insisting that I limit the time I listen as he didn't have a whole lot of batteries with him. It was sweet audio heaven to spend the evening under headphones, listening to the whole of Mike and the Mechanics' self-titled debut album from 1985. For the duration of that tape, I was far removed from the drudging reality of life on the Border, lost in the strains of *Silent Running* and *Taken In*. The evocative *All I Need Is A Miracle* and *You Are The One* made me think with longing of Kimberly – how my heart ached for her!

A small roaming convoy of Buffels acted as a water-replenishment service and mobile canteen. Every three to four days, the convoy would come from the main base, where water supplies were sufficient, and meet us at certain secure points in the bush to exchange our empty water cars with full ones. At the same time, rat-packs for the next few days were dropped off, our weekly danger pay was distributed to us in cash, and our mail delivered. Our letters home were collected for posting. The visiting Buffels were stocked with drinks and sweets we could buy, and as their arrival coincided with the delivery of our danger pay, there was always a scramble to place orders for ice-cold Cokes and Bar Ones the day before the convoy was due to arrive, which we would pay for from our just-received cash.

Although it was a forbidden practice, we often made use of the community wells to supplement our water supplies. We would lay low and observe the well for a while, waiting for a local to come along and draw water for themselves or their stock. This usually happened early in the morning or late in the afternoon. Convinced that the water was safe for consumption, we would replenish our water bottles and wash our faces.

I seldom had the opportunity to engage in any activity resembling a bath during my time up there. From time to time, we would manage to stockpile some water before resupply came through. At the exchange of water cars, we would take advantage of the remaining water in the outgoing water car in order to give ourselves what passed for a bath in the bush. Similar to what we'd done during training at Omuthiya, we would dig a shallow hole in the ground and cover it with a bivvy. Five to ten litres of water would be poured into the shallow depression and one of us would lie in it and wash as well as he could. When he was done, he would lift his bivvy filled with now-dirty water and toss it aside, and the next bloke would line the hole with his bivvy and repeat the exercise. Out on patrol we sometimes came across the network of concrete-lined irrigation canals in that part of the world, which made for excellent bathing. Further afield, we would come across stock watering dams, or if we were really desperate, we sometimes asked the locals if we could use their stock watering cribs, made out of large hollowed out tree trunks, to wash ourselves. Without soap, we would try to hand wash ourselves and rinse the dirtiest parts of our browns. We would usually go commando, so we only had our socks to rinse.

But mostly, I just had to get used to the feeling of being unwashed in the bush. We would wear the same clothes for days on end, and we were all caked with dirt. I used to save just enough water every day to wash my face and hands before sleeping.

We had been in the bush for two weeks, and I needed a bath – whichever way it came! All three sections of our platoon got together at a large waterhole, somewhere deep in the bush, which was like a small earth-walled dam. Guys were posted as sentries and to watch over the Buffel and generally keep their eyes peeled, while the rest of us hauled off our dirty, sweat-stained clothes and jumped *kaalgat* into the water. What bliss! We swam about and revelled in the tepid freshness of the water, and even Lieutenant Pretorius, Platoon Sergeant Coetzee and Corporal Potgieter joined in the water celebrations. Such opportunities simply had to be taken when they presented themselves. It was our only bath in many days of walking incessant and gruelling patrols.

We knew that our time in South West Africa was almost over, after which we would at last be making the return journey to South Africa and

Infantry School for the last training of the year.

From the various villages we came across, we started purchasing little knick-knacks to take home with us, mementoes of our time here at the edge of South West Africa: handmade bows and arrows, leather quivers. I suspect we were swindled. The Owambos caught on to a lucrative little business here, convincing the servicemen deployed in their countryside that the trinkets they were buying were authentic Bushman artefacts, when in reality, they were quick knock-offs created especially for sale to these white invaders dressed in brown.

Sometimes, to ease the boredom of being out on patrol, we would negotiate the use of a couple of *dikwiel* bicycles from the locals, bartering goods from our rat-packs in exchange for a quick spin on the bikes. We had become a little complacent. The few weeks we'd been deployed here gave us the clear notion that we wouldn't see much action in our area of responsibility. We had gone a little "native", but not *bossies*.

Then the news arrived that we were to move into Angola for our last week of deployment. This was unexpected.

With renewed excitement, we moved up from our area in four Buffels. We passed to the east of Hurricane AFB and 51 Battalion HQ at Ruacana, from which we had previously heard music blaring at night. We met up with replenishment Buffels on the main C46 east-west border road, where we exchanged our near-empty water car for a fresh one.

Coordinates: 17°23'25.71"S 14°28'27.67"E

We crossed over the *kaplyn* ("cutline"), a thin strip of land cleared of all vegetation, on the border between South West Africa and Angola, into Angola's Cunene Province at a point we were convinced was unlikely to be mined or under observation by the enemy. "How could you have known that?" you may well ask. Simply put, we randomly chose the densest virgin bush and basically drove over it with the Buffels. The water cars bounced over the flattened bushes and odd tree stumps created in the wake of each of the Buffels' massive wheels – it was slow going, but it worked! We were in Angola! We had now invaded their sovereign soil. I realized we'd better watch out now, this was bandit country.

We had been sent there to follow up on the classified map our lootie had been producing for the past three weeks. The area we found ourselves in, here in the far south of Angola, was entirely unpopulated. There was nothing here but bush, thick bush, as far as the eye could see. Tasked with monitoring the area for evidence of possible terrorist activities, we would hopefully intercept travelling insurgents before they crossed the border into South West Africa and made their way towards their intended targets. I assumed this strategy was reproduced west and east of our position by other platoons who had recently been stationed near the border to carry out similar functions. Part of me was hesitantly excited by the fact that we might have the opportunity to put into practice all we had been preparing for during our long and intense ambush training at Omuthiya.

The sun had almost set. Without much light to progress any further into that rugged and foliage-choked terrain, the lootie stopped us about two kilometres in to set up temporary base in a spot he deemed appropriate.

It must have been about 01h00 when I woke from a restless sleep punctuated with nightmarish images of being ill-prepared under an attack. I knew immediately that something was wrong. My stomach was coiled up in an intense cramp. No sooner had the cramp passed than I had a sudden urge that couldn't be ignored. Clambering out of my sleeping bag and rushing from the trench, I dug a small and shallow hole as quickly as I could, whipping off my browns just in time. I had diarrhoea! Oh boy! I closed up the hole and returned to my sleeping bag. Twice more over the next hour or two I had to jump up to relieve myself, and by 03h00 a massive headache had descended on me to complete the picture.

I dozed on and off until around 05h00, when, just as it was getting light, I lifted my aching head to look around. What a sight! The guys were all looking decidedly green around the gills, every one of us suffering from gyppo-guts. The water from the new water car we had taken charge of the night before was obviously contaminated, and now, dehydrated and ill, we were unable to replenish our fluids. We were parched and shrivelled and extremely uncomfortable out there in the bush.

The lootie radioed in to logistics to report the problem. The team there wasn't willing to drive with a fresh water car into Angola, but they agreed to meet us on that main C46 east-west border road back in South West Africa later that same day. We spent the morning sleeping fitfully in the scant shade of the trees and Buffels, irritated as much by the flies as by our bellies. In the afternoon, we gingerly climbed aboard the Buffels and retraced our tracks – slowly and cautiously, not for fear of the enemy, but rather of the effects of the bumpy ride on our queasy stomachs and throbbing heads – and crossed the border back into South West Africa.

The sum total of my Angolan experience: an unproductive incursion that lasted an interminable day!

***

It was 1990, the year Nelson Mandela was released from prison and a year since the Bush War had ended. I had gone into a bar with some friends to ponder the future of the white man in the country, when, out of the corner of my eye, I spotted a man whose face was familiar to me. I looked closer and it dawned on me: this man was the spitting image of the staff sergeant of my dream.

I approached the deeply-tanned man, who was alone at a table, nursing a beer as he stroked his considerable moustache.

"Excuse me, sir," I said. The man brought his piercing, steely-blue eyes to rest on me. "Were you in the Bush War?" I asked.

The man looked me up and down and, deciding I meant no harm, answered, "Ja, I was there." His gruff voice was flavoured with a strong Afrikaans accent.

"You weren't, by any chance, a staff sergeant, were you?" I asked.

"Ja, I was," he answered. How uncanny! Then and there I told him of the dream I had had, and what the staff sergeant in my dream had predicted.

I finished telling the story and grinned. "You know," I said. "The staff sergeant in my dream was wrong with his prediction. Things are very different in Namibia now."

The ex-staff sergeant nodded, took a sip from his bottle of beer, and then pointed the neck towards me. *"Engelsman,"* he said, catching me off-guard with his eerie echo of my dream. "I held that same view," he said. "Same as that staff sergeant in your dream."

"But, Staff," I said, automatically addressing him as though we were still in the army. "You realise that SWAPO won the elections after all? By fifty-seven percent!"

"Alright, *Engelsman,* I confess," he said. "I too made a mistake in my prediction. But your imaginary staff sergeant and I were right about SWAPO breaking their promises." I motioned for the man to continue, settling into a chair next to him. He obliged. "On the day when the peace accords were supposed to have come into action last year," he said, "SWAPO defied the agreements therein and sent 1 600 soldiers across the border to attack South Africa's army. They failed – South Africa, with the UN and the international

203

community, wiped them out – but still ..." He gave me a meaningful look before finishing his beer and setting the bottle aside. "You know," he went on thoughtfully, slowly beginning to stroke his considerable moustache. "Cuba has agreed to pull its troops out of Angola by July next year?" I nodded to indicate that I did know.

"Staff," I said. "Aren't communists known for abusing negotiations and deceiving the opposition?"

"That's right," he replied. "Their motto is "peace is war continued by other means"." He gave a wry chuckle, rubbed his stubbled chin and leant back in his chair. "They are wily," he went on. "They get past international control and monitoring mechanisms easily."

"You know, *Engelsman*," the ex-staff sergeant really seemed to be hitting his stride. "SWAPO may have won the elections, but they had to give up the war. They realised we couldn't be defeated.

"During the most intensive period of fighting towards the end of the Bush War in 1988, including Operation Savannah, FAPLA and the Cubans lost almost five thousand men, almost a hundred tanks, more than a hundred armoured vehicles, nine aircraft and other Soviet equipment valued at more than a billion rand. A billion rand! South Africa lost less than thirty-five men, three tanks, five armoured vehicles and three aircraft." I whistled through my teeth to convey my astonishment. *"Ja, nê?* We were certainly not defeated on any battlefield. Nor were we driven out of the country." He gave a throaty grunt. "SWAPO lost its support from its communist allies when the Berlin Wall fell last year," he went on. "The countries involved realised that it was just too risky to carry on with the war. It was costing too much – in money and lives. Plus, Russian-style communism was crumbling.

"The Cubans," the old man said, "the Cubans were convinced that they would never defeat us, so they started a propaganda and diplomatic campaign to disguise their setbacks and losses. Think about all their lies – claiming that they beat us at Cuito Cuanavale and the battle for the Lomba River. They even tried to pull a fast one over Fidel Castro! I almost feel sorry for the Cuban brass that were executed by Castro – they had to fabricate stories about beating us. At least, by attempting to deceive *el Presidenté* off their own bat, they unintentionally ensured that not more men were executed."

"But SWAPO continued to try and control the locals, not so, staff?" I enquired. The staff sergeant nodded.

"You're right," he said. "Before the elections, SWAPO told Namibians that the UN had recognised it as the legitimate representative party of that country. SWAPO threatened to continue fighting if it didn't win the elections."

Here the ex-staff sergeant raised a forefinger. "But," he said emphatically, "since coming into power, the leading SWAPO officials have changed the party's policies whenever it suits them. To date, they have yet to have a formal congress. It's been impossible for any internal, objective person to find a platform to criticise the leadership. SWAPO's power is unchallenged. Not the UN, the support groups or the churches have spoken out against the party." Here the old man shrugged. "I guess they fear rocking the boat," he said.

The old man signalled to the bar tender for another beer while I thought about SWAPO and their blatant abuse of power. The beer arrived, and the ex-staff sergeant interrupted my thoughts.

"*Jy weet,*" he said, taking a swig from the green bottle and wiping his mouth with the back of his hand. "SWAPO has always encouraged hatred for capitalists and wealthy people." He shrugged expansively, cocking his head as if to say "just as expected". "But," he aimed the bottle towards me again, "SWAPO's true nature emerged when it started forcing people to denounce their Christianity and the existence of God. Now can you see why South Africa fought so hard to defeat SWAPO? They anticipated this problem long before it happened."

"But, Staff," I said. "I'm a bit confused. If everyone had to withdraw from the war, who won?"

"Well, *Engelsman,*" he replied. "To be honest, no one won the war. The SADF did exceedingly well in its military strategy and tactics. We won almost every fight. After Ongulumbashe, SWAPO never had the chance to start a single base in Namibia. There were no safe areas where its forces could recover and set up an alternative government. We pushed back SWAPO's bases in Angola hundreds of kilometres. South Africa's strong force on the border prevented SWAPO from crossing into Namibia. The SADF's goal to limit SWAPO's access to Owamboland was a huge success. Also, the casualty figures alone showed a victory for us."

"So we were the victors?"

"No, no!" the old man insisted. "The Owambos still voted for SWAPO, made it the ruling party. We were there to prevent SWAPO from getting into power, and we failed."

"So SWAPO won?" I was confused by what the old man was saying. Again he shook his head.

"No. You see, SWAPO's long-term goal wasn't just to govern. It wanted unquestioned power without opposition, it wanted a one-party dictatorship. But the election was mostly regarded as democratic. There are now opposition parties in Namibia. So, in the end, none of the role-players succeeded in achieving their aims."

"I see," I said. "So, in a way, we won. But in another way, SWAPO won." The ex-staff sergeant chuckled and shrugged his agreement. "Does that mean," I asked, "that the war was a waste of time? Because communism is still controlling Namibia."

"Ja," the staff sergeant nodded gravely. "You're right. Those communists are very hard to control. Once they get a foot in the door, they take over. We tried our best, but in the end we really had no choice. We had to leave Namibia to its fate."

I thanked the old man for the chat and wished him well. As I rose from my seat to leave, he took hold of my arm and looked sternly at me. *"Engelsman,"* he said. "Know this: Angola was Castro's Vietnam."

Chapter 16

"Ek verklaar, geen skerppunt ammunisie, leë doppies of enige dele daarvan in my besit nie, korporaal!" We were at Grootfontein, on our way back to "The States". We were going home!

"I declare, no sharp-point ammunition, empty shells or any parts thereof in my possession, corporal!" We were being inspected by several stern-looking corporals for contraband: anything illegal from the enemy's equipment or our own. But the inspection amounted to nothing more than declaring that we carried nothing. Most of us lied.

"I declare, no sharp-point ammunition, empty shells or any parts thereof in my possession, corporal," I stated, standing to attention. As a joke, I added, "Except for a Bushman bow with arrows." He gave me a look which said, *Spare me your bullshit humour!* and ushered me on with some irritation. *"Ek verklaar, geen skerppunt ammunisie, leë doppies of enige dele daarvan in my besit nie, korporaal!"* Those who caved to their guilty consciences and declared the contraband they carried were just told to dump it into one of several ammo crates nearby.

"Ek verklaar, geen skerppunt ammunisie, leë doppies of enige dele daarvan in my besit nie, korporaal!" I passed through "customs' with two coloured flares, one illumination flare, a bunch of R4 rounds and one 35-round magazine. Two years later, I found the flares and cautiously fired them off: two on Guy Fawkes' night and the illumination flare at a New Year's celebration. They went off without a hitch. Many years later I got rid of the live rounds and magazine.

In mid-October we had travelled down to Grootfontein from the Oshivelo Base in brown liveried SAMIL 100s with caged trailers, in which we sat surrounded by our kit, our shirts open to catch the last of the South West African sun's rays. On arrival in Grootfontein, our bush hats now replaced with green berets, we neatened up our browns in preparation for the inspection. After making the declaration to the corporals, we boarded an orange, white and blue SAFAIR Boeing 737 in an orderly fashion. I was relaxed and happy to be returning to South Africa.

Aside from the locals and the *Dankie Tannies*, which hardly counted, we had encountered no one of the female persuasion during our time out of the country, so the smart and sassy air hostesses in their blue-grey SAFAIR uniforms and expertly applied make-up were a tonic to our eyes. They dazzled us with their smiles, and my spirits lightened immediately. As I passed them at the door to the aircraft, I inhaled their perfumed presence deeply, anticipating a most enjoyable flight: being served by these heavenly maidens while reclining in my seat. This fantasy was not to be realised, though. As soon as we had been settled into our seats, the two sexy flight attendants departed after delivering our lunch, disappearing as quickly as the morning mist. Our "lunch" was no more than a stapled-shut, brown paper bag, the contents of which included a bag of Simba potato crisps, a small bag of Simba peanuts and a fruit juice. While I chomped and sipped my way through "lunch", I speculated on what might be happening in the cockpit, where those two lovelies had disappeared.

The flight was smooth – no droning turbo-props to deafen you – so I relaxed, listening to the quiet chatting of my fellow-soldiers around me. Some of the guys dozed.

There were so many reasons for the end of our stint on the border to feel good. The tedious daily activities had got to me after almost two months, although, if I am honest, the time had been rewarding in its own way. I would never forget the landscape we had trudged through daily – so rugged and beautiful – very different from anything I had come across in South Africa. I also had a sense that I had done well up there, standing up under the discomfort and pressure of the rigorous training and stark conditions. And most importantly, the end of the border signalled a great milestone in my national service: my first year was almost over.

Knowing that I would see Kimberly soon was cause for great excitement in me. I had been lonely on the border as only a soldier can be. Surrounded by mates, I had never actually been alone, but even the company of Ian couldn't compare to the satisfaction I got from having Kimberly close by. I was buoyed by my renewed commitment to our relationship, and eager to start planning our future together.

The experience of the dreaded border now behind me, I felt confident about returning to familiar ground. I had made it ... we had made it. A fractured bone or two and some blisters were the worst of the company's wounds of war, and we were returning as "main *manne*". *Die Grens* had been a unique experience and one that left an indelible impression on me. I felt I was returning to South Africa a changed man.

If any member of my platoon or Bravo Company had come to the border hoping for a Bush War fire fight, they were sorely mistaken: we were there at the wrong time of the year. Most of the SWAPO-PLAN incursions up there were undertaken during the rainy summer season, and we were there at the end of winter. Had a shootout taken place, it would most likely have been due to compromising a guerrilla lurking behind in a local community from a previous incursion, or coming across a recce-type from a SWAPO-PLAN camp, although my platoon's experience with the forlorn FAPLA soldier had been an eye-opener for me. We had been briefed that the SWAPO recces were psychologically strong and equipped with the latest Soviet gear, and they were assumed to be more bush-savvy, better disciplined and more motivated than their Angolan counterparts. We had been given the impression that the Angolan liberation forces were generally a push-over. Word on the ground was that the SWAPO forces were preparing for insurgency within a few months, and that the SWAPO forces the SADF would face had been trained in Russia. The suspected areas of their activity certainly included the areas our forces were based, but this was not the time for their activities, and by the time the rainy season arrived to disguise their movements and hide their tracks, we would be safely back in our own country and back to our training at Infantry School. It was the officers and NCOs deployed there later that would be expected to contain the incursions with their troops.

Later, I would hear stories that would dishearten and disappoint me, stories that caused me anger towards the perpetrators, for bringing disrepute to those of us who abided by a higher moral and ethical code. I heard of villagers suffering poor harvests and dire circumstances because SADF Casspirs laid waste their crops in the pursuit of suspected insurgents. Stories of students roughed up by SADF soldiers, or missing months of classes because their teachers had been taken away for questioning by the SADF. Once, I was told how comops guys would make a show of publically thanking SWAPO activists by providing gifts such as maize meal, for spying on behalf of the SADF, just so that they would be subjected to brutal retaliation from their comrades. Tainted by the false identification as a spy, the activist's family would be beaten and raped before the perpetrators turned on the suspect and murdered him.

But this was all to come later. On returning to South Africa, I felt like I had survived an ordeal, proven myself to myself and my superiors. I was returning with a new appetite for life and a renewed commitment to my future with Kimberly.

Landing after just over two hours in the air, we were loaded into several SAMIL 50s to make the journey back to Infantry School. The blokes were in good spirits and we sang a few victory songs along the way.

The NCO companies got one stripe just before they went up to the border. They always carried their stripes with them, although they weren't allowed to wear them. Soon after our return from the border, when I was returning to our bungalow with Ian from the tuck shop one evening, one of these about-to be-ranked NCOs wearing his stripes illegally had tried to pull rank on me by insisting in Afrikaans that I was to *strek* him, because he had this little floppy adornment and I didn't yet have anything. Initially, I just ignored him and walked on, but he persisted, coming to stand directly in front of me, wagging his finger under my nose. My patience was wearing thin. I told him that his actions could see him kicked off the course – if the incident was to escalate into a fight, we were both in danger of being kicked off the course – but he wouldn't listen and continued his tirade.

Perhaps he was full of Dutch courage, who knows? Finally, I told him, in no uncertain or particularly wholesome terms, to stuff off.

"Next year," I said, seething, "I'll make you polish my lootie's pips, if I feel like it!" With that, we brushed him aside and walked away. He just stood there looking stupid. This always happened with imminent NCOs – they used to try and pip the graduates at the post, but it was the closest any of them ever came to it with me.

That weekend we were granted a pass. I longed to see Kimberly and feel her warm presence in my arms, but a mere weekend wasn't enough time to make my way to Pretoria. We all wanted to celebrate our return to normality, though. So, together with a couple of mates, I planned a weekend break at the coastal resort of Plettenburg Bay.

Some of the guys were given permission to leave early on Friday morning for good merit. I don't know why I was one of them. Perhaps Pottie was concerned that as a one-pip lootie, as I soon would be, I would give him gas. Regardless, Pottie and I had reconciled our differences during our time on the Border, and even Lieutenant Pretorius treated me with a little more decency now that we were back.

Mark, an English-speaking chap from another platoon, was making his way home to Port Elizabeth in his small, white, canopied Ford bakkie, and I convinced him to drop me off in Plett, which was just off the N2 to PE. Wearing my civvies and sporting a fresh haircut, I picked up a vehicle from the Avis Rent-a-car offices. After a leisurely and satisfying Wimpy lunch, I set off to meet up with Ian and Adi and the others, who had hitched a ride with some other guys also on their way to Plett.

Using our unspent danger pay – which had by then added up to a substantial amount – we booked two rooms at the luxurious Beacon Isle Hotel. It was just what I needed after the border! We lounged on the terrace at the swimming pool, drinking beers and watching the waves crash on the rocks below. It was a perfect welcome home to South Africa: one of the most expensive hotels on probably one of the most expensive real estate areas in the country at the time, and I felt like I owned it!

A little eatery with the appropriate name of *Why Not?* became our second home for the weekend, where we enjoyed the coldest ales, the best red wine and the greatest meals – not to mention the pleasant view of some of the most stunning beauties on two legs. The place was truly restorative, to body, mind and soul! You could stumble from the Beacon Isle Hotel across the bridge over the high water zone near the beach, across a parking lot and sink down in one of their welcoming chairs to the smiling "Hello! What can I get you to drink?" from a pretty waitress.

Ian and I stocked up on nearly a dozen bottles of Nederburg reds: Cabernet Sauvignon, Baronne and Pinotage. We guzzled these as we walked from one public place to the next, bottles in hand. We were horrible! Knowing full well that we were contravening the laws of public decency, I discounted any threat of retribution, practically daring anyone to challenge me. I guess I had become a bit full of myself following my stint on the border, but I had made up my mind that anyone who tried to stop me from drinking in public would be given a hiding and sent home to mommy crying. What an oaf I was! My behaviour was making a mockery of myself and all the decent national servicemen who were trying to have a pleasant time down there.

That night we decided to head off to the Formosa Inn, a night club and restaurant with a reputation for a great party. Still slugging liquor by the bottle, I found it necessary to steady myself against table tops as I made my way through the establishment, the room swimming before me. Coming across two pretty young women enjoying a meal together, and convinced as I was of my animal magnetism, I tried to strike up a conversation.

"Well, hello there!" I thought I was being suave. In retrospect I was probably just being coarse. "Are you two enjoying your dinner, then?" They looked up, forced a smile, returned to their meal, trying to ignore me. "Would either of you fine young things like a swing around the room with me?"

"No, thank you," said the young woman on my left, trying hard to be polite but firm – but it was all lost on me in my state.

"Oh, come on!" I said. "You should see my moves on the dance floor!"

She spoke a little louder, "No, thank you. We're not interested!" She turned back to her dinner companion. I swayed alongside the table, but didn't get the hint.

"Just come and have a dance, won't you?"

When she spoke this time, the unfortunate target of my attentions sounded decidedly strained. "Please, just go," she said. "You're drunk. We don't want to dance with you. Can't you see that you're disturbing us?" It finally penetrated my drunken mind that I wasn't going to get what I wanted. I shrugged a shoulder and lurched onto the dance floor, clumsily grabbing the nearest girl for a dance.

I had some fun dancing and there on the dance floor my drunken oafishness was more disguised. Some of the girls seemed to be enjoying my free-spiritedness as I danced wildly, bumping and grinding against them. My judgment wasn't impaired. It had vanished.

Still smarting from the slight the two diners had given me, I was determined to get my revenge. My vision was blurred and my balance was shaky, but I managed to climb onto the nearest table and make a bleary pronouncement:

"Ladies and gentlemen," I bellowed drunkenly to one and all. "Consider this a public service announcement." I had the attention of just about everyone in the vicinity. I thought they were rapt with my captivating presence. I suspect they were just amazed at my dreadful behaviour in a public place. I thought I saw Adi cringe. "These two fine young ladies, here," I pointed the beer bottle in my hand towards the two young women, "they are off limits." The table threatened to be overturned, but I managed to right it with some quick-thinking moves. My balance restored, I returned to the matter at hand. "That's right, guys. Don't even try your luck," I said, pausing for effect. The two were looking at me with wide eyes, their hands frozen around their glasses in mid-sip. Blearily I announced to my now-captive audience, "I am sorry to disappoint you all, but I believe these two beauties are lezzies!" At the suggestion that they had dismissed me because they were lesbians, I saw the one who had spoken grow red with fury. Giving me looks like daggers, they grabbed their purses and departed as I challenged: "Prove me wrong!"

Adi, by now, had made his way to my side and was pulling me down from the table, just as the manager arrived with some heavies to pull the two of us aside.

"I think the two of you should be going home now," the manager said with barely concealed contempt. To Adi, he said, "Your friend here needs to sleep it off."

"Hey!" I lurched forward into the manager's face. "I don't want to leave!" Adi was pulling at my shoulder, but I shrugged him off. "And you can't make me!"

"Actually, sir," he replied with exaggerated politeness. "I believe I can." He nodded to the thickset men behind him, who stepped forward and crossed their arms. I was brave with alcohol, though, and couldn't be persuaded.

"I believe my mates from the army here tonight outnumber your brutes," I shouted at the manager. "Want to take us on?" The manager couldn't hide the flicker of concern, but stood his ground all the same. Adi was holding me back by my shirt.

"Mike!" he shouted into my ear. "You've had too much to drink. Let's go, man." Ian, who had come to see what all the fuss was about, agreed, and they each took one of my arms and led me to the stairs at the exit.

At the car, I fumbled in my pocket for the keys. Finding them, I aimed them shakily towards the keyhole in the driver's door.

"No ways, man, Mike!" Adi took hold of my wrist. "You're way over the limit! I'll drive."

"Nah-uh," I slapped his hand away. "I'm okay, man. I'll drive." I tried to smile to give him a sense of confidence in my abilities. Adi and Ian exchanged glances, Ian shook his head.

I took the wheel and sped out of the parking lot. At the next traffic light on the main road I almost took out another car.

"Stop!" Adi screeched. "Just stop. Right now!" He slammed the dashboard with his fist. "You're out of your ever-loving mind, man!" Realising he was right, I submitted.

"Okay," I said weakly. "I don't feel too good. I'll let you drive."

A cruel and blinding white light pouring into the room woke me the following morning. Scraping my eyelids off the eyeballs beneath, I took stock: swollen sandpaper tongue, blinding headache. I had a massive *babbelas*. I swallowed a handful of paracetamol and returned to the bed with my eyes covered, waiting for the pain to subside. I heard the door open and looked up to see Adi and Ian eying me with little sympathy.

"You remember what happened last night?" Ian asked.

"Arghh! I'm trying not to!" I groaned into the sheets. "I made a fool of myself, didn't I?" Ian snorted.

"You were a jerk, man!" He gave a brief outline of the events, and I winced at the memories.

"Oh, man," I said, pulling the sheets down and looking at them both. "I have been such a moron! Sorry." They both chuckled.

"I think your barbie and the regret you're gonna feel will be enough penance," Adi said. "Come on. You need a fry-up." What good mates – they forgave me quickly.

We spent the rest of the morning swimming and relaxing by the pool overlooking the Indian Ocean. With the harsh glare and the hot rays of the sun beating down on me, the only thing to ease my throbbing head was more alcohol, so I ordered some hair of the rabid dog that had bitten me; a drink or two, to ease my mind. I downed those *regmakers* in quick succession, hoping that they would pick me up. The pain slowly dissipated as the alcohol coursed again through my veins. I felt remorseful, and wondered if Adi didn't see me as a bit of a liability as a friend, but my remorse seemed to evaporate as we spent the evening savouring the luscious fruits of the vine, again.

Chapter 17

When we got back from that notorious pass, there was very little left to do.

Shortly after our return, we officially received our candidate officer tabs, although I had already started getting the pay of a candidate officer while I was still on the border. We were now allowed to wear them around Infantry School. We called those shoulder tabs *kakpapier* ("toilet paper") and we were now *kakhuis offisiere* ("shit-house officers"). The shoulder tabs and boot bands carried no rank – they were just a kind of marker to designate us as officers-in-training. For this reason, the bands were regarded with derision by one and all.

We spent the better part of three weeks undergoing some urban counter-insurgency training, or "urban coinops" in SADF terms. This training was supposed to prepare us to deal with riots and civil unrest, presumably in the townships, where the anti-Apartheid conflict had intensified and turned these ghettos into all-out zones of terror. What made this training memorable was: riot drills in ill-fitting and uncomfortable hard plastic riot helmets with visors; claustrophobic and ill-fitting black rubber gas masks, and vehicle movement drills on and off Buffels through open areas. When a Buffel wasn't available for our training, we "played" at being in one, going through the drills and boring routines. I felt a bit silly during these "pretend" sessions, like I was a grown man involved in a boy's fantasy game. One group would be designated the "soldiers", the other the "rioters". If I had to choose, it was more liberating and fun to be a rioter, where we could muss up our uniforms, shirts hanging out, web belts removed, bush hat brims tucked in under the crowns leaving a peak resembling Cuban-Marxist guerrilla revolutionary caps. We threw small stones harmlessly, to mimic Molotov Cocktails; half-bricks at the shields held by some of the "soldiers", and looked the part of rag-tag rioters. As "soldiers" we learnt how to undo one side of our R4s' straps – usually used to sling our weapons over our shoulders – and tie it to our wrists so that we couldn't be easily unarmed by the enemy. But this training felt ineffective after our stint at the border. It was like it had been tacked onto the end of our first year to fill time. Even the ranks seemed vaguely disinterested, and we all picked up on this attitude.

Once, the platoons of Bravo Company were loaded into Buffels and taken out to Bhongolethu Township on the southeastern outskirts of Oudtshoorn to "see what it was like". The Buffel I was in went no further than the entrance to the township, which seemed quiet at the time, before Lieutenant Pretorius instructed the drivers to depart so as not to incite the residents. By that stage we were all NAAFI ("no ambition and fuck all interest" – a term that was used frequently at that time) anyway.

A couple of days into urban coinops, I made an appointment to see the *dominee*. Having decided I was going to propose to Kimberly, I thought I could enlist his help in convincing my lootie and the top brass to send me closer to Pretoria to be with my future-wife. Arriving a little early, I waited for my appointment in one of the little thatched gazebos near his office.

I had been waiting listlessly in a grey plastic chair for no more than five minutes when I was joined by a fretful looking *troep* from Foxtrot, who took a seat opposite me on a chair matching my own. We nodded to each other.

"You waiting for the *dominee*?" I asked, a bit pointlessly, considering we were in the *dominee*'s waiting area.

"Yes," he replied. Another moment passed in awkward silence. I tried to make small talk.

"Foxtrot, hey?" I said. He gave a nod. "You don't look like a fly-half," I grinned to show I was kidding. The guy was lean and looked fit, but had none of the bulk of a rugby player.

He chuckled.

"Nah," he said. "I walk." I must have looked bemused, he continued: "I have provincial sports colours in walking." He smiled. "You a teacher?" he asked, as if to change the subject.

"Nah," I shook my head. "Graduate. BSc," I said, "Wits. And you?" "I'm a teacher. UCT."

I leant forward and held out my hand. "Mike Warren," I said. He gripped my hand firmly.

"Gavin Fish." We chatted a bit about ourselves, our studies. The silence settled again.

After a while, I plucked up the courage to ask him why he was seeing the *dominee*. He took a moment before replying, narrowing his eyes as if composing his thoughts.

"I hope he will help me get a rural posting next year," he said at last. "Being forced to operate in the townships would conflict with my Christian beliefs." I nodded sagely, but didn't really understand what he was saying.

"You didn't apply for exemption from national service on religious grounds?" I asked.

"Well," he seemed to be thinking again. "It's not that I object to national service, you see," he said. "I don't mind doing the training. I won't mind carrying out my duties elsewhere. I would just prefer not to be sent into the townships." Here he paused and looked at me with a long and steady gaze. He seemed to be trying to gauge my response to what he had said. After a while, as if having drawn some conclusion about me, he spoke without taking his eyes from mine. "They're South Africans, you know," he said, "in the townships. Just like you and me."

"Warren!" It was the *dominee*, calling me from his office. I was sorry to leave Gavin and his conversation. We gave each other expressions which suggested "here we go" and I left him sitting in his grey plastic chair.

Urban coinops was followed by a low-level command and control course, where we were introduced to discipline, methods of instruction and the like. We all enjoyed the course, because it was low-key and we knew it signalled the end of our year. Our time would soon be taken up by preparations for the passing out parade, which would last a couple of weeks.

Vormingsopleiding, or instruction in etiquette, took up some of our time during this period. This was to prepare us to behave like officers and gentlemen in formal situations. We were taught table etiquette, like which cutlery to use for each course. We were given a two-hour lecture on wine – we weren't allowed to actually taste the wine, but we were told about it in great detail. Port was made available and we were instructed on how to pass the decanter and pour from it. Cigars were brought out and we were shown how to smoke them, although never having been a smoker, I wasn't bothered to learn. After a couple of dry runs, we were treated to a formal dinner in the officers' mess hall, to put what we had learnt into practice.

At the end of *vormingsopleiding*, as the culmination of our etiquette training, we were given the opportunity to take part in a formal function at the Army Women's College in George. The event wasn't compulsory – those who were married or who were disinclined to take part because they were *vas* with a girl were excused. I went along out of sheer inquisitiveness.

We left Infantry School late one Friday afternoon in our step-outs, looking very smart indeed. We travelled to George in several canopied SAMIL 50s, and by the time we got there, the sun had almost set. We were herded into the foyer of a hall, where light refreshments were served. The atmosphere was strained, as around a hundred officers-to-be from Infantry

School mingled awkwardly with the *soldoedies* (female soldiers) or Botha Babes from the college. The term "Botha Babes" originated from PW Botha's support of women volunteering in the army as their contribution to the cause, his daughter Rozanne being a leading example.

The women wore ugly khaki and brown step-out uniforms. These *boeremeisies* were very average-looking in their uniforms. Only a few seemed pretty. No alcohol was served, and all our platoon commanders and their equivalent ranks looked on with eagle-eyes to ensure that none of us disappeared around a corner or behind some bushes. I don't know if this was considered an opportunity for us to make use of our new *vormingsopleiding* skills, or a very misguided attempt at giving the guys some fun, but either way, it was a stiff affair!

A little later, the doors to the hall were opened and *sokkie* music was broadcast over the PA system. A number of the Afrikaans guys took the opportunity to *langarm* around the hall with the strange creatures in khaki skirts and unflattering brown shoes. Being English-speaking, I had never been taught nor had the desire to learn how to do this close "wind-surfing" dancing so popular with the Afrikaners. A bunch of similarly disadvantaged English guys stood around outside, and we chatted amongst ourselves. It rates as one of the most unmemorable evenings I have ever had the misfortune of spending in the company of the opposite sex.

One afternoon, we were called to the mustering area in front of Bravo's lines, where Major Drost addressed the assembled men. First, he made it clear that where each of us was to be posted in the year to come was a decision made from above. We would not be able to challenge that decision once it had been made. Then he suggested that the decision-makers would like to give us the opportunity to volunteer for certain posts if we were so inclined, and that they would take our preferences into account. Each of us was given a slip of paper, on which we were instructed to write our names, our force numbers and our top three choices in order of preference. Then he reminded us that there was no guarantee any of us would get to be posted according to our wishes. The chief of the army, he said, had reported that most of us would be required for border duty, and we should brace ourselves, because as much as eighty percent of us would end up on the border for most of the next year.

I watched some of the guys wrestle with this exercise, thinking hard about what they wanted and whether they should volunteer for a particular post. I remembered the lesson I had learnt at the beginning: never volunteer for anything in the army! I also doubted our choices would carry much influence. I wasn't keen on being posted to the border in South West Africa. It was too far away from home and Kimberly, and I knew the guys on the border would have very long stints without passes. I also had no desire to return to Infantry School. Not only was it still too far from home and Kimberly, but our experience there had been very different to what we now knew normal operational duty was all about. On the little piece of paper I wrote my choices down: 1. Pretoria. 2. Near Pretoria. 3. As close to Pretoria as possible.

Sometime later, we were again called together and informed who was posted where for the following year. Some of the guys had opted to go to the parabats or weapons units. Military intelligence was there to recruit volunteers for that unit. Then the guys who had chosen or were selected to remain at Infantry School were called out. A big deal was made about these guys being the cream of the crop. Ian was one of them. I congratulated him, and in his matter-of-fact, good-humoured way he simply shrugged his shoulders and said, "It could've been worse, bud!" I was relieved not to be considered for Infantry School – I found it very *paraat* and without much practical value. The two-pip loots posted to Infantry School would have to contend with a degree of pretentiousness. I had no doubt that Lieutenant Pretorius would have resisted any suggestion of me staying on at Oudtshoorn, anyway. As it turned out, less than forty percent of the guys ended up on the border for their second year. I thought the threat of sending the majority of us to the border was just a tactic to scare guys into volunteering to stay on at Infantry School.

Soon there were very few of us left standing in the company lines waiting to hear our fate. Eventually my name was called. Lieutenant Pretorius said that the *dominee* had spoken to him about my situation, he had considered my request, and I was fortunate to be posted to 113 Battalion (113 BN). I had no idea what it was, but I thanked him and left. I asked around, "What in the blazes in 113 BN?" Most of the guys had never heard of it, but someone said he had heard it was based near the Kruger National Park. Another guy said he thought it was a black battalion. This sounded like good fortune, to me. I had made a stand and basically got posted closer to home and Kimberly.

During those last few weeks at Oudtshoorn, I had a lot of time to reflect on the year. I knew that I would leave here with nothing but relief: there was very little about Infantry School that I would miss. This place had come to embody a type of incarceration for me, a punishment for some unknown transgression. At times it felt like I was being punished for the accident of my birth: I could no more claim responsibility for being born a white English-speaking male in a fiercely contested South Africa, than accept blame for the battle waging amongst her citizens. Here in a historic town in the Klein Karoo, my punishment took the form of a complete and agonising removal from society and all the things I loved. I had felt physically and mentally trapped between the Swartberg Mountains to the north and the Outeniqua Mountains to the south. Every day for a year, as we assembled in front of the Bravo lines, I saw the Swartberg Mountains in front of me: stunningly beautiful, majestic and immovable. All it did was play on my psyche: a hulking representation of all that blocked my way to Kimberly and my life in Pretoria.

I started the year expecting the worst, but I had survived. It had been incredibly tough, physically and mentally, but now, at last, it was coming to an end. PT, inspections, lectures, drilling and more lectures; early mornings and long days; there was barely a moment's rest. I wrote more exams at Infantry School in a year than I wrote at university in four. We were slowly transformed from carefree students into functional – albeit reluctant, on my part – soldiers.

Much of what I learnt at Infantry School was useful, but a load of the bull that was dished up to us was of no value whatsoever. In many respects, the training we received at Infantry School was misguided: I mean, all the pedantic inspections, excessive PT sessions, *rondfoks*, *opfoks*, verbal abuse, brainwashing ... were these things really important to the objective of Infantry School? Did these things really contribute to the production of good officers? A lot of the seemingly pointless and mind-numbing activities were actually nothing but time-wasters and time-fillers with the aim of messing a *troep* around. I think that we would all have been more productive without these sideshows.

I had not ingratiated myself at Infantry School. I suspect there were men there who were as glad to see the back of me as I was to see the last of them. I remembered some of the chaps who had left during the course of the year. I think that some of the guys that should have left didn't. Some of the *manne* in Bravo's platoons, our lootie's wonder-boys, did not have what it takes to be a good officer. These suck-ups became favourites because they were quick learners, physically tough or willing to submit unquestioningly to the army's nonsense. I came to view them as lacking in integrity, and I wouldn't have chosen to serve under them in a situation of conflict for anything. I knew that reason, responsibility and common sense were far more valuable to a soldier with rank, and I understood that many of our superiors had been conned because they themselves had had insufficient operational experience.

I had mates at Oudtshoorn, but the relief of leaving the place, I knew, would sadly be greater than any of the friendships I had made. We were strangers, flung together under strange circumstances. Friendships arose out of necessity rather than a sense of fraternity, and such relationships don't usually have the substance to last beyond the situation. Unity amongst the members of my platoon never took hold. We did eventually learn to work together, after strong hints from our corporals, and many failed attempts at going it alone. But true camaraderie never came about organically. The nature of our training, the environment of the army and Infantry School, and the mentality of some of the platoon members precluded this. It was every man for himself, and to hell with the rest. Infantry School is hardly an environment to promote lasting friendships!

I had grown to despise the "us and them" mentality of Infantry School – an attitude I knew was the same everywhere in the army. Division was pervasive, based on language, background, education, rank ... anything that could be used as a means of discrimination, was used. I felt the impact of this discrimination often at Infantry School. The *oumanne* gave me grief because I was a *rower*, the PFs made my life difficult because I was a national serviceman, the Dutchmen gunned for me because I was English. In the army, it was impossible to escape discrimination.

But now, I was halfway through my national service: one year down, one to go. All the training, the *rondfok*, the *oppies* were finished with. In the year to come I would be ranked and I would call the shots. I would no longer be dictated to by officers and NCOs like those at Infantry School – only commissioned officers more senior than a two-pip lootie would hold sway over me.

What the year ahead held for me I could never have guessed.

But now, literally counting the days until this would all be over, I was increasingly anxious to leave. Those last few weeks were a strange time of limbo for me. The more I was chomping at the bit to go, the slower the time seemed to move. Together with Ian, I became a regular and big-time spender at the *snoepie* every single evening: drowning my sorrows in chocolate bars and Simba crisps.

As Ian and I weren't involved in any of the displays that were to be staged over the course of the passing out parade weekend, we stood a lot of guard duty at the main gate. It rained on and off during those weeks, a gentle but gloomy rain which made evenings in the guardhouse quite cold, even though summer had well and truly settled into the Klein Karoo.

Passing time in the darkness, the statue of the infantryman bathed in its ominous red light keeping me company, I remembered my first passage through this boom on the back seat of Derick's cream-coloured Honda Ballade. Just ten short months had passed since that long-ago January day, but I felt like a lifetime had gone by in the interim.

Oudtshoorn is roughly 1 200 kilometres from Pretoria. I had been warned by those who had gone before me to avoid travelling there by train at all costs, so I was lucky to have found a ride with Derick. When Derick arrived to fetch me from my parents' house early on Sunday morning, I had been horrified to discover that our travelling party numbered three with the inclusion of none other than the one-testicled stud Barry, Kimberly's fling from two years before. It was to be a thoroughly surreal experience. As if the journey wasn't going to be awkward enough, what with me having to bend my six-foot-plus frame into the rear seat of a car designed with the comfort of your average-sized Japanese traveller in mind, I would now have to contend with the presence of a guy I had nothing but contempt for. It was too late to change my travelling plans. I accepted my fate with some resignation, but I patently refused to speak to Barry for the entire journey. Poor Derick had to act as mediator and interpreter.

Derick, perhaps wisely, hadn't warned me that Barry was to be joining us on the trip. He must have known Barry's history with Kimberly. I didn't know whether I was pissed at him or not, but I was relieved that Kimberly hadn't come to see me off. As we rounded the corner near Kimberly's house, I wondered if she was watching through a window. I would have loved to have witnessed her reaction on seeing the scoundrel Barry in the passenger seat as we drove by.

The journey began in tense silence. I guess we were all preoccupied with thoughts of what was to come. My head was full of imaginings based on my one and only personal experience of the military at my dad's Voortrekkerhoogte cricket match when I was eight. I felt some reservation about the year ahead – who wouldn't, driving into the unknown? I watched the landscape slide by as the city gave way to black formal settlements and then farmlands.

I tried not to think about Kimberly's indiscretion with Barry, but from time to time I found myself staring at the back of his head in anger. I imagined the satisfaction of punching him out cold and shivered at the realisation of how deep my hatred for him ran. It was only in retrospect that I saw how, by casting Barry as the architect of her infidelity, by convincing myself that he had led her astray, I was merely making excuses for her.

Sometime after Bloemfontein, I tried to figure out where Derick's head was about Infantry School. I liked Derick. He had been in the same res as Barry and me. An eccentric and affable red-head, he had studied zoology and botany. At the time, I wondered how he would hold up in the army. Although he had an edge of biting sarcasm, he was in no way a fighter.

Derick was a pacifist and a dreamer – I bet he would have preferred to stroke frogs and hug bunnies, perhaps wrap his arms around the odd indigenous tree, to spending two years as a cog in the Apartheid fighting machine. I knew I was a dreamer, but I considered myself less of a softie than my friend, the anti-violence, peace-loving carrot-top. As it turned out, Derick and I wouldn't cross paths again during our year in Oudtshoorn.

I shifted my position, resting a shoulder against Derick's seat.

"Hey, Derick," I said. He flicked me a look in the rear-view mirror. "How d'you feel about this Infantry School thing?"

"Well ... I wish we didn't have to do it at all," he said, scratching the back of his neck absent-mindedly. "I guess we must just make the best of a bad situation, hey?" He caught my eye in the mirror again. "You worried?" he asked.

"Sure, I'm worried," I replied. "Aren't you?"

"A bit," he answered. "It seems weird," he grinned, "considering I've been in res for years. I'm worried about being homesick."

"Ja, me too," I confessed. Barry gave a gentle snort of derision, but I ignored him. "Plus, I'm gonna miss Kimberly. A lot." Barry shifted slightly at the mention of her name. "And I hate that we don't know when we'll get a pass."

"I reckon we'll get to go home after basics," Derick offered. "They always do that. Shit, you know, I'm worried I won't make it through basics!"

"Me too, bud!" Some time passed in silence as we all thought about it. My voice was soft when next I spoke: "I'm worried about where I'll be posted next year," I volunteered. "What if I'm sent to some hectic region on the border?"

"Or worse – to the townships," Derick added. "Exactly," I said.

"Ag, don't be wusses," Barry had finally decided to contribute to the conversation. "Thousands of guys have done this before us," he said. "We'll be fine, man." Derick and I made eye-contact in the mirror again, but it seemed the stud had had the final word on the matter.

I slipped back into the rear seat and returned to the passing scenery and my thoughts. The Great Karoo had a soporific effect. I woke more than a thousand kilometres from home with a crick in my neck.

We arrived in George late that afternoon and bought takeaways at the local diner. Having eaten our fill, we drove another half hour or so to the picturesque seaside town of Wilderness, the sun setting behind us. Under cover of darkness, afraid that the cops might be alerted by a concerned citizen, Derick parked the car in a public parking lot on the beachfront. We had no plans for accommodation; this was to be our resting place for the night. Before turning in, I stood barefoot on the white sands of an empty beach, listening to the surf in the breeze of the summer night. I tried to burn into my memory the feeling of being free.

We woke early on Monday morning feeling stiff and tired. The crick in my neck had turned into a spasm and I would surely have enjoyed the services of a chiropractor were they available to me. We loped over to the nearby beachfront ablutions with its defaced and rusted "Whites Only" sign. On entering we surprised a coloured hobo, who hurriedly exited in a cowering manner, probably anticipating a reprisal of sorts. He needn't have worried. We were Witsies. We wouldn't have dreamed of giving him a clip 'round the earhole – or worse – that he feared. My shave and shower were quick and cold.

Doubling back on our journey of the previous day, we passed again through George before hitting the N12 to Oudtshoorn and Infantry School. The drive was short and uneventful, undertaken in the silence of excited apprehension of the unknown. Part of me was relieved to finally be facing the start of my national service. The road from George to Oudtshoorn is little more than eighty kilometres, but traverses through some of the most varied and beautiful landscapes in the country. Derick's Honda struggled under the weight of three large guys as we slowly climbed the magnificent, scenic Outeniqua Mountain Pass, and then descended into the *fynbos*, succulents and thorny scrub of the Klein Karoo.

Travelling down a long, dipping U-bend, we followed the railway line past ostrich farms as the N12 became Langenhoven Avenue, finally arriving in town around seven. There was little conversation as we ate a Wimpy breakfast of eggs, bacon, toast and their famous frothy coffee. The beauty of a Wimpy is getting exactly what you expect.

In silence we got into the car after breakfast and in silence we drove towards Infantry School.

Almost a year had passed, and now I experienced mixed emotions as I handed back my rifle, my *trommel* and all my battle gear. This was the symbolic end to my year at Infantry School, and as such was undoubtedly a cause for celebration. But I had developed something of a relationship to these things. Knowing how I had taken care of my kit through thick and thin – especially my R4, which had become a kind of extension of me – I had a strange feeling of ownership, as if I should be taking these things home. The feeling soon passed, however, and I was buoyed by the sense of letting go. Escape from here was literally a day or two away.

Chapter 18

The passing out parade was a huge event at the end of November. Parents, wives and girlfriends were invited to witness a show that lasted the whole long weekend, and included rifle drill demonstrations, weapons demonstrations and the Infantry School Band.

The band was made up of the more senior graduates, recruited from Bravo Company, and only under exceptional circumstances was a musician from another company recruited. Adi was in the band, and they practiced solidly for two weeks before the big day.

The rifle precision display drill entailed wearing white gloves and spinning a mock R4 in all directions, slapping thighs and boots, all while standing in formation. It was very impressive, but a little too much like drum majorettes for my taste, so I didn't volunteer when we were asked. Kerry did, though. He had to practice his butt off! The rifle drill demonstration was rehearsed at the local sports stadium.

Ian and I enjoyed free time while the guys in the band and the rifle display had to practice. All we had to do was practice marching in preparation for the marching display through the town. In the lead-up to the parade, we spent hours practicing marches in and around Oudtshoorn. We were given the run of some of the town's streets and avenues to practice. We marched without weapons. During the last week before the Freedom of Oudtshoorn march, we would set off at dusk, around 18h00, march from the base through the town and back out again, returning after dark at 20h00.

The weather was unusually cold and cloudy when my parents and Kimberly arrived in Oudtshoorn late on Thursday afternoon. Kimberly was staying with her Uncle Alan and his wife in town, but my parents had been unable to find accommodation nearby. It seemed that all the hotels and guest houses had been booked up months in advance in anticipation of this event. They drove on to George, where they stayed in a guest apartment.

On a bright and sunny Friday morning, Infantry School exercised its right to the freedom of Oudtshoorn, and the whole school marched through town looking downright impressive. People stood on the pavements clapping and cheering, and I spotted Kimberly and my parents waving and smiling at me from the sidelines.

After the march, I introduced my parents and Kimberly to Ian and the others. It was now lunchtime and we were allowed to mingle with family and friends in town. The afternoon was free time, set aside for us to be with our families, and my parents took Kimberly and me to a local restaurant. I couldn't keep my hands off Kimberly, I kept touching her and taking her hand under the table. She blushed, trying to remain prim and proper in front of my folks. Lunch was followed by a trip to the foothills of the Swartberg to explore the world famous limestone Cango Caves that penetrate almost four kilometres into the mountain range.

I returned to base in the afternoon to march with the others to the local sports stadium where Infantry School put on a show. Families were seated in the main grandstand, while we sat to the side of the sports field to watch the events.

The passing out parade took place on Saturday morning – a very gung-ho affair. We looked smart in our step-outs, as we marched past the green metal grandstands placed on the grass sports field below the main parade ground with the eyes of our parents, wives and girlfriends on us. We each received our two stars or stripes, one for each shoulder, from the officer commanding, who shook our hands and repeated, "Well done, soldier. You've got your rank. *Mooi so!*" My mom and Kimberly each proudly fastened a silver star to an epaulet as my dad clicked the camera. I was now officially a first lieutenant.

A weapons demonstration took place in the training area on Saturday afternoon. I wasn't involved in the execution of this exercise, so I was allowed to join Kimberly and my folks as they drove along the road to the demonstration in my dad's Volkswagen Passat. I was used to traversing this road at a run or – on days we were more fortunate – by SAMIL 50.

The area was filled with Ratels and Olifant Tanks – the school had pulled out the whole kit and caboodle to impress the visitors. As we entered the area, little packets of yellow Styrofoam earplugs were handed out to us – just like the ones we used on the shooting range. I showed my folks and Kimberly how to insert the earplugs, and advised them to put them in quite firmly, as all hell was likely to break loose.

The demonstration started with platoon weapons, and the guys used several M79 Grenade Launchers – the infamous *snotneus*, Patmors, automatic FN MAG machine guns which glowed red-hot as they put the hammer down, Milkor Multiple Grenade Launchers – the Meerkat, Claymore mines and various grenades. I was impressed by how well the guys who had been roped in to do these demonstrations performed – they made us soldiers proud.

The platoon weapons were followed by displays of the larger ordnance, and even I was caught off-guard by the massive blasts and spectacular displays. As many as eight Milan anti-tank missiles were fired off – during the rehearsal as well as for the main event. I leant over to Kimberly.

"You know," I said. "One of my lieutenants told me that just one of these Milan missiles costs the equivalent of three small BMWs." Her eyes widened. "And they fired off at least four for the rehearsals, too! Can you imagine how much money was blown?"

The man to my right, a staff sergeant, heard me and interrupted. "You're right about the cost of these missiles," he said. "But all this ordnance is close to its shelf-life. It would have to be disposed of, anyway, so it's not such a waste."

The explosions were accompanied by spectacular phosphorous and coloured smoke grenades, lending the atmosphere a surreal effect as the smoke billowed and lingered. The smell of cordite was overpowering. I was amazed. They even had the 81 mm mortar guys there. It was a really sensational event to impress the visitors. What a display!

Kimberly and I chatted a bit more to the staff sergeant, who had been at Oudtshoorn for many years. He was most well-informed about every weapon used at the display and had fascinating stories to tell. Close to the end of the show, he pointed out two little metal crosses with a small oval plaque attached to each, a little distance from where we stood.

"Did you notice those?" he asked.

I shook my head. "I hadn't noticed them, staff." I said. "What are they?"

"Some years ago," he said, "two relatively senior infantry officers were sent to blow up old ammunition here, at this very site. They miscalculated how much was there and remotely detonated the cache from what they thought was a safe distance. The people in Oudtshoorn thought the base itself had blown up! Not a trace of the officers was ever found." He shook his head sadly.

In the evening we were given a couple of hours to go out with parents, wives or girlfriends, but we had to be back that night. Some of the guys and I went to a local night spot with Kimberly in her uncle's car. We had a blast dancing to *Electric Avenue* and *Do You Feel My Love* by Eddy Grant. Two years after the army, I would dance to Eddy Grant's anti-Apartheid anthem *Gimme Hope Jo'anna* at night clubs, disregarding the sentiments of the song. It was just a great party song with a catchy reggae beat. Maybe we too were expressing some rebellious, anti-establishment sentiments. On that night, though, we all celebrated the end of our first year of national service. The guys really *smaak*ed Kimberly, a fact that made me both proud and a little jealous. I acted a bit over-protective, but she lapped up the attention. I still have a photograph of us guys that night, snapped by Kimberly as we all partied.

The guys were expected to report for a special church parade at 09h00 on Sunday morning, after which they would be sent on. Some were already leaving for their new posts, while others were going home. I had been given permission to leave early on Sunday morning to return to Pretoria with Kimberly and my folks.

Sunday, my last morning in Oudtshoorn, finally dawned. Ian and I said our goodbyes.

"Cheers, bud," I said, as I gripped his hand in a firm shake. "All the best, hey." The moment was awkward. We had become close during that first year of national service. But we were still tough guys, and I couldn't bring myself to admit that I would miss my buddy.

"Ja," he grinned. "You too. Stay out of trouble, man!"

My dad's car drew up to the main gate where I stood ready and waiting to take my leave of Infantry School. Somehow, I'd managed to cram all my stuff together into my *balsak*. I heaved it into the boot and took my place in the rear seat beside Kimberly. I didn't look back as my dad pulled away. It was such a relief to be leaving, like I was escaping prison.

I spent the journey home chatting to Kimberly and enjoying the warmth of her presence, slipping into silent retrospection when the other occupants of the car went quiet.

The December pass was good. Kimberly was already on holiday, so we got to spend a lot of time together, relaxing and doing all those things that made me feel normal. I tried not to think too much about the fact that I would soon be leaving again. I was expected at 113 BN before Christmas. Part of me was excited to begin this new chapter, but I also longed to stay here where Kimberly was, where my life was.

Author's Interjection

Herbert Warren, my great-grandfather on my father's side, was born to Hannah Warren in 1873, the illegitimate son of William Booth, founder of the Salvation Army. That Herbert was sired by Booth is disputed by the Booth family, but is certain to be true.

Herbert was never officially recognised as William's heir, and Hannah, William's secret extra-marital plaything of a lower station, was shunned as a whore for bearing a child out of wedlock. Family legend has it, though, that William must have contributed to Herbert's upkeep and Herbert might have been the beneficiary of some kind of inheritance when William was "promoted to glory" in 1912.

As a youngster, Herbert earned money by singing in pubs. At the age of thirteen, he joined the British Navy as a cabin boy and sailed off to see the world. He joined the Derbyshire Rifles, a volunteer corps associated with the British Army, when he was eighteen. It was while he was stationed in County Meath, Ireland, with the Derbyshire Rifles that he met and married Elizabeth Wheeler, and the couple relocated to the Island of Malta in the Mediterranean when Herbert was posted there.

During the second Boer War, Herbert, by then a sergeant major, was called to South Africa. Stationed at Diamond Hill, close to Bronkhorstspruit, he was tasked with rounding up the last of the stray *Boer* guerrillas. Herbert fell in love with South Africa, and he and Elizabeth chose to remain here when the war ended. He was appointed the station master for the South African Railways at Premier Mine near Cullinan around 1910.

Later, Herbert and Elizabeth settled in New Muckleneuk, Pretoria in the house next door to the one I would later grow up in. It was rumoured that William Booth had provided the money, or a large portion thereof, for Herbert to purchase that property. In Pretoria, he lectured aspiring engine drivers at the Pretoria Technical College until retirement, striking up a friendship with his Irish-Afrikaner neighbour, O'Neil, which would last a lifetime.

I have never truly understood what motivated my great-grandparents to settle in Pretoria, the predominantly Afrikaans-speaking capital of South Africa. A neat city that is the seat of the South African government, Pretoria is sometimes compared to Washington DC. It is made up of peaceful, leafy suburbs that are a magnet to a conglomeration of government departments, foreign embassies and corporate and NGO headquarters. Despite a fairly large community of English-speakers in the city, there prevails an attitude of disdain towards us.

I was born to English-speaking parents, second-generation South Africans of Anglo-Irish and Anglo-Dutch heritage, in the aspiring middle-class neighbourhood of Nieuw Muckleneuk. Following a municipal election in which the Nationalists had won by a landslide, the predominantly Afrikaans-run municipality dropped the original "New" of the suburb's name, to replace it with the Dutch word *"Nieuw"*, apparently meaning the same thing. The name now tied the Dutch adjective to the Scottish word "Muckleneuk" – even the smallest things were being changed by the Nationalists after 1963.

The first school at which I scraped my knees on the tarmac while still wearing nappies was the Menorah Nursery School, a Jewish pre-school affiliated to the nearby Shul, Temple Menorah, and run like clockwork by the battleaxe of a principal, Mrs Wolfson. The school conveniently abutted the rear of my parent's property and, curiously, had a policy which allowed goyim like me to attend. A small team of black staff were employed to carry out the menial work of gardening and cooking in the kosher kitchen, but no black children or teachers were allowed.

Pre-school was followed by primary school, and the zoning policy of the Transvaal Education Department (TED) of the time compelled me to attend the nearby Waterkloof Primary School, a whites-only, English-medium, co-ed public school where the kids of working, middle-class parents mixed freely with the offspring of the upper-crust residents of Waterkloof Ridge. Waterkloof Primary was presided over by the strict but genial Principal Salmon.

Afternoons were often spent visiting Arno Naudé, an Afrikaans boy some years older than me who didn't seem to mind English-speakers like my sister and me. Arno had quite a following. Many of the neighbourhood kids would congregate at his parent's house to hear what he was up to. It was with Arno that I learnt how to fly balsa wood planes with small fuel-driven engines that were controlled by strings. I loved flying those planes around in the nearby park and on the local Afrikaans primary school rugby field, finally crashing them into the ground rather than executing a proper landing. Arno also had a massive Scalextric set which we once set up in my folks' back garden. Arno taught me how to make sherbet by mixing Eno with icing sugar. Arno was my hero in those days, and I thought he was a genius.

Later, the Inghams moved into the house across the street, a corner property with a swimming pool. Mark, Justin and their young sister, Lisa emigrated from Britain with their parents, and seemed to me to be worldly-wise and liberal. Mrs Ingham's collection of yoga books boasting photographs of gravity and anatomy-defying poses by infinitely flexible female yogis in the nude were borrowed by her two naughty sons to show me. My senses were totally warped by those images, fascinating and shocking my pre-adolescent mind in equal measures. Mr Ingham's rather more sedate collection of electric model trains that ran on yards and yards of track were more appealing to my impressionable mind, though. Hot summer afternoons were spent swimming and reading war comics with the Inghams. Young Justin benefitted eagerly from my developing skills and passion for the game of soccer. We would sneak over the fence into the grounds of the local Afrikaans primary school to play. One day, the school's headmaster managed to come right up to us before we could skedaddle, filling us with fear of reproach and retribution, only to be told that we were welcome to play there!

My two best friends at primary school were Jeremy Cooke and Lionel Kruger. Halfway through primary school, Lionel and I started to notice the other sex. With cautious curiosity, I started paying attention to the pretty girls around me. Lauren Leathern, a pretty brunette a year ahead of me who could bat a rounders ball like nobody's business! Lesley Rothman, with the longest golden hair I'd ever seen. Susan Johnstone and Lesley-Anne Pedlar. But by far, the fairest of them all was Carol Cunningham, nicknamed "Coo", the most popular girl at school who all the boys took a fancy to. My wild imaginings seemed to be tantalisingly close to realisation when she agreed to dance with me on the night of our Valedictory Dance. Who knows where I found the courage to ask her, but she agreed and I sampled a moment of pure heaven as she lightly rested her arms on my shoulders while Abba crooned about a *Dancing Queen*. Unfortunately, barely a chorus had ended before another boy cut in, and I was shunted to the sidelines from where I watched a succession of sweaty-handed boys cut in on one another to have their moment in the arms of Coo. She must have danced with at least five of us before the song was over!

My first love was an ex-Rhodesian girl, a blonde gymnastic beauty that went by the name of Janet Thompson. We were introduced by her best friend Michelle Swart at Michelle's party in standard six, and we were soon swapping youthful love letters filled with coy anticipation. Janet soon realised she was quite the popular girl and rapidly moved on to the *breekers* and main *manne* at school.

Louise Bilbo became my new friend for while, until she, too, started hanging out with the enemy. I decided the older girls at school were a safer bet, and two blondes, Paige and Elsa, became the unknowing recipients of my remote but attentive affections. In my later years in high school, I took a secret fancy to the girl who would become head girl when I was in matric, Tanya Ritter, who was the daughter of an Afrikaans father and Canadian mother. Near the end of my standard nine year, I met Kimberly.

When I was twelve years old, my parents, wanting to shake off the classist fetters of that old established neighbourhood and start afresh, moved to the relatively new suburb of Lynnwood Glen in Pretoria East. My high school years would be spent at The Glen High, another whites-only, English-medium, co-ed public school, which I was compelled to attend because of the zoning policies of the TED. Those years saw a succession of principals at The Glen, beginning with the affable Mr Batty, who handed over to the disciplinarian Mr Brown, who in turn handed over to the regimented Mr Penzhorn. All the while, the sports-mad deputy head Mr Wilcocks waited in the wings.

Our new neighbours in Lynnwood Glen included two British girls, Carol and Donna Baker, who wasted no time in giving me their attentions. Not the prettiest creatures I'd ever encountered, I was flattered nonetheless, and I couldn't move in our own backyard without being beckoned from across the boundary wall to join them for a chat. This state of affairs came to a rapid end, though, when Mrs Baker entered our yard unannounced one day to retrieve a stray ball from her two sons' soccer game, only to receive a nasty bite to the rump from our dog. A heated exchange with my mom was followed by the eruption of war between the neighbours, leading to us being reported for keeping racing pigeons without licence and me having to destroy the poor birds' cage and let them go. Name-calling became the order of the day, and lost soccer, cricket and tennis balls and other youthful projectiles were never returned unless we surreptitiously sneaked them back under cover of darkness. The Bakers thankfully ended the impasse when they returned to England just before the first democratic elections, probably fearing a black backlash on whites.

To begin with, I excelled in high school. I was top of the class, vying only with an equally competitive girl, and immersed myself in whatever sport I could, playing cricket and soccer and doing athletics. In standard seven, I took seven wickets for the loss of only thirty five runs against Clapham High School – although we still lost the game! Later, I received a cricket trophy in recognition of my skills on the field. I guess I was somewhat more than a realist then – perhaps an optimist – and a leader of sorts among my circle of friends. I had an opinion on everything. I was a model student, infused with potential, and my future looked bright.

By standard nine, however, something had changed. I was riding an oversize motorbike, my Yamaha Enduro 175cc scrambler, Kimberly and I were dating. I was acting macho, and I was on the slippery path downward, receiving poor scores and averages. Memories linger long, and when it came time to choose prefects in matric, I was bypassed for even a nomination, my actions counting against me amongst my teachers and peers.

I thought of myself as an intellectual rebel ... without much of a cause. My dislike of authority had taken root and I questioned every vestige of authority at every turn. In an argument, I would try to out-reason my opponent, sometimes descending into derision and sarcasm when I faced losing an argument. These traits would not serve me well in my two years in the army.

As a child, I felt safe to roam anywhere I pleased. But one couldn't escape the fact that prejudice and segregation were everywhere. The all-white English-speaking community of Pretoria, because of their fear and intolerance of any other group, created an enclave for themselves, which, by virtue of the community's evident sense of self-importance, one would swear was an offshoot of the British Monarchy itself. English-speakers derided anyone who didn't mimic their own pretentious attempts to speak the Queen's English. They were know-it-all, I-told-you-so types who were quick to discriminate against anyone who didn't fit into their view of the world. According to them, Afrikaners were not to be trusted.

A person with an Afrikaans-sounding surname that was clearly English-speaking was deemed okay by the English-speaking community. A surname such as Labuschagne, for example, a throwback from the French Huguenots who settled in the Cape in the eighteenth century, is a common South African family name which is usually pronounced the Afrikaans way, "La-bu-skag-nee" with a guttural "g". If you called yourself "La-bu-shayn", however, and especially if you threw in a cultivated toffee-nosed phonetic inflection for good measure, you were clearly separated from the vile middle- or working-class Afrikaner, and thereby judged to be acceptable to the preposterous

English community.

The insularity of the Afrikaans community did little to advance my bilingualism. As disinclined to mix with outsiders as the English were, Afrikaners sought to retain the purity (however dubious) of their race, and feared contamination from the *rooinekke* and their *duiwel se taal* (devil's language). This suspicion and dislike of the English can largely be attributed to the Anglo-Boer Wars of the late 1800s and early 1900s, during which the *Boers* resisted Imperial oppression and suffered unspeakable injustices at the hands of the British.

My own great grandmother on my father's side, Amy Tossel, who was the first white child to be born in Kimberly, experienced first-hand the cruelty of the British soldiers when she was incarcerated in a concentration camp "for her own safety" during the second Boer War. Amy was English, and her family had made a small fortune digging for diamonds in Kimberly, but the British soldiers cared less. They stole her prized-possession: a necklace with ninety-four gold Kruger Rands.

It is ironic that Afrikaans, known as kitchen Dutch until the middle of the last century, was a language almost certainly first spoken by the Malay slaves in the Cape Colony, who used it to communicate with their Dutch masters. What is never mentioned these days is that it was also referred to as *kombuis kaffer* or "kitchen kaffir", a term which carries some weighty connotations in post-Apartheid South Africa. The first people to call themselves Afrikaners were, in fact, the South African coloureds of the early eighteenth century, and this name was only adopted by the Cape Dutch, *Voortrekkers* and their descendents more than a century later. During the Apartheid years, the number of coloureds who spoke Afrikaans as a first language exceeded the number of whites whose home language was Afrikaans. It would seem that there is more that connects us than divides.

In the sixties and seventies, the prevailing politics were not a concern to the English-speakers in Pretoria, as long as black people were kept in their place and continued to provide cheap labour. We were more interested in doing business and making money. Thanks to the Nationalists, labour would continue to be cheap to acquire and easy to control. If South Africa was going to be successfully developed, it would be due to the ingenuity of white men on the backs and sweat of black labourers.

A few bleeding-heart liberals in the English-speaking camp stuck up for the downtrodden black populace, but much of their concern was feigned and bigoted in any event. For most English-speakers, the fact that black people had been relegated to the locations and homelands suited them wholly. English-speakers, as much as any other white community in the country at the time, subscribed to the view that no right-thinking, progressive society could allow such a common herd to infest the ordered and functional areas occupied by whites. Laws were designed to keep the black man *kraal*ed in order to ensure the status quo was maintained. Black people were kept out of sight, and therefore out of the minds, of white people, who thus supported implicitly the segregation policies of Apartheid.

The confluence of English-speakers and Afrikaners has seldom been a happy one. A legacy of intolerance approaching hostility has permeated every generation following the wars, and considerable resentment remains. I had a few Afrikaans friends in my early years, neighbourhood friends whose parents did not object to them interacting with English speakers, but sadly for me, these tolerant families were few and far between.

I had only one black friend, our maid's grandson, who would come and visit his granny every now and again.

The only other black people I encountered as a child were the domestic workers and gardeners employed by the families of me and my friends. Thousands of domestic workers lived in the tiny outside rooms of Pretoria houses. These rooms were referred to as *kayas*, a Zulu word meaning "home" now bastardised to refer to the second-rate accommodation provided for blacks in the white suburban landscape. Domestic workers – who were commonly referred to as "maids" – cared for white people's children as if they were their own, but by law were not permitted to house family members or friends in their *kayas* overnight or for any length of time. The South African Police, or SAP, were always on the lookout for such disregard of the law, but in any event, their white madams would not have tolerated this sort of fraternising. Maids refrained from gathering in groups of three or more on street corners for fear of regularly patrolling police vans containing white and black policemen who would harass them for their passes and question their intentions of holding such "meetings".

By the time I reached high school, I had no real Afrikaans friends remaining and only infrequent interactions with Afrikaners my own age. Nor did I have any black friends. Perhaps self-righteousness, disdain and aversion had already taken root in me as a pre-adult English-speaker? Certainly, by the time I began university I had no Afrikaans or black friends to speak of.

The only black peer I ever encountered during those years was Harold, who worked in my father's garden on Saturdays.

***

Discrimination has been practiced by one group of humans against others throughout the world, over the entire course of recorded history. We have found reason to bully, exploit and marginalise people on the basis of their religion, race, social standing, language, or culture, both within the boundaries of single countries and across borders. Historically, racial segregation has been practised in China, England, Germany, India, Italy, Latin America, Rhodesia, the United States and South Africa, among others. Racial segregation is still being practiced in modern Fiji, India, Malaysia, Mauritania, the Middle East, Yemen, the United States and yes, even still in South Africa, after almost twenty years of so-called democracy.

The global super-power and supposedly the most advanced nation in the world today, the United States of America, has been practising racial discrimination for centuries. It was only in the 1960s that the full inclusion of blacks into their society was initiated, and old habits die hard ... America still finds herself dealing with the same issues today.

It was only in South Africa that the boldly calculated and poorly misguided move was made to systematise the process of racial segregation by writing it into its laws and edicts, forever sealing the country's fate as the pariah nation of the free world before 1994 and leaving her citizens continually facing the reminders and consequences of those ill-fated practices subsequent to our "liberation". This is the "legacy of Apartheid".

The world has been fixated on unpicking every nuance of Apartheid, but when it comes to nations such as China and Russia, where activities that are found to be distasteful to the free-world are practiced, these countries merely thumb their noses at the critics while the free-world wrings its hands impotently.

***

In the early nineties, as South Africa prepared for the momentous occasion of our first democratic elections, I returned to those old questions that had haunted me before going to the army. Like many others, I suspect, I pondered the meaning of a "new South Africa", a "liberation" organisation at the helm of a newborn democracy. My mental eye inevitably filled with stark images from the "independent" north. I wondered how Apartheid could ever be overcome, how South Africans would ever achieve reconciliation.

Would the new dispensation find it in their hearts to honour the fallen SADF soldiers who had lost their lives in defence of Apartheid? Would they realise that giving recognition to combatants on either side of the divide was imperative for true nation-building? Or would their own militants be the only beneficiaries of tribute?

Would South Africa's "liberation" lead to a modern, reverse Great Trek, with whites leaving the frontier lands that their forefathers had fought for so long ago to return to the Western Cape, the land of their origin on the southern tip of Africa? Or would whites simply depart these shores in great numbers, fearing retribution such as occurred in many other parts of Africa as the colonial shackles were shrugged off? Perhaps the African continent has not seen the last great trek yet?

How would the nation of South Africa look, post-Apartheid? Were we destined to become a nation devoid of virtue, dancing to the beat of criminals and savages, the unread, greedy and vulgar? Would we become the barbarians?

Would the new South African government want the convenience of supping with the Devil, its old communist supporters? I feared this may be the case, imagining the ANC remaining hostage to their past relationships with communist and despotic countries that had supported them during their struggle years. The ANC would need a long spoon!

I wondered if everything that worked at the time, the infrastructure, resource-management, provision of services, would be used as a blueprint for a non-racial and integrated South Africa. Would those things that worked still be functional after democracy?

And what if all my fears for the country were realised? Would South Africans revolt? Would we show the ANC-led government that it can't do as it pleases? Would we be brave enough to vote with our rands: withhold taxes, establish ratepayers' associations, hold the government responsible? Could we do as the Dutch did to the Spanish so long ago: withhold all taxes until the services they should fund are received?

I was realistic enough to know that corruption can afflict all and any. It is a fact of our common humanity. A government could not and should not legislate morality. I knew that the "victors", as always, would rewrite history to suit their own ends, but I hoped the "vanquished" would be given the space to explain themselves.

I certainly would never have pictured a post-Apartheid South Africa in which the ANC's original, noble ideals of justice and equal rights would be replaced with practices diametrically opposite: cronyism, nepotism, corruption, greed, incompetence, continued support for unsavoury allies such as dictatorships and rogue nations, and the immoral political doublespeak of today's ANC-led government. I couldn't have anticipated that this behaviour on the part of our leadership would lead to nothing but the entrenchment of apathy amongst black citizens, cowed and ignorant under the yoke of ANC despotism driven by the desire for total control over the legislature, judiciary, security forces and all organs of state and the media. Worse, that such a government would perpetuate racist policies, now aimed mainly at whites, ironically aided in many instances by their former enemy: scores of now compliant and colluding Afrikaners. How could I have known that the ANC would continue to rely on their struggle credentials? That they would act like a liberation movement, while using the legacy of Apartheid as a continual excuse for poor performance and non-delivery of services to the poor? I could not have predicted that mediocrity would be celebrated and failure promoted, or that this would result in the lowering of life-expectancy and the increase in widespread poverty. South Africans expected a government made up of a collective of dedicated and selfless politicians accountable to the majority, the poor people who elected them. Unfortunately, this is not what we got.

The celebration of one hundred years of the existence of the ANC is an auspicious moment. But achieving liberation for the masses without the concomitant freedoms of economy and education seems like a hollow triumph, an empty commemoration, rubbing salt in the wounds of the expectant and unserved majority.

As the saying goes, the faces may have changed, but the system has, in many respects, remained the same.

My fears for the country seem to have been founded in some truth. South Africa may have thrown off the shackles of Apartheid and her citizens celebrated with the rest of the world at the dawn of the Rainbow Nation, but the fact remains that much of the country's citizens have been failed by the promises made by our early years of democracy. The "freedom" we all looked forward to has become a "free for all", in which the old adage that "the poor get poorer and the rich get richer" holds true. True, that is, for all except for the politically connected few. These fat cats, business people and politicians alike, who have shunned the principles of the Freedom Charter that drove the dismantling of Apartheid, continue to spout the revolutionary rhetoric that inflames the working class, all the while ensuring that their own material ambitions are realised at the expense of the people they claim to speak for.

All we are achieving in our current situation is an ever-increasing polarity between races and classes. Although Apartheid has been all but overcome in terms of legislation, our leaders' inadequate attempts at redressing the imbalances of the past have done nothing but further entrench the hatred and disunity that has come to characterise our land. The much-vaunted Rainbow Nation has steadily lost its lustre.

True democracy demands an understanding of responsibility. Freedom can only be achieved within the reasonable limits of morality and goodwill. Every South African continues to be affected by the deeply dysfunctional thought processes that Apartheid engendered, but the current feedback-loop train of thought and analytical processes is itself tainted by the legacy of Apartheid, and as such, is nothing but a diversion from the real work of growing this land.

It is time that the ANC is relegated to the dustbin of history, just as the Nationalist Party has been. It is time that we make allowance for more progressive parties to emerge and take over the reins, parties who have proper governance as their focus, no longer harking back to any credentials borne out of the liberation struggle. The revolutionary has no place in our maturing democracy. He is a relic and out-of-touch with modern South Africa and the changing world in which we find ourselves. But, like the Nat supporters of old, the struggle loyalties linger long.

I am no politician. I am merely a concerned citizen who has witnessed a changing South Africa. But I am alarmed at how the general population have adopted a general wait-and-see attitude towards the governance of this country, pinning their hopes on the chance that things will improve rather than actively changing allegiance and casting meaningful votes for parties that could genuinely make a difference.

South Africans need to be encouraged and supported to engage in moving the country forward. Unity between our citizens is imperative. Our country is plagued with urgent ills, and our racialising of these issues serves no observable purpose. By continuing to view our circumstances through lenses clouded by the pall of Apartheid, we lose sight of the fact that solving the problems we face in our land would benefit every single one of us, not just "the poor blacks" or "the previously (historically) disadvantaged". Every South African must work to break free of the restraints imposed on us by our history in order to find our common hopes and dreams for the future. This is what our constitution aims to provide for us, however inadequately these principles are being put into practice.

South Africans need to grasp the notion that improving the lives of my fellow-citizens improves my own in direct proportion. To truly rid the country of the hangover of our past, we need to remove the artificial boundaries that divide us on grounds established by the architects of Apartheid, in order to meaningfully and successfully address the issues that plague our society. We need to accomplish these things so that every single individual faces a future that is an improvement on their past.

Certainly, our leadership is inadequate and indisputably plagued by festering wounds – greed, cronyism, lip-service paid to upliftment in the face of rampant corruption, to mention but a few – but these things will never change as long as the public is engaged in petty banter about race and Apartheid. This ongoing dispute, invoking reverse discrimination or what might be termed something akin to "revenge-heid", only serves the interests of those who wish to keep us all occupied and looking the other way as they fleece the public coffers to line their pockets and manipulate the systems to ensure the continued benefit and protection of themselves and their own.

We live in a land of huge potential. Finding our commonality is imperative for the success of our nation.

Chapter 19

It was Sunday 14 December 1986. Travelling in a northeasterly direction on the N1 in Roberta's funky little blue Renault 5, I passed through Naboomspruit, then Potgietersrus and on to Pietersburg. Roberta had kindly allowed me to borrow her car to get to 113 Battalion. I would be returning to Pretoria in the middle of January to attend my sister's wedding, so I wouldn't have the car for long.

Turning onto the R71 just before Pietersburg, I headed east past the Pietersburg Skydiving Club, where I had jumped out of that plane, and on past the Zion Christian Church stronghold of Moria. Soon after passing Haenertsburg near the Ebenezer Dam, the road drops dramatically in a series of twists and turns through afforested land on the edge of the escarpment, past the picturesque Magoebaskloof, and through the town of Tzaneen. Leaving Tzaneen in an almost easterly direction, still on the R71, I passed through large white-owned citrus orchards which gave way to several rural black settlements.

On this first trip, I inadvertently took a tar road that runs parallel to and just north of the *Groot Letaba Rivier* or Great Letaba River. Had I known, I might have continued a short distance to a turnoff designated R529, near the settlement of Letsitele. Fortuitously, after some distance, there appeared a small signpost indicating the direction to Letaba Ranch Game Reserve. Having turned right, I soon crossed a bridge over the Great Letaba River, where I turned left onto the tarred surface of the R529. The Great Letaba River runs parallel to and just north of R529 for some distance. Before long I came across a holiday resort in the middle of nowhere, called Eiland ("Island"), which lies on the southern bank of the Great Letaba River, surrounded by the beautiful bushveld scenery of the Hans Merensky Nature Reserve. When Eiland first opened its doors to the public, it was a whites-only family camping and day resort, boasting natural mineral and hot water springs with pools. Barely having passed Eiland, the tarred road suddenly gave way again to a wide red-brown sandy road. It didn't escape me that the tarred road designated as R529 was there only to serve as a convenient access to Eiland for white holiday-makers.

I travelled onwards, trailing a cloud of dust behind me, past one turn-off to my right and then crossing two unmarked and dangerous intersections, near the settlements of Nondweni and Mahale, respectively, eventually arriving at the main gate of the Letaba Ranch Game Reserve late in the afternoon. The gate was opened for me by a rather inattentive and sloppily-dressed black game ranger, who was part of a group of locally-sourced staff that served at the game ranch.

The Letaba Ranch Game Reserve, located about twenty kilometres north of the mining town of Phalaborwa, is today incorporated into the Kruger National Park. In those days, it only abutted the Kruger National Park on its eastern boundary, and it was strange to me that 113 Battalion's base camp was contained within the reserve.

Passing through the Letaba Ranch Game Reserve gate, bearing left at a fork in the road, I travelled almost two kilometres on a gravel-strewn drive, arriving at yet another barrier. A small black and white signboard mounted on the boom announced my arrival at 113 BN, together with the strange insignia of the battalion: a blue shield bearing a pair of yellow ladles joined by a chain. I was met at the boom by two black infantrymen, nutria-clad and casually armed with R4s. I wore civvies that day, as the safety and security policy of the SADF forbid conscripts from wearing their uniforms when travelling privately, unless expressly required by a higher authority to do so. The guards politely asked me my business there and instructed me to sign a register before allowing me access to the base.

"Welcome to 113 BN, lieutenant!" one said as they both saluted me. "Just so you know, us Shangaans also call it Letaba Ranch" as he pointed his finger back and forth between him and his buddy, grinning broadly. I grinned back and entered.

Coordinates: 23°39'34.41"S 31°03'02.18"E

Hardly anyone was present on my arrival at battalion headquarters. I scouted through the camp, coming upon a series of long mobile homes on wheels, or caravans, each containing a number of small cabins. Just a stone's throw away was a rather uneven parade ground which sported patches of sand intermingled with flattened wild grass. Guessing that these were the officers' living quarters, I persuaded the sergeant on duty to give me a key to what appeared to be the best of the unused, uninhabited and sun-faded mobile homes, unlocked the door and dumped my kit in one of the hot and stuffy cabins.

The camp was perched on the eastern bank of the Great Letaba River. The officers' quarters occupied the western and southwestern boundaries of the base, close to the entrance to the south. I emerged from the caravan, and decided to walk along the riverbank, which was dotted with large and beautiful indigenous riparian trees. From this bank to the thickly vegetated opposite side, the riverbed reached more than a hundred metres, but the water in the river itself was only about twenty-five metres wide and flowing sluggishly. The heavy summer rains, which typify the climate of this part of the world, were still due.

Reaching the northwestern point of the camp, I came upon the officers' mess hall, recreation room and bar, which were contained in a large, thatch-roofed structure, partly built on wooden poles in case of flooding, causing the building to jut out an elevated patio towards the river. Standing outside the officers' mess and looking eastwards, I could see several low buildings, a small sign on a wall indicating that these were the administrative offices. Following the eastern boundary of the camp southwards with my eyes, I saw, partially obscured by a corrugated sheet metal and diamond mesh fence, the quartermaster's stores, and behind that, the mess hall and recreation hall for the troops. In the southeastern corner of the camp I could see a number of long prefabricated buildings or bungalows, which I took to be the troops' barracks.

More than twenty-five years have passed since that long-ago day when I went exploring my new surroundings in that base in the Letaba Ranch Game Reserve, and the only remaining evidence that 113 BN ever existed is the almost circular shape of the original camp, demarcated by roads and paths which have not yet grown closed with vegetation. The buildings, which were all prefabricated, or constructed from wood or steel panels, have long since been dismantled; perhaps taken apart by the SADF in its last days, or by the new government, in its systematic environmental programme of rehabilitating old SADF bases that were used as operational training areas, or stripped for construction material by the locals. Some concrete floors may remain, but they have most likely been broken up – whether by hand or nature. Today, 113 BN is all but a memory for those who were there, its base a lymphoma excised from the landscape. The scar remains, but the passage of time will ensure that it shrinks and shrinks, until it is necessary to scratch at the surface to find its trace.

After I had been wandering about the camp for about an hour, who should arrive but none other than Gavin Fish. He strode towards me with his hand outstretched, grinning. We greeted each other with the warmth that accompanies the chance meeting of acquaintances in a strange place. Gavin's wish had been granted. He was not sent to any unit that would require him to carry out urban coinops in the black townships, but to Letaba Ranch, a rural posting, as he had requested. I was relieved to see him.

Soon Gavin and I were joined by several other guys from Oudtshoorn. Anton Maas, who had been in Platoon 3 with me, was there. Ross Johnstone and Rick Parfitt were also all officers from Infantry School. With a few exceptions, such as my friend, the *plaasjapie* from Malmesbury, Lieutenant Maas, and two other pleasant but unremarkable Afrikaans blokes from Infantry School, we were a large contingent of English-speaking looties. Later we met two one-pip loots, Mark Cowie and Jason Smith, who were both imports from other SAI camps. There were no NCOs, and we would shortly learn that, apart from one or two senior white PF NCOs, all the corporals and sergeants at 113 BN were black.

I suggested the guys all get keys to the caravans from the sergeant on duty. We discovered that the best mobile homes and some "nice" prefabricated bungalows, those positioned under the shady trees on the river's edge, were already occupied by the loots that were the previous year's intake. The guys selected their accommodation from what remained, and we settled in as best we could. Gavin, Ross, Parfitt and I shared the caravan closest to the entrance to the base.

The first of the resident loots to return to camp that Sunday was Lieutenant Ehlers, a dark-haired young Afrikaner who stood at 6'5" with size fifteen feet – talk about a giant among men! A one-pip lieutenant and July intake from the previous year, he was friendly and helpful; I suppose we would have called him a tame Dutchman at Infantry School. He warned us to watch out for the resident two-pippers, who were due to get back to camp later that evening. They had almost finished their two years' duty and Ehlers told us that they were an arrogant and dismissive bunch. Needless to say, they were all Afrikaans, to a man.

As the sun started to dip, two corporals came by to invite us to eat in the troops' mess hall at 18h00, as there would be no dining service in the officers' mess that evening. As the two-pippers had not yet returned from their pass-outs and the PF officers were only due in camp at 07h00 the following morning, we decided against donning uniforms and made our way across the parade ground in our civvies. On entering the mess hall, we were greeted by distant and somewhat malevolent stares from the black troops gathered there.

I nodded and smiled at some of the guys as we made our way uncomfortably to an empty table, but I had the distinct impression that we were not welcome. The food was the standard army fare accompanied by custard and jelly – certainly not on par with what we were used to at Infantry School, but we were glad to have it anyway.

After supper, we retired to the caravans and caught up with each other. There was no hot water or electricity, and the beds were without linen. After a cold shower, I spent a restless night in my sleeping bag, tossing and turning on an unfamiliar mattress, as much from the stifling heat as from being plunged yet again into an unknown situation. I calmed myself by thinking that at least now I would be the one giving orders as a commissioned officer.

I awoke to a cloudless Monday morning, shaved in cold water and donned my browns which were still adorned with Infantry School insignia. Just before 06h00, the other loots and I went to the officers' mess for breakfast. Coffee and rusks were waiting at a self-service table for us, and our meal was shortly served, comprising greasy eggs, bacon and fried tomatoes. We were upbeat with expectation, and the conversation was light hearted.

As we were finishing our breakfast, a group of five two-pippers arrived. We greeted them and one or two seemed friendly enough, but soon these were joined by a guy who seemed to be the leader of the pack. He strutted into the mess hall with self-importance and I immediately felt the mood amongst the others change to palpable disdain towards us, the new guys.

"Lieutenant Contempt", as I lost no time in labelling him, was shorter and more portly than the others, but what he lacked in physical stature, he made up for in derisory comment.

"*O, kyk wat het ons hier,*" he said in an irritating falsetto ("Oh, look what we have here!"). *"Die nuwe ouens!"* ("The new guys!") He gave a loud and forced laugh. His voice changed to harsh and commanding, *"Staan op, een-sterre! Salueer!"* he insisted we should stand and salute him. We all looked up from our plates with *Oh, come off it!* expressions. I had to suppress a chuckle. I guess he was hoping for a bunch of anxious and overeager newbies to fall for his bluff and jump up to salute him, just so that he could sneer *"Wat die donner dink julle doen julle?"* He hadn't counted on a couple of English-speaking, smartass officers from Infantry School.

Ross spoke to him in pointedly polite Natal English, "I believe we're seated at the table, *sir*," the final word was loaded with scorn. "A salute would be uncalled-for." Lieutenant Contempt's expression changed to mocking.

"Oh. Englishmen, are we?" He said with a laughable attempt at an

English accent. Pulling a chair out from the table at which his mates sat, he straddled it backwards, leaning his folded arms across the back. Facing us, he gave us a look dripping with conceit.

"Well, well, well." I wondered if he saw the amused glances we exchanged amongst ourselves. He wagged a finger in our general direction. *"Julle ouens lyk 'n bietjie nat agter die ore."* You guys look a bit wet behind the ears, he told us. *"Hier gaan julle by die kaffers afkak, Boet!"* he said, talking to all of us, but looking at me. You lot are going to suffer with the kaffirs here, he said. Turning the chair around, he rested an ankle over his knee and rubbed his chin. Switching to English, he said, "But yous are *mos rooinekke*," he said, butchering the language unforgivably. "Maybe yous will enjoy it here, with your kaffir brothers, eh?" He and his buddies laughed. *"Miskien sal julle nogal van hierdie houtkoppe hou? Kry vir julle!"* he spat ("Maybe you'll really like these wooden heads? Well, you lot can have them!"). They hooted and chortled at this. I got the distinct feeling he was continually focussing on me as he spoke. Was he threatened by my imposing height? Or insulted by my obviously English ways? Or did he regard me as the leader of the new loots? He really riled me, and I wanted to get up and punch him one! Somehow I maintained my dignity and composure, and gave him a dismissive look instead. We ate in uncomfortable silence.

Breakfast finished, I left the mess hall with the other loots. There was much muttering amongst us when we got outside. We all agreed that those two-pippers were a bunch of wankers, especially Lieutenant Contempt. We made our way to the officers' caravans and hung around just out of sight with a view of the parade ground on our left and the entrance to the camp on our right, observing the activities unfolding in the base and keeping our eyes peeled for the arrival of the PFs. The PFs stayed in town in Phalaborwa and travelled just over twenty kilometres to 113 BN each weekday. Lieutenant Ehlers had told us they seldom came to the camp on weekends, and if they did, only on a Saturday morning.

First to arrive were two captains, who parked their little sedans behind the admin buildings and disappeared inside. We assumed these were admin-types. Next came a compact, faded-blue BMW, out of which emerged a short and wiry major with light hair and a blond moustache – he looked like a mixture between a fox and a ferret. Last to arrive, in a big Mercedes, was what looked like the battalion commander. He was a large man, easily as tall as me, but at least twice my width. He had pitch-black hair, a black moustache and a very dark complexion. His expression matched his dark colouring, and he looked as though he might thunder at any moment.

It seemed to be a given in the SADF that white PFs – especially NCOs from the rank of sergeant upwards and all officers – wore moustaches. Perhaps it was the *manne* factor, as if sporting a Magnum PI was an indication of the wearer's machismo. I wondered if the guys ever compared notes, debating the merits of the down-comb compared to the centre-part, or advised each other on the best *snor*-maintenance techniques. I just thought upper-lip adornment looked ridiculous, especially when it provides visual evidence of the moustachioed man's last meal.

Gathering up the courage, we marched over to where the two ranks were talking on the little concrete walkway outside the admin offices. We saluted and introduced ourselves.

"*Welkom, manne,*" the sandy ferret-face said. "*Ek is Majoor Muller, en Kommandant Jooste*" at this he indicated towards the large man on his left, "*is ons bataljon kommandant.*" We engaged in awkward small talk in a mixture of their broken English and our poor Afrikaans, until, just before 07h00, scores of troops began assembling on the parade ground. The troops were followed by the black ranks: several company sergeant majors, sergeants, dozens of corporals and lance jacks. Forming into about six to twelve blocks of three rows each, I calculated the battalion to number at least three companies, possibly more. Promptly at 07h00 a company sergeant major brought the whole ensemble to attention. Another company sergeant major politely asked us to form up on the parade ground to one side of the companies gathered there, and we complied. The two-pippers then joined the scene and each one stood by what appeared to be their respective platoons.

Under the watchful gaze of us one-pippers, the *oranje-blanje-blou* of the South African flag was raised and everyone saluted. The incongruity of the situation was not lost on me: these black soldiers saluting the flag that was a symbol of their oppression. I wondered if the same thought occurred to anyone else.

Orders were then given for parade inspection, and, lo and behold, Lieutenant Contempt himself was the lieutenant on duty, reporting with his company sergeant major to the commandant. His cockiness made sense now.

While we were on parade, at around 07h30, a number of cars began pulling into camp and parking in front of the admin offices. With astonishment, we watched as the doors opened to reveal a procession of young and middle-aged, smartly dressed white women who click-clacked into the admin offices in their heels. We soon learned that these women were civilians who worked in administration and stores. One woman in particular stood out as a real beauty. She was tall and slender with fine features and raven hair. I watched as she made her way to the door, flicking her hair and stealing a glance towards the parade ground as she crossed the threshold.

After parade, we were instructed to go to the administrative offices in order to open up our personal files. After watching the arrival of the young women and following their passage into the admin building, we were only too happy to oblige! It was like a breath of fresh air to deal with these young lovelies in the midst of the overwhelmingly stale and masculine military environment. The long-legged brunette was called Stienie, and she told me that she was married and lived in Phalaborwa with her husband. She was sweet and friendly, and I found it hard to concentrate in her presence. After providing various personal and military details, we tried to drag the process out as long as possible, offering the ladies our histories and questioning them about theirs. The women began to feel relaxed in our company, and soon they confided in us that they were all rather afraid of Commandant Jooste. He was moody and could fly into a rage at the slightest provocation – it seemed he was quite the dictator. An image of the commandant began to take shape in my mind. He was clearly a man not to be trifled with. If you found yourself on the wrong side of him, he could make your life hell. For the duration of December and whenever we were in camp the following year, Stienie was always very friendly towards us when we encountered her.

After meeting the administrative requirements, we were told to go to the stores to collect our new kit. If Infantry School had required us to be sharp and carry out every instruction on the double, 113 BN was almost the complete opposite. Here, everything seemed to be done at half the pace. We ambled into the quartermaster's stores and found it relatively neat, but with large piles of various kit items all over the place, as if there was insufficient shelving to store it all. We were handed our bits and pieces, and I looked in amazement at the old canvas webbing in my arms, just like the webbing I had seen in the seventies *Vasbyt* pictures at Infantry School. At Infantry School we were kitted out with the latest apparel. Without thinking, I said, "Are you serious? Are we using this old stuff?"

To my surprise, a corporal behind the counter came back with, "Oh. No, actually. Come this way, lieutenant." I followed him to some hidden shelves near the back of the store. He indicated to a shelf full of webbing. I couldn't believe my eyes as I pulled at the contents of the shelves. It was the same as what we had used at Infantry School. "The old webbing is for the use of troops and NCOs," the corporal explained. "This is for the officers' use." Apartheid made its presence known in logistics and supply. I would come to learn that discrimination was rife at 113 BN, and it was seldom overt.

The emblem on my green beret now changed from the *bokkop*, or springbok head, over a green and off-white bar, to a red-orange flame on a brass background over a blue and yellow bar.

That afternoon, the two-pippers left 113 BN, bringing an end to their two years of conscription. We had the good fortune of only having to tolerate their company for a day! The following day was 16 December, the Day of the Vow, a public holiday commemorating the Battle of Blood River and practically a holy day on the calendar of the Afrikaner nation. With hardly a goodbye, the two-pippers had handed in their kit, emptied their cabins and left, hoping to get home as quickly as possible before the holiday. We scrambled to get the best mobile homes and bungalows they had just vacated.

No PFs or civilians were at the camp the next day. In our civvies, we played pool and drank beer in the officers' recreation hall.

For the next three days we ambled around the camp, regularly going from the administrative offices to the stores and back again. Each morning at 11h00 we were given a Tsonga class by Sergeant Matimba Maluleke, a smart and well-groomed black man in his mid- to late thirties. The idea was to teach us basic conversational Tsonga, which is the language of the Shangaans, so that we could communicate better with our troops. It was tough going. After a few days the proposed advanced class was dropped, with the dapper and well-educated Sergeant Maluleke telling the major that we must all be illiterate! As with all language beginners, we quickly picked up some of the more interesting words that could be used to good effect, but rumour of our lack of verbal skills soon ricocheted around the camp, and wherever we went we were met with knowing grins. Even the commandant and NCOs were not above giving us looks of sarcastic amusement.

We had only been at Letaba Ranch for a few days when Mark Cowie, who was operating in another company, called me over and asked me to go with him to take a look at the troops' toilets. Arriving at the ablution facilities, I discovered all the doors locked.

"Man, why are they locked?" I asked him, baffled. Cowie was unlocking them one-by-one.

"Take a look," he said, disgusted. I stepped into a cubicle, looked into the toilet bowl. To my amazement, it was filled with rocks.

"What in the blazes is this about?" I asked Cowie, going into the next toilet, and then the next, and the next. All the toilets were similarly trashed.

"It's the troops," Cowie said. "They've been wiping their arses with rocks!" He was outraged. "Like they're in the bush, man! I decided to lock the toilets. If that's the way they want to behave, then they can crap in the bush, just like they're used to."

"Look, Mark," I couldn't help it. I was laughing quietly at the absurdity of it: the ruined toilets and Cowie's indignant fury. "Let's go have a chat to your company sergeant major. I reckon someone must just make sure the troops have toilet paper and know how to use it." It took some time and gentle ragging, but I eventually got Cowie to see the funny side of the incident. Soon we were both laughing, but I couldn't help feeling that the guys had been let down by their NCOs. It seems like such a basic right, toilet paper. I couldn't understand why the troops hadn't just asked for more, but they had obviously made the best plan they could under the circumstances. I made a mental note to speak to our Company Sergeant Major Mthombeni about the situation.

At the end of our first week at Letaba Ranch, Major Muller told us looties to prepare to meet our company captain, who was expected in camp late Sunday or early Monday. That weekend, as we had no formal company duties yet, and the NCOs were dealing with the troops, the loots decided to treat ourselves to a night at Eiland. We felt we owed it to ourselves to have a looties' weekend off before starting with the rigours of our second year of national service. Six of us departed in a couple of cars on Saturday morning, and we spent our time at the resort resting, braaing, reading, swimming in the hot and cold pools and drinking beer and listening to music. We returned to camp on Sunday afternoon refreshed.

Captain Chris Engelbrecht finally arrived late on Sunday afternoon. He was hardly in the camp when we got the message that he wanted to meet us. He was an interesting character – in all the time I was to know him, I could never figure out if he was trying to become a PF or if he was doing a longer stint to reduce his quota of camps for the future. National service worked like this: After two years of unbroken service, a serviceman would have one year off, during which no service was expected. Thereafter, 720 days of service had to be contributed in the form of yearly camps of one to three months long. This could mean as many as eight to ten extra years of army camps after completing your first two years of service. Not a pleasant thought for a young man.

Captain Engelbrecht was of Afrikaans origin, in the vein of a *verligte*

Afrikaner. Us English-speaking guys would most likely have labelled him a very tame Dutchman. He was not the most handsome chap; he resembled a blond-haired cross between Charlie Chaplin and Albert Einstein. He sported a large, slightly hooded nose above two small puffy lips, topped off with a droopy blond moustache. His eyes were small, peering from behind thin-rimmed spectacles. He wasn't very tall, and verged on the portly side of stocky. He lisped ever so slightly and had a tendency, when talking animatedly, to let the spittle fly. Physical appearance aside, Captain Engelbrecht had the most wonderful character, which soon endeared him to us all.

On Monday morning after parade, Captain Engelbrecht told us to make ourselves especially presentable for the following day's parade, which meant highly-polished boots and clean browns. Having not yet assumed any duties with the troops, we reckoned we would be given orders to formally take over our individual platoons. With the two-pippers having left, the company sergeants and corporals were drilling the men and overseeing their activities.

Mid-morning, we were bundled into a couple of SAMIL 50 trucks with the troops and driven along the gravel road towards Phalaborwa. A few kilometres out of base, the trucks stopped at a desolate area to the right of the road that must have belonged to the SADF. Here the troops were assembled, and Captain Engelbrecht asked us lieutenants to provide the troops with demonstrations of and instructions for the use of various weapons. First, I showed the men how to use a 75 mm rifle grenade. Later, wooden crates displaying Portuguese writing on the side were brought off one of the SAMILs, and when they were opened, I saw they contained high explosive hand grenades and M79 *snotneus* grenades concealed in separation trays, covered with curly wooden packing shavings. These grenades were of a type I had not before encountered, but looked similar to those we had trained with at Infantry School. I wondered if these were salvaged from the enemy in some cross-border military operation in Angola. Perhaps the SADF was disguising its imported weapons from SA-friendly sanction-busting countries. Or maybe they were attempting to disguise weapons containers locally. My mind echoed with speculation.

The training exercise was a great success. At lunchtime, a SAMIL 20 arrived from 113 BN with a meal for us all and mango juice in large silver urns. I leant against one of the trucks as I ate, surveying the surrounding bushveld, and thought to myself that things could be worse. I felt that I might actually be able to make a difference with these troops.

On Tuesday morning, when the troops had been mustered on the parade ground, we were nominally placed in charge of a platoon each. Standing at our platoons with our designated corporals, we were called by name, one-by-one, by Captain Engelbrecht, to receive our two-star epaulets. My name was called and I marched up to the Commandant, saluted him, and then shook his hand as gave me my bush-epaulets: two yellow stars each on two shoulder boards of soft brown material. The commandant acknowledged each of us in turn by mispronouncing our surnames, except for Maas and the other two Afrikaans looties. I was now officially a second lieutenant. We returned to the weapons demonstration area that morning feeling pretty chuffed with our two pips!

On Wednesday morning we learnt that all the troops would be going home for Christmas and New Year, as specified in the five-year contract they had each signed with the SADF. The vast majority of the troops were Shangaan, staying in and around Giyani and Namakgale, while some lived as far north as the "homeland" of Venda, and others as far south as Acornhoek. After lunch we watched as the men boarded several SAMIL 50s in their civvies, their December paycheques in their pockets. Turned out in their smartest shoes and pants, they cheerfully waved goodbye to us with a chorus of *"Totsiens, luitenant"* as the trucks rumbled out of the gate and out of sight, billowing dust clouds behind them that hung in the hot air for an age.

With the camp suddenly emptied of troops, the PFs soon followed suit, driving out of base and home to their families for the holidays. With a skeleton staff of NCOs on duty, our daily duties were now suspended, and we wondered around in casual wear, enjoying the peace and quiet of the deserted camp. On Thursday, Christmas day, we played pool and drank beer in the officers' recreation hall. The sounds of Juluka's 1982 hit *Scatterlings of Africa* and Toto's 1982 hit *Africa* played off a lootie's tape-deck as we sat on the patio of the officers' mess, watching fish jumping, antelope drinking and the sun sink slowly over the Great Letaba River. It was pleasant and relaxing.

We watched night fall on the river as Klymaxx's 1986 hit single *I Miss You* wafted across the bushveld, and I wished I was home with Kimberly.

We really got to know Captain Engelbrecht that evening. He was a truly engaging person, asking about us and our families with genuine interest. He told us that he had been a teacher at Clapham High School in Pretoria, and that he kept contact with several of his pupils on a regular basis. He seemed to have a way with the ladies, too! That evening after supper in the officers' mess, he showed us letters he had received from some of his female students to prove the point. From that day, he became affectionately known to us as "Cappie".

Cappie must have been sizing up our contingent of loots, because he soon made a decision, choosing four of us to be the looties of his company, Charlie Company: Gavin, Ross, Maas and me.

Mid-morning Boxing Day, the commandant arrived in camp wearing his light-blue and yellow, military-issue 113 BN tracksuit. He didn't appear to be in a good mood. He called Captain Engelbrecht for a meeting and they disappeared into his office. A short while later, Cappie emerged looking bewildered but elated. He instructed Charlie Company to pack up our gear, put on our browns and prepare to leave the camp. Together with several NCOs, we loaded a couple of SAMIL 50s and a SAMIL 20 with food rations, camp equipment and metal and wooden crates containing a variety of ordinance and munitions, including a whole lot of R4s.

The SAMILS started their engines and we prepared to clamber onboard. "Cappie," I asked, "where are we going?"

To which he replied, "We're off to Gumbu Mine, my friends!" We had no clue what or where Gumbu Mine was, but Cappie's enthusiasm was contagious. "It seems," he continued, rubbing the palms of his hands together, "that the commandant conspired with the major to have us vacate the camp."

"What did he say, Cappie?" Maas asked in a thickly accented brei. Cappie chuckled.

"He said, *'Vat jou manne en weg is jy, Kaptein! Weg, weg ek sê – uit my basis uit!'*"

Chapter 20

Exiting the main gate of Letaba Ranch Game Reserve, our small convoy of brown-liveried trucks turned right a short five kilometres on, onto a sandy road at the intersection before the village of Mahale. We soon crossed the Great Letaba River and travelled due north on a network of gravel roads, passing the Kruger National Park on our right. As our convoy travelled all the way up through Giyani and beyond, locals, young and old, smiled and waved to us as we drove by. As I waved and smiled in return, I wondered at this friendly acceptance of the brown uniforms on SAMILs. According to the outlawed black liberation movements – ANC, PAC, AZAPO and others the SADF was the agent of the Apartheid government, the military might by which the legislation of oppression was enforced. Were these friendly locals untouched by the political rhetoric? Could they be genuinely accepting of us?

At the request of the NCOs travelling with us, the SAMILs made brief stops at several of their villages en route so that they could pick up some personal effects. These interludes made me feel a little uneasy; I wondered what kind of reception an uninvited convoy of SAMILs carrying soldiers would get from these communities. But Cappie had no qualms about our visits amongst the locals, and carried out some splendid comops while we were there.

We passed through deeply rural parts of Venda, across mountainous terrain on winding gravel roads which seemed to have no end, until we came to the eastern portion of the Madimbo Corridor, a narrow section of land spanning nearly thirty thousand hectares and running alongside the Limpopo River in the far north of the province. Having no foreknowledge of the history of the Madimbo Corridor, in time I would learn that the Apartheid government had forcibly removed the original Venda and Shangaan inhabitants of this area from the late sixties until the early eighties. Having thus dispossessed the locals of their land, the SADF established a military restricted zone in an attempt at curbing guerrilla cross-border movements. These removals and the so-called "betterment strategy" of the Apartheid government – in which people were banished to the homelands based on their assumed shared ethnicity – appeared to have achieved the Apartheid state's objective of divide-and-rule. The legacy of this strategy sadly lasts beyond the demise of Apartheid, and the original inhabitants are to this day pitted against one another in a dispute over who has the right to lay claim to the region. The Madimbo Corridor has been described as a place of congregation which has been turned into a zone of exclusion.

Aside from the fertile regions on the banks of the great river, the Madimbo Corridor featured semi-arid terrain with sparse vegetation, pedologically characterised as sandveld, with generally poor to medium fertile soils and limited surface water sources. The Corridor was bordered to the drier west by private, white-owned, commercial farmland and the town of Messina, and to the marginally wetter east by the Kruger National Park. Messina was the most important town of the region, and a strategic bastion of the SADF.

By late afternoon, we came to the sisal line barrier. This man-made barrier was composed of a roughly fifteen metre deep strip of tough and pointed sisal plants, protected on each side by a fine square-mesh fence topped off with outward pointing strands of razor wire. The cleared planting area for the sisal line and the gravel observation road to its south are both still evident today, although the plants that formed the barrier are all but totally eradicated. Crossing over the observation and service road, the trucks stopped while Cappie alighted to unlock the two double gates in succession so that we could cross the barrier. Following a dirt road, we soon turned off to the left onto a narrower dirt road, which descended for some distance before twisting and turning towards a dense area of trees and thick bush. We were approaching the Limpopo River.

Coordinates: 22°20'02.98"S 30°59'40.64"E

Arriving at Gumbu Mine, we dismounted the SAMILs and stood in stunned disbelief. We found ourselves in the ruins of a compound of small mining houses, their crumbling white and grey walls pockmarked with numerous bullet holes. The faded red and grey corrugated iron roofs of some of the little houses were partially or completely missing, the rest had been shot through so that the late afternoon sun spilled through them like colanders. On a nearby kopje about a kilometre north of the compound, we could see what little was left of the mine manager's white-walled house, partially obscured by trees and bushes.

"Surely you're joking, Cappie?" I broke the astonished silence. Cappie just grinned.

"Make yourselves at home, my friends," he said. Pointing at a larger building close to the entrance to the compound, he added, "I dibs the room adjacent to the ops room!"

Gumbu Mine, it turned out, had been used over the years by various SADF units, mostly Special Forces, for live weapons training exercises and as a launch pad into Zimbabwe for covert military operations. Due to the latter-day rehabilitation of Gumbu Mine, incorporating that anthropological footprint into an environmental reserve, there is no evidence of its cluster of buildings today, just a semblance of a track that was once the road leading into the camp, and the marks left by a bulldozer where those little houses once stood. This collection of houses remained Gumbu Mine to the men of 113 BN, to whom this was temporary home many times over the years. As regulars at Gumbu Mine, the NCOs had already chosen the houses they were to occupy for our stay here. Gavin and I chose the remains of a little house that was still mostly intact, slightly elevated on a concrete slab, just a few houses on from the command centre or ops room that Cappie had chosen. Ross and Maas took the other nearly intact house. We scouted about a bit to get our bearings, then ate a cold supper and prepared our new homes as best we could.

Night fell and we lit candles in our houses, but this was almost unnecessary. The camp was glowing from the light of the full moon, the sky a luminous backdrop silhouetting the kopjes which surrounded the site. In the ops room it was all lights shining with a diesel-powered generator running outside, battery-powered lamps on standby in case of a generator malfunction. Cappie had prepared the room with 1:10 000 maps of Gumbu Mine and 1:50 000 maps of the surrounding area. He gathered us together to brief us about our responsibilities here, but orders were light as the troops weren't around. The key things, Cappie stressed to us, were to be on our guard and to carry our R4s with us at all times. After the briefing, we sat companionably in the ops room, drinking coffee and eating rusks and chatting.

Surprisingly, until the New Year when the troops returned, guards were not posted at Gumbu Mine to keep watch through the night. I guess the threat couldn't have been too severe. Either the intelligence provided from the Intel Units at Messina, Pietersburg and Pretoria was that reliable, or the SADF was labouring under its arrogant belief in its own invincibility. Either way, Gumbu Mine came to feel like some kind of weird holiday camp to me, an outlandish theme-park designed to keep us occupied during this strange time of limbo, when all I wanted was to be at home enjoying the summer holidays with Kimberly and my mates.

On Saturday morning we were curious to explore our surrounds. Cappie gave us permission and instructed Sergeants Mathebula and Mnguni to accompany us as guides. The little settlement at Gumbu Mine had been built several decades before, after the discovery of graphite deposits in the area, but after the depletion of economically profitable reserves of the mineral, the mine was closed and the houses abandoned. The compound was partly situated in a conclave of kopjes which today form part of the northern boundary of the Matshakatini Nature Reserve. To the north, a narrow *poort* gave access to the Limpopo River, where the small tributary that made its way through the west of our camp met the great waterway. The ruins of the mine manager's house overlooked the compound from halfway up the southern side of a fairly high kopje which marked the sweep of the river bend to the north. Across the tributary to the west was another almost conically shaped kopje. To the east of the camp was an elevated stretch of open land.

The vegetation alternated between sparse and thick stands of Mopani and acacia trees and bushes. Tall and thickly growing alien scrub wattle, originally planted by the miners to provide fuel and mining materials, lined the road at the entrance to the camp on the southeastern side and had now spread far and wide off the track.

Following the course of the tributary in a northerly direction, we tried to avoid walking in the narrow riverbed, but this was difficult to do as the banks were mostly choked with indigenous vegetation. Our route turned sharply to the west before the stream met the Limpopo River. The great river itself was still bone dry, the wide bed a mix of coarse and fine sand interrupted here and there by low outcrops of rocks. We discovered that along the easterly curve of the river which turned in a northerly direction, accessibility on the South African side was narrow with high, incised banks, and the thick vegetative cover on the Zimbabwean side made a good site for a possible sniper or reconnaissance unit to be concealed. Deciding to avoid exploring or patrolling this area altogether, we continued in a westerly direction, where a wide section of reed-covered bank at the confluence would mask our comings and goings from any prying eyes.

That night, the four of us looties retraced our steps down to the river. We lay on our backs on the riverbank − a particularly comfortable patch of grass and soft sand below us, a piece of driftwood at our heads. From time to time I surreptitiously reached down to touch my R4 resting next to my right leg, reassuring myself of my immediate security. The moon had risen to meet the dark night, suspended in a sensuous cosmic embrace. Sharing a pair of powerful field binoculars, we gazed up at the moon in all its reflected splendour. With not a cloud in the sky, every detail was visible. It felt as though I could just reach out and touch that giant ivory orb. The South African hit from '81 *Man on the Moon* by the band Ballyhoo came to mind, and I gently hummed it. The others first chuckled as they recognised the tune, then soon joined in to make an a cappella quartet of dubious ability.

Over the next few days, we explored the riverbed a little further each time. A few kilometres upriver to the west, in a northwest facing bend, we came upon a wide and shallow outcrop of rocks which formed an island in the middle of the dry riverbed. Here the underground water is forced to emerge from its hidden course and make its way over the bedrock, creating a series of cool and inviting pools. We lost no time in stripping down and wallowing in the pools buck-naked, always sweeping the far bank with our eyes for signs of movement. I was more concerned about hippos and crocodiles than snipers, but we saw none there. The setting was so ruggedly beautiful that we could easily have been lulled into a false sense of security.

Sergeant Mathebula took me aside during this time and warned me to be on the lookout for *nyoka*. *Nyoka* is the Swahili word for "snake", but in this instance, Mathebula was referring to the deadly black mamba, a species which is particularly prevalent in that part of the world. The scorpions and some spiders of the region are also deadly, and it became standard practice for me to shake out my boots before donning them in the mornings, just to be sure none of these had made a home in them. Set amongst the unspoiled bush of the country's far north, Gumbu Mine and its environs were home to such varied wildlife, that at times I felt as though I was on safari. The cricket-laden night-time air was punctuated by the grunt of *yingwe* (leopard) and eerie laugh of *mhisi* (hyena). At dawn the kopjes would echo with the bark of *umfene* (baboon), and in the quiet afternoons the scrub became the playground of troops of cheeky *nkau* (vervet monkeys). During my time there, I would come across impala, waterbuck and kudu, often scattering away before us as we patrolled the riverbed and bank. When the first summer rains had abated and the river had dried up almost completely, herds of wildebeest (*nkonkoni*) and buffalo (*nyarri*) moved along the length of the river, crossing between South Africa and Zimbabwe and proving borders to be nothing but the artificial construct of governments. Tracking the spoor of these animals while on the lookout for evidence of human movement became a pastime which would both fascinate and calm me, and I eagerly became fluent in the visual language of the region's ecosystem.

Aside from our explorations of the riverbed, much of that first weekend at Gumbu Mine was spent quietly chatting or writing letters to our girlfriends. The nearest public phones were in Messina, roughly 120 kilometres west of us by road, so we had no choice but to resort to written updates. I enjoyed the letter writing: it was both a necessary connection to home and a means to while away time with thoughts of Kimberly. Gavin was an avid writer and spent ages writing to his girlfriend Cathy in Cape Town.

Gavin and I set up a little portable radio-tape player in our lodgings, powering it by half-spent A52 and A53 batteries from tactical field radio handsets – strictly not allowed, but we did it anyway. My self-compiled mix-tapes brought a sense of normality to our strange setup, and the various hits of the mid-eighties I'd recorded began to sound pretty odd as the batteries lost their final bit of juice. One tape in particular was played over and over during my time there, and my memories of Gumbu Mine are set to the poignant soundtrack of Mr Mister's *Broken Wings* and *Kyrie* and *Don't Forget Me When I'm Gone* by Glass Tiger. *Something About You* by Level 42 and *Addicted To Love* by Robert Palmer were upbeat tracks that kept me going, and when I needed a pick-me-up, Billy Ocean provided it with *When The Going Gets Tough (The Tough Get Going)*.

I discovered that sometimes, late at night, we could pick up an FM station or two. This required some ingenuity and perseverance on my part: attaching a long piece of copper flex to a wire coat hanger clipped through a hole in the corrugated iron roof, I would manipulate the tuning knob and antenna simultaneously until just the right arrangement brought us the static-burdened voices and fresh music broadcast from faraway civilisation. It was like an umbilical cord to the life I had left behind.

On Monday, we left Gumbu Mine for Messina in a SAMIL 50 with Cappie. We made our way to Messina Sector Head Quarters, where Cappie was expected for a meeting with their top brass and intelligence officers.

Messina Sector HQ was also the home to 116 Battalion, a black battalion like 113 BN. After dropping Cappie off, us looties and Sergeant Mnguni went with the driver to explore the town of Messina, where we picked up a few personal items, chocolate bars, gum, cold drinks and beer, and cigarettes for the NCOs.

We left Messina on the N1, turning left onto the R525 (now the R508) and then left again onto R525 (still the R525 today), on which road we passed the Tshipise Family Resort. Then part of the Overvaal Group of resorts, Tshipise was a whites-only holiday facility featuring natural hot mineral springs, frequented mostly by Afrikaans and Zimbabwean families. Many white Rhodesians who had fled south after Zimbabwe's independence had packed what little they had into caravans and towed it over the border into South Africa. Coming across Tshipise, they simply stopped, made camp and had stayed on, many of those families only moving on years later to other parts of the country. Tshipise's other claim to fame was hosting the making of the 1978 *Wild Geese* movie, which I could still recall having seen in 1979, starring Richard Burton, Roger Moore, Richard Harris and Hardy Krüger. Passing long stretches of agricultural land parading row upon row of citrus trees fed by strong boreholes, the cultivated terrain eventually gave way to a bushveld vista dotted with baobab trees with their root-like branches reaching for the sky as though upturned by giants. Turning off the R525 just short of the Kruger National Park's Pafuri Gate, we re-entered Gumbu Mine some time after dusk.

Back in the ops room, I took the opportunity to examine the cadastral maps Cappie had pinned to the walls, comparing them to some aerial photographs of the area. Running my finger over the Limpopo River from the point at which the tributary west of our camp joined the main waterway, I could distinctly see a dirt road running north-south on the Zimbabwean side. I would later learn that this road was suspected of being used by operators smuggling illegal refugees into South Africa. It was possible that insurgents used the endpoint of this road as a drop-off point to begin their trek down south into South Africa. Every time I walked down the banks of the tributary to the river, I looked for possible human spoor, but the sand was too loose and deep to really get a sense of anything there.

I got to know Gavin very well while we were sharing a house at Gumbu Mine. At the time I thought I had chosen him to buddy with, but in retrospect it was probably the other way around. Gavin was different from the rest of us. He was patient and modest, sensitive to social-military interactions. Kind and self-controlled, he always did things in a balanced manner – even eating and drinking in moderation. While the rest of us were at times ill-mannered, coarse, crude and bad tempered, Gavin was always respectful, thoughtful and restrained. He had a sense of decorum and responsibility. Gavin never found it necessary to make excuses or misrepresentations for any of his actions. Like the band Marillion's one song illustrated, I thought Gavin to have a heart of Laurium.

In the quiet afternoons and free evenings, Gavin and I would listen to music and talk. We spoke about our families, our girlfriends, our plans for the future. Gavin was dating a girl he had known from high school, just like me and Kimberly.

"Gavin," I said, one evening, "how long have you known Cathy?"

In his typically measured way, Gavin responded, "We've been dating a long time, Mike," he said, "I've known her since high school."

"Are you planning to marry her?" I asked.

"For sure," he replied. "I just haven't made firm plans to get engaged to her yet."

"Why not?" I asked.

"Well ... I wanted to finish this army thing first," he said, "but I don't know if I can wait."

"What's the big deal?" I asked. "Why can't you wait?"

"Well, Mike," he seemed to be uncomfortable. "It's a physical thing ..."

"What do you mean, Gav?" I thought I had misunderstood him. "Do you mean you guys haven't "done it" yet?"

"Uh-huh." I was incredulous. "You mean, you're both virgins?"

"Uh-huh." I was perplexed. I decided to stop my interrogation of him. A strange feeling of guilt crept over me. I was suddenly ashamed about having been sexually active with Kimberly. Not just once or twice, but having been quite experimental and voracious. I didn't want Gavin to ask me anything that personal.

I changed the subject, hoping he wouldn't pick up on why I had skirted the issue.

"Gav," I began, "when I met you in that gazebo at Infantry School, when we were both waiting to see the *dominee* ... what was that really all about? Why didn't you see your way clear to doing township duty? Do you have a problem with going into the townships and sorting out those rabble-rousers?"

Gavin was careful with his response. "You see, Mike, my beliefs – personally and as a Christian – don't permit me to participate in such things," he said.

"What do you mean?" I asked. "Do you consider the actions of the army to be wrong?" Again, his response was slow to come.

"Not entirely," he said at last. "I believe we need to protect this country and its people against communism and its influence." He was looking at me now with a steady gaze. "My objection is to the presence of the army in the

townships. The duty of the army is to protect its citizens, not target them."
"Okay," I said, digesting what Gavin was saying. "But what about the troublemakers who incite people in the townships against us, against the whites? How should they be dealt with?"

"That's a hard question to answer," Gavin admitted. "But by deploying the army to the townships, even under the guise of a "State of Emergency", the government is essentially escalating political resistance to Apartheid to what amounts to civil war. We, as conscripts, are being asked to carry arms against our fellow citizens, and that doesn't feel right to me. Can you imagine how it must be for them? Can you imagine it was you and your family under threat from the SADF?" Silence descended as I contemplated Gavin's words. For the first time, I considered how it must feel to face the army in your neighbourhood, to hear the sounds of war from your kitchen, to hide under your bed in fear. Gavin interrupted my thoughts. "The actions of the government," he said, "are really polarising this nation." Finally bringing across a real truth, he said, "We'll never create peace from the barrels of our guns. This conflict can only be overcome by the uniting of our hearts."

"But tell, me, Gav," I asked. "Weren't you afraid that you would be reported to military intelligence? Weren't you afraid that you would be kicked off the course at Infantry School, or sent to DB or jail?"

"You know, Mike," Gavin said. "I would have done what I did anyway. I don't feel that I had a choice. I was morally obliged to stand by what I believe is right."

"Boy," I said. "You really do feel strongly about it."

"I do," Gavin responded. "I think the road we are currently on is leading to the destruction of our society. It's time we started working together to unite this country."

"Man. You've really got guts." I told him.

At this, Gavin smiled a beatific smile for an age in that candlelit room, before responding, "Nah. I'm blessed with courage, but not of my own making or doing."

"Huh?" I grunted. "What do you mean by that?"

"Mike, are you a Christian?" I was surprised by Gavin's question.

"I suppose I am," I responded. "I mean, I went to church for many years when I was young. Sometimes I pray to God."

"Do you know," he asked, "that before the foundation of the world, God knew and planned for your existence?" I looked at him with some doubt. He smiled at this, and continued. "God is all-knowing and all-powerful," he said.

"So, are you saying that you have courage because of God's plan for you?" Gavin nodded. "Okay," I said. "And do you know what that plan is?" "Well," Gavin was thinking again. "I trust that God will reveal his plan to me as the time is right. For now, all I know for sure is that I must remain committed to the principles of my faith." He changed tack, "Mike, are you aware that God sent His only son, Jesus Christ, born of a virgin, through the Holy Spirit, in order to die for your sins? We were all separated as enemies of God because of original sin in the Garden of Eden. The only way back to a right relationship with God was for His Son to be a sacrifice for our sins." "Ja, Gav, I know all that from my Sunday School Bible lessons," I said. "Yes," he responded. "But are you born again?"

"I've heard of churches that practice that sort of thing," I said, "but I don't know what it means."

"Being born again means that you are a new man in Christ," Gavin explained with patience. "Christ takes away your old nature: the old man is gone and There's a new man in his place. You actually change and take on the nature of Christ. He replaces your heart of stone with a heart of flesh." "Wow. That sounds amazing," I said. "And that's where you find the courage to stand up for what you believe in?"

"That's right," he said. "Any and all your good works are meaningless when you aren't born again."

"So how does a person become born again?" I asked.

"Actually," he responded. "It's not up to you." I gave him a questioning look. "Only God, by His amazing grace, can give you the ability to recognise your sinful nature. You are made to understand that you have offended a mighty and holy God. He saves you." Gavin paused here, watching me intently.

"And then?" I asked.

"Then, you respond to God's call by realising that you must repent and ask His forgiveness. You must truly repent of your miserable, worldly, sinful ways – of offending a Holy God. You know, Mike, there is no one on earth, except Jesus Christ, who hasn't sinned. Because of sin, every one of us has a fallen nature. But God, in his endless love for you, has the power to raise you up from that situation, from being dead in your sin. And he will bless you with eternal life."

"Eternal life?" I questioned.

"Eternal life," Gavin repeated. "When God calls his faithful home to a life in eternity with Him. The only way to be saved from a life of sin and have eternal life is through Jesus Christ. There is no other way to the Father except through His Son. When you accept Jesus Christ into your life, you receive the fullness of the Holy Spirit. The Holy Spirit dwells in you and acts as a guide in understanding the road you will now walk. This walk is one of sanctification, where each day, by obedience to the Word of God in your life, you earnestly pursue a life of righteousness. When you become a true believer, your life will be characterised by good works."

"And you begin by repenting of your sins?"

"If you truly repent of your sins and humble yourself before the Almighty, He will not let you fall away. God's grace knows no bounds. You are now a true believer, part of His flock. He is the Shepherd and He will look after every one of His sheep. He will look for every lost sheep." Gavin's words were echoing around my head. For the first time, I was thinking, really thinking, about faith and the nature of God. I had spent so many years taking religion for granted, not considering its meaning or value in my life. I was humbled by the sincerity of Gavin's convictions. Then he uttered what sounded like something he knew by rote, perhaps saying it as much to himself as a reminder, as to me: "Repentance brings salvation; God's forgiveness provides access to the Promised Land; sanctification provides healing, a relationship with Christ and a lifelong holy walk."

"Here," he said, holding out his Bible. "Read this passage." I looked down. He had turned to the Book of John, Chapter 3 Verse 16 in the New Testament. I started to read it to myself. "No," Gavin said. "Read it aloud." I read, "For God so loved the world; that He gave His only begotten Son, that whosoever believeth in Him should not perish, but have everlasting life."

Something began to niggle at me. It was Kimberly. How did my relationship with Kimberly figure in God's plan for me? I thought I felt overwhelming love for her. But now I wondered, was it just lust? Gavin interrupted my thoughts.

"So Mike," he said. "What do you think of everything I've said?"

"I'm not sure, yet, Gav," I replied. Tiny ripples of anxiety were the only inkling of turmoil deep below the surface. "I think I need to mull over it all for a bit."

"No problem," he said. "Whatever you choose to do is fine. If it's meant to be, it will be." He began to make himself comfortable in his sleeping bag. "I'm going to get some shut-eye," he said. "Goodnight, Mike." He blew the candle out.

I lay there in the darkness thinking about all Gavin had said. His words, spoken with such authenticity, had stirred the waters of my soul, kicking up the settled soil and making my vision muddy. As if I had reached out for the safe anchor of a rock and found it slick with algae, the firm grasp I felt on my life slipped for a moment, and in its place was doubt and fear. I had to reassure myself. Thoughts of Kimberly helped me to regain my composure. *I'm okay*, I thought to myself, *I'm fine. I have Kimberly, and that's all I need.* Pleased with my reasoning, I turned on my side. *I'm alright, God,* I said under my breath. *I'm a reasonably moral and decent person. I'm sure you know me that way.* For good measure I added an *Amen.* I closed my eyes in the assurance of my own ways: as long as I knew of and about God, He would have to look after me and accept me as His friend. After all, He created me. He would have to be there for me.

It wasn't until a little more than thirteen years later that the seed planted on that day would germinate and I would finally see the light of Christ, when, by the grace of God, I realised that I was indeed a sinner; lost and separated from the blessings of God. That's when I called on Christ to save me. I repented of my sins, put my trust in Christ and believed in Him. I declared Christ my Lord and Saviour – what a blessed event!

I took my first racially integrated shower at Gumbu Mine. Actually, it was more of a slap-dash wash in a large, red fire-bucket on a concrete slab in the middle of the bush. We had brought along makeshift overhead shower dispensers, but these were ideally suited for placement in an elevated position, like in a tree. We were using a coal-fired donkey to boil water for cooking and we discovered that by really stoking the coals, we could heat several gallons of water at once, providing hot water to wash ourselves with at the same time. Gavin and I shared this bathing exercise with Sergeants Mathebula and Mnguni, the other looties and several corporals looking on with much laughter and amusement. Aside from the mirth, it seemed quite natural for us men, black and white, to bathe alongside one another under a glorious Madimbo sunset.

To keep fit, we ran in our PT gear and *tekkies* on the track exiting the camp, turning around where it met the intersection at the top of an incline, to make a trip of nearly three kilometres. The first few times we ran this route, I found it quite taxing, my R4 heavy and awkward in my hands. I was amazed at how quickly I had become unfit, but kept my mouth shut, not wanting the others to think I was lazy. A couple of days into this routine, Ross piped up and complained about how difficult he was finding it to run with his rifle. It turned out the others felt the same way, and it was with some relief that we all agreed to leave our weapons behind at camp when we next ventured out for our jog. We took care to observe our surroundings as we went, but I felt a little vulnerable without an R4 immediately to hand, as much to a chance encounter with a *yingwe* as a terrorist.

New Year was not what I had ever experienced before. Used to exciting parties with mates, it was strange to be stuck in the bush, and even stranger at a place called Gumbu Mine. Cappie invited us to join him that night in celebration. With a hot toddy, coffee and biscuits, we chatted away until late.

Chapter 21

The first of the troops and several corporals returning from their December pass arrived in two SAMIL 50s around mid-morning, Friday 2 January. Some in browns, some still in civvies, they greeted us distantly, showing their regard for Cappie with friendly nods and smiles in his direction. After forming up for a brief pep talk and reminder of the rules of the camp from the senior NCOs, the troops were billeted in little rooms in grey-white buildings with their faded red and grey corrugated iron roofs near the NCOs quarters.

After lunch, Cappie asked the loots to give the troops a full platoon weapons demonstration in the deployment area. No problem, this was our bread and butter! Following the NCOs to the elevated stretch of open land east of the camp, the men settled on a slight rise facing north across an open and marginally depressed expanse of ground. Ammo and ordnance boxes were brought out, and we opened them to find 75 mm rifle grenades, high explosive hand grenades, MAGs and M79 *snotneus* grenade launchers. From a safely demarcated area, we began by firing the rifle grenades towards the ruins of the mine manager's house. The rifle grenades flew several hundred metres, exploding into the depressed expanse between where the troops sat and the house on the kopje. A few hand grenades were thrown. Then we fired the MAGs across the gap, hitting rocks and trees around the building, almost a kilometre away. Next we fired the *snotneus* grenade launchers. With each demo of a particular piece of equipment, we gave a couple of the more willing troopers a chance to try it out. We guided the men on proper use of the weapon, all the while explaining to the group the appropriate safety measures to take in handling each weapon. In that confined terrain the explosions were deafening, and I could see the men flinching, some looking downright scared. Then Cappie produced his trump card, the sergeants hauling out an RPG-7 rocket launcher and a crate of rocket propelled grenades.

It must have been around 15h00. The sky was turning black as banks of menacing clouds made their way towards us from the west and northwest. The light was fading fast. The first rains of summer were expected: a momentous meteorological event on the seasonal calendar of that dry bushveld region.

Grinning broadly, Cappie raised his eyebrows in the direction of the loots, a silent dare which was enthusiastically taken up. Practically elbowing the rest of us out of the way, Ross leapt forward to have a go, whilst Gavin primed the rocket grenade. Aiming the weapon at the dilapidated house on the kopje opposite, he fired ... and missed. An audible *Aah!* went up from the troops. Gavin had a go. He hefted the launcher onto his shoulder, as I helped prime the grenade. He took his time taking aim, fired ... and just missed. An even bigger *Aah!* was heard from the troops. I wanted a go. I had a strong desire to leave my own mark on Gumbu Mine, a macho hankering to add to the damage left by generations of SADF soldiers over the years. I took the RPG launcher from Gavin, and, kneeling as I had been taught at Infantry School, I shouldered the device while Gavin primed and loaded the rocket. I felt the weight of the loaded launcher on my shoulder, aware that I held the power of destruction in both hands. It was at once exciting and fearsome. The remaining smoke and acrid smell of the last launch wafted over me and the troops as I took my time aiming through the launcher's two sights, alternating with each eye between the focus area and the wider view of the terrain and my target. I took a breath and squeezed the trigger. I heard a *Woosh!* and there was a puff of smoke as the grenade left the barrel of the launcher, the force of the kickback knocking my right shoulder backwards. The RPG launches a grenade at a speed of over a hundred metres per second, and a rocket can reach up to three hundred metres per second in flight. I followed the projectile with my eyes, its spinning trajectory leaving a thin plume of smoke as it sailed towards the house. In a matter of seconds, a fiery flash blew chunks of brickwork and mortar into the air and I heard *Blam!* as the grenade hit the mine manager's house and self-destructed. Smoke and dust drifted on the breeze. What a shot! A whoop and a cheer went up from the troops. Cappie was impressed and even the senior black NCOs gave me a sideways glance of acknowledgement and a nod of the head: *Well done, Mlungu!*

With the inclement weather threatening, the troops were assembled and quickly marched back down the elevated portion of veld towards the base, where they were dismissed. Cheerfully chatting and laughing as they went, it was clear that they had enjoyed that show of power and strength. Large and heavy drops of rain began to fall.

Back in the ops room, a radio message from Messina Sector HQ reported that the Limpopo River at Beit Bridge was already flowing strongly and we could expect the turbulent waters to come past our base within the hour. Cappie began to explain that moisture laden air coming from as far as the equator would move down through Botswana, replenishing the Okavango swamps and delta in its advancement southeast, through western Zimbabwe and on, towards the northern and northeastern parts of South Africa.

He continued. The Limpopo River is sporadically fed year round from a number of tributaries upstream, but it receives the majority of its highly variable flow during the summer rainfall season. Its primary contributor during this time is the highly ephemeral Shashe River, which forms the border between Botswana and Zimbabwe and meets the Limpopo between the Weipe Militarised Zone in the east and near the conical Dongola Mountain in the west.

Although the Limpopo River and the whole area in general had apparently been going through a period of prolonged drought with little rainfall and subsequently minor and sporadic flows in the river for a number of years, the inclement weather with those heavy clouds looked very promising.

We decided to hurry down to the river as the rain began to fall, to witness the miracle of dry turning to wet. We sat on some large boulders at the river's edge, and just as we had been told, a wall of muddy brown water approached from the west, churning and foaming as it devoured the riverbed. Several hundred metres across and almost waist high, the water was travelling towards us at a speed of about three metres per second. It took my breath away. The swirling waters passed by us, eddies carrying dead branches and logs in their wake. Crossing an expanse of boulders on the riverbed, it soon formed rapids, which frothed and spluttered, and in a matter of minutes, the river was in full flow, the cloudy water passing by with a strength and speed that was mesmerising. I calculated that the volume of water passing by must have been close to seven hundred cubic metres per second. The Limpopo River flows with this strength, on average, just once a year. I felt fortunate to have witnessed such an awe-inspiring event first hand. We stayed a while longer, marvelling at the power of the swollen waters, until the rain started to pelt down in earnest and we hurried back to camp.

The first main exercise – the weapons demo – had now been dealt with, and Cappie seemed pretty gung-ho about it. The rain was pattering lightly on the corrugated iron roof as we met in the ops room that night, Cappie giving us a rather animated briefing on our roles and responsibilities for the duration of our stay at Gumbu Mine, based on the intelligence he had obtained at his meeting at Messina Sector HQ.

Using a coarse-scale map of southern Africa, Cappie explained that Angola, Botswana, Mozambique, Tanzania, Zambia and Zimbabwe were the so-called "frontline states" supporting the ANC, some even hosting military bases for *Umkhonto we Sizwe*, or MK for short, the armed wing of the organisation, within their borders.

"Any action taken against these terrorist-supporting states," he said, "should be seen as part of the strategy for the protection and security of South Africa." After a pause, he added, "We need to be of firm resolve." I thought he sounded a bit too much like the PF top brass heard rambling on the radio and TV and quoted in the newspapers, but I didn't like to say anything.

Cappie spread another map out over the trestle table. This map showed in greater detail the curve of South Africa's border as it followed the course of the Limpopo River flowing past Botswana, then Zimbabwe, and into Mozambique. Running a finger along the river's trajectory, Cappie explained how the river itself formed the first line of defence in the SADF's filter-system controlling access to the country from the countries to the north. The borderline front included the Western Transvaal and the Northern Transvaal. The Kruger National Park, part of the Eastern Transvaal and bordering Mozambique, had no natural geographic barrier, and had its own man-made defences. The town of Messina, together with the Sand River, was the mid-point of that northern borderline front, and the whole military area was divided up into sections controlled by various SADF battalions, predominantly black.

Cappie used a 1:10 000 finely detailed map to outline our area of responsibility while at Gumbu Mine. From a point a few kilometres to our west, he traced his finger along the Limpopo River eastwards, following a wide, distinctive U-bend. I could see that this section covered a particular area along the Madimbo Corridor towards the Kruger National Park. Tapping his index finger at a point on the border just before the Kruger National Park, Cappie explained that the easternmost extremity of our area of responsibility fell there. The regions beyond our area of responsibility to the west and east fell under the responsibility of Madimbo Base and Mabiligwe Base respectively. 113 BN's Charlie Company's first line of defence was the riverbank, which we would patrol almost entirely on foot, reacting to any irregular activities, attempted crossings or contact occurring in this region.

Cappie continued with this map: the second line of defence was the area from the Limpopo River up to and including the sisal line barrier a few kilometres from the river itself. Just south of the sisal line, for several kilometres until the border with the homeland of Venda, was also at times considered part of the second line of defence. Here, we would patrol the dirt roads, tracks, gullies and open areas on foot and by vehicle. Landmines, he was at pains to reassure us, were not a threat in this region as they were out west of Messina beyond Weipe and further, including irregular incidents in the Vhembe Militarised Zone, up to the Pondrift area. Pointing to the town of Messina, Cappie told us that the SADF had, just a few years earlier, installed a Norex electric fence which was monitored by SADF operators at the Messina Sector HQ. The fence ran either side of the town, on the border between South Africa and Zimbabwe, for a distance of approximately sixty kilometres each way. This electric fence, or "Ring of Steel" as it had been named, was meant to keep guerrilla insurgents and illegal immigrants out, while preventing disease-infested cattle straying across from Zimbabwe. Apparently, he said, plans were already underway to extend this fence to cover the whole of that northern border, and rumour had it that, he paused for dramatic effect, the voltage would be set to

"lethal".

Later that year, I had the opportunity to visit the operations room at Messina Sector HQ and chat to the officer in charge of remotely monitoring the electrified fence. The ops room looked like the main control of a space shuttle, with banks of flashing lights and knobs filling panels arranged against the walls of the room. Schematics were pinned up on the sides of the panels. One of the operators explained how the lights indicated the status of the fence by sections: a green light indicating that section of the fence was fully operational, without incidents or power surges; an amber light warning of faults or anomalies that needed to be checked out, while a red light alerted the operator to a possible incident along that particular section of fence, at which point the local SAP or SADF unit covering the area would be radioed to respond. There was apparently also an electric fence running between the Kruger National Park and Mozambique, operated from Komatipoort. He added that the electric fence, in conjunction with the sisal line, offered an extended physical security barrier.

"Is the charge of the fence lethal?" I asked.

"Well," he hesitated. "It certainly can be, depending on what voltage we set it at and how contact is made with it. You see, the lightest of touches may just result in a short, sharp shock. But if a person had to, for example, grab hold of the fence with one or both hands, the charge would induce a high voltage shock which would be extremely painful, most likely deadly." I remembered my physics, where it was really the amperage that was more important than the voltage – the higher the amps, the more deadly.

"Has it killed any insurgents?" I asked. The officer shifted uncomfortably, looked around.

Tugging at an ear, he spoke quietly.

"Actually, the only casualties of the Messina Sector fence to date have been baboons, some antelope and the occasional illegal immigrant. The insurgents ... they're too sharp for this apparatus." I was quite surprised by this revelation, and he must have seen it in my face. "It's my opinion," he went on, "that it's really just a psychological reinforcement, you see. It seems to provide peace of mind to the white farming community in this area. Besides, power surges from time to time cause entire sections of the fence to be out of operation ... sometimes for days ... while maintenance crews are sent out to repair it. But I have been reliably informed that all is set to change very shortly. The contactors are about to extend the fence further to both the east and the west, and concurrently increase the reliability and the capacity or boost of the charge."

On leaving the ops room, I had formed the distinct impression that the fence was a bad idea. Not only was it restricting the movement of wildlife in the area, but it actually harmed the poor baboons who were its primary victims. Then I thought about how gruesome it would be to find the lifeless body of some unfortunate refugee still clinging to the fence, which stood between him and his hopes for a better life.

113 BN was not expressly required to patrol the third line of defence, which stretched south of the sisal line all the way to Venda, including all the roads, towns and bus and taxi stops in the area, spanning up to thirty kilometres at some points. We would only be deployed in this area based on specific intelligence information from Messina Sector HQ.

Beyond the military restricted area, south of the Madimbo Corridor, the land was made up of mainly white-owned farming lands and game ranches, except for that northern portion of Venda Homeland to the east. Cappie told us that both black inhabitants and white farmers, along South Africa's borders with Botswana and Zimbabwe often assisted the SADF and SAP by reporting suspected crossings of insurgents and illegal immigrants into their areas. He also said that the SADF and SAP had arrangements with the headmen of most of the villages adjacent to the border to report any untoward activities. The Madimbo Corridor's Leeudraai area was apparently a common smuggling route into South Africa from Zimbabwe, and routes into the country through this region were utilised by human traffickers from Zimbabwe, one of which passed close to Gumbu Mine.

On Saturday morning, under an overcast sky and occasional drizzle, I stood with the other loots to watch as the NCOs mustered the troops for Roll Call, the day's orders and Sick Report. They were a bit of a motley crew, not the neatest bunch, and certainly a far cry from the spick 'n span troops of Infantry School. The company was around 160 members strong, and the men were divided between us four loots more or less equally, each of us leading a platoon of between thirty three and thirty six men. It didn't occur to me at the time, but Cappie must have taken care when assigning men to their platoons, trying to make the most of the pairing of officer with soldier. Many of the guys in my platoon, it would turn out, were difficult characters, and I suspect Cappie put them under my control thinking that, at 6'3", I was not to be trifled with.

I was introduced to my platoon by Corporal Maluleke, the lance jack assigned as my second-in-command. Although the men were mostly Shangaan, there were some Ndebele, Sotho, Venda, one or two Zulu men and one Swazi amongst them. The surnames were interesting and took some getting used to. I took to keeping a pocket book of all their names, besides the company Roll Call register, to aid me in getting to know them. There were also many names duplicated, so we all got into the habit of identifying those with initials and surnames to avoid confusion. Amongst my men were Baloyi, Chabangu, Chauke, Hlongwane, Khoza, Lubisi, Mabasa, Mabena, Mabuza, Makondo, Maluleke, Masuku, Maswanganyi, Mathebula, Mhlongo, Mkhize, Mnguni, Mnisi, Mthembu, Mthombeni, Mtsweni, Mulaudzi, Ndlovu, Ndou, Ngubane, Ngwenya, Nkambule, Nkosi, Nkuna, Ntuli, Phiri, Rikhotso, Shabangu, Sithole, with a few repeats. Some of the guys were young, fresh and eager, while others looked a bit long-in-the-tooth. I found some looked at me with downright hostility, as if challenging me to just try them. There were the dozy-looking faces of what we called *vaakseuns* at Infantry School. In fact, it seemed to me that there was no difference in behaviour and attitude whatsoever between these troops and the *troepe* I had been with at Oudtshoorn. I pictured myself, a year ago, mustering alongside my fellow soldiers, just like these guys.

That weekend and over the next few days, more and more troops returned in dribs and drabs. Some arrived having hitched a ride in locals' cars, others arrived on foot. A couple of guys pitched up a week late, citing no money to get back. Others turned up several weeks later, having tended to crops and cattle before returning. One or two returned months late, having tried unsuccessfully to find employment elsewhere. It seemed there were a few cases of soldiers going permanently AWOL, never to be heard of again. Enquiries were made amongst the others, but those who never returned weren't pursued further.

I confess to mixing names and faces up a bit to begin with, but after a week or two, I got the hang of who my men were and started to get to know them better. My lance jack, Maluleke, was a great help. A young, bright and keen chap, he was fluent in English and Afrikaans and generally liked to please, only I would come to discover that he was prone to bouts of self-pity.

Saturday afternoon was free time for all of us, and, not wanting to miss any opportunity to swim in the Limpopo River while it was flowing, I hurried down to the river with my fellow officers – this time with PT shorts and swimming trunks. The water was less muddy than the day before, and although still flowing strongly, the river was more settled. We carefully edged into the water from the safety of the grassy bank. The water was refreshing – even a bit on the cool side. We made our way to large grey-white boulders which formed rapids at the edge of the river and wallowed like hippos in the turbulent flow. I couldn't shake the thought of a rogue crocodile on the hunt for some fresh prey ...

We returned to dip in the river again on Sunday morning after breakfast and a Bible reading from Cappie. This time, the river was reduced to about half the depth it had been when the floodwaters first arrived, but it was still flowing strongly. I still couldn't shake the thought of a rogue crocodile on the hunt ... and my imaginings were augmented with images of snakes swimming down river.

"Tomorrow morning, we're taking the men out to the sisal line road," Cappie announced to us loots on Sunday evening in the ops room. "The men look a bit *slapgat* to me after their pass, and I think it's time we do some route marching to get discipline back into the company ... and your troops need to get used to you as their new platoon commanders." We looked at each other with a little confusion.

"But, Cappie," Maas objected. "Who will patrol the river?" Cappie just laughed.

"There's no real need to patrol the river at the moment," he explained.

"On both our western and eastern sides, the river is narrow, but flowing with such strength, no one could make it across on foot. No one would dare to cross at the wide and shallow sections to our immediate north – they would have to literally walk through our camp! We have a couple of days, maybe a week, before the river subsides a bit and we will need to begin patrolling." It would turn out just as Cappie had said.

For the next ten days, the river continued to flow, the volumes dropping off rapidly. By 12 January, the river was barely a trickle and we began to patrol the riverbed over the mud hollows where the river had churned out new patterns on the riverbed.

Sick Report on Monday morning brought with it a shock for me. One of the troopers raised his hand.

"*Luitenant,*" he said. "*Ek het 'n probleem!*"

I spoke to him in English, "What is your problem, *troep*? Do you need to see the medic?" He hesitated.

"Uhmmm ... *Luitenant*, can I speak to you in private, sir?" I was a little peeved, but I motioned for him to come towards me. He beckoned for me to follow him to a corner behind the ops room, away from the prying eyes and flapping ears of the others.

"Okay, soldier. What's your problem?" I asked again, hands on my hips. "*Eish, luitenant,*" he was unbuttoning his browns, avoiding my eyes. "*My piel – hy's seer!*" ("My penis is sore") he said, dropping his rods and revealing the most enormous pecker I'd ever wished never to see. When I recovered from the surprise of getting to know one of my men far better than I had anticipated, I noticed that his privates were covered in suppurating sores that were oozing pus. I flinched, backing away and knocking over a chair. Composing myself, I picked up the chair and sat down on it.

"*Troep*, do up your pants! Have you been to see the medic?" I asked, quite redundantly, as it was quite clear to me that he hadn't.

"No, sir." I'm no doctor, but there was no doubt in my mind that he was in need of some medical care.

"Well, I think you had better make your way to the medic, soldier. This is not something I am qualified to deal with." He looked despondent.

"They won't treat me, sir."

"What?" I was incredulous. "What do you mean, they won't treat you?"

"It's true, sir. They won't treat me. They say it's my fault for sleeping with *nyatsi* whores on pass." While I understood the logic of the argument, I was outraged that a medic would refuse a man treatment. "Lieutenant," the *troep* pleaded with me, "please will you speak to the medics for me?"

I lost no time marching over to the medics' station.

"Who's in charge here?" I barked at the skinny young medic seated in the front of the ambulance. I followed his eyes over towards the rear of the vehicle from where emerged a man in his late thirties, dressed in browns. The man looked puzzled.

"That would be me," he said, then extended his hand. "Corporal Chauke", he oozed obsequiously, ignoring the imperative to salute me, being that I was of higher rank than him.

"Corporal Chauke," I shook his limp hand. "I'm Lieutenant Warren. One of my men is in need of your assistance. It appears he has an STD." At this Corporal Chauke clicked his tongue and shook his head.

"Yes, lieutenant," he said. "You will find that this is a common problem after the men have been on pass. An unfortunate state of affairs, I'm sure you'll agree." Here he smiled a scornful smile, the corners of his mouth turning down in a strange and inappropriate smirk.

"So, shall I send him over to you, then, Corporal Chauke?" I asked, ignoring his opinion. The smile disappeared and he knitted his brow. "Actually," he said. "During my time here, it has become my policy not to treat STDs." I couldn't believe my ears.

"I beg your pardon?" I said.

"You heard me, lieutenant," Corporal Chauke said. "I won't treat the men for STDs." I looked at him with disbelief. "They should know better," he went on. "If they want to behave like common dogs and take up with any dirty bitch, then they deserve their diseases." I was stunned by his disrespectful language and flabbergasted by his attitude. "I won't waste my medical supplies on such things," he finished, folding his arms in defiance. I gathered myself together and spoke with controlled rage.

"Corporal Chauke," I said. "Let me remind you that these medical supplies are not your property, and you are not authorised to make policy on behalf of the SADF." I waved across the parade ground to the poor trooper awaiting his fate, motioning for him to come over to the ambulance. "Now, I insist that you give my man the medical treatment he requires, or I will be taking this up with the Captain." Chauke's mouth twisted into a disapproving pout and he gave me a look of narrow-eyed resentment. The *troep* arrived, breathless, and Chauke grudgingly administered the necessary jab. It soon emerged that from the moment we first met, Corporal Chauke and I would be on a collision course.

Over the next two days, having heard about the incident with their mate, several more men came to see Gavin and me, dropping their britches to reveal their painful and diseased equipment, and asking for our assistance in getting treatment. We weren't expecting the troops to be engaging us in their personal issues already: we barely knew them! We had only met them three days ago. It was the strangest beginning to a trust that would be built up, little by little, with the men in our platoons that year.

Following my head-to-head with Chauke, Roll Call and breakfast, the four platoons clambered onto several SAMIL 50s and, with Cappie in a SAMIL 20, rode out to the sisal line observation and maintenance road, approximately ten kilometres west of Gumbu Mine. When the men had all debussed, Cappie instructed the SAMIL 50s to return to base. He formed the company up along the length of the road, each platoon forming a rectangular block of three lines and separated from the next by a stretch of about thirty metres. Formed up like this, the troops covered almost 250 metres of that dry and dusty road beside the sisal line.

Cappie then gave the instruction for the men to begin marching east, back along the way we had come. Gavin, Ross, Maas and I marched alongside them on their right. Cappie rode along with the driver in his SAMIL 20, but from time to time he would get out to march along with us. When he did, he ambled alongside us in a gait that was half march, half walk. He had a hard time keeping up with us.

The road was very gravelly, making sure-footedness a challenge. Over some sections of the road, our boots caused fine brown-white dust to waft up, clogging our noses, drying our mouths and giving us ashen faces. We looked like ghosts – especially the black guys!

Cappie struggled to keep up with us, drifting even further back as we consciously picked up speed in order to outpace him. His ego was a bit bruised, but he steeled himself and showed a brave face, all the while trying to keep up with us. I took pleasure in marching away from him – he was acting too PF then: shouting at the troops and at us loots, threatening no water breaks (read: "smoke breaks") if we faltered or broke ranks, and generally throwing his weight around.

I hated every moment of this marching on the sisal road. I was sweating and chafing and getting sticky from it all, but I kept my poise, faltering only now and then when the dust and oppressive heat got to me. If Cappie saw a lootie or a member of their platoon falter, he'd shout at the poor lootie, who in turn would have to shout at his troops. I hated this. I didn't want to be a shit towards my men, and I especially didn't want to give them any reason to dislike me. I cursed Cappie and the *bliksemse* SADF under my breath, imagining telling him and his bloody army to piss off.

Up and down that road he made us march, covering kilometre after kilometre with only a short break for lunch, which was brought to us by one of the SAMIL 50s, and an even shorter siesta under the Mopani trees after lunch. It was late afternoon when Cappie finally radioed the SAMIL 50s to come and fetch us.

For two whole days he made us march up and down that road.

By Tuesday night we were tired and our feet ached from the relentless marching on the sisal line road. The loots joined Cappie in the ops room for an officers' meeting.

"Tomorrow morning, we're taking the men out to the training area near Madimbo Airfield to do attack formation exercises," Cappie announced. Looks of relief settled on our faces: no more marching on the sisal line road! Attack formation exercises could be enjoyable, too, especially when live ammo was used.

That Wednesday morning, following Roll Call and breakfast, the four platoons at Gumbu Mine again clambered onto several SAMIL 50s and rode out to the nearby training ground, a dilapidated firing range on the other side of the sisal line, just south of the Madimbo Airfield.

Gavin lined up his first section, their R4s loaded with a 35-round magazine each. There was no MAG for left-flank support, and perhaps it was just as well. A point near the front of the range, about two hundred metres away, was selected as the target. The order was given for the exercise to begin, and the men at the ends of the section fired off a rifle grenade each towards the intended target, the signal for the line to begin advancing. Gavin and I ran behind the men bellowing, *"Hardloop!"* ("Run!"), trying to gee-up the laggards as the line moved forward in its staggered motion. Our bellows quickly changed to "Stop! Stop!" as we realised the line was distorting and the men at either end of the section were closing in on the middle. They would have been firing into each other before they reached the 200-metre point and secured the objective of the exercise. We brought the exercise to a rapid halt.

Gavin and I met halfway between the ends of the line to discuss our observations of the exercise. As it had been when I was taught the fire and movement drills at Infantry School, the drills were explained half in English, half in Afrikaans, and then carried out in Afrikaans. I told Gavin that it had occurred to me that the disastrous progress of the drill might be put down to a problem with language, and he agreed. We made our way to Cappie and the other loots to put forward the suggestion that it might be language that was hindering the men's progress. Cappie gave us permission to teach the men the drill in English, using English commands.

We did several dry runs that morning, and by lunchtime we were happy with the men's progress. It was clear to me that no one had previously taken the time or effort to train these soldiers properly. I suggested to Gavin and Cappie that we retrain the men, and we spent the three days during the river's full flow training at the Madimbo training ground. The rapid progress of the men in all four platoons proved that the decision was right. It was good to feel that we had made a difference: their standard of training was vastly improved, which boosted their morale and, in turn, led to us being able to achieve so much more with the guys during our time there.

Before we were to begin our regular patrols along the river, Cappie gave orders for us to spend a Saturday doing comops in the zone between the Madimbo Corridor and Venda, almost to the Mutale River – the third line of defence. Following intel received from Messina Sector HQ, each platoon was instructed to take a SAMIL 50 into the perimeter zone and walk as a unit in and around several of the villages that lay in a suspected direct line linking insurgent trails from Zimbabwe, across the river and through the militarised zone, down into and through Venda. Our job, besides doing comops with the locals, was to be there as a presence, a show of force, to let the locals know that the SADF knew that insurgents were accessing that area.

Coordinates: 22°23'49.68"S 31°02'20.12"E

My platoon walked for an age in the heat, moving south to the northern-most bend in the Mutale River and beyond.

On the return leg of our journey, we arrived at the northern point of the village of Bende Mutale. By then, our water was all but depleted. Approaching the headman's compound, I was struck by the neatly swept area and finely decorated huts. We were welcomed into the compound by two regal women, and shown into a fairly large communal area with a low wall around it, at the centre of a curving row of adjoining huts. Inside, I greeted the headman and explained our reasons for being there through Lance Corporal Maluleke. The headman was friendly and hospitable, and as Venda tradition would have it, he asked me, as the most senior member of our group, to sit down with him and share his Umthomboti out of his ceremonial calabash. I was chuffed to be given the royal treatment, and relieved that I would quench my raging thirst! Not knowing that this traditional beer is made from fermented sorghum, and has a thick texture like watery gruel, with a heavy earthy and alcohol taste and a sour odour, I graciously accepted the calabash from the headman's first wife and drew a long sip from it. Oh my goodness! It was horrible! I did my very best to keep a straight face, but I'm sure my lemon-look gave me away. Smiling a toothless grin, the headman put his hand at the bottom of the calabash and tilted more of the contents into my resistant mouth. I gulped it down, sighed and wiped my mouth on my sleeve, hoping to convey satisfaction rather than revulsion. I took hold of the calabash firmly and passed it on to Maluleke, who, being a non-drinker, made an appropriate smiling apology to the headman. By now the troops, not wanting to miss out on such a wonderful opportunity, were clamouring to have a taste. I started to tell them to back off, but the headman said something out loud, to which they all gave a gleeful shout and clapped their hands. Chuckling, the headman gave an instruction to one of his other wives, who disappeared into a hut and returned lugging a massive plastic container. The troops jumped to help her. Bringing out several calabashes and a large wooden ladle – much like those depicted on the 113 BN insignia – she proceeded to dip into the vessel and ladle the contents into the calabashes. Boy, how the troops grinned as they drank the stuff!

When the encounter came to an end, I thanked the headman, and took my leave of him. My tired and aching feet couldn't carry me out of the place fast enough. I rushed back to the SAMIL ahead of the troops, with whatever decorum I could muster, and searched frantically for the extra water bottle I knew I had left in the cab. Finding the water, I rinsed my mouth thoroughly, spitting into the dusty vegetation behind the truck, and then thirstily gulped down what remained. Trooper GJ Nkuna caught me in the act and grinned – he knew! I grinned back and shrugged a shoulder as if to say, *"Oh well!"* and he laughed.

That evening, we were informed by Cappie that we were to begin patrolling the river on the Monday. The river's flow had subsided considerably and the skies had cleared. After a braai of lamb chops and *boerewors* that evening, we sat down to draw up patrol rosters and area maps showing platoon responsibilities.

On Sunday, after Roll Call, Sick Report and a Bible reading delivered once again by Cappie, we all had time off to reflect, chat and write letters while listening to the music which palpably connected me to another life. I clearly remember hits such as *Alive And Kicking* by Simple Minds and Pet Shop Boys's *West End Girls* juddering from my tape deck with its make-shift power supply. *Stuck With You* by Huey Lewis And The News and *Sledgehammer* by Peter Gabriel were other regular accompaniments to our free time, along with *Sara* by Starship and Falco's *Rock Me Amadeus*. Letters home from Gumbu Mine were never censored – we posted them ourselves at the local post office during our regular trips to Messina. On Sunday evening, we informed the troops of the orders for the week.

Monday morning at 06h00, having risen early and had a quick breakfast, us loots were ready to move, but many of the troops were taking their time and lethargically mustered for Roll Call. Some hadn't even bothered to arrive and were still asleep in their quarters. Cappie shouted at Staff Sergeant Hlongwane, who in turn shouted at the rest of the NCOs to get a move on. The late sleepers were unceremoniously pulled from their sleeping bags and dragged to the rest of the company, eventually standing to attention half dressed and half awake. The last to arrive for Roll Call was Phiri, who loped over towards us without urgency, the NCOs yelling at him to pick up the pace. Giving them a look of disdain, he sluggishly joined the others. Almost as tall as I am, Phiri was proving to be a bit of a lazy lurker, always following orders with the greatest of reluctance. I realised that dealing with these guys was going to be a roller coaster ride.

After a number of successive mornings of Phiri arriving late for morning inspection, Cappie had had enough. He ordered Gavin and me to lock Phiri up for a few hours, in order to teach him a lesson and to try and instil respect for orders in the man. The detention barracks or DB was nothing other than a corrugated iron hut with a padlock. He put up quite a resistance, but eventually Gavin and I managed to unceremoniously push him in and lock the door. Lo and behold, less than an hour or two later, we saw him strolling around camp, carefree as a bird. None of his mates owned up to helping him escape that day, but we realised he had one or more close allies. I knew then that I was going to be in for a tough time with Phiri.

We carried out an abbreviated inspection, giving their clothing a quick once-over, counting their sharp-point rounds and checking that their rifles were in good order – the conclusion was far from satisfactory, all present and none-too-clean respectively, but we needed to get a move on, so we let it all slide just for a day. By the time we set off, it was past 07h00. At that time of the year, the days grow hot quickly up there in the north, and the recent rains had increased the humidity to uncomfortable. By 10h30, walking out in the sun would be almost unbearable.

My platoon was charged with patrolling the point furthest west from the camp, and I set off at quite a pace in order to make good time. We made our way along the western and north western stretch of the Limpopo River armed with our R4s. I carried two fully-loaded magazines, while my men carried only ten to fifteen rounds each in one magazine. I wondered why the troops were allocated fewer rounds. Was it because the SADF intelligence concluded the threat of enemy contact or incursion as minimal? Or was it because they didn't trust the black troops not to abuse or lose their ammunition? I never openly questioned the policy, however, simply applying the rules as best I could.

I was impressed by my men that day – they could really walk! They seemed to make a silent challenge: *C'mon, lootie, let's see if you can walk as fast as we can!* I didn't take up the dare, though, preferring to rely on the quality training I had received at Infantry School: pace yourself, ensure you are wearing good boots and fresh socks, and be sure to drink small amounts of water often to avoid dehydration. When I sensed the guys wanted to push too hard, I halted them and questioned them about the area, asking them to tell me about spoor on the riverbed or the vegetation on its banks. A number of them claimed they were particularly skilled at reading their environment and were eager to show me what they knew. Pausing in this way several times on our route took the sting out of the patrol and aided me in maintaining control of my platoon.

I got the distinct sense that Phiri was not fooled by my strategy of halting the troops to test their knowledge of the bush. Each time I stopped them to question them about the area he would give a throaty *harrumph!* followed by a disdainful click of the tongue and a word under his breath to his nearest *maatjie*, ending in a chuckle.

"*Xigono lexi xa munhu wa ntlhohe, xi ti endla ntlhari!*" I heard him mutter a few days later on patrol, when I had stopped the men to discuss some aspect of fieldcraft. A handful of the men sniggered.

"What's that, Phiri?" I demanded. Phiri avoided my eyes. "Nothing, lieutenant," he responded, trying not to smile.

On our return to base, I called Corporal Maluleke aside to ask him in private what Phiri had said. I repeated the phrase to him as best I could. Maluleke lowered his eyes with embarrassment.

"I think, lieutenant," he said. "Phiri said something like, "This white dumbass thinks he's clever." I was incensed, but because this was all hearsay and speculation after the fact, I couldn't place him on orders. I resolved to keep a watchful eye on Phiri, to keep him on a short leash. I wished I had paid more attention to the Tsonga classes back at 113 BN.

The riverbed was not yet dry, the mud at the edges of the floodplain just beginning to crack as the last of the rainwater subsided. It was the perfect condition to spot footprints. Coming across a set of barefoot impressions, I questioned the men about them. GJ Nkuna offered the simplest explanation: Zimbabwean stock herders must have been trying their good fortunes on the South African side of the river. A few metres away, the spoor of goats could be clearly seen running alongside the river's edge, and I felt relieved to know that at least some of the guys had a reasonable grasp of fieldcraft.

We soon arrived at our furthest point of patrol where we took a fifteen minute water break before retracing our steps back towards camp. If we were being watched it didn't matter, our patrol was intended to be nothing more than a show of force. On successive days that week, I practiced some backtracking manoeuvres with the guys and showed them how to vary a patrol route by emerging from the bush at random points along the riverbank. I took care to avoid walking the same route twice.

Before long, we all got the hang of things and started to enjoy our daily routine. We marched out just before dawn and again for an hour before sunset. We were in a good groove!

Chapter 22

My sister was getting married in Pretoria on Saturday 17 January, and I was granted a pass to attend the wedding. I confirmed my arrangements with Cappie, and he organised a lift to Letaba Ranch in one of the SAMIL 50s going to fetch supplies. Arriving at base just before lunch time, I pulled on some civvies, jumped into Roberta's little blue Renault 5 and with pedal to the metal, I happily charged homeward.

As always, my first port of call was Kimberly. Varsities were still in recess, so she was at home in Pretoria. Thoughts of her welcoming smile – once coy, now sensual and inviting – filled my head: how I loved to see her face light up when she saw me! I was excited as I made my way up the street to the junction of her road with mine. I found all of Kimberly's family at home and after greetings all around and handing Roberta her car keys with grateful thanks, I encircled Kimberly with my arms in an affectionate hug. Her response was not the warmth I expected. She was hesitant and reserved. A rush of concern constricted my chest. Crazy thoughts flashed through my mind. Was she embarrassed to show affection in front of her family? Was she falling out of love with me? Was there someone else? But I reasoned the panic away, putting it down to my own readjustment to normality. I told myself to go easy on the girl.

Saturday morning saw the Warren household in a flurry of activity. My family had not relied on my presence at the wedding in case I had been unable to get a pass, so I had nothing to do but watch as the women – my mother, the bride and her two bridesmaids – scurried about with last minute preparations. I put on the cobalt-blue suit I had worn to my graduation ceremony the year before. Just after lunch, the old, new, borrowed and blue in place, flowers and veil at the ready, a vintage Rolls Royce drew up to the pavement and parked, standing by to transport the bride to the Brooklyn Methodist Church. I hung around just long enough to see my sister preparing to get into the Rolls, then took off to fetch Kimberly in my mom's car. I looked with longing at my Honda XL600R scrambler as I reversed my mom's car out of the garage. I felt I could have done with a good long ride just then, speeding off towards nowhere-in-particular without a care in the world, relishing in the sense of freedom that comes from the open road and the

289

scrambler's engine growling beneath me.

Kimberly was beautiful in a dark blue, short-sleeve dress which reached below the knee, a fine silver necklace and pendant I had given her resting below the hollow of her neck. She had chosen to wear a large, wide-brimmed straw sun hat, an unusual choice which I thought looked rather odd and out-of-place. As we settled into a pew in the church, I noticed that few women were wearing hats at all, and those that did sported headgear that was rather more conservative. It crossed my mind that Kimberly was becoming a bit eccentric, following in the footsteps of her mother and grandmother before her.

The congregation held its collective breath for the arrival of the bride. The appointed time came and went and the flock became fidgety and restless. At the front of the church, the groom must have had the jibbers, wondering what was keeping his betrothed. Eventually, with some relief and more than a little confusion, I spotted through the large double doors at the entrance to the church, the bride emerging from an emerald green Mercedes Benz. I was to learn later that my father and sister had taken their seats in the Rolls Royce, ready to depart for the church, when, having barely driven around the corner, the old car began coughing plumes of acrid smoke from behind the dashboard. My sister had leapt out of the car for fear of catching her voluminous wedding dress alight, and just in time too, as the vehicle began belching flames and smoke. The chauffeur scrambled about in search of a fire extinguisher. As luck would have it, a friend of my sister's husband-to-be was just pulling up to the house in his Merc, and my father and sister lost no time in jumping into the fancy sedan. Having narrowly escaped ruining her white frock and her wedding day, my sister issued a command to get her to the church on time.

The church ceremony was followed by a reception at the Manhattan Hotel near the Pretoria Railway Station. In those days, it was a sought-after venue for wedding receptions, and weekends were booked months in advance. Kimberly and I drove there together in my mom's car, some trivial matter igniting a silly argument on the way. As we joined the rest of the guests, we stopped our bickering, but her quiet resentment of me continued, and made the whole event uncomfortable. I was at a loss to understand why she would be so difficult, especially considering I would be leaving so soon to return to 113 BN, and slightly hurt that she didn't make an effort to enjoy our short time together.

Following a wonderful meal and the inevitable speeches and toasts, the music began. After we had all watched the newlyweds with delight as they took their first dance, the DJ opened the floor and I tried to make reparations to Kimberly by asking her to dance. We had always enjoyed dancing together, and I was hoping to mend the discord between us. She refused my offer offhandedly, and turned her back on me to continue chatting to the person beside her. Wound up by Kimberly's rejection of me, I excused myself from the table and went around the room greeting the guests I knew and introducing myself to those I didn't.

Coming across my mother's cousin, Jenny, I joined her table where the mood was much lighter and the conversation animated. Jenny was older than me, and was studying at Wits with Kimberly. We struck up a conversation about her studies and her time at res. Jenny told me that she'd seen Kimberly about, and I asked her to keep an eye on my girlfriend. I was relieved to think that Jenny would be able to look out for Kimberly in my absence.

A little while later, the blushing and animated bride came to fetch me, saying she wanted to introduce me to a colleague of hers. Taking the hand of a very pretty, dark-haired girl, I was introduced to Karien, who had a friendly smile and greeted me in English with a light Afrikaans accent. We connected immediately and had a pleasant chat. Karien was single, perhaps a year or two younger than me, and I got the distinct impression that this was a set-up on the part of my sister. I wondered why my sister would try and set me up with another woman while I was clearly committed to Kimberly. In retrospect, this should have set off alarm bells. Perhaps my sister knew something based on her womanly intuition?

It didn't take long for Kimberly to come rushing over and butt in. She bustled up to us and demanded to be introduced. I complied. Sensing the tension brought by Kimberly's arrival, Karien excused herself from the awkward company, and I experienced a moment of regret at seeing her go. From that moment, Kimberly didn't let go of me, but hung on my sleeve for the rest of the afternoon. Part of me wanted to shake her loose, to free myself from her clasp, but being a decent bloke, I put on a brave smile and tolerated her behaviour.

I had no desire to spend the evening with Kimberly. Making an excuse about being tired, I dropped her off at her folks' place and turned the car onto the Mooikloof road heading out to Bapsfontein and Delmas. On the car stereo, Phil Collins insisted on *One More Night*. Passing Tierpoort, I turned back onto Lynnwood Road. My mind was occupied with thoughts of Kimberly and our strange afternoon together. For more than a year, I had suffered the tension of being physically removed from her. Now, I realised that we were becoming emotionally estranged, and the thought filled me with sadness. I had hoped that Kimberly and I would one day soon take to the floor for our first dance as husband and wife, but now I wondered if this was ever going to happen. Foreigner's *I Want To Know What Love Is* filled the car with sorrow and I realised that I didn't know Kimberly any more. This cold and changeable woman was so different from the girl I loved; the woman I ached for. The Kimberly I carried with me during my national service was sweet as honey, my refuge in times of loneliness.

After lunch on Sunday, I went around to Kimberly's house to say goodbye. After a brief chat and a stiff goodbye, I left Pretoria in my mom's Jetta, distressed and vulnerable. My relationship with Kimberly was in crisis: it was teetering on the brink of disintegration. With profound unhappiness I drove on, thinking all the while about Kimberly and our years together. I slipped another of my mix tapes into the tape deck, and I found resonance in its playlist: *If You Love Somebody*, Sting sang out to me, *Set Them Free*. His sentiments seemed like good advice.

I reached Letaba Ranch just before dusk and parked the Jetta under a shady tree. That night, lying in the small cabin on the river, I listened to Steve Winwood's *Back In The High Life*, the heat and darkness weighing in on me. A superb album from a master of blue-eyed soul, the slightly upbeat tracks with lilting, melancholy melodies provided the perfect soundtrack to my blue mood. The last haunting ballad on my tape, *My Love's Leavin'*, brought on emotional overload, and I found myself weeping with real sadness for the first time since I was a child.

On Monday morning I pulled myself together and went for breakfast at the officers' mess. I asked one of the NCOs responsible for logistics whether any SAMILs were scheduled to go up to Gumbu Mine, to which his response was positive, saying that one was expected to go there after lunch. I had a suspicion Cappie had pre-planned this convenient lift – what a guy! Following my disappointing weekend in Pretoria, I was eager to get back to Gumbu Mine and make the most of the experience.

I was greeted heartily by the other loots and Cappie. This felt more like it: a band of brothers, offering a guy acceptance and common understanding. We had a job to do. We found ourselves together in a situation not of our choosing, but we would work together to make the most of our circumstances.

Life at Gumbu Mine continued unabated. The week of my return, my platoon was still walking the furthest patrol to the west along the river. We patrolled early morning and noon, every weekday. Saturdays and Sundays were more relaxed, with one or two sticks being sent out as a skeleton patrol. We took it easy on the weekends, bothered only by the flies, but even those weren't half as bad as the flies I had experienced in South West Africa.

My platoon of 33-odd men was easily divided into sections of 11-plus each. With Corporal Maluleke and I each leading a section, I needed to find someone from amongst the men to lead the third section. Cappie had made it clear that he expected us to make this kind of selection, to identify suitable candidates for further training. Try as I might, I never managed to find the right guy for the job. I would place one of my men in charge of the section, and inevitably, within a week, he would have to be replaced. It was no fault of theirs: the troops were just unwilling to take orders from a man with the same rank as themselves, from a mate. Besides, many of the men were functionally illiterate, and being an NCO requires both verbal and written communication skills. I was frustrated by these circumstances, and suggested to Cappie that some basic language and writing courses in English and Afrikaans for the troops would be beneficial. But my suggestions were met with a shrug of the shoulders.

"It's the Commandant," Cappie said. "He's our problem." It would seem that Cappie had tried suggesting this course of action before and gotten nowhere fast.

Over the next weeks, we adjusted the patrol rosters, trying to give the guys an easier time without compromising our duties or the security of the area. We swapped areas between platoons and reduced the number of sections patrolling simultaneously.

I wrote to Kimberly less frequently. When I found myself in Messina during an afternoon, I chose not to phone her at her res to see how she was doing as I had always done in the past. Perhaps I was waiting for her to apologise; to realise that she had wronged me again and ask for forgiveness. But the apology never came. Days turned into weeks, and still all I got from Kimberly was the odd letter that didn't ring true, her words hollow and distant.

I still spent many hours listening to the mix tapes I had brought along to Gumbu Mine. Listening to music in my little run-down house gave me the opportunity for much reflection. Those evenings were infused with the sensation of longing: whether for Kimberly or just for life to return to normal, I couldn't say. I had no proof that I was being cuckolded by

Kimberly, but the fear that there might be someone else in her life haunted me. At the same time, I realised that she might just be tiring of our long relationship and ready to spread her wings.

One morning, just before lunch, Cappie had left for Messina Sector HQ and I was sitting in the ops room poring over a map at the table. I was engrossed, tracing out new patrol routes to cover some gaps I had encountered in the field. A footfall close to me snapped me out of my preoccupation, and I looked up to see Major Muller looming over me. Caught by surprise, I leapt to my feet and saluted, to which he responded by losing his temper. The major swore at me with some choice Afrikaans words, causing me some confusion, until it dawned on me that I wasn't supposed to salute him while not wearing the appropriate headgear. As I was bare-headed, without a beret, *staaldak* or *boshoed* on, I was supposed to only *strek* him: straightening up with my arms next to my sides or straight out in front of me on the table, hands clenched in fists. It seemed to me that this was a minor error in protocol on my part, but the major made such a huge song and dance about the faux pas, you'd have thought he had discovered some kind of treason taking place at Gumbu Mine. This being my first real interaction with the man since the day we met at Letaba Ranch in December, it didn't contribute to my positive opinion of him. I really despised the PFs: they epitomised everything I hated about the army! He had come to inspect the base, check up on Cappie and the looties, and see that the troops were disciplined. He wasn't there for more than an hour or two before he left again. I was always glad to see the back of the likes of him.

The only human spoor we came across during our patrols belonged to Zimbabwean stock herders, who were far too clever to be caught by us. We would see fresh footprints in the dust, but as soon as we started tracking the spoor and trying to catch up to their owners, the gait would change, the distance between steps increasing, as they made their way back to Zimbabwe, their goats driven quickly before them. It was no use radioing in to one of the other platoons to cut them off, the herders knew where our sections were operating because we had been intentionally obvious in our patrolling. It was possible to send the SAMIL 20 with its awesome 4x4 capability after them, but, as Cappie reasoned, "What for? If we catch them all we'll do is chase them back over the river. Let them be."

I was fascinated by the wildlife and became adept at watching for spoor in the dust. I saw the tracks of many different buck, and from time to time I came across the spoor of buffalo. Big cats were scarce, but I did encounter the spoor of leopard on occasion. It was exciting to spot such spoor. I would imagine the size, weight and age of the creature, and wonder where it was hiding from us. Was it watching us?

One afternoon, I was patrolling the riverbed with my platoon. Having reached the furthest point, we were returning to base when I suggested we split up into sections and return to base via different routes. I wanted to break the inevitable monotony, and knew I could trust Corporal Maluleke to do the job properly. We checked his radio and battery, all was A-Okay. I sent Maluleke and his section out to my right, slightly inland. The other stick, under one of the better troopers, I sent out to my left. They would walk close to the centre of the river, slightly exposed to the Zimbabwe border. Theirs was a quicker route than what I chose for my own section: we would be walking in the sandy riverbed, close to the South African bank.

I sent out the spotter or point man to walk ten metres or so ahead of my stick, where he could effectively do reconnaissance. I walked in the second last position, monitoring the men's patrolling abilities and watching that they behaved themselves. As I had been trained at Infantry School, my eyes were continuously scanning the terrain ahead, staying alert for signals of anything untoward before us. The recent floodwaters had eroded a bank on a horseshoe bend in the river, leaving a number of islands, the tops of some standing at least three metres above the riverbed. Surviving trees stood towering out of these islands, their massive root systems exposed, great caverns carved out of the recesses between root branches. We came to a particularly narrow section where two islands almost abutted, the space between neighbouring root systems just large enough for us to pass through in single file. As the point-man in front entered the narrow root-choked passageway, I looked to the left and ahead, past the men immediately in front of me, in the direction we were moving. At first, everything looked fine, but a glint caught my eye and I looked again. I blinked and looked again, not daring to believe what I saw. I caught my breath. I almost froze, but I knew that if I'd given away what I'd seen, pandemonium would have broken out, so I kept quiet and continued, the anxiety and fear mine alone to bear.

The sun was above and behind us to the west. Peering into the dimness between the tree's roots, my eyes slowly adjusted and made out a shape. There, at shoulder height on our left, almost totally hidden by the surrounding roots, I saw the outline of an enormous black head, a pair of dark menacing eyes watching our movement. He was waiting in ambush; in an instant, death could strike. As the men passed him by, he moved not a muscle, didn't flinch. Only his eyes followed our every movement. A cold shiver ran down my spine in the blazing heat and extreme humidity. I spoke a prayer under my breath. I couldn't warn any of my men in time. I silently clicked off the safety catch of my R4 and cocked it.

We passed one by one through the corridor of roots, passing his hideaway, his ambush zone. I somehow managed to walk, leaden legs carrying me ever closer to the enemy, lying in wait. He was tactically positioned to launch a surprise attack on us. I tried to make out whether he was alone, but couldn't see if he had a comrade.

I felt vulnerable. Was he waiting especially for me? Did he know I was the one in command? Had I given away that I'd seen him? I held my breath as I passed, my finger on the trigger, sneaking a furtive glance at him out of the corner of my left eye. He was stunningly well camouflaged, his weapons mere inches from my face and left shoulder. Despite my fear, I couldn't help but marvel at his almost perfectly concealed body, how well he had managed to get into and between the massive roots. Expecting him to strike, I felt my back arch in anticipation. Emerging from that tangle of roots, I was relieved. Nothing had happened.

Somehow I managed to remain composed. Removing the magazine, ejecting the round before clicking the safety catch back onto safe and waiting until we were safely some way off, I gave the signal for the men to stop and crouch into a kneeling position. I beckoned them closer to recount our narrow escape.

"I'm telling you," I countered their startled *auwu*s and *eish*es. "He was at least four metres long," I held up my fist, "his head was the size of my fist!" The guys were keen to go back and take a look, some seeming to disbelieve me. Phiri especially doubted my story; I could see him sneering in dismissal. I led them back towards the passage of roots and showed them gingerly where he was hidden. His cover broken, sensing danger, the enormous black mamba retreated, snaking off behind the roots and out of sight, but not before they'd all seen him.

In camp that night, tall stories were brewing as my men relayed their close-encounter with the *nyoka*. I watched with amusement as one trooper paced and measured off what must have been a distance of six or more metres, another held up his hands about a foot apart to indicate the head-size. All these incredible measurements were accompanied by gasps and loud whisperings. I realised I was witnessing the beginnings of a legend.

My life in that strange little camp at Gumbu Mine continued in much the same fashion, until one afternoon, late in February, Cappie returned from Messina Sector HQ with news that we were to deploy to another, more active area not far from Gumbu Mine. Mabiligwe Military Base was just six kilometres east of Gumbu Mine as the crow flies. The company stationed there had come to the end of their deployment, and we were to take over the patrolling and monitoring of the area. We would be joined by other 113 BN companies, with the likes of Looties Parfitt, Mark Cowie, Jason and others, and Cappie was to take charge of them all. On Friday, we packed up camp and, just like that, it was as if we'd never been there. I left with little nostalgia; I was excited about the change. But as we exited the camp, I looked out the passenger side of the SAMIL cab in which I sat and thought I might miss the raw beauty of Gumbu Mine's surrounds, and strangely, even those little bullet-riddled houses, which had been "home" for more than two months . The base would not be deserted for long. Soon, another company or battalion would arrive, settle into those ruins, and carry out their daily activities much as we had. No gap would be left in the SADF security system on the Limpopo River.

The road from the sisal line to Mabiligwe is not a straight line. From the sisal line, following a wide curve to the left, the road rises and falls as you go through a series of undulations. About halfway to the camp, you crest a rise and see Zimbabwe in the distance, and, shortly after, the base itself.

Coordinates: 22°20'32.76"S 31°03'09.38"E

Settling into Mabiligwe base was easy. We had all the comforts we could have hoped for at a base in the bush. Had we been in civvies, we might have looked the part of tourists on safari.

After warmly greeting the other 113 BN looties who'd joined us there, we had a look around. Several cats emerged from the buildings and greeted us tentatively. Mabiligwe was perched on an elevated portion of a fractured quartz-rock outcrop. Being an SADF permanent base, it was made up of several bricks and mortar buildings, a wooden building, and several green canvas army tents. The officers' quarters was a long brick and stone building looking out over the Limpopo River just 120 metres to the north. To the left of this building was a signal or radio room, housing long aerials, which was used to send and receive information from Messina Sector HQ. Close by was an indoor ops room, where Cappie would pin up his maps that night. Abutting the officers' quarters to the east was our open-air ops area, covered by camouflage shade cloth, where we would plan our movements using those sand models we had learned to construct at Infantry School and in South West Africa. A large area which functioned as a parade ground and volleyball court was situated south of the officers' quarters. Near the entrance, to the southeast of the camp, was the medics' tent and to the southwest was a grouping of tents which would house the troops. A shower truck was positioned between the troops' tents and the officers' quarters. Ablutions were shared, except for the toilets. As officers, we would be privileged to have our own toilets, whilst the NCOs had theirs covered by tents. All the ablutions were serviced by French drains. Several other buildings dotted the landscape, the wooden one being used as a kitchen, the others, stores. It was a very neat and practical base, which had the air of an established safari camp. Today it functions as a game ranger post for the contested Makuleke-Kruger Contractual Park.

That first evening at our new base we braaied. We chatted amicably as we ate lamb chops and drank beer. Jason told us an incredible story which had recently taken place while he was stationed at 113 BN. While rummaging in one of the dark corners at the back of the store in search of a new sleeping bag to replace his old malfunctioning one, he thought he heard hushed talking and a stifled giggle. Thinking the noises were strange and unfamiliar in those surroundings, he set off to investigate, following the sounds to the back of the stores. Creeping quietly towards a corner and peering around it, he came across an unforgettable sight: There, pressed against a large pile of old canvas webbing, was Stienie, the commandant leaning over her with his right hand up her skirt and his left fondling her breast through her blouse. The commandant's face was nuzzling Stienie's in a fumbling attempt to kiss her. Jason was shocked, and didn't wait to see what would happen next, but reversed quickly and quietly, and left the stores. It was hard to imagine someone as attractive as Stienie, and married to boot, having it on with the commandant, who was also married.

My mind went back to my first day at 113 BN, when those civilians had arrived on the base while we were on parade. Then, my eyes had caught something between Stienie and the commandant – a small and knowing smile from her, a restrained grin and imperceptible wink from him – and even then I had wondered if there was something going on between them.

It would soon emerge, from the other women on the base, that the commandant was a regular skirt-chaser who had made a nuisance of himself by hitting on them inappropriately. They suggested that Stienie was not a willing conspirator with the old brute, but was only trying to protect her job. Later that year, our suspicions were confirmed when Stienie unexpectedly resigned. On enquiry, the women in the office told us that her husband, on threat of divorce, had forced her to resign when he discovered the goings-on between her and the commandant.

I would catch up with Lieutenant Mark Cowie the following year, when we had completed our two years of national service. We met at Farm Inn, a popular nightclub in Pretoria in those days. There, Mark would deliver some distressing news about Jason. While on a camping trip to the Okavango in Botswana with his folks, he and his girlfriend were in a small boat in shallow waters when they had inadvertently drifted through a herd of hippos. The boat was flipped by the alpha bull, and the couple fell into the water, whereupon they were charged by the bull. Jason got between his girlfriend and the bull, giving her the chance to escape as he stood his ground facing the hippo. The bull went for Jason, gouging into his side with his tusks before flipping him through the air like a rag doll. Jason's girlfriend, meanwhile, made her way back to Jason's parents, who called for help over a two-way radio. Jason was airlifted by helicopter to Gaborone, then to South Africa for specialised treatment. Fortunately, Jason survived the ordeal, but bore massive scars from fending off that hippo.

Before the troops were mustered for parade early on Saturday morning, I set off with Gavin and the other loots to explore the Limpopo River. It looked much the same as it did at Gumbu Mine, except that its course followed an almost straight northwest to southeast route alongside the base for between eight to nine kilometres, disappearing around a gentle bend to the east. Looking westwards, I could see the dry riverbed emerging from behind the northernmost kopje at Gumbu Mine.

Back at the base, from its more elevated position, I surveyed the surrounding area from a better vantage point. The terrain was a lot flatter here than it had been at Gumbu Mine, which would prove easier to traverse by foot. The vegetation was more like veld than bush, and the grass and shallow rocky outcrops were littered with fragmented quartz rocks of various sizes, evidence of a tremendous geological event in the area, eons ago.

Beyond my view from the base, just over three kilometres to the east, we would later discover that the military zone came to an abrupt halt against the border with the Kruger National Park, a very high and robust game fence marking the boundary. The game fence ran across a steeply-elevated area and over a dagger-shaped kopje, ending on the South African bank of the

Limpopo River where it was anchored by a massive green painted pole. At the foot of the kopje was a large depression which formed a type of wetland delta, with a large sandy pan, which drained the surrounding area when the irregular rains of summer arrived. The park stretched beyond the sisal line to the south, creating an overlap with the barrier, several kilometres westwards. This seemed to me to be an intentional physical security overlap, preventing insurgents and refugees from gapping it across that area. Another natural but smaller delta-like drainage system lay to the west of the base just over two kilometres away, beyond which lay rugged and hilly terrain, all the way to Gumbu Mine.

Our area of responsibility totalled about twenty two square kilometres, which we were expected to cover daily. Patrols would begin on Monday morning, and, after a "welcome to Mabiligwe" braai early on Saturday evening, we sat down to draw up patrol rosters and area maps showing the various platoon responsibilities.

As I was relaxing in my quarters late that night, my blood ran cold as I heard a distant and chilling scream. I closed my book and listened, waiting to hear more. No more screams came, but unidentifiable bangs from far-off echoed through the night air. When sleep eventually came, it was restless and disturbed.

On Sunday morning, I mentioned the strange sounds I had heard the night before, and Gavin reported that he had heard them, too. Later, just as the sun was beginning to set, we decided to take a walk down to the river to investigate. Looking across the dry riverbed towards Zimbabwe, to a point almost due east, we saw nothing aside from a small kopje poking out from the dense surrounding bush.

Back at base, we told Cappie what we had heard and asked him what was out there. He told us that it was Robert Mugabe's notorious Chikwarakwara camp, a so-called police detention centre and prison. According to Cappie's intel, the base was used to torture any suspected collaborators and would-be refugees that were unfortunate enough to be caught before they managed to cross over into South Africa. It also functioned as a launch pad for terrorist operations into South Africa. I found this hard to believe, but as the weeks and months went by, we heard the occasional disruption and I was slowly convinced of Cappie's explanation.

On Monday morning, we inspected the troops' clothing and webbing, counted their sharp-point rounds and checked their rifles, and by 06h30, we were on patrol. My platoon exited the base to the east, rounded the bottom of camp, and then set off westwards along the river front, keeping off the service road and tracks. As the sun emerged, it was clear that the day would be cooking-hot out in the bush, so I made sure that we made it to our turning point quickly, just beyond the small delta-like drainage system, a few kilometres away.

Coordinates: 22°19'53.34"S 31°01'43.45"E

As the men rested under some tall riparian trees in the dense bush at our turning point, I scouted around carefully in the brush near a small rise that heralded a kopje to the immediate south. I found two wire snares tied to the base of some trees, and concluded that these could only have been placed there by Zimbabwean poachers, or perhaps some rogue SADF members, who had since left the area.

I returned to the men and had them thoroughly search the surrounds. Eight wire snares of varying degrees of strength were found, set to catch anything from a wild hare to a medium-sized antelope. Fortunately, none of them had been triggered. Feeling like we'd done our bit for the environment, we returned to camp with our prizes. Cappie took one look at our loot and said in a matter-of-fact voice, "You'll probably find all of them back there again tomorrow ... Certainly before the week's out." I was disappointed.

We made good use of our time on patrol, exploring the area and keeping the troops fit and disciplined. I was impressed with my platoon's behaviour out there. Armed with my R4, confidence in my men growing, I began to feel pretty invincible. Us loots became quite relaxed about our role at Mabiligwe. The easy-going atmosphere here gave us the opportunity to get to know the men under our command a little better, getting the hang of their distinct personalities and quirks.

GJ Nkuna was probably the oldest trooper in my platoon, Masuku coming a close second. At close to double my age, GJ was well built and rugged, with a physique like a middleweight prize-fighter. He was of average intelligence, but always reliable and respectful. Masuku, on the other hand, a short man with toadying habits, gave me the impression he was compliant only until my back was turned – not an attitude to inspire confidence in a man. ET Hlongwane may have shared initials with the famous extra terrestrial of the 1981 film, but he looked more like a baby-faced teenager, especially because he was one of the shortest in the platoon. He always seemed to be in a *dwaal*, forever daydreaming and not paying attention. He admitted that he often dreamed of wanting to "go home" on pass. The Nkuna twins were good looking lads, but almost complete opposites. Nkuna the younger was high spirited, enthusiastic and cheerful and seemed to follow my orders with genuine enthusiasm. I never got the sense he was trying to please with ulterior motives. I nicknamed him "Smiley". Nkuna the elder tried hard to be a positive and obedient trooper, but was cursed with a worrying nature which gave him an almost permanent scowl. I nicknamed him "Grumpy". Mabunda, very thin and taller than most, with a head disproportionately large in comparison to his body, reminded me of a praying mantis. He and his mate, Rikhotso, shared a similar trait: they both tended to be slow and confused in reacting to orders. Despite this, Mabunda wore a huge grinning smile most of the time, and I liked him for his unsophisticated ways. Then there was skinny "Sad Sack" Mathebula – if anyone was going to gyppo, it would be him. A real *sluiper*, as we would have called him at Infantry School, he would avoid exerting himself at all costs, and the minute you turned your back on him, he would slink off to sleep under the nearest bush.

Phiri was an anomaly. He was almost as tall as me, with a permanent scowl etched across his face. He had a dark, almost pitch black skin, explained by Sergeant Mnguni as due to Phiri's father being from "up north". I admit that these facts made me a little nervous about him, an irrational reaction, perhaps, but it was reinforced by his defiant and sometimes hostile attitude. He would look at me with such intensity that I felt as if his gaze bore right through me.

Phiri's disdain for any and all authority was clear. He inevitably arrived last to Muster, entering the squad formation in a shabby and *slapgat* manner. He was slow to follow commands and would try to rile the NCOs by feigning temporary loss of hearing, responding to an order with "What was that again, Sergeant?" The troops would titter and the NCOs would seethe. I often heard the black sergeants warning him – not in English, but their tone said it all. With me, he kept trying his luck by muttering comments under his breath to bring sniggers and furtive looks from his *maatjies*. I tried to ignore it, knowing that insisting, "What's that, Phiri?" would only draw from him a "Nothing, lieutenant," and give him the ammunition he wanted to annoy me.

He tried to whip up other less-than-compliant troopers into low-intensity revolts against the ranks. *Sluiper* Mathebula started mimicking Phiri's tardiness, and before the week was out, he had four mates employing the same strategy. He managed to influence his little gang of cohorts to react to commands with laziness, and some even picked up his habit of muttering disrespectfully under their breath.

I was not amused by Phiri's behaviour and approached Cappie with my concerns.

"Cappie," I said one day, when we found ourselves alone in the ops room. "You don't have any concerns about Phiri, do you?" He was straightening up the room and didn't pause as he responded.

"Phiri? Well, of course, with these guys there are always concerns, aren't there? Is there something bothering you, Mike?"

"Well ..." I spoke cautiously. "He's quite a handful, you know." Cappie nodded.

"He is, yes," he said. "Can be quite the troublemaker, too." He stopped what he was doing and looked at me. "I purposely put him under your command, you know." He said. "I think you have what it takes to control him." I was pleased and troubled at once. Was I capable of living up to Cappie's expectations?

"Yes, but, Cappie," I began. "Aren't you afraid that Phiri might be a ... you know ..." I dropped my voice. "A spy?"

"Like I said, there are always concerns with these guys," Cappie replied. "And Phiri, especially, with his dark skin and shifty ways. I have also wondered whether Phiri isn't a mole. But it occurs to me that he draws too much attention to himself with his bad attitude. If he's an *agent provocateur*, or a spy as you suggest, he isn't a very good one!" Cappie chuckled at this, but I wasn't reassured.

"But, Cappie," I said. "If he's a spy – a good one or not – he could be putting the whole company in danger. Shouldn't we be more concerned?" Cappie shook his head.

"I'm glad you have your eyes open, Mike. You're a good officer ... you think." Here, he tapped an index finger on his temple. Then he wagged the same finger in my direction, saying, "And I trust you to figure out how best to handle Phiri. If we had to start interrogating Phiri to find out if he was a spy, we might be doing ourselves more harm than good. Having him under our noses and under our control is more to our benefit, spy or no spy." He patted my upper arm and smiled, "You should be more concerned about his poor discipline and cheek!"

Two weeks into our stay at Mabiligwe, our patrolling area changed when half of Charlie Company, under Ross and Maas, was deployed to patrol the Kruger National Park from inside the game fence. The patrol route on the Kruger side of the fence stretched along the Limpopo River all the way through to the Levuvhu River at Crooks Corner, where Zimbabwe, Mozambique and South Africa's borders meet, and beyond. This increased 113 BN's area of responsibility to almost a hundred square kilometres. Gavin and I were now accountable for the whole of the Mabiligwe area, until platoons rotated and we had our chance to be posted to the park. I was envious of Ross and the boys when they departed for Kruger, but I would later discover that it wasn't quite the safari experience I imagined.

I returned from patrol one day to find Cappie slumped in a chair in the ops room, his fingers pressed to his eyelids as he quietly sobbed. I froze, alarmed and unsure of what to do next. Fortunately, Gavin walked in just then. He was far better at offering consolation to the distraught than I could ever be. He looked at me for explanation, but I shrugged ever so slightly and told him with my eyes that I had no idea what was going on.

Gavin acted immediately. Walking over to Cappie, he tenderly put his left hand on the distressed captain's shoulder.

"Hey, Cappie," he said quietly. "What's the matter?" Cappie's weeping intensified, and he dropped his head onto his arms on his desk. He raised his right hand in which was clasped a photograph. Gavin took the picture: it was of a young brunette, smiling into the camera with beguiling innocence. "She's gorgeous, Cappie," he said. "Who is she?" Cappie didn't reply immediately, but cried into the desk. Gavin was kind and patient, leaning on the edge of the desk as he waited for the weeping to subside. Eventually, Cappie lifted his tear-stained face, sniffed and wiped his eyes with the palm of one hand.

"That's Jackie," he said in a faltering voice. "She was my pupil at Clapham High." Cappie's face scrunched up in agony, his sobs barely contained.

Gavin waited a minute or two, then said, "And Jackie is why you're so upset?" Cappie closed his eyes, nodded. He pulled a hanky out of his pocket and blew his nose. Sighing, he looked at Gavin and me sorrowfully. "She's dead."

We were stunned. Pulling up chairs, we whispered condolences which were hopeless and inadequate. After a minute, Gavin asked the question which had filled my mind: "How'd she die, Cappie?" He touched a raw nerve, and Cappie's tears began to flow again.

"She committed suicide!" he wailed.

I was dismayed: the girl in the photograph was so young, so beautiful. Imagine losing a friend this way! In the tragic air of the ops room that afternoon, I silently mourned the death of this young stranger. My heart broke for Cappie, who cared so deeply for Jackie that her death struck him down with a physical force. Without speaking, Gavin and I waited for Cappie's strength to return, pondering the brevity and fragility of life. When he was able to speak again, Cappie told us how Jackie had jumped to her death from the block of flats built over the Sunnypark Shopping Centre in the Pretoria suburb of Sunnyside. It seemed that she had suffered months of personal troubles. While Cappie remembered his friend, Gavin and I kept him company and comforted him.

It took a couple of days for Cappie to recover from the blow of Jackie's suicide. He was unable to focus on his responsibilities at Mabiligwe with his usual efficiency, and Gavin and I did our best to pick up the slack and give him time to grieve.

Chapter 23

Coordinates: 22°20'07.40"S 31°02'05.16"E

The sky was cloudless. Even as we set off in the early morning, I could tell it was going to be another scorcher of a day. We faced yet another boring patrol on the same route, and I did my best to motivate the guys, but it was always hard in the oppressive heat of late summer.

We made faltering progress, my men whining like belligerent kids all the while. Sometime after 08h00, hardly two kilometres into patrol, I looked down to find Smiley Nkuna on my left.

"Lieutenant," he said cautiously. "It's hot. We're thirsty. Please let us take a break?" I didn't respond immediately. I was reluctant to agree to stopping, but I didn't want to increase the guys' resistance to me. Hoping to bolster the platoon's spirits, I grudgingly agreed to let them have a break, and pointed out a young thorn tree about fifty paces on.

We paused around the tree, the men scattered about in its inadequate shade. I stayed on my feet, anxious to keep moving but glad for a long drink of water. After ten or fifteen minutes, I tried to get them moving again. "Alright, men," it was hard to strike the balance between commanding and bullying, but I always liked to try. "Let's get moving. We can stop again at the halfway mark." Some of the guys moved to obey. I tried to encourage the others. "Hey! You lot! On your feet. It's time to go." A handful of men were standing by, weapons ready. Others were slowly getting to their feet. Phiri stayed where he was, propped against the tree, his rifle resting in the Y of two branches, butt on the ground, eyes closed as if he'd never heard me. "Phiri! Come on!" He opened an eye to squint at me sullenly. "Let's go." He ran his left hand over his brow and eyes, the thumb pushing his sweat-stained bush hat to the back of his head. I tried to stifle my irritation. "Phiri!" I walked towards him, nudged his boot with mine. "Let's move!"

He waved an insolent hand at me, clicking his tongue with a long drawn-out click. I was incensed by his disrespect.

My instinct in these times is to shout, like an angry parent to a toddler, but my experience had taught me to be more self-controlled. With restraint, I spoke quietly but firmly.

"Phiri," I said through clenched teeth. "I won't talk again." I needed to maintain authority in the face of Phiri's insolence, keep a hold of my position in front of my men. I got no response from Phiri. I raised my voice a fraction. "Phiri! On your feet now, or I will teach you a lesson!"

Discipline amongst the troops of 113 BN was a tough balance to strike. Unlike the conscripts I encountered at Infantry School, these guys were here by choice. The option to simply quit was open to my men in a way it never was to us. The threat of an *oppie* was enough to get us to comply with instructions with speed, the more severe the threat, the quicker our compliance.

With my men, however, I was disinclined to use the threat of an *oppie* unless there was no other means of gaining their obedience. I knew that empty threats did not work, and giving one of them an *oppie* might end up working against me in the long run. It was important to me to preserve the respect of these men.

Phiri had pushed me further than I had yet been pushed.

"Would you like to take your weapon for a run?" I asked him. Imagining having him complete the patrol doing knee lifts to touch his outstretched weapon brought me some satisfaction. "I will give you a rifle *oppie* like you have never experienced, *troep!*" He emitted another long click and sneered.

"*A ndzi nge yi kwalaho, musatha-nyoko!*" ("I'm not going anywhere, son-of-a-bitch"). This wasn't the first time I regretted being so slack during our Tsonga lessons. There were some chuckles and snorts from the others. I had to stop this now.

"Phiri! I will not tolerate you disobeying orders! This is your last chance, boy."

I guess I must have got to him. He was on his feet and in my face in a second. Barely inches from me, his finger almost up my nose, his voice was heavy with threat.

"Lieutenant," I could feel his breath on my face. "I am going to shoot you." He caught me by surprise, but I wasn't going to be intimidated.

"I'm warning you, Phiri ..." At this, he seemed to be overcome with rage. Stepping away from me, he grabbed his R4 and waved it about with bravado.

"I'll shoot you, lieutenant!"

I heard some of the other men gasp at Phiri's brazen behaviour. Someone spoke his name, as if to caution him. *Probably Smiley Nkuna*, I thought. Phiri brought the weapon to bear on me, aiming somewhere near my head, and I went into automatic mode. Time seemed to slow down, as they say it does in crisis. I zoned in on Phiri and the barrel he had pointed at me.

I could have brought Phiri down in an instant. In one fluid motion, I could have clicked the safety catch off with my right hand thumb, whilst cocking the rifle and curling my index finger around the trigger. I was certainly provoked enough. Here was one of my men threatening mutiny. I had a rifle pointed at me, and there seemed to be little motivation on the part of the others to stop Phiri from pulling the trigger. Although, to be fair, had he landed a shot, it would probably have been more by accident than by design.

I visualised how I would bring my rifle to bear on him, and then shoot him *smack!* – between the eyes. I had been trained, far better than Phiri had. I knew that I would be able to deal with the extreme event if it became necessary.

Being taller than Phiri, I raised myself up still further. Standing almost on my toes and leaning in towards him, I said in my coldest, hardest, most steely voice, "Just you try, Phiri. We'll see who comes off second best!"

In that moment there was no fear. I didn't fear Phiri shooting me, I didn't think he would, or even could. In any event, he would be more than stupid to even try – he would have been locked up in no time, and even if he was lucky enough to stand trial, he didn't stand a chance at getting off for shooting his superior, a white man whose skin was far more valuable than a black skin during those Apartheid years. Even if he dropped his weapon and ran – as he undoubtedly would have done, typical bully that he was – he would have faced a lifetime on the run.

I looked hard at Phiri for what seemed like an eternity. I watched Phiri's eyes flicker, watched the resolve fade from his face. He knew that I had called his bluff. He had no option but to back down. A nervous smile crossed his lips. He gave a goofy chuckle and waved a dismissive hand at me.

"Just joking, lieutenant," he said, an absurd attempt at retreat. I held my gaze steady, watched him squirm with discomfort. I took a deep breath. "Phiri!" I said. "Go back to base immediately and report to Captain Engelbrecht." I took my eyes off him for the first time since the start of the incident, scanned the faces of the men watching us. "Nkuna!" both twins saluted. "Smiley Nkuna. Come here," he made his way towards me. I looked again at Phiri, "Accompany *Skutter* Phiri here to the base, without delay." Smiley was only too happy to be of service.

I radioed back to base, explaining to Cappie what had happened.

"Send him here, on the double!" Cappie said straight away. I tapped Smiley Nkuna's shoulder and indicated he should move. As they disappeared around some bushes, I turned to the rest of the platoon.

In a measured and calculated voice I said, "If any of you ever disobey orders, or threaten me, as Phiri has just done, I will stuff you up." I spoke louder, almost shouting. "Do you understand me?" Rows of wide eyes in ashen faces watched me silently. "You will get the worst *opfok* of your life!" To drive the point home I said, "If any of you ever try your luck with me, I'll make sure you're kicked out of the battalion. And you will never get another job in the army again!" I had never seen a bunch of guys so taken aback and fearful. I paused for a second for dramatic effect, scanning their faces with piercing intent, then turned to go. "Let's move!" I barked.

The patrol continued in silence. I walked with purpose and indulged in no chat. As I walked, I was thinking – and quietly raging – over what had happened with Phiri.

It was not that I was afraid that Phiri would, in fact, shoot me that got me raging. What had triggered my anger was his blatant disregard for my authority and his outright defiance. Phiri had always been troublesome: sullen and insubordinate, but now his behaviour took on a new colour. He was a bully who thought I would be easy prey. I wondered if by trying to earn my men's respect by showing leadership rather than autocracy, I had let Phiri think I was weak. Had he succeeded in intimidating me in front of his peers, he would always have had one up on me, as well as the unquestioning submission of the men. Why would one with such a problem with authority enlist in the army?

I doubt he would have tried his luck with me had I been an Afrikaner. The Afrikaners, especially the PFs and Dutchmen, could be brutal. Give them an excuse and they would gun for you ...

We returned from patrol to find Sergeant Mathebula giving Phiri an *oppie* with a sandbag, Corporal Chauke looking on with a grin. I remembered my *oppie* at Omuthiya in South West Africa. Mathebula must have been at it for over an hour with Phiri. I walked over to where they were and stood quietly for a minute, watching Phiri strain. He was exhausted. Dust had caked on his lips, his shirt was drenched in sweat. I walked over to Sergeant Mathebula, holding up a hand to indicate I wanted to talk. As Phiri neared us, I stopped him.

"Phiri!" He dropped the sandbag, gave me an unsteady *strek*, but in his state he could barely stand.

"Lieutenant!" he said, his eyes lowered to the ground. "You still want to shoot me?" Phiri shook his head.

"No, lieutenant!" He was hoarse. He was broken.

I shouted. "Do you want to shoot me, Phiri?" He shook his head earnestly. "No, lieutenant," he whispered. I spoke to his tormentor.

"Sergeant Mathebula, that's enough. Thank you." I turned to go, but Mathebula stopped me.

"But, lieutenant," he protested. "I haven't finished."

"You have, Sergeant. Let the man go," I replied. On Phiri's face, relief and concern did battle.

"Lieutenant," said Mathebula, "Phiri has had this coming for a long time. He's a troublemaker." Corporal Chauke was chuckling, nodding his head in agreement, egging Mathebula on. "He's given all us NCOs nothing but trouble for months now. I want to give him what he deserves." I was appalled by their spitefulness.

"Thank you, Sergeant, but you have done enough." I wasn't going to be swayed. "Let Phiri go back to his tent."

From that point on, I had the sharpest platoon out there in the bush. When I barked an order, there was an instant response. For a while I enjoyed their prompt and unquestioning obedience. After all, this was the army. You don't question orders unless you want to get nailed. But I started to feel that my relationship with my men had lost the human element. The bond that arises from respect rather than fear was missing. I didn't want to be an ogre. I didn't want to be like so many of the other white guys in the army: instilling fear to maintain compliance. I wanted my guys to follow me, their leader, out of respect for me, not out of a sense of self-preservation. If Gavin could do it, so could I.

Following the incident with Phiri, I never consciously turned my back on my platoon, especially Phiri, again. I was careful to ensure a safe distance between me and my men. For a couple of days, Phiri was sullen and withdrawn, but whether this was a result of remorse for his actions, or because he felt sorry for himself, I never did find out.

At the end of our third week at Mabiligwe, I was relieved when Cappie told Gavin and me that he would be sending us out to operate from temporary bases in the field. I really liked the idea – I had been finding life at the base a bit tedious. Mabiligwe was a comfortable base – certainly more comfortable than Gumbu Mine – what with real beds to sleep on and marginally more sophisticated ablution facilities. I had also enjoyed playing volleyball with the guys (I earned myself a reputation for a mean spike which always caught the opposing team by surprise). But I was ready for a new challenge and welcomed the idea of a change in setting and routine. Gavin felt the same way.

We were to spend a week at a time at our temporary bases, taking it in turns to return to base for R&R for two or three days before heading out again. At the start of the next week, our platoons stocked up with five days' worth of rat-packs and departed from the base. Gavin's platoon set up camp quite near the base, patrolling the river front. With my platoon, I went down to the riverbank's edge near the low-lying kopje adjacent to the natural delta-like drainage system, the turning point of our recent patrols. Cappie had graciously provided me with an outdoor stretcher to sleep on, a luxury the troops didn't have.

Out in the field, I took to scouting the surrounding area in the dead of night with my night-vision goggles. Through the goggles, the stars and partial lunar reflection lit up the landscape in eerie shades of green, as though illuminated by cosmic floodlights.

I was awoken from my sleep in the middle of the first night by strange noises and shuffling coming from the riverbed. I spoke quietly to GJ, who was posted on guard duty.

"Pssst! Nkuna!" He turned slightly towards me. "Yes, sir?"

"Did you hear that?" I asked. GJ grinned, white teeth flashing in the faint moonlight.

"Don't worry, lieutenant. It's only *nyarri*." I grabbed the night-vision goggles and took a look. There they were: a herd of twenty or more buffalo, walking out towards the middle of the dry riverbed, just a hundred metres from where we slept. I watched as the herd slowly made its way past us, the pungent smell of the beasts lingering long after they had disappeared.

The incident was repeated on the second night. And again on the third. I couldn't understand what the herd was doing there, until I realised that we had set up camp directly in their path. Coming across our camp from the Kruger National Park side of the river, they must have chosen to walk still further westwards along the riverbed until they were satisfied that they were far enough away from us to re-enter the bush to access the veld grasses on which they foraged. If there is an animal you don't want to mess with, it is the buffalo, let alone a herd of them. Buffalo can keep a pride of lions at bay, and a wounded buffalo is extremely dangerous, known to backtrack on its hunter and make him the hunted. This herd had obviously got wind of the humans in their way. Realising there were a number of us camped out there, they had opted to circumnavigate us rather than barge their way through our camp. We had to be careful, though, never knowing if one of the herd would decide to charge us, or worse, the herd stampede us.

During that first week out at temporary base, Kimberly turned twenty-one. My day was taken up with poignant thoughts of her. How I wished I could be with her. I wondered if she was as consumed with thoughts of me, as I was of her.

One afternoon, I decided to give the men a treat and sent the Nkuna Twins back to base to pick up some refreshments: a Coca Cola and chocolate bar each. The twins left shortly after 16h00 with their rifles, their empty canvas webbing ready to be filled with goodies.

Much later, the twins returned at a pace, holding onto their bush hats and R4s, looking harassed. They were breathless and jabbering about *nyarri*. It took some effort to calm them down, and as their composure returned, their incredible story unravelled.

On their return journey, loaded with their bounty, the Nkunas had rounded some bushes about halfway and inadvertently walked straight into the herd of buffalo that had been roaming our surrounds of an evening. Freezing in their tracks, the twins watched as the frightened buffalo scattered – all but one large male, who stood his ground, snorting at them and digging his front hoof into the ground. Then the bull charged. Grumpy ran one way, Smiley the other. Choosing his victim, the buffalo followed Smiley, bearing down on the poor frightened soldier with his ominous up-curved horns and massive bulk. He easily caught up to the fleeing Smiley, who, looking over his shoulder, saw the bull's black eyes and felt his hot breath on his neck. Twisting his curved horns downwards, the buffalo flicked his head sideways and made a move into Smiley. Smiley knew he was a dead man. Next thing he knew, Smiley felt himself flying through the air, only to land atop a dense thorn tree shaped like an upturned umbrella. Lying flat on his back more than two metres off the ground, Smiley kept still, not daring to move. Convinced he must be bleeding to death, it slowly occurred to him that the only pain he felt was from the thorns pricking him through his browns. Hearing the buffalo snuffling and snorting below, he braved a peek over the edge of the dense leaves, branches and thorns. The buffalo was pacing around the tree, disturbed and confused. He could still smell the presence of his quarry, but was unable to find him as he lay petrified in the tree above the circling bull. Smiley tried not to breathe, holding onto the branches below him and willing the buffalo to leave. Eventually, the great bull gave up, and went off to join the herd, now some distance off.

Grumpy crept gingerly out from behind some bushes in search of his brother's lifeless body. Finding no corpse, he scratched his head and looked around, as confused as the bull had been, until a small and shaky voice asking for help reached his ears from above. He looked up and could just make out the shadow of Smiley through the almost impenetrable foliage of the thorn tree. Grumpy helped his brother down from his perched hideaway, and hugged him close with relief. The two quickly gathered up the scattered Cokes and chocolates, and ran all the way back to us.

The story was recounted to an open-mouthed audience. Recovering from the shock, I asked Smiley if he'd been hurt. He whipped off his shirt, revealing a long welt on his back, just at his right kidney where the buffalo had grazed him, the skin miraculously unbroken. It seemed the buffalo had managed to get its horn between Smiley's body and webbing, and the canvas straps had acted like a slingshot to hurl him to the top of the thorn tree, sending soda bottles and candy bars flying through the air.

The coke bottles fizzed when we opened them using the wire-cutters on our R4 bipods as bottle-openers, and several of the chocolate bars had been flattened, but we didn't mind – we'd just heard the best story ever! No fictional encounter, Smiley had survived a genuine on-the-very-brink-of-death episode, and was here to tell the tale. I knew the story would be recounted with relish by us all for generations to come.

When we returned to base after our first week in the field, Cappie told me he had decided to institute a bit of a refresher course in fire and movement to keep the troops on their toes, much like we'd done at Gumbu Mine. I thought it was a good idea. Cappie had arranged for one of the looties and his platoon deployed in the Kruger Park to relieve Cappie of his position at Mabiligwe Base during the day, so that he could join Gavin and me and our platoons for the training exercise over the next few days. Our first morning back at the base, after Roll Call, Sick Report and breakfast, we all clambered onto several SAMIL 50s to drive with Cappie out to the dilapidated old firing range that served as our training area when we were stationed at Gumbu Mine. We started out early, as the days were still very hot. We would need to take a break from training during the hottest time of the day between 11h00 and 14h00, time we would use for lectures, lunch and a half hour rest, after which physical training would resume.

I began the morning with a refresher lecture using a flip chart, followed by a description of the drill using a sand model. I really wanted to depict clearly for the men what was expected from them. I didn't want a repeat of the fiasco that had been our last fire and movement training there. I knew the guys better, now, so communication was easier, but my encounter with Phiri weighed heavily on my mind. I was afraid that he would use the exercise to shoot me intentionally; then claim it was an accident. I was extremely cautious, doing everything by the book.

I drilled them through the exercise, doing a dry run with each section. It looked okay, but I knew the real thing would be the test of my training. After the dry drill, I told Cappie I thought we were good to go live. Rounds were counted and dished out to each man. I lined up the first section of twelve men, R4s loaded with 35-round magazines. We didn't make use of a MAG for fear of the guys being caught in the crossfire.

With the order to begin, the men at the ends of the section fired a rifle grenade each towards the chosen target about two hundred metres away. The exploding rifle grenades signalled the line to begin advancing. Running behind the line as it made its staggered but ordered advance, I was amazed to see how well the guys were carrying out the drill. They reached the 200 metre point up front having performed an almost perfect exercise. I gave the order for the men to secure their weapons and marched them back to Cappie, who was smiling broadly.

"Well done, men!" he said, to their delight. "That was one of the best fire and movement drills I've ever seen!"

The next section was gearing up for their turn – they were eager to prove they were equal to their forerunners. The competition was on! I gave the order to begin, the rifle grenades exploded, and the section advanced on the target in the staggered formation, executing the drill as well as the previous section had. By the time I had taken all three sections through the drill, it was impossible for Cappie and me to choose which had performed the best. I was amazed – these guys would have given the Infantry School recruits a run for their money!

I spent the rest of the afternoon and the next morning putting the guys through the drill as many times as I could.

The second day of training was as successful as the first. The sun was inching towards the horizon as the third section took their places for the last fire and movement drill of the day, Phiri among them. As the guys stood waiting for the starting order to come, I saw intent and focus etched across their faces. The guys were so "in the zone" that nothing would have stopped them. When they had passed the 200-metre point and secured their weapons, I turned to them, saying I had never seen anyone perform a fire and movement drill better than what I had just witnessed – not even at Infantry School – and I meant it. With a hoot of victory, GJ Nkuna and Phiri rushed towards me, grabbing me by the waist, and lifting me effortlessly onto their shoulders. I laughed as I was bounced and swayed as the section broke into a spontaneous dance of victory, whooping and ululating. I was blown away. Gavin had his camera with him and snapped the moment of triumph, with Cappie running alongside, whooping it up with the rest of them. I sensed that the trust between me and my men had returned: I was their leader and they respected my position. But, more importantly, they respected me as a person.

Chapter 24

During the R&R days back at base, I volunteered to join the SAMIL 20 delivering water and rat-packs to the platoons stationed in the Kruger National Park – it was a pleasant way to alleviate the boredom of camp life and a chance to catch up with Parfitt, Ross and the other looties. Corporal Chauke was required to come along to attend to any sick reports from the troops in the bush, but I mostly ignored him and his smarmy ways. I sat up front with the driver, Corporal Chauke sat in the back with the rat-packs. It made me smile – that was where Chauke belonged! I got along famously with the drivers. I made regular stops at the Pafuri Gate, the most northerly entrance to the KNP, striking up a friendship with Mark, the thickly-bearded game ranger. We chatted many hours over freshly brewed tea in his double door, blue and white Kruger National Park guest reception caravan, which was permanently stationed under a thatch roof with concrete steps into the camper. The SAMIL driver was always glad for a little time off, taking a siesta under a shady tree nearby, or engaging in animated conversation with the local workforce, especially the women.

The first time I joined the team making deliveries, we entered the park through the Pafuri Gate and shortly turned left off the road towards the Limpopo River on a *twee-spoor paadtjie* that could hardly be called a road. There were various routes to get into the park, but, as always, I asked the drivers to go the long way around, so that I would have the opportunity to do a little game watching en route. On the twin-track, I had Ngobeni stop the vehicle. I was going to drive! He tried to protest, saying I needed a special military vehicle operator licence, but I dismissed this, saying I would take full responsibility with Cappie should anything go wrong. He reluctantly swapped places with me, giving me a quick rundown of how to apply the exhaust brakes.

Anyone who thinks they have experienced 4x4 driving because they cruise the suburban highways in a luxury Landy has no idea what 4x4 really means! Driving the SAMIL 20 is the ultimate off-road experience. A permanent 4x4 vehicle with a ground clearance of almost half a metre, the SAMIL 20 weighs five and a half tonnes and carries an off-road payload of up to two tonnes. Close to three metres in height, this beast of a vehicle is tough and imposing, and I had always admired it. I was stoked to have the opportunity to drive it. It was a synch! Despite its size, it felt much like driving a large car or small bus.

I saw surprise on the faces of Ross and the boys when the SAMIL 20 arrived at their base with me at the wheel. I only ever drove the SAMIL 20 on the gravel tracks, hopping out to let the driver take over when we came to tar roads. Pretty soon, I was driving the SAMIL 20 all over the northern part of the Kruger Park, making deliveries and relishing in the power and agility of the gigantic lorry. I would charge down those gravel roads with that powerful air-cooled six-cylinder diesel engine growling away, and I learned to operate the exhaust brakes quite effectively. With time, I progressed to the heavier SAMIL 50 personnel carriers. The other looties refrained from emulating my SAMIL exploits – whether they were too scared or too *paraat*, I don't know, but whatever their reasons, they missed out!

Coordinates: 22°21'06.45"S 31°05'35.48"E

Gavin and I finally got our chance to be based inside the Kruger National Park in April. My platoon was located just the other side of the fence from Mabiligwe. As close as this area was to Mabiligwe, the landscape was very different. The vegetation here was far denser than across the fence, and difficult to traverse by foot, so we made use of the roads in the park to patrol. This meant we had to be very wary of where we walked. Based on my experience of walking each day in the bush, I developed my own patrol protocols. I made use of a primary and secondary spotter. The first spotter – one of the troopers who had keen eyesight and the ability to concentrate for long periods during the patrol – was positioned fifteen to twenty paces in front. It was his responsibility to observe the ground and terrain ahead of the section. Not far behind him was the second spotter, who would "read" the bush around us, to look out for signs of anything amiss. It wasn't so much that we had to meticulously look out for and avoid spoiling the tracks of illegal immigrants through the area. It wasn't even that we might be ambushed by insurgents or encounter landmines. The biggest danger posed to us while on patrol in the park was nature itself. A black mamba would most likely flee approaching danger, but if cornered or sensing it had the advantage of attack, it might go for the oblivious soldier. Following the Nkuna twins' experience, I was wary of tripping into a herd of buffalo. Coming upon a pride of lions at a kill could be fatal. Even with the weaponry we carried, I knew the best practice was caution.

Our temporary base was set up under some tall trees, facing north towards the river. To our right, about a hundred metres away in an easterly direction, was an open expanse of grass, favoured by grazing herbivores. The patch was like an oasis, almost completely hidden amongst the trees and vines, and quite close to the gravel road that passed behind us in a large horseshoe, roughly from east to west. Beyond the grass oasis, some distance from us, was a natural depression which, even in this dry spell, held water due to the dense brush and foliage that hindered evaporation.

This close to the riverbank and so well sheltered from sunlight by the bush, our camp was exposed to heavy morning mists. To avoid waking up soaked-through by settling moisture, I set up my bivvy against a palm bush like a makeshift tent in the middle of the temporary base. All around me in a *laager* formation, I placed the members of the platoon, two by two. There was hardly a risk of being shelled by mortars or engaging in a fire-fight with insurgents at Mabiligwe or in the Park, so we didn't need to dig trenches. I allowed my men to place old fallen logs on the perimeter of the *laager*, more as a psychological barrier than as an effective physical barrier.

One afternoon, not long before dusk, I was preparing one of my delectable culinary masterpieces from a rat-pack, when Phiri gave a "Psssst!" and motioned us with a hand signal to stop what we were doing and look.

Following the direction of his finger as he pointed towards the bush, I saw several figures, barely detectable in their grey-brown camouflage, making their way slowly towards us from the Zimbabwe side of the Limpopo River. They were almost hidden by the undergrowth and steadily-growing shadows, and as they drew nearer, they seemed to materialise out of thin air like ghosts, the largest walking point, slightly ahead of his section. They didn't seem to have seen us.

I silently motioned to the guys to drop to the ground. Some were behind the logs nearest the advancing spectres, the rest of us on the far side, now a little exposed. Having dropped onto our bellies, we lay motionless. I had taught the guys, if they were ever to encounter a situation like this, to quietly take the safety levers off their R4s while lying in wait, ready at a moment's notice to cock their weapons and fire if necessary, but only on my command. Our browns were perfect camouflage in that dense undergrowth, but I wondered if our scent would give us away. I had heard stories from South West Africa about the keen sense of smell of SWAPO combatants avoiding the most adeptly concealed SADF ambushes set for them, just because

Johnny had brushed with Colgate before going out on ops. There wasn't a hint of a breeze in the early evening air, though, so our presence remained concealed. I don't think any of us had ever been so close to an eland bull. Just ten metres away from us, I could see that he stood over two metres tall, and must have weighed nearly a tonne.

I watched as he stopped in his tracks, looking directly towards where we lay, his dewlap impressive and his horns imposing. He didn't see us or smell us. If he had, he would have disappeared into the undergrowth in a flash, so we must have been downwind of him. But he was bothered by something. Eland are extremely skittish, and inclined to flee at the slightest hint of danger, but a bull may well charge when cornered. Their sharp, spiralled horns function like rapiers: you don't want to be on the receiving end of a charge by an Eland bull. We lay still and watched as he stood. He seemed to be mesmerised – we certainly were. A few minutes passed, then he turned to his left and passed us by, his harem following him towards the inviting patch of grass to our east. Later, I realised that the logs must have puzzled the animal, appearing out of place on his trail. Not knowing how they had arrived there, the bull took a minute or two to reconfigure his route. I was mightily encouraged at how well my men had reacted in the circumstances, and more so by their ability to quietly return to our meal preparations with hardly a whisper or a rattle of a tin. We were blending into the environment well.

Being bored I decided to grow a moustache. Although typically regarded as the "badge" of a PF, I thought that it might make me look older, perhaps more commanding; a "badge" of an *ouman*. I'd grown scraggly facial hair in the latter part of my varsity days, but now I wanted a *snor*. Slowly but surely, I cultivated that blond caterpillar above my top lip, as the hair on my head also started to grow beyond what was standard and acceptable military length. Haircuts were generally left for pass and mostly at our discretion as to length.

While we were deployed in the Park, we didn't need to shave unless we wanted to. I would stay in the bush with my troops until we all had the chance to go back to Mabiligwe for R&R, wash our clothes and clean ourselves up.

I read many books, mostly novels, after our patrols, just to break the endless daily monotony. Early on, Smiley Nkuna enquired as to what I was reading and if I could teach him to read English – so, for the days we were out there, each afternoon, I would teach Smiley and a few of the others how to read English.

I don't know why they were ever popular, but I had light blue *tekkies*, akin to American basketball sneakers. After patrol, I would quickly and with relish take my boots off and put on those sneakers, wearing them each day with my browns – I think that this was both a comfort and rebellious issue – rebellious because I had hated wearing my boots all the time during some of our Infantry School phases, and now, here I was making my own choice what I would and wouldn't wear, bringing a bit of civvy-wear into my life out there in the bush – they certainly were comfortable even if they reeked a bit!

At times we would scout around the immediate area and farther afield, more out of relieving the boredom than actual interest – in this way I found some elephant bones, but not without getting stung on my upper lip by an angry and potent (with venom) hornet that had been squatting on the calcified white femur when I picked it up – this was a huge source of pleasure for the troops who thought I looked hideous with my fat top lip!

***

"Okay, girls!" It was John, Michelle's new boyfriend. He was topping the girls' glasses up from a bottle of semi-sweet wine. "Let's do a poll." He smiled a wicked smile. "Helmets or polo necks?" It was 1984 and we were back at his uncle's holiday house in Rustenburg after seeing Chicago live at Sun City. It was after midnight and we were all amped from the show. Seeing a world-famous band was a rare opportunity for us South African youngsters during the time of the world's cultural boycott of the South African government. And Chicago didn't disappoint. We had sung along to the familiar songs, watching with wonder as Peter Cetera held the audience in the palm of his hand. After the show, we had some fun at the casino playing the slot machines. None of us were serious gamblers, we were just having a good time. Sun City was an entertaining outing for us. Located in Bophutatswana, one of the Apartheid government's so-called homelands for the black dispossessed, Sun City was the brain child and cash cow of local businessman and celebrity Sol Kerzner. Ol' Kerzner appeased artists' consciences by convincing them that playing the holiday resort was in no way equal to performing in Apartheid South Africa, and proceeded to rake in the bucks as South Africans who could afford the trip and had the urge to see an international band flocked to his venue by the thousands. I guess the bucket-loads of cash he offered the bands went a long way towards convincing them of his somewhat faulty logic. We paid no attention to the political game-playing. We were just thrilled to be able to enjoy a concert of international standards.

The girls all giggled at John's suggestion, the wine lubricating the conversation so that we all dared to go where propriety would normally have prevented us. Right now, that was a frank discussion about the male apparatus and whether or not girls preferred it circumcised. We were relaxing at the counter that separated the small kitchen from the lounge area, the cool night air kept at bay by sitting close and partaking of a sociable drink. Michelle looked at her boyfriend disapprovingly and refused to take part in his childish game. John shrugged and looked at Diane. She blushed and mumbled "Polo necks," through a coy smile, looking at her boyfriend. He laughed.

"Kimberly, my girl," John looked our way. "What about you?" Kimberly was bold, as she laughingly stated her preference. I was shocked. Then I remembered Barry, her one-testicled paramour. She had convinced me they had just kissed. Now I knew better. The bitter taste of bile and deception made me nauseous. I couldn't look at her. I didn't even hear what the other girls' responses to the question were.

***

Memories of that weekend in Rustenburg were dredged up when Kimberly wanted to join several others going to Sun City to see some or other international band that was playing during my pass just before Easter. I opted out, not wanting a repeat of that weekend three years ago. Kimberly was disappointed, and the remainder of my pass in Pretoria was none too comfortable. The situation wasn't improved by the fact that Kimberly was evasive about her twenty-first. She told me she'd had a party at her folks' house on the Saturday, and those of her friends that were there were suspiciously quiet about the whole affair. At my request, she showed me the photos, none which made me mistrustful. I never thought to push any of the girls for information. Her twenty-first seemed to be a mental and emotional watershed between us – indicative of a conscious separation between her life, back in civvy street, pursuing her own agenda and interests, and mine, governed by the military, where I could do little to influence day-to-day happenings. That pass turned out to be frustrating for me, as I found Kimberly to be passionless and uninterested. I felt the distance between us in so many ways now. Physically, our interactions, as few as they were, lacked the ardour and excitement of our earlier relationship, and gave me little satisfaction and no real pleasure.

I decided to return to Letaba Ranch after my Easter pass with my Honda XL600R scrambler. I wanted to have my own transport available to me while I was there, and I couldn't continue borrowing other people's cars. I couldn't afford to buy my own car, either. I had convinced Cappie that the bike would be effective for use in our local ops – I had a way about me in those days, I could make anything sound like a dream if I put my mind to it. Cappie was sold on the idea, concerned only that a civilian vehicle should be used in a military zone. I answered this by saying that without the licence plate on, no one else needed to know.

The ride back was long and uncomfortable. A scrambler is not a long-haul touring bike: its pillion seating ergonomics and handlebar position are not conducive for comfortable riding over protracted distances. By the time I hit the dirt road passing Eiland, my bum was totally numb. It had been raining in the area, and as it was late in the afternoon, the light was dim under the overcast sky. Just ten kilometres away from my destination, I drove the last stretch standing up, giving my backside much-needed relief and popping wheelies across the larger puddles on the dirt road, which had turned to mud.

I spent another lonely night in my cabin in the mobile home on the river. Listening again to Steve Winwood, I shed no tears, feeling nothing but profound sadness and a sense of acceptance that my relationship with Kimberly was really shaky, acknowledging the distinct possibly that it was probably on its way out.

The next morning, a couple of troopers helped me lift my Honda onto a SAMIL 50. I secured it with tie-downs and we departed the base towards the Madimbo Corridor and Mabiligwe. I arrived to warm greetings from my mates, and I quickly stashed the Honda away near the officers' quarters.

113 BN platoons were systematically redeployed to the Mabiligwe area over mid to late April and early May, with almost all the sections out in the Kruger National Park recalled, except those immediately adjacent to the Mabiligwe area and on the river. General elections had been called by Prime Minister PW Botha, the *Groot Krokodil*, to take place on 6 May, and the SADF were gearing up to be on high alert during this period, expecting infiltration from Zimbabwe. Cappie relayed the intel he had been given, ordering us to be on the lookout for guerrilla insurgents crossing over the border, carrying mini-limpet mines and other ordnance that could be used to create terror in the Republic in the lead-up to the elections. The authorities believed the insurgents would try to access the country between Gumbu Mine and

Mabiligwe, making their way to Venda, where they would be lost in the crowds and probably aided by sympathisers. From there, the terrorists would make their way to Pretoria with their deadly cargo, where they or other operatives would plant the bombs as part of a concerted effort to cause terror among civilians and derail the elections.

As a means to beef up our battalion during these sensitive times, an 81 mm mortar team was to be deployed to Mabiligwe with us. Cappie charged me with the responsibility of escorting the team from Messina Sector HQ, and I relished the idea of getting away for a while. I left in the afternoon with a driver in an open-back SAMIL 50. We stopped in town to stock up at the local supermarket and bottle store before making our way to Messina Sector HQ to meet the loot and his team. The loot was an English-speaking dude who had done his training in mortars. He had light-coloured hair and was a tad podgy by infantry standards. I got the idea he had been drinking before we arrived. He greeted me in a friendly enough manner and I said, "Let's go." He and his team jumped up onto the back of the SAMIL and away we went. I stood on the back of the truck with the team. The late afternoon air rushing through my hair was an improvement on sitting in the stuffy cab.

No sooner had we turned off onto the R525 than he opened a beer, clipped on a full 35-round magazine, cocked his rifle and began firing it into the air, whooping it up like he was some kind of renegade cowboy. The driver immediately slowed down, thinking something had happened. Trying to be polite, I asked the jerk to stop indulging in his moronic idea of fun, but he continued to fire off that whole magazine. Realising there was no reasoning with a drunk, I held my tongue. Eventually he gave up. Perhaps he had been cooped up too long and now, being deployed, was acting like a total lamebrain. We finally arrived back at Mabiligwe, none too soon for my liking.

Coordinates: 22°19'53.34"S 31°01'43.45"E

The next day, I returned with my platoon to our familiar spot furthest west from the base; Gavin and his platoon were again stationed closer to Mabiligwe Base, patrolling the river front. This time there was no sleeping stretcher for me; the nights were to be spent lying in ambush along the banks of the dry riverbed. The whole of our company was now concentrated on the Mabiligwe and Kruger National Park front.

I reorganised my three sections into two, concentrating section two, codenamed Whiskey Two, under Corporal Maluleke, to the west of me, in the direction of Gumbu Mine. About three hundred metres away from me, Maluleke's stick was positioned almost two metres above the riverbed, on the edge of the riverbank. They were well hidden beneath the thick brush and trees where we had found those snares. With Whiskey One, I settled just east of the buffalo trail, less than a metre above the riverbed on the edge of the riverbank. The whole platoon faced north across the border, towards Zimbabwe.

Night fell and we took up our positions under a moonless sky. My section spread out to cover a distance of almost fifty metres, seventeen prone bodies taking cover behind driftwood logs. Our firing arcs created a kill zone of about 150 metres across and a hundred metres in front of us. The men had been given two full 35-round magazines each. Between 20h00 and 06h00, each section member would have a turn to do guard duty. Lying at one end, Smiley Nkuna two metres to my left, I scouted the area with my night-vision goggles.

We passed the first two nights in this manner without incident. Occasional banging and intermittent bellows came from down-river and across the border where the Chikwarakwara detention centre was. These ominous noises set my imagination on fire, putting me on edge, imagining the worst rape, torture, murder – and when sleep finally came, it was fitful and disturbed by dreams filled with terror.

Close to midnight on the third night, my ears pricked as I heard the faint sounds of a vehicle drive up to a point almost directly across the riverbed from where we lay. I trained my night vision goggles onto the spot and in the different shades of green and black, made out the distinct outline of a pair of headlights, which lit up the viewfinder with the faint reflection of ambient cosmic light. I guessed the vehicle to be about six hundred metres away, on the far bank, in Zimbabwe. Without having seen its headlights, which had deliberately been switched off before coming down to the riverbank, I was suspicious.

"Psst! Smiley!" I whispered to my left. "D'you hear that?" Smiley had been asleep. He sniffed, shook himself awake.

"Eh ...?" I slithered closer to him, held the goggles out to him in my left hand.

"Check," I said, and pointed in the direction of the headlights. Quickly alert, Smiley lifted the goggles to his eyes, just as the engine across the river was cut. He nodded, handed the goggles back without taking his eyes from the spot. I looked again through the lenses. Taking shallow breaths, I tried to fill in with my ears what my eyes couldn't see. Aside from the usual noises of night time in the bush, I could hear nothing untoward.

A minute passed. Then five. I didn't see or hear anything to explain the situation. I decided to radio Maluleke, but before I had raised the handset to my lips, the tap-tap, tap-tap of a lone R4 rang out in the still night air. It was coming from his section. Smiley and I looked at each other in alarm. "What the heck ...?" I said. A minute later, another R4 joined in, firing two rounds at a time, just as I had taught the guys. "Crap! That's the other stick!" I said. "What's going on?" I heard another R4 start firing. And then another. Before long, the whole section must have been firing, a cacophony of shots resounding over the bush. Smiley and I were on our haunches, our hands clasping our weapons. By now, all the men in my section were awake and muted questions were making their way up and down the line. Soldiers trained at Infantry School would have taken a second or two before all rifles were blazing. This sounded to me as though the shooters weren't convinced about their target or its identity. I had received no radio warning from Maluleke that he was about to engage. I got on the radio. "Whiskey Two, this is Whiskey One, come in!" I clicked the talk lever off. Silence. "Whiskey Two! This is Whiskey One. Come in!" Nothing. I swallowed the rising panic. "Whiskey Two! Maluleke! Can you hear me?" Still no response. Through the goggles, I could see tracer rounds lighting up the viewfinder with their bright red magnesium tails, every third or fourth cutting through the darkness towards a point across the river. They could only be coming from Maluleke. I knew I had to act.

I got on the radio. "Bravo, this is Whiskey One, come in, Bravo." I was relieved when the radio crackled to life in response.

"Bravo to Whiskey One, I read you. Over." Mabiligwe Base was awake – they must have heard the commotion down on the river.

"We've just had what appears to be contact. Over."

"Give the coordinates. Over." I spoke the coordinates into the radio, then, "Give me eyes. Over."

"Copy that. Over." I held my breath, counted silently. I had reached eight when the 81 mm mortar went up from just over two clicks away at the base. The magnesium flare drifted on its parachute several hundred metres above us, flooding the ground with its eerie white-yellow glow. It was spot on target. The metallic voice from base came over the radio.

"Bravo to Whiskey One, eyes launched. Keep us updated. Over." On the dry riverbed I saw nothing except for the shadows changing as the flare drifted by. By now, the panic had subsided and I was focused. I clicked back onto the radio.

"Whiskey One to Bravo, repeat eyes. Over."

"Copy that. Over." This time I had only reached three when the second flare zipped upwards, shedding its white-yellow radiance over the terrain.

The rocks and trees seemed to come alive in the moving light, but I saw nothing untoward. Another flare went up. I was frustrated. I had already decided to find out firsthand what the heck was going on when I heard Cappie's voice come over the radio.

"Whiskey One, this is Charlie Bravo. Come in!" I could sense he was uptight. His anxiety drifted the two kilometres over the terrain from the base like the flares before it.

"Whiskey One to Charlie Bravo, I read you. Over." In his state, Cappie lost all sense of radio discipline.

"Mike! What the hell is going on?!"

"It appears Whiskey Two have opened fire. Over." I could just imagine Cappie's red-faced spluttering.

"Well, what is it? What do they say?" "Whiskey Two aren't responding. Over."

"Well, you'd bloody well better get over there, and fast!" "On my way. Over."

"Keep us updated," he said, and then as an afterthought, "... over."

I hastily briefed my section to hold tight. "... And don't fire!" I said, as another flare went up. "Don't fire, unless you're actually being fired on." Leaving my radio with them, I set off, loping at a half-crouch under the cover of the riparian bushes. The mortar crew popped another flare across the area, then kept them coming, so the light was like weak but constant daytime, creepy shadows passing over the nearest kopje on the Zimbabwean side. Clutching my R4, adrenaline pumping, I covered the 300-metre stretch to the other section. Acrid gunpowder smoke hung thickly in the air; empty shells littered the ground. By the time I spotted Corporal Maluleke, his men had stopped firing. I braked too late and bumped right into Maluleke, grabbing his radio.

"Bravo! Hold fire! Hold fire! Over." The mortar crew must have shot at least ten flares since I had called for illumination.

The area gradually darkened as the last flare gave up its light. Cappie was impatient over Maluleke's radio.

"Mike! Mike! Are you there?!"

"Charlie Bravo, this is Whiskey One. I'm at Whiskey Two. Hold while I investigate. Report to follow. Over." I lay on my belly on the riverbank in the darkness and breathlessly asked Maluleke what had happened.

"I was asleep, sir. We all were. Phiri started firing and woke us all up. We thought he must have seen something, so we started firing in the same direction." That explained the slow start to the firing. I called Phiri with a hoarse whisper, beckoned him over when he looked our way. He scampered low towards us, dropped on his stomach beside me.

"Phiri!" I said. "What happened, man?" Phiri was fired up, out of breath.

"I was on guard duty when I saw a car or bakkie," he said. "It came down ... right down to the edge of the river, without lights." I was nodding. So far, just as I had seen. "Then it switched off, and I heard voices."

"Okay, Phiri," I interrupted him. "I saw the vehicle too, but I didn't hear voices. Could you hear what they were saying?" Phiri shook his head.

"The voices were hushed, lieutenant. But it sounded like they were coming closer. They were coming this way, lieutenant! All of a sudden, the voices stopped. I got nervous. So I shot in their direction." I wasn't angry with Phiri for disregarding procedure, but I was puzzled. The guys had been taught to wait until they could make out that the enemy was in the kill zone, not more than a hundred metres away, preferably as close as fifty metres. Phiri and the rest of the section had fired across an international border to a mid-point that was easily 250 metres away. I realised that this could be a major political incident that South Africa didn't need.

I radioed a report to Cappie.

"Okay, Whiskey, copy that." Cappie's memory of protocol had suddenly returned. "Incident will have to be reported to Hotel Quattro. Prepare a sitrep and send it to me early in the AM. Change your coordinates, but stay close by. Over and out." The order to remain in the area was contrary to what we had been taught, but I realised that we wouldn't expect any mortar rounds to hone in on the shooters' position. SADF intel was reliable – here across the Limpopo, the Russians, Chinese and other communist countries hadn't supplied the insurgents with the required firepower required for retaliation. Their support, I supposed, was concentrated on the more volatile region of the South West African-Angolan Border.

None of us could sleep that night. I wondered if we would find any bodies or discarded weapons at dawn… Early in the morning, Cappie radioed an instruction to send the troops back to the base, but told me that I would have to remain at the site of contact until a group team from Regional HQ in

Pietersburg arrived to investigate the matter. I kept Smiley and GJ with me, more for the company than as fire support. I sent the others back to base, carefully handing my handwritten situation report to Lance Corporal Maluleke, with instructions to give it directly to Cappie. It was late in the afternoon after a long day of waiting when a white military Toyota bakkie finally arrived. Two moustaches got out, both captains, PF and, of course, Afrikaans. With their eyes already scanning the empty riverbed, their attitude was accusing from the start, and I took an instant disliking to them. They didn't even bother to greet my men.

"*Dag, luitenant.*" They nodded curtly in my direction. I saluted them.

"*Sê vir my,*" the taller, dark-haired of the two wasted no time getting down to business. "*Wat het gisteraand hierso gebeur?*" He asked what happened here last night. He put his hands on his hips and looked at me expectantly. I deliberately spoke in English, recounting Phiri's story in as much detail as I could, while the second PF made notes on a clipboard.

"So," the first said in English. "No wounded, no dead?"

"No, sir," I replied. He sighed, wiped his hands briskly on his thighs.

"Let's go take a look at the contact point," he said. I indicated to the two Nkunas to follow. "*Ag nee, los hulle hier.*" It was the captain with the clipboard. "*Hulle hoef nie saam te kom nie.*" I reluctantly instructed my men to stay where they were, stressing that they should be alert, and led the two three-stars towards the middle of the dry riverbed. As we walked, the taller said to the other, "*Ongelukkig is daar nie beter soldate om op dié grens te plaas nie, né?*" To which the second nodded ruefully. I couldn't tell if he was disparaging me or my men by questioning the calibre of the soldiers here on the border, but either way, I was livid. Somehow, I managed to hold my tongue.

Arriving at the middle of the riverbed, the moustaches started looking around. I thought they were reckless, the three of us making easy targets for a sniper hidden in the bushes across the river, but they didn't seem to care. I wondered if they were brave or just stupid. I kept low and watched the far bank carefully as the terrain was reconnoitred. The dry sand didn't hold prints well at all, and there was little to see. Hundreds of depressions littered the bed, but it was impossible to tell if any of these were made by human feet or by a herd of buffalo. I kept getting sceptical looks from the two captains as they scouted about.

"Maybe the guys were firing at ghosts, hey?" the taller eventually asked flippantly. I chose not to respond, not trusting myself to be respectful. "*Daar's niks hier om te sien nie,*" ("There's nothing to see here,") he said to his partner, and they turned towards the southern riverbank to go. Just then, I saw, lying in a depression in the sand close to the point of supposed contact, hidden behind a low sand bank, a small red object, which, on investigation, turned out to be a cigarette lighter – pretty new by the looks of its glinting plastic coat.

"Uh, Captain," I said, lifting the lighter from its resting place and holding it out towards them. "Did you see this?" They both turned to look. "I found it here," I said, pointing to the ground where it had lain. Their eyes looked to the ground, then rose to look at me. The taller man cocked his head as if to say *"And?"* I answered his silent question with one of my own.

"Well, what is it doing all the way out here?" He gave me a smile that was at once sarcastic and indulgent.

He said, *"Luitenant, dit kon op 'n klomp maniere hier beland het.* It could've been lying there for days, even weeks. Maybe it was dropped by a herd boy, eh?" He pocketed the thing, anyway.

As the arrogant PFs departed, I turned to Smiley and GJ.

"Don't worry about them," I waved a hand in the direction of the rapidly diminishing bakkie trailing dust clouds. "They don't have a clue what they're doing." To this day, I wonder what actually happened out there that night.

Following our midnight incident on the river, Cappie suggested I stay at the base with my men for a few days. I didn't know if this was punishment, or instructions from above. Either way, I was frustrated, but thought better of complaining to Cappie. Being stuck at the base felt limiting at a time when some action was expected in the area. To alleviate the restlessness and monotony, I took to riding out on my scrambler to the sections patrolling the riverbanks. After checking in with the guys, I would turn the bike onto the gravel road, leaving it just before the base on a track leading to a far western kopje that dominated the area, overlooking the Limpopo River. I gunned the bike on the dirt roads and around the bends. This little daily excursion was a real treat for me, bringing with it a feeling of something akin to freedom. Once, standing on the top of the kopje, as I looked out towards Zimbabwe, I remember being struck again by the sheer rugged beauty of the area. The bush sang out its symphony of insects and birdsong, a gentle breeze playing around my ears and in my hair, and I experienced a moment of sublime contentment. I took a moment to acknowledge that I was privileged to have been selected to spend my second year of national service here in an environment so different to what the average conscript experiences. I thought of the men in my platoon, and felt a real sense of pride. They had really flourished under my lead, and I appreciated them for being so different in so many ways to what I was used to. I silently thanked them for the challenges they had brought me, as I realised how far we had all already come in just a few short months, although the time passing felt interminable. Taking my leave of the kopje, I breathed in a long breath of the clean river air, hopped back onto the bike and made my way back to base.

I parked my scrambler, and as I made my way towards the ops room, I felt the middle finger of my left hand stinging uncomfortably. On examination, I saw it was quite swollen. I turned the hand over, held it up to the sunlight, and there, just above the knuckle on the second phalanx, I found a small mark on the skin. I assumed I must have been bitten or stung by some small bug while riding and shrugged it off, thinking it would come right in no time.

The following morning, I woke to find the finger more swollen and sensitive than the day before. I showed it to Corporal Chauke, who was as perplexed as I was. He agreed it must be a bite or sting and daubed it with calamine. By the third day, my finger was as thick as *boerewors* and terribly painful. I went over to the medics' tent. Chauke shook his head, stumped.

"It must be a thorn from one of those acacias," I suggested. "It must have pierced my finger as I rode past." Chauke and his sidekick medic laughed loudly at this. I looked at them for an explanation for their mirth.

"No man, *Mlungu!*" Chauke chortled. "That's impossible!" Scratching lightly at the mark which made the centre of the wound, I discovered it was slightly raised, the skin around it taut. It occurred to me that, as I was receiving no medical attention from the medics, it might be time to take my treatment into my own hands. I squeezed hard on the swollen skin around the red puncture, and couldn't believe my eyes when it spat forth a foreign object, black and sharp, in a stream of pus. I held it up for all to see. It was clearly the broken off end of a devil thorn, almost ten millimetres long and about as thick as a toothpick. It had turned from white to black in the moist confines of my wounded finger.

Coordinates: 22°22'06.47"S 31°03'29.39"E

Early in May, as the *Groot Krokodil*'s general election was looming, I had taken to riding out at daybreak each morning on my bike, doing my own version of patrolling, riding slowly as I looked for footprints along the Limpopo River bank. On these rides, I usually found nothing, and on this

331

particular day, it was the same. But something made me think to ride all the way back to the sisal line, where I followed the minor maintenance and service road in an easterly direction on the northern side of the barrier. About four clicks from the base, where the road dips away towards a wide and sandy gully that feeds into the wetland area to the east of the base, out of sight from the access gate through the sisal line to Mabiligwe, I saw them. Two sets of footprints, both the recognisable tread of a *tekkie*, leading towards the fence, then bunched close together with multiple imprints just below a gaping hole where the fence had been cut with wire cutters. I drew in a sharp breath as the implication of these signs dawned on me. I knew I couldn't get through the gate, as it was locked, so I parked my bike and jumped off to follow the prints. Climbing through the gap in the fence, I made my way through the sisal barrier, experiencing first hand just how easy it was to sidestep the sharp points of the leaves and duck through gaps where the sisal wasn't growing properly.

I made it all the way to the other side and saw where the footprints exited the barrier. To mark the spot, I fetched the red handlebar pad from my scrambler and fixed it to the fence on the southern side as a marker. I had no radio with me, so I raced back to the base and breathlessly told Cappie what I had seen. Cappie sprang into action, calling Sergeant Mathebula and another sergeant who was also a tracker. Grabbing our R4s and fully loaded mags, the four of us jumped into the SAMIL 20 and raced down the road at breakneck speed, Mathebula at the wheel.

Passing through the now-unlocked access gate, we turned left towards the Kruger National Park on the main southern maintenance and service road, stopping when we spotted my red crossbar pad. The two sergeants hopped down to take a closer look at the footprints. Sergeant Mathebula pointed out how the footprints were quite deep in the soil at points, explaining that this indicated the travellers may have been carrying extra weight. He estimated the spoor to be a couple of hours old. Cappie thought the trail should be followed to see where it led, so the tracker ran ahead of the SAMIL 20 as we made our way in the general direction of the Bende Mutale village, south of Mabiligwe Base.

I began to think that the prints would lead us all the way into the village, where they would disappear in the confusion of the evidence of the locals' everyday life, but after crossing the tar of the R525, several kilometres before the village, they suddenly turned southeast, heading away from the village and back towards the Kruger Park. We came to the large fence abutting the

Kruger Park's game fence in an area marked by scores of deep dongas and rises that even the SAMIL 20 was unable to access. The sergeants found a gap in the fence through which the pair had wriggled. At this point, the area was no longer under our jurisdiction, and Cappie told us it was now in the hands of the SAP. He radioed in to Messina Sector HQ to report what we had come across. I was disappointed, feeling like we had come close to achieving something, only to have it handed over.

The general election took place just a few days later. There was some pressure from the ANC and other resistance movements in the shape of increased random terrorist attacks, mass action and violence all over the country. Up at Mabiligwe, we heard the reports but we were mostly unaffected. I guess the election results were pretty much a foregone conclusion, despite the resistance. None of us were given the opportunity to exercise our right to vote.

Not long after the general election, a report came through from Messina Sector HQ describing a fire-fight between police and two armed insurgents which had taken place near the village of Bende Mutale, not far from Mabiligwe. According to the report, the terrorists were making their way back to Zimbabwe through Venda. They must have entered South Africa sometime prior to the elections. The two were intercepted by the police, who opened fire when the men made a dash to run. One fleeing terrorist was killed outright in a hail of bullets. The other was shot and wounded as he attempted to throw a grenade at his pursuers. Before he could be captured, the wounded man was blown to bits by the grenade in his hand – whether by accident or by design, no one will ever know. Thinking about the two dead terrorists, I couldn't help but wonder if I had followed their entry into the country as I tracked those footprints in the sand that day in early May.

Chapter 25

The ancient Limpopo River is intersected by the more youthful and faster-flowing Levuvhu River at the northern-most point of the Kruger National Park. The confluence of these two great rivers marks the site at which the three countries of South Africa, Zimbabwe and Mozambique meet. Here, where the land tapers to a point between converging riverbeds, is Crooks Corner, which, at the turn of the twentieth century, was a haven to all manner of shady characters: outlaws, determined to evade capture, and poachers, who would smuggle ivory and rhino horns for the black market. Crooks Corner was wild and secluded, its proximity to three international borders making evasion from the law literally a hop, skip or boat ride away into another country and out of the pursuers' jurisdiction. Cecil Barnard, possibly the country's most notorious ivory hunter, made Crooks Corner his hideout in the twenties when he was on the run from rangers and police.

Coordinates: 22°25'52.96"S 31°17'57.71"E

Following the General Election of '87, my platoon was stationed on the northern bank of the Levuvhu River, not far from Crooks Corner. The high alert security status that accompanied the election had come to an end and things at Mabiligwe returned to normal, the Company again divided between Mabiligwe and the far northern and northeastern portions of the Kruger National Park. The banks of the Levuvhu River were steep, several metres higher than the banks of the Limpopo where we had been patrolling in April. Our temporary base was under some fever trees, just off a small pathway forged by the feet of humans, not animals. In those days, a police outpost was located at Crooks Corner, just across the river, but we were given express orders to stay as concealed as possible and have no contact with the SAP around our area of patrol, for concern over giving away our routes and position.

The area teemed with wildlife. A dense covering of trees lined the river's course – a multitude of fever trees dotted with the odd baobab, accompanied by dense undergrowth – and all manner of birds took shelter here, their varied calls setting the bush to whooping and babbling as the sun rose each morning. Hundreds of vervet monkeys chattered away in the treetops. It was autumn, so the river was dry, but the odd muddy pool became waterholes which attracted a wealth of buck and monkeys. From time to time, I would spot a crocodile lounging in the shallows of one of these pools, but crocs and hippos were scarce at that time of year, having moved below the confluence into the Limpopo River itself, where baseflow from the Levuvhu seeped out to form bigger pools in the great riverbed. I was always delighted to come across the prehistoric features of a legavaan, the shy monitor lizard which was common in the area.

Because the terrain was so thick with trees and bushes near the river, we patrolled the riverbed itself. Any insurgents or refugees wanting a fast route into South Africa would be forced to do the same, almost always at night. I didn't once encounter human spoor on patrol in this region, but the riverbed would often be peppered with the spoor of lion and leopard, hyena and occasional hippo. We encountered elephant, buffalo and giraffe spoor further inland and upstream of the Levuvhu River, where the bush was less dense. The area left an indelible imprint on my mind, for its stunning scenery and wealth of wildlife.

After an uneventful week on the banks of the Levuvhu River, I returned with my men to Mabiligwe. While back at the base, I would head out on my Honda when I needed some solitude, or rejoin the SAMIL trucks making delivery trips to the field if I felt like company.

On one of these trips, in the Kruger National Park, I was travelling as passenger alongside Sergeant Mathebula, making rat-pack deliveries to the sticks out in the bush. As we crested a steep rise onto an open expanse of savannah, the longest black mamba I have ever seen slithered across the two-track spoor right in front of the vehicle and into the veld on our right-hand side. Easily equalling the length of the SAMIL 20, it must have measured just less than six metres long. Mathebula slammed on brakes, and – I don't know what possessed us – we both jumped out and started chasing the fast-moving serpent. Mathebula had a head start on me, and I watched him galloping at full speed as I brought up the rear. Startled by the SAMIL and its noisy engine, and now with two crazy figures chasing after it, the black mamba picked up speed and raced along at more than double the pace we were running, travelling with its head a foot or more above the ground. Before we came close to it, the snake disappeared around the base of a large baobab tree, just beyond which was thicker acacia shrubs. I caught up to Mathebula and we gave each other a look and fell about laughing at the absurdity of our actions. We were fools. The snake could so easily have turned on us.

A few days later, Cappie stormed into the ops room, red-faced and flustered.

"*Reg, julle,*" he dropped a pile of files and paper on the table. "*Motorfiets-ry by Mabiligwe is oor!*" Whenever Cappie reverted to speaking to us in Afrikaans, we knew we were in trouble. He moved his hands outwards in a gesture of finality and said, "No one may ride that bike anymore." He turned to me, pointing his finger. "Especially you, Mike!" My mouth opened and closed in silence, like a gold-fish. If Cappie noticed my confusion, he ignored it. None of us knew where this was coming from. It was late in May and Cappie had been to Messina Sector HQ for one of his meetings. Parfitt spoke first.

"Meeting go well, then, Cappie?" In his prickly state, Cappie didn't notice Parfitt's teasing tone.

"No, the meeting did not go well." Cappie enunciated his words carefully, rolling his eyes. "The brass have got wind of Mike's escapades on the bike. And they are not impressed." Us loots looked at each other. I gave a shrug, organised my face into an expression of innocence.

"How'd they hear, Cappie?" Gavin asked.

"*Sit, julle.*" Cappie wagged his hands in our direction. "Hlongwane!" He called.

"Yes, sir?" The response came from outside the door.

"*Koffie, asseblief.*"

"Yes, sir." Cappie sat at his desk and took a breath.

"The police," Cappie said, raising an eye-brow in my direction. "Huh?" I grunted. I couldn't connect the dots.

"A coin-ops team in the Madimbo Corridor caught a pair of Zimbabweans crossing the river," Cappie explained. "A man and a woman. They were handed over to the SAP who interrogated the two. Turns out," here Cappie closed his eyes, and lifting his glasses, pinched the bridge of his nose. "They were spies, operating under direction from MK, aided by Mugabe's ZANU-PF government." He looked up again. "They've been watching the SADF units deployed on the river and they had precise information on all our patrol activities here," he shrugged. "Not surprising, since we haven't been trying to conceal our activities. But ..." He looked meaningfully at me, "... they specifically mentioned "the tall one who rides the big red motorbike"." I gave Cappie an apologetic look. "They detailed all the dates, times and routes of your rides, Mike." Cappie was reproachful. I was alarmed. "Needless to say," he continued, looking at the others. "There were a few thorny questions for me to answer." He pursed his lips, drummed his fingers on a file in front of him.

"Sorry, Cappie." I really was sorry. It must have been a very uncomfortable exchange for Cappie.

"Anyway," Hlongwane came in with Cappie's coffee, Cappie nodded thanks and had a sip. "There is some other news," he said, grimacing from the hot drink. "I'm leaving Mabiligwe tomorrow." We all spoke together in shock.

"What?!"

"Cappie! What do you mean?"

"Tomorrow?" Cappie shushed us, waving his hands again.

"I'm going to Pretoria. I'm doing some advanced training there. I hope it will put me in line to become a major." We all responded together again. "Congratulations, Cappie!"

"Wow, that's great!"

"Ag, thanks guys." Cappie was smiling now. "I'm very pleased about it, yes." He picked up his coffee and leant back in his chair. "I don't know how long I'll be gone. Probably a couple of months." He took a sip from his mug, shook his head. "But I'm worried about you guys." He wiped his mouth. "I don't know who they will be sending here to replace me." Putting the mug back on his desk, he looked at us with real concern. "But you'll be fine." He said. "You guys will be fine. Just stay off that blerry motorbike!" He grinned at us, we chuckled. "And I'll be back. I promise you that. Before the end of the year, I will be back at Mabiligwe."

I must confess to feeling a little concerned, and I suspect Gavin and the others felt the same. We were so lucky to have Cappie in charge, and it was partly his leadership and companionship that made Mabiligwe and my second year of service tolerable. I knew the matter of his replacement was pretty much luck-of-the-draw, and in the army, I came to expect the worst.

Cappie took his leave of us in the early hours of the morning before we set off on patrol. We hung around the base on our return, waiting anxiously for Cappie's replacement to arrive. Late in the afternoon, a SAMIL 50 arrived at Mabiligwe, and Lieutenant Pienaar – soon to be christened "Lieutenant Psycho" – alighted in his browns and boots, sporting the purple beret of the parabats. *Oh, no,* I thought. *Not one of those!* A real-live macho man. We would learn that he came from the 44 Parachute Brigade at Walmansthal, just north of Pretoria. I noted that he had the same rank as us, and wondered what possessed the authorities to send a lieutenant – and a parabat, at that – to command us in Cappie's absence.

The new arrival surveyed his surroundings through his small slit-eyes, a twist of dissatisfaction settling about his lips as he drew his conclusions about the base. As always, Gavin was the most welcoming amongst us, and he greeted the lieutenant with a firm handshake before making introductions. Then he pressed Staff Sergeant Hlongwane forward, instructing him to help the lieutenant with his *balsak* and show him to his quarters. I watched the two figures retreating towards the officers' quarters with a bad feeling. Hlongwane had no similar qualms, good naturedly chatting away to the blond-haired man, offering to show him around and urging him to call on Hlongwane if there was anything he needed.

The staff sergeant returned with instructions for us to meet the lieutenant in the ops room in ten minutes. We ambled over and awaited Pienaar. He swept into the room bringing an atmosphere of tension with him. Just shorter than me and a bit bulky, he stood with his legs astride, hands on his hips, and asked in Afrikaans what our routines at Mabiligwe involved. Between us, we tried to explain the existing arrangements to him in our best Afrikaans, but soon reverted to English.

"And why are you lot here at the base?" he asked. "Why aren't you operating from temporary bases in the veld?" We explained to him how we alternated platoons, several at a time in base while the others were out in the field at temporary bases on the Limpopo River and in the Park.

"This is how Captain Engelbrecht has been operating," Gavin finished. The new commander clearly disapproved of the existing arrangement. A born-and-bred, hardnosed Afrikaner, he probably resented being lumped with so many English-speaking looties. He was dismissive.

"Well, Captain Engelbrecht is no longer here, *manne.*" Pienaar was unjustifiably curt. I thought it was typical of someone out to prove themselves, changing a strategy that clearly worked. "I have different plans for you lot," he said. "You'd better forget about what you've done 'til now." By the end of our first conversation with him, Pienaar's features had arranged themselves into a sneer which seemed to remain there for the duration of his stay at Mabiligwe. I guessed we were headed for some kind of showdown.

We got to know the man a bit better over the next few days as he tried to get a feel for how things operated at Mabiligwe. My first impression of him was pretty much spot-on, but I was still shocked at the tone he took with the NCOs. Commands were barked with little respect, and orders not followed to his satisfaction were followed with threats of violence and deprivation. It was worse with the troops. Too slow to Muster? The troops were threatened with no lunch. An order had to be repeated? The offender was in line for an *oppie*. *Vloekwoorde* were bandied about like adjectives, and amongst the loots, he referred to the troops as *"kaffers"*. My nickname for Pienaar stuck quickly and didn't budge. It would have been better if he had been consistently foul-tempered, but his moods were entirely unpredictable. Psycho, indeed!

Pretty soon, the NCOs confided in Gavin and me. They didn't like him and his manner got their backs up. Plus, he was making the troops restless and difficult. We tried to reassure them.

"Be cool," Gavin said. "Just try not to upset him."

"It won't be forever," I added. "He's just here temporarily." They tried. We tried. But the rollercoaster of his moods wore us all down.

With the embargo on riding the Honda still in place, catching a glimpse of my beloved bike gathering dust under an old blanket in a corner of the base would fill me with a longing to rev it down the gravel roads and be rid of this regime for an hour or two. Ross asked me if I wanted to sell the bike to him. He thought it would be useful on his dad's farm in Natal. I took a couple of days to think about it, although I knew immediately that it was time for me to let it go. With a heavy heart, I accepted Ross's offer, and he organised transport to take the bike away when next he went on pass. I put the cash he gave me for the bike aside with the intention of using it to buy myself a car.

We had spent three days cooped up at the base with Psycho's erratic behaviour when he announced, with venom, that he wanted us out of the base immediately. We were all taken aback, but I, for one, was relieved. I knew it would be far better to spend my time constructively with my men out in the field without having to deal with the shadow of old Psycho. Gavin and I had our troops pack up their gear, loading up a week's supply of rat-packs, and departed the base for our usual positions in the Mabiligwe bush. It felt good to get away from the stifling and unpredictable environment under Psycho's tyranny, but his pettiness made itself known when he insisted on sitreps from us every hour, on the hour, despite the fact that nothing was happening.

"Sheesh man! He's a nightmare!" I said to Gavin when we met up on the Limpopo River, halfway between our camps, to commiserate with each other. "It's a relief to be off the base!" Gavin was his usual tempered self. "Well, he certainly is different ..."

"Different? Gav, he's a nutter!"

"You know, Mike, he is difficult, but let's not exaggerate." Gavin grinned good-naturedly. I didn't feel his empathy for the man.

"It's no exaggeration, Gav. He's like a little Hitler. And you know his attitude will have repercussions with the men." Gavin nodded at this. "You're right. We're going to have to manage this with care," he said. "We must convince the guys that we're looking out for them, that we're on their side, without getting Psy ... I mean, Pienaar's back up."

"I hear what you're saying, Gav, but how do we do that?" I asked.

"Well, Mike, I don't mind if you let off steam about Psy ... I mean, Pienaar with me. But try to be respectful in front of the troops." I saw Gavin's logic about this, and nodded in agreement. "And with Psy ... uh, Pienaar," he continued, "we must all just keep our noses clean. We don't want to give him any ammo to target us unnecessarily." I hated the idea that this meant I would have to be meticulous in following orders, that I would have to keep my mouth shut when I encountered injustice. "Just remember," he said, "and remind your troops, too, that this is just a temporary situation. Psy ... Oh, you know who I mean – he won't be here forever."

"Man, I miss Cappie!" I said.

"Me too," said Gavin, giving me a playful elbow. "Me too."

Returning to our temporary field base one afternoon after patrol, my men and I performed our routine safety check on our R4s. This was the same drill that got me into trouble at Infantry School with Lieutenant Pretorius the year before. This entailed first removing the loaded magazine from the rifle, then, in a safe position, pulling back on the bolt carrier operating mechanism to eject any round that may be in the chamber, and finally pulling the trigger to make doubly sure that the chamber is empty. The weapon can then be placed on safety. We had done this countless times without incident.

This time, I decided to get the guys to really clean their rifles, the way I had been shown at Infantry School. We all sat on dead tree trunks that formed a large, almost-square perimeter near the riverbank, a short distance from our temporary base. I sat on the largest tree trunk, facing north towards Zimbabwe. Just as I began dismantling my weapon, a live round whizzed past my right earhole, not five inches away. I froze, stunned. Then I looked at the men and saw them all motionless in their places, looking at me with astonishment. The culprit, Mabunda, dropped his weapon, his hands on his head, his mouth open. I realised that he must have carried out the safety drill back-to-front, first pulling the trigger and then pulling back on the bolt carrier operating mechanism, thus loading a round into the chamber with the magazine still attached. Thinking he had cleared the chamber, he set about cleaning the rifle and, inadvertently pulling the trigger, shot a round off towards me and my innocent ear (which, thankfully, was unharmed).

Regaining my composure, I knew I had no choice but to radio the main base and tell Lieutenant Psycho what had happened. It was with uncalled-for glee and malice that Psycho insisted Mabunda return to base for an *oppie*. I wasn't happy about this, knowing that in the safety check with the men I had overlooked Mabunda's rifle safety drill actions. But I recognised that this transgression demanded corrective measures and that this would be doled out in the form of an *oppie*, unfortunately for Mabunda, from Psycho.

I spoke first to Mabunda, making sure that he understood why he was being disciplined, then sent him back to the base with Smiley Nkuna. They returned about two and half hours later, just as the sunlight was beginning to fade. Poor Mabunda looked like he'd received a real working over. I felt sorry for him. I liked him. He apologised to me, and I reassured him that I knew it was an accident. Making sure that he would take extra care in the future, I gave him a nod to let him know that I understood and forgave him. He was relieved and gave me a wide grin, showing his bright white teeth. I realised that I had narrowly escaped injury, even death, had the bullet penetrated my skull, and it reminded me that life could be snuffed out in an instant.

The year was close to its halfway mark, and winter was approaching. Although it was still very pleasant out in the middle of the day, with temperatures hovering around the 23°C mark, the nights were getting cold. To stave off the cold air from descending on me in the dead of night, I erected a bivvy above my stretcher, strung from the branches of the trees under which I slept. I felt sorry for my guys, though, who slept with only an inner and a sleeping bag on a groundsheet, but they laughed off my concern, calling me a softie. Yet again, I was amazed by their resilience.

Coordinates: 22°34'46.32"S 31°14'58.53"E

After a week in the Mabiligwe bush, Psycho got it into his head to move Gavin and me to the Kruger National Park, south of the Levuvhu River, slap-bang in the middle of the most unpleasant part of the Park. Here, the base was surrounded by the thickest Mopani trees and bushes I have ever seen. Around a coarsely-gravelled, open area, the bushes had been cut away and cleared, creating a semi-permanent base. Those persistent little black Mopani flies hovered in the air around the base in their hundreds, and I shuddered at the thought of how many there would be in the height of summer – probably thousands!

Several green canvas army tents were already erected by the time we arrived at the camp. There were beds with mattresses in the tents for the loots and NCOs. An open area in front of the tents acted as a sort of parade ground cum mustering area, the troops having been ordered to demarcate walkways and functional areas with the many stones found there. Open-air showers were constructed for us officers, using large brown plastic screens enveloping two makeshift overhead shower dispensers, suspended from the branches of two of the numerous Mopani trees in the camp. The troopers had to each find themselves a spot around the perimeter to make their own: Lieutenant Psycho had no care for their comfort and was in no way going to allow them to enjoy the relative luxury of the tents. A large SAMIL 50 water bowser was stationed there, which would collect fresh water from Mabiligwe and deliver it to the various encampments stationed along the Zimbabwean and Mozambican borders with the Park.

The base abutted a very stony gravel access road that led some way off towards the two power lines coming in from the Cahora Bassa Hydro-electric scheme in northern Mozambique. The lines themselves were no longer functional, the Civil War in Mozambique having rendered them useless through countless acts of sabotage of the pylons over the years, but they acted as a navigational aid for the illegal immigrants, who followed them at a distance to trace their route into South Africa. Our purpose here was to stop and capture these would-be refugees.

Even though our main task there was as a rapid response or reaction force to support the various platoons and sticks deployed in the Park with any of their requirements for assistance or backup, patrolling in the immediate area and surroundings of the Mopani base camp was difficult. The stones, the gravel road and the thick bushes made walking extremely difficult and spotting spoor almost impossible, but Gavin and I did our best to keep the troops motivated and kept our frustrations to ourselves. It didn't help that walking patrol was extremely hot and bothersome. Despite the pleasant daytime temperatures and the gentle late autumn sun, there was little wind and the dry heat seemed to suck the air out of our lungs when walking patrol. We sweated liberally and there was the ever-present danger of overheating. Many "patrols" were simply done by Gavin or I riding with the driver in the water bowser, as he went to replenish deployed platoons and sticks in the bush, scouting the terrain, near and far, looking for any sign of human activity.

Several times during our daily patrols we came across evidence in the veld of the recent presence of illegal aliens, their belongings abandoned in the bush as they hurriedly disappeared at our approach. A tattered bag would open to reveal baby goods: a grubby blanket, a babygrow, a cheap pacifier. Occasionally we would find a pot of still-warm maize meal left behind on the smouldering ashes of a campfire. We knew that chasing them through the bush was a waste of time, as they would drop everything and run to avoid capture. The best we could hope for was to relay a radio message to one of the deeper-lying southerly platoons, giving them the general direction of the refugees' scatter, hoping that they could intercept them.

Once, the grisly sight of a human adult thigh bone and a crushed skull told of the gruesome end to a refugee's life in the jaws of a predator, the remains dragged away by scavengers. I shivered when I thought of these unfortunate folk, unprepared and defenceless in the wild and hostile bush.

I reckon for every one we caught, at least as many as four would evade capture. Those refugees that were unfortunate enough to be captured by us were invariably deathly-thin and ill. Sometimes an entire family would be gathered under a tree in our camp, their faces devoid of expression as they waited with resignation for the relevant authorities to collect them for repatriation. I felt sorry for them. I knew I would do the same if I was in their position. Driven away from their rural homes in Zimbabwe and Mozambique by conflict, terror and starvation, these people were literally fleeing for their lives. South Africa, the terrible Apartheid nation that the world so reviled, represented to these people their only chance at a better life.

When we weren't on patrol, I found this base particularly boring. Gavin and I took to mustering the troops for morning and evening parades, wearing only our black shorts and *plakkies*. I read, but there is only so much a person can read. I listened to music, but the same old tapes eventually became tedious after countless replays. We tanned in our underpants, lying on towels draped over stretchers, but our lily-white torsos and regular intake of the anti-malarial, Darachlor, repelled those weak rays. We even had a table set up outside our tent with a white tablecloth for the early morning and evening meals. Gavin and I looked for any excuse to keep ourselves and our minds occupied, and we took to venting our frustrations on a fitness bar between two poles erected by the NCOs. Both quite competitive, we started a challenge of ever-increasing dare, competing to see who could do the most push-ups and pull-ups, eventually attaching a twenty-five kilogram fire-extinguisher to our web belts to up the ante in the great pull-up contest.

A young one-pip loot from another SAI camp joined us at the Mopani camp around the middle of June. Dries Bekker was a good-looking guy, and we all guessed he got on well with the ladies. He was a bit aloof to begin with, but we did our best to include him. It would soon emerge, however, that Bekker was a bit of a loafer who liked to take gaps where he could.

While we were stationed here, Lieutenant Psycho took to using the SAMIL 20 as his personal vehicle, allocating an unranked driver as his chauffeur. Barely a week into our stay, he sent word via radio that he was joining us in camp. I privately wondered if he didn't trust us to do the job. He arrived in his limo wearing his purple beret, as ever (he never wore a bush-hat), and selected a tent separate from the one Gavin, Bekker and I shared. Although Psycho had left Ross and Parfitt nominally in charge of Mabiligwe base, he had brought along a stronger radio transmitter than the normal A53 VHF/FM short-range tactical field radios we carried, in order to run Mabiligwe from deep in the bush.

In all fairness, Psycho tried hard to overcome his personal issues with us out there. He made an effort to engage, especially with Gavin and sometimes with Bekker, in conversation, which was rather difficult and stilted and mostly limited in topic to music and physical exercise. I could tell that Psycho viewed Bekker as his inferior, being only one pip, but this opinion was balanced by the fact that they were both Afrikaners. On that level, Bekker was his "brother". He seldom engaged with me, and if he did, he used Gavin as a conversational proxy, never directly addressing me if he could avoid it.

"Fish," he said to Gavin on one occasion. "Who has a better build, here, me or Warren?" I had to smother the laughter that was threatening to escape from my lips. I was never endowed with a well-defined and large muscular frame, being somewhat lean all my life. In the army I had become fit and strong, though, and was at that time quite sinewy and toned. Old Psycho, on the other hand, was showing the signs of a developing belly and flab around his waist. Clearly none-too-keen on exercise, I did not on a single occasion witness him partaking in a patrol. But Gav, good old Gav, was his usual tactful self.

After a pause to carefully select his words, Gavin replied, "Uhm ... well ... you definitely have the bigger build." He smiled angelically at Psycho, whose command of the English language was not sufficient to convey the ambiguity of Gavin's statement. Psycho looked satisfied, even smug, but Gavin later apologised to me.

"You know I didn't mean to offend you, hey, Mike?" He said. "Psy ... I mean, Pienaar really put me on the spot with that question."

"No, I know, Gav," I replied. "Don't worry. Besides," I punched his shoulder gently and laughed. "You were just being truthful. He is definitely bigger than me!" Gavin smiled, possibly a little uncomfortable at his deception of Psycho, but I knew that he had saved us both from a whole lot of spite we would've been in for had he spoken the truth.

I took a ride with the SAMIL water bowser to replenish the water at all the temporary bases, Corporal Chauke joining me to tend to any sick reports. I needed to escape the lingering oppressive atmosphere at the camp that had started to stifle me. I could even tolerate the irksome Chauke, if it meant a break from the camp.

On our return journey that afternoon, some distance from the camp, I spotted a heap of rags next to the gravel road that hadn't been there when we passed by earlier. Realising the heap was in fact a person, I ordered the driver to stop and dismounted the SAMIL to cautiously approach the bundle. I made out the outline of an emaciated man in rags, lying on his side on the ground with his hands under his head in the dust. As I came nearer, the man turned his head and stared with his vacant eyes which rolled about in their hollows. He didn't stir to run, clearly so hungry and thirsty that he had no energy left.

"Just wait there a minute," I said, uselessly, knowing he wouldn't be going anywhere and not sure if he even understood me. I returned to the SAMIL and filled the little fire bucket attached to the water tanker with water. Returning to the emaciated man, I knelt beside him and cradled his head with my left hand as I poured a sip of water into his dry mouth. He lapped at the liquid with obvious relief and sank back onto the ground.

The man was not old – perhaps in his mid thirties – but looked closer to fifty. Nothing but skin and bone, his eyes were wild and staring. Thick, white spittle had collected and caked at the corners of his mouth. As I knelt beside this wasted, dying man on the side of the road, my nostrils were affronted by his smell. His threadbare clothes reeked of shit and sweat, and the sweet smell of rot rose from his breath and body. Knowing not to rehydrate him too quickly, I helped the poor man into a sitting position to give him another sip of water from the fire bucket. Leaning against me, he let out a dry sob and covered his eyes with a hand. I didn't know if it was an expression of grief or relief.

I returned to the SAMIL and radioed base. Psycho told me to bring the man back to base. The poor man, as if starvation wasn't bad enough, would now have to face the arrogance and contempt of the little Hitler. I gave the man another sip of water, then gently eased him to his feet. I helped him to the SAMIL, practically carrying him, but when I tried to open the door to the cab, Corporal Chauke actually held onto the door handle to keep me from opening it. Irritated, I yanked at the door and just about pulled Chauke out of his seat with it. "What are you doing, man?" I demanded.

"Lieutenant," Chauke complained. "You can't put him in here!"

"Why on earth not, corporal?" I moved to help the man into the cab. Chauke covered his mouth and nose with one hand, waving the other in our direction.

"He stinks, lieutenant!" he said. Chauke was right. I could barely breathe without gagging. But I was surprised at his lack of empathy for a man in dire need. "We won't have him in here with us!" Chauke finished, closing the door with finality. I couldn't argue with Chauke.

Making a plan, I showed the man how to climb up onto the side of the bowser using a short metal ladder with three foot-rails. There a person could stand, on the three-rung ladder, above the diesel tanks, just behind the cab on the driver's side, holding onto the piping and steel struts. The figure in rags looked at my gesticulations blankly. I tried miming the action. Still nothing. Finally, I called on Chauke to come and try to converse with the man. Chauke repeated my instructions in Tsonga, then listened as the man spoke slowly and laboriously, shaking his head with despair.

"He says he doesn't have the strength to climb up, lieutenant," Chauke said at last. I sighed, looked at the figure. He couldn't have been more than fifty kilograms. With much difficulty, but finally convincing him, I enlisted Chauke's assistance, and together we pushed him up onto that platform, each of us turning our heads away as we did so, trying not to breathe the stench in. There the man stood, his legs shaking from weakness rather than fear, and I knew that he would be unable to hold on all the way back to base. Climbing up behind him, I stood at his back, shielding him from falling off as the SAMIL made its way back, the turbulence created by the moving truck making it bearable for me to breathe.

As we arrived in camp, Lieutenant Psycho was standing at the entrance, his hands on his hips. When he saw me standing behind the man, he gave me a look drenched in disapproval and disgust. I took no notice of him, waving at Gavin who returned the gesture.

I called to Gavin and several helping hands came to get the man off the vehicle. Gavin led him off to a shady spot under a large tree and gave him more water. As required by procedure, a sentry was placed on duty to ensure the captive didn't escape, but I laughed at the silliness of it. To begin with, we spooned small amounts of rehydration fluid into his mouth – boiled water reinforced with trace amounts of salt and sugar. When this seemed to be working and the man could focus his eyes again, we tried giving him small amounts of food. We knew not to feed a starving person too much or too quickly – there is a danger of choking or vomiting. The man showed his gratitude with the faintest smile and ate slowly.

As he ate, Maluleke probed him gently about his story. A Zimbabwean, he had fled his village in Matabeleland South with his wife, his baby boy and his brother. They travelled southwards as part of a larger party escaping the horrors of starvation and intimidation wrought by Mugabe's notorious Fifth Brigade. I listened to Maluleke translating as the man recounted the terrors he had witnessed in his homeland and how his only hope was to forge a better life for his little boy south of the border. When his brother fell sick, the family was abandoned by the other travellers. Making their way slowly towards the Limpopo River, his brother all the while getting sicker, they had barely crossed the river when his ailing brother was cornered and mauled by a lone rogue lion. In the panic, our captive was separated from his wife and the baby. For three days he had been wandering in search of them, but he was overcome by hunger and thirst and had lain down on the side of the road in preparation for death when we came across him in the SAMIL.

Later that afternoon, as it was getting dark, a yellow SAP bakkie arrived and the emaciated man was bundled carelessly into the closed canopy at the rear, a barred box that looked like nothing so much as a cage. As I watched the policemen loading the man into the bakkie, I saw, peering out from the gloomy interior several sets of eyes, fearful and hopeless, and thought of the stories each pair had to tell of their trials and journey into South Africa – how many were as heartbreaking and hopeless as our emaciated man's? How many tragic stories were carelessly disregarded, as illegal aliens were packed off back across the river to face who-knows-what-kind of treatment in the countries they came from?

During the next few days, while out on patrol or travelling the dust roads in the SAMIL, I kept my eyes open for a trace of the mother and child, but there was none.

At the beginning of July, after spending three weeks at the base in the Kruger National Park, Psycho decided he wanted to take leave, so we dismantled the base and returned to Mabiligwe. The day he departed Mabiligwe in a SAMIL 50 with his chauffeur I was so thrilled, I wanted to throw a party. The atmosphere in the base was immediately easier, and we sat in the officers' quarters with the NCOs chatting and laughing about Psycho and our relief at his departure. Us loots tried to remain neutral during the conversation – the man was an officer, after all, and it was decorous to protect our ranks – but the NCOs took one look at our expressions and laughed and pointed. There was no hiding how we felt. They knew we felt as strongly as they did about Mr Purple Beret. We had a braai that evening, a celebration of our freedom, revelling in the sense of relief.

Gavin had been given charge of the company in Psycho's absence, reporting from the signal room to Messina Sector HQ and taking care of communications between the various bases out in the bush. All the NCOs sparked to keep morale and discipline up, only too happy to help Gavin and all us loots out. It was a sweet respite and a pleasant week. Everyone was quite *rustig* and Mabiligwe returned to a semblance of normality.

All too soon, we got word that Psycho was set to return and we were to send a SAMIL out to Messina Sector HQ to fetch him. News of the lunatic's impending arrival sent shudders through the camp and we all braced ourselves for his return.

We greeted him affably when he arrived, and to our surprise, he looked refreshed and behaved most pleasantly towards us all. For just a moment, I wondered if we had misread the man, and resolved to give him the benefit of the doubt. Spending some time with the loots, Pienaar brought out tapes he had picked up during his pass. It was on one of his tapes that I first heard John Fogerty's *Eye Of The Zombie* album from 1986 – not usually my choice of music, but when I listened to it, I really quite liked it. His collection also included Paul Parker's double album of disco music, with its catchy track *Right On Target* from '82. Pienaar graciously offered for Gavin and me to borrow any of the ten tapes he had brought along. I was amazed by the gesture.

Then Pienaar brought out what he clearly regarded as his trump: the February 1987 issue of *Penthouse*. Those were the days of extreme censorship in South Africa, when *Scope* was the only version of a skin rag that could be legally purchased – a very watered-down version of men's magazines, featuring images of topless women sporting stars where their nipples should be. I had perused the odd copy of *Scope*, reading on its pages appeals from the publishers for the government of the day to lighten their stance on the soft porn industry and specifically mentioning *Penthouse* and *Playboy* among them. As I paged through Pienaar's copy, however, I realised that this was no soft porn we were looking at. The photos left little to the imagination.

The looties all crowded around the magazine to get a look, laughing nervously and making dirty jokes, when I looked up and caught Gavin watching us quizzically. I realised he didn't have clue what the excitement was all about.

"Gavin," I said. "It's full of pictures of naked women." Gavin blushed and I laughed, holding up the centrefold to give him an eyeful. "This here is a friendly blonde from Canada showing us what she's been gifted with!" Gavin gasped with astonishment at what he saw and quickly averted his eyes with embarrassment, blushing a deep crimson. The guys jumped at the chance to tease the poor innocent, and I let them have a little fun before telling them to stop. "Okay, guys," I said, moving over to Gavin's side in solidarity. "Let's not taint Gavin with this filth – he'll have to tell Cathy what he's been up to and she won't like that!"

That *Penthouse* did its rounds amongst the loots, until someone discovered that it had gone missing for some days. This caused much ragging among the guys, as we each poked fun at the others about lifting the skin mag and hiding it under a pillow. It eventually emerged that Corporal Chauke had got hold of it, and we all took it as licence to rag him endlessly about it, asking how his Canadian "girlfriend" was treating him!

The initial ease we all felt with Pienaar on his return didn't last, and the pleasant atmosphere soon gave way as Mr Congenial couldn't sustain the good nature and Lieutenant Psycho returned. He had tried to be one of the boys, showing off by getting great music and banned publications, but the act didn't last, and like the proverbial Jekyll and Hyde, he quickly reverted to his old ways. I felt both embarrassed and sorry for him. He seemed to me like a schoolboy trying to win over friends.

Once again, he sent us all off into the bush so that he could have the run of the base. I got the impression he had a particular ire for me, that his orders for my platoon were some kind of retribution. We never got along. I didn't like Psycho, and I made no attempt to conceal the fact.

His instructions were very specific. My platoon was to pack rations for two whole weeks. We were to leave all manner of scented toiletries behind: no deodorant, toothpaste or soap was to be used. Water would be restricted, only to be used for drinking or cooking. The thought of going weeks without showering or cleaning my teeth was not a pleasant prospect – cleanliness always being high on my list of priorities. Besides the restrictions on water, it was safer not to give ourselves away to sensitive and well-trained olfactory senses.

In the cool of the winter morning, my platoon and I climbed onto a SAMIL 50 and drove all the way past the Mopani-bush base to a point about a click from the border where the Cahora Bassa power lines crossed the border from Mozambique into South Africa. Here, our orders were to patrol the entire area around and along the lines for several kilometres inland, looking for the spoor of insurgents and illegal aliens. The land here was very flat, with a sandy, reddish soil.

Suspended over this landscape, the first and second power lines crossed the border at 22°32'15.41"S 31°23'35.08"E and 22°32'13.82"S 31°21'21.97"E respectively, then veered off in a southwesterly direction. I chose to set up base and operate closer to the second power line, which lay nearer the border just off the main access and maintenance road. This meant that we could cover the southern-most power line on our morning patrol first thing, make our way to the northern line, and then turn back, ensuring that if anyone had come through the previous evening, we would pick up their spoor sequentially along either line. Operating the other way around, we would have lost more than double the time, picking up the spoor at its earlier position.

Several times I found that refugee tracks simply followed the path of least resistance, and if they had managed to pip us by a few hours because of a late night or early morning ingress, I would make a rough calculation of where they should be with the help of my men, whose tracking skills had advanced dramatically. I would radio one of the other platoons' sections further southwest and warn them, hopefully leading to the refugees being intercepted before they came to the rugged terrain not far from the Mopani base camp and their tracks simply disappeared.

At the start of our deployment here, I was just relieved to be away from Mabiligwe. Out in the bush with my men, I was master of my own fate, and could take charge and make decisions with the greatest chance for success. But I tired of the area very quickly. I felt enclosed by that landscape and during the day, the only sense of a horizon I could get was by looking down the arrow-like service road either way, or looking above the Mopani trees and bushes at the electrical pylons sticking out of the landscape intermittently, like lone alien sentinels.

I found the flies tiresome and never got used to having to swat them away incessantly, so I always relaxed as soon as dusk fell and they disappeared. Suppers, prepared using Esbit tablets to heat the coffee in the fire buckets and food in the dixies, had to be finished before night fell. Once darkness came, it was not recommended that a soldier simply up and exit the camp to pee, as the guard on duty might shoot at him as he relieved himself. So we ensured that ablutions were completed before the light went, taking a spade and toilet paper to a designated area a short distance southwest of our TB. No light was permitted during the night-time hours for fear of giving away our position. At least at night, the cosmos was aglitter in all its array of lights.

I would stay awake until about 22h00, lying atop the ridge of red sand next to the road, peering down through my night vision goggles towards the border. I saw mostly single buck walking aimlessly about in the dark. The area was unable to support much vegetation aside from the ubiquitous Mopani trees and bushes. Even the animals were scarce, and birds here were a rarity. From an aesthetic point of view, it was the least attractive setting for a temporary base I had seen all year.

One evening a strange rasping sound reached my ears as I slept in the dead of night. I surfaced from a cold, dreamless sleep. *What are the insurgents up to?* I wondered. *Have they devised some cunning way to find us? Are the hunters becoming the hunted?* I shook off the sleep and tried to locate the origin of the sound. *Maybe it's a hyena gnawing at the toe of someone's boot ... Maybe it will bite his toes off!* I listened more carefully and realised the sound was coming from uncomfortably close-by, perhaps an arm's reach from the left side of my head. I had to find out what it was. I nudged my R4 with my right elbow, reassuring myself that it was close by. Moving slowly and quietly, I reached my right hand down to the thigh pocket of my browns where I kept my small torch. Pulling the torch up over my chest and slowly past my face, I covered the lens with my left hand before switching it on. I opened my fingers a crack and cast a sliver of a beam in the direction of the sound.

Before turning in for the night, I had dumped a hessian bag containing the empty rat-pack packaging from my evening meal just left of where my head now rested. In the faint light from my torch, I made out, gnawing loudly at the fabric of the bag, the biggest red roman spider I have ever seen, easily bigger than my splayed-out hand. The creature had obviously picked up the scent of the remains of my supper, and was now doing its best to get into the bag. I prodded and poked it with my R4, but it was so engrossed in trying to get through the sack-cloth that it paid me no attention and continued scratching and gnawing.

Now, spiders aren't my favourite creatures under the sun, but I always give a living thing the benefit of the doubt, as long as I'm not being attacked. During my time out in the bush there, I often felt creepy-crawlies tracking across my face in the dead of night, a sensation which would make me grimace with revulsion and cause me to swat at my face to remove it as quickly as possible. Unfortunately for Mr Red Roman, I had reached the end of my tether with these creatures of the night. Seeing my boot lying conveniently close by, I grabbed it and in one swift movement, banged the heel squarely over the unsuspecting spider, snuffing out his life in an instant. I whacked the now-dead arachnid twice more to be certain he was a goner. The mess was repulsive, but I was satisfied that at least I would sleep in peace for the rest of the night. I was wrong, however. My dreams were populated by giant red romans that were chasing me through the bush – I was trying to escape them wearing rat-pack wrappings for clothes.

The hot days and cold nights dragged on out there. I was dirty, sticky and *gatvol* of walking patrols day in and day out. My clothes were caked with salt and sweat stains and had begun to chafe at my skin. I was starting to detest the Mopani bush and all its flies. One day, late in July, Gavin arrived in a SAMIL 50.

"Jump in, he's gone!" he said looking down from the passenger side of the cab.

"What do you mean, "he's gone"?" I asked, looking up at his grinning face. "He left this morning." Gavin was smiling widely. "We're getting a replacement in a day or two." I can't describe the joy and relief the news brought me.

Arriving back at base, the other officers and NCOs avoided coming close to me and my men, walking in big circles around us and teasing us for smelling bad. I thought they were having us on. We all piled into the shower truck together to take a hot shower. It was stupendous to stand under the shower head, taking a good ten minutes to scrub down and really get clean. Emerging shaven, spotless and feeling like a new man, I went to the officers' quarters to retrieve my browns. They weren't there. Puzzled, I looked around my room, under the bed, in the passage, they were nowhere to be found. Opening the front door, I found them lying in a heap on the pathway. Someone had chucked them out. As I bent to pick them up, I gagged. Before cleaning up, I obviously hadn't been able to smell myself. Now, the smell of my clothes was unbearable. I wanted to throw them away or burn them, but one of the corporals suggested I should leave them overnight in soapy water in a half forty four gallon drum that we used for washing our clothes, stirring them with a large wooden stick every few hours for a few minutes at a time. By morning, the soap had seeped through the grime and stains, but I still had to give them a good go with a scrubbing brush. When I was done, my shirt and pants had turned a few shades lighter, now more of a light, sandy brown than nutria. I discarded several pairs of underpants and socks which were beyond saving.

It was a relief that Psycho's dictatorship of Mabiligwe had come to an end. We reckoned we couldn't get anyone worse than him to command us again. A day later, Captain van der Walt arrived. Short and stocky with a mean, hard look, he was Afrikaans, but his spoken English was excellent. After greeting everyone and getting a rundown of how things operated, he informed us that before the week was over, we would all be departing for Sterkrivier, somewhere between Potgietersrus and Naboomspruit. We would be retraining the troops in all aspects of battle handling, and we would be undergoing evaluations of our own training skills while we were there.

Captain van der Walt had a short fuse and he could be a right bastard at times, but he was more stable and reasonable in his interactions with us and with the troops than old Psycho had been. I found him to be approachable, and he was open to our suggestions regarding operations and training. He was certainly an improvement on his predecessor, but we all missed Cappie and his warm camaraderie.

As we departed for Sterkrivier, I wondered if we'd see Mabiligwe and the Kruger Park again.

Chapter 26

The drive to Sterkrivier from Mabiligwe is just over 380 kilometres, but it took almost five hours in the cumbersome SAMILs. Driving on this long stretch of road felt to me like I was going home, but twenty kilometres south of Potgietersrus, we exited the N1, shortly turning northwest onto the Sterkrivier Road, which connected the portion between the R35 and the R518. Emerging from several twists through a narrow *poort* shadowed by a series of very high kopjes, the road straightens out for some distance. We rumbled along, the Sterkrivier Dam to our left, which is fed by the Sterkrivier or Strong River. Not far along this straight stretch tarmac, we turned off due west into an SADF-owned training area, a short distance before the one-horse town of Sterkwater.

Coordinates: 24°16'54.97"S 28°52'29.60"E

The landscape was gold with dry winter grass, but it would be lush green savannah during the summer rainfall season. Here, the kopjes were more prominent than at Mabiligwe and the Kruger Park, making the surrounding area almost mountainous. It was a relief to be rid of the incessant Mopani flies which were absent from this region, although there were a fair number of houseflies and the odd horsefly – which could inflict a nasty bite if you didn't swat at it.

There was an already established field base, with tents for a field kitchen, officers' ablutions and living quarters. We even had an officers' mess tent with a fridge that operated off a generator. It was certainly a well-equipped field base, having previously been established for military training purposes, which probably took place all year round. All we had to add were a few more tents and the other logistical odds and ends we would require. I could see we would be comfortable. But my heart sank when I saw where Charlie Company would be sleeping: in the veld! Spring was around the corner, and its arrival was hinted at in the warmth of the sun and the gentle reawakening of the veld. But it was still early August and the nights could be uncomfortably cold. I felt sorry for the guys, and knew that having them sleep out could cause trouble.

Our stay at the Sterkrivier training base was expected to be about six weeks long, after which there was a rumour that we would all be given a pass – officers and troops alike. Captain van der Walt explained to us that our time here would be spent training the men in various battle-handling skills, section and platoon tactics, both in lecture format and out in the field. There would be no patrolling here. We drew up a company roster for sentry duty.

The Sterkrivier period started out well enough, despite grumbles from the troops about their sleeping arrangements. The first morning was slow, as the guys struggled to get out of their beds in the chill of the early morning. After a late and poor inspection we got to work, the officers lecturing their platoons on all infantry related practices and aspects. Out in the field, I made use of a flip chart to draw diagrams and write out various steps, but I had to go over the theory of battle-handling many, many times over. The guys were struggling to grasp the concepts in this format. I also did sand model exercises with my troops, much as I'd done as a recruit at Infantry School and on the South West African Border, and as I'd done with my men back at Gumbu Mine. These seemed to help click the concepts into place for the guys.

When I emerged from my tent before the troops mustered on the second morning, I drew a quick breath at the sight of the camp. The area was littered with rat-pack wrappings and tins from last night's supper. Hurrying towards the nearest group of soldiers preparing for the day, I rounded up a couple of the early risers who were already dressed and sent them out to clear up the rubbish, hoping the captain hadn't yet caught sight of the mess. The troops were slow to Muster again, and I could see that many of them were sloppily dressed.

The third morning was no better, with early morning inspection a failure because many of the guys hadn't cleaned their rifles. It dawned on me that the men had engineered a type of go-slow, slack attitude because they were cheesed off that the officers were staying in tents while they were sleeping in the veld. I wondered how we were going to handle this without making the situation worse.

"*Manne!*" It was Captain van der Walt. He was approaching us loots where we were standing outside our tent chatting. We saluted his arrival. "I'm not impressed with your men." My heart sank. I had hoped I might have the opportunity to have a quiet word with the other officers and the men about what I had seen happening before the captain picked up on the company's carelessness, maybe encourage the guys to shape up without resorting to any extreme disciplinary measures. "They're getting sloppy, and I won't have a slack company under my watch. You guys better get your men acting like soldiers, or I'll have you sleeping in the veld with them!"

"Yes, sir, captain." Looking at the other officers' faces, I realised that none of them were surprised, either.

"I don't need to tell you what I'm referring to, do I?" The captain glared at us, his hands on his hips. We all shook our heads.

"No, sir."

"Good," he said. "Let me just say that there are four things I want you to take care of," he counted them off on his fingers. "One, the camp. Two, your men's punctuality – no more late mornings!"

"Yes, sir."

The Captain continued, "Three, their browns, and four, their weapons." Van der Walt took a long pause here as we all shifted uncomfortably under his gaze. "Right. I'll give you until tomorrow. Then your men better be back on form, or you will pay the price. Do you understand?"

"Yes, sir," we were all emphatic.

"Good. Don't say I didn't warn you." The Captain returned our salute brusquely and turning on his heel, stormed off towards the kitchen.

Us loots discussed the problem amongst ourselves. Getting the men to shape up was going to be tricky. I certainly didn't want to end up sleeping in the veld. The few creature comforts afforded us officers here at Sterkrivier weren't much, but after spending so much time in the bush, they were worth hanging onto. I was *gatvol* of being out in the bush. But there wasn't much we could use to motivate the guys and get them to cooperate with us. Eventually, we decided to use the pending leave as leverage, threatening to revoke or reduce it if they didn't cooperate. But we all knew that this was a bit of a gamble. None of us wanted to stay behind to oversee any errant troopers who were refused pass.

For a day or two, the troops seemed to shape up somewhat, but it didn't take long for the sloppiness to return, and no amount of coaxing from us officers seemed to change the prevailing attitude. Captain van der Walt turned to us after evening Muster one day, fuming at the *slapgat* troops. "Your men don't listen!" He bellowed at us. "*Vanaand gaan julle by julle troepe slaap!* Go make your beds in the veld!" We were pissed off, and we let the troops see this.

The following day we drove the men as hard as we could out in the field, doing Infantry drills and battle exercises until they were out on their feet. We spent two nights sleeping out in the field, frozen to the bone, after which the troops realised that they would be made to suffer for their attitude and decided to sharpen up their behaviour. For those two days, we practiced mostly a few dry drills and then a few live exercises. Us loots also realised that the guys had become a bit *slapgat* over the weeks, and we intensified the training. We returned to our tents after two nights in the cold, but sustained the momentum of training for a while, and after a week and a half, the guys were looking as sharp as ever. Retraining had its merits.

Soon the pattern of training was such that we could have done it blindfolded. The troops became quite proficient and by the third week, Captain van der Walt was so impressed that he took to leaving us over the weekends to go home to his family.

Since Captain van der Walt was absent over the weekends, we would cast lots to see who would stay in the base, and the rest of the officers would pile into Ross's car to go out for the evening. The first time, Gavin and I went with Ross to a nightclub in Pietersburg. There wasn't anything by way of nightlife in Potgietersrus, and Pietersburg wasn't that far to drive. Pulling on blue jeans and a smart shirt, Gavin in his smart white shoes, me in my grey shoes, we exited the base with some excitement. It was great to get out of camp for a while. We arrived at the nightclub only to discover that it was more like a *sokkie* – Afrikaner guys and gals doing the *langarm* around the venue to a few of the current Top Forty hits and several Afrikaans *liedjies* that suited this type of dancing. Gavin knew more-or-less how to dance that way, but Ross and I had never wanted to learn how to windsurf like that. English-speaking kids danced loose-style. But the music wasn't all that bad and the beers were cold, and we ended up enjoying the break from army life up at the Sterkrivier training base.

On another occasion, Ross and I spent a Saturday visiting my mother's cousin whose husband worked at the Ruto Flour Mills in Pietersburg. My mother's aunt and uncle from England were visiting their daughter and three kids, and we spent a pleasant day in the company of my family – Ross relaxed and chatted away to everyone as if he belonged.

During all this time training, the prospect of Commandant Jooste and Major Muller coming to evaluate us hung over our heads. Eventually the day arrived, but only Major Muller stayed to assess us – the commandant using the opportunity away from home and 113 BN to visit elsewhere. The major observed each officer and his platoon during theoretical and practical sessions.

On the first day, I stood in front of the flip chart facing my men, Major Muller looking on from the sidelines. As I always did, I carried out the lecture in English, but it occurred to me, halfway through my presentation, that I might have made a bad judgment call in this regard. It might have been my imagination, but I felt like the major's eyes were drilling into me from where he sat. Knowing the army's preference for *Die Taal*, I should perhaps have considered lecturing in Afrikaans for the major's benefit. Deciding it was too late to change tack, I finished the lesson in English.

The following day, when it was time for my platoon to do the practical, Major Muller instructed me to stand back and let my lance jack take the men through a live fire and movement exercise. I stood on a rise facing the kopjes to the north with a view of the live training area beneath me. The major walked behind Corporal Maluleke, who walked behind the section as they moved forward through the veld, their R4s chattering away, rat-a-tat, rat-a-tat, rat-a-tat. The section proceeded in formation from left to right in front of me. As the line progressed down a wide valley, the men entered the tallest yellow thatching grass I have ever seen – you could have hidden a herd of elephants in there! From within that stretch of grass, the men were almost entirely hidden from view, and their view looking out was surely obscured – the kopjes I faced were likely to have been the only part of the horizon the guys could discern from their perspective. From where I stood, I saw the ends of the line, where the men were progressing at a faster rate than those at the middle, veering inwards. In time, the ends of the line would have been moving in towards each other, and with their R4s all firing, a sure catastrophe was imminent.

"Stop!" I rushed down into the valley shouting as loudly as I could. "Maluleke! Stop! STOP!" I ignored the fact that I was countering the orders of Major Muller. The firing ceased and the men turned to me in surprise. I ran up to Major Muller pushing my way through the long grass, panting, more from the adrenaline rush than from the exertion of sprinting across the veld.

"*Wat die donner dink jy doen jy?*" He demanded ("What in the blazes do you think you're doing?").

"They were moving in towards each other, major," I began explaining between gasps of breath. "I was afraid there would've been a terrible accident if I didn't stop them." The major was furious.

"You talk *kak*, Warren!" he shouted. "How dare you interfere with my orders! Don't you ever do that again!" Spittle exploded from his lips and a

359

droplet came to rest on his chin. He was pointing an erect finger at me, his eyes practically bulging out of their sockets in rage. I was stunned. I couldn't believe he was willing to allow such a disaster to happen. "That's it!" he said, turning to the troops. *"Basis toe!"* ("Back to base!"). The troops began to form up slowly, as if unsure of the command.

"But, major," I objected. "They haven't finished. You haven't even started with the rest of my platoon." The major looked at me with narrowed eyes. *"Ek gaan nie meer evalueer nie, Warren,"* I couldn't believe he wouldn't finish assessing the platoon's performance. My scorn for Afrikaners like him grew in intensity in that moment, and I felt my poor opinion of them was justified.

Later in the afternoon, Captain van der Walt informed me that I had failed my evaluation. Taken by surprise, I asked him if he knew why. The Captain sucked at his lips, empathy flickering briefly across his hard face. He nodded.

"Yes, Warren," he said. "The major expected you to deliver your lecture in Afrikaans."

"But, sir," I objected. "It was cleared with Captain Engelbrecht that the troops could be taught in English. They weren't following well when we lectured in Afrikaans." Van der Walt nodded.

"Ek weet," he said. "I know. But the fact remains, Major Muller expected the lecture to be in Afrikaans." I thought this was petty. I had delivered the lecture successfully and my troops had understood. This should have been sufficient grounds to pass me, regardless of whether the instruction had taken place in English or Afrikaans. Once again, the army made me feel like being English was equivalent to having a disability.

"Sir," I pleaded with Captain van der Walt. "Please will you ask the major if I can redo the lecture for him?" The Captain looked at me with an expression that said *"No!"* I tried my luck, appealing for his help. "Captain, I know that I can do the lecture to the major's satisfaction in Afrikaans. Please, sir, ask him to give me another chance?" The captain put his hands on his hips, and I heard his toes tapping on the lino floor. Eventually, he made up his mind.

"Okay, Warren," he finally agreed. "But you better not be wasting my time. Or the major's!" A little while later, the captain returned to let me know that the major had agreed to my request.

"But this is your last chance, Warren," he finished.

The major sat looking at me with a mean expression as I stood in front of the flip chart. I was to give the presentation without the troops. I started by explaining to the major how the training at Gumbu Mine at the beginning of the year had been slow and ineffective, and how Gavin and I had approached Cappie to request that we deliver the lectures in English. I also told him how the troops' execution of the drills had improved significantly with this change in strategy. I didn't know how much of my speech made an impression on Muller. He just sat there quietly, his face unchanging, his arms folded across his chest. Then I did the presentation for him in Afrikaans, and, soon after, he left the camp. When I asked Captain van der Walt whether I had passed, he reported that I had, but told me that I had scored the lowest of all the loots. I was angry. I knew this was an attempt on the part of the major to get back at me for stopping the exercise in the veld. He clearly regarded the incident as a challenge of his authority, and was now responding with petty vindictiveness. *Screw you, Major Muller,* I thought. *Screw you and your stupid bloody army. I don't give a damn about your training evaluations.* I was insulted and this made me furious. I knew my own capabilities – I had seen the effects in the improvement in my platoon – and I was convinced that I was better than the major's evaluation. I consoled myself with the fact that my national service was nearly over, I wouldn't be doing this kind of training again. I also knew that the major was pulling rank on me for no justifiable reason. I thought he was being childish and the incident added just a little bit to the resentment that was building up within me for the petty authority that characterised the army.

"I've been missing you, Babe!" It had been over four months since I had seen Kimberly – longer than we had ever been apart before. I got a lift into Potgietersrus to call her from the orange payphone outside Wimpy, with John Waite's 1984 song *Missing You* playing on the radio in the background – how apt! "It's been so long since I saw you!" Her voice was like a tonic.

"I know. I've been missing you too, Michael."

"Listen, I've got a pass next week. Why don't you come up here and fetch me? It's not so far. You could stay the night on Saturday." She giggled. "Stay with you at the base?" she asked.

"Ja. It'll be fun. I'll introduce you to everyone here, you can see where I've been. Come, Babe. I'm longing to see you."

"Okay," she sounded hesitant but keen. "I'll have to organise to borrow a car ... Maybe I could get Wendy to drive with me? Can she come?"

"Ja, bring Wendy. I'll see you Saturday then?" I was excited.

There was just one week left at Sterkrivier. I would be seeing Kimberly on the weekend and I was going to be home on pass for my birthday in a couple of days. I felt like life was improving, especially as we took it easy in camp that last week.

We had the troops congregate on the parade ground. It was Friday, and we were all going on pass. None of us knew why Captain van der Walt wanted the troops mustered just before lunch. The sun shone warmly on us and a fresh breeze stirred the veld. Spring is a good time to be in the bush.

Van der Walt joined us, grinning like a Cheshire cat.

"I thought I'd give you guys a bit of a demonstration," he said. "Call it my parting gift to you. Watch this!" He presented a grenade, his fingers curled around it – we assumed it was a smoke grenade – and he proceeded to lob it into the centre of the mustered troops. As he did so, the breeze changed direction slightly, and the acrid smell of teargas reached my nasal passages. *It's a bloody teargas grenade!* I thought. *What a jerk!* The captain, us loots and many of the troops were wheezing and coughing, tears streaming down our faces. He thought it was funny. We thought he was a twit.

Kimberly arrived with Wendy early on Saturday afternoon in her mother's brown Datsun 120Y. All the concerns I had been harbouring about Kimberly and our relationship were temporarily set aside – it was just so good to see her after such a long time. She seemed happy to see me, too, and the tiniest spark of hope ignited in my mind. I looked long at Kimberly after kissing our hellos, giving my eyes enough time to take in every delightful feature: her brown hair was longer, and I thought it made her look more grown up. I couldn't stop touching her, as if confirming that her presence here was not just a dream.

I showed the girls to a tent I had prepared for them and they left their overnight bags there. Then I took Kimberly's hand and led her and Wendy off to show them the camp. In the officers' mess, I introduced the girls to the loots who were having lunch and left Wendy chatting amiably with the guys, taking Kimberly to introduce her to my troops. The guys were sweet with Kimberly, welcoming her to the camp and teasing her about her boyfriend.

"She's a very fine *wansati*," old GJ Nkuna said, shaking Kimberly's hand with warmth and grinning. He wagged a finger in my direction. "You're a lucky man, lieutenant. Be sure you take good care of her." GJ winked at me and we all laughed.

After a braai that evening, when everyone had gone to bed, I sneaked Kimberly out of their tent for a cuddle in the officer's mess tent.

On Sunday morning we left the Sterkrivier training base in Kimberly's mom's car with Gavin who was hitching a ride to Jan Smuts Airport. He was flying to Cape Town to visit Cathy. The roundabout drive to Pretoria via the airport was a very pleasant one, and I was looking all the more forward to spending some time back in civilisation and in Kimberly's company.

On Sunday evening, Kimberly returned to her residence at Wits. I stayed on in Pretoria to begin the hunt for a second hand car. I was lucky. Just down the road from my parents' house at Glenwood Motors, I found a white Ford Escort 1600 GLE which had belonged to the Chilean Embassy in Pretoria. I went for a test drive on Monday morning, and besides the bonnet coming unclipped while I was driving and a bit of an indistinct manual gear change, it seemed a perfect fit. I decided to buy it with the savings from the sale of my Honda. I was proud to now own my very first car which I had purchased with my own money.

Friday was my twenty-fourth birthday. Kimberly had asked me to accompany her to a formal dance for the residents of her res that evening, and to one of her good varsity friends' twenty-first birthday party in Pietersburg on the Saturday, so I packed enough clothes for the weekend and made my way to Joburg in my newly acquired, second hand Escort.

I knew Kimberly would be busy with preparations for the dance, so I stopped off to visit Harald at Knockando, my old res. We caught up over coffee and rusks, sharing our stories of varsity and the army. He agreed to let me bunk in his room that night, as I knew Kimberly wasn't allowed to have men visit her in her rooms. Talk of the dance that night led the conversation easily to Kimberly.

"You have much contact with her, Harald?" I asked him, poking around a bit to find out how she was when I was far away.

"Ja, quite a lot lately, actually," Harald replied. "She and Kim have become quite friendly." Kim was Harald's girlfriend. "They are a formidable pair when they are together!" he said, with a twinkle in his eye. "They talk non-stop and they can bully a guy into doing just about anything they want!" He chuckled. It was a relief to me to think that Harald might be around Kimberly a lot, keeping an eye open on my behalf, so to speak. I laughed along with him, imagining the two of them running circles around Harald.

At lunchtime, two cute brunettes arrived. They weren't allowed into the men's rooms, so Harald introduced them to me out on the landing above the stairwell. They were Rachel and Andrea, friends of Kim's.

"This is Mike," Harald informed them. "He's Kimberly's boyfriend, here on pass from the army."

"Oh, right," one responded, leaning on the balustrade.

"Yeah, we've heard about you," said the other. They both looked at me with curiosity.

"Hey, guys, I gotta go," Harald said. "I promised Kim I'd help her take some stuff over to the auditorium for the dance. I won't be long." Harald looked at the girls and pointed a thumb in my direction. "Mike here will keep you company while I'm gone. See you later," Harald left with a wave, and I smiled awkwardly at Rachel and Andrea.

"So you're Kimberly's boyfriend, huh?" Andrea said. I nodded. "You know her, then?" I asked. They both nodded.

"We're at res with her. She's our res mother," said Andrea. Kimberly had been elected the student head of her residence, "res mother", by her buddies there. I hadn't been surprised when she wrote to tell me. She was a popular girl.

"So you've heard of me, hey?" I tried to be cool, not sound like I was fishing for information. They both looked away.

"Sure," Rachel looked back at me, smiling slightly.

"Only the good stuff, I hope?" I gave a chuckle, but the girls just went on smiling uncomfortably. Silence settled around us and I began to feel anxious. Why were Andrea and Rachel being cagey? I tried to fish some more.

"So, Harald says Kimberly and Kim are close?" I asked. They both seemed relieved at the change of subject. Andrea gave a snort.

"Inseparable!" she said. "At the res, we call them "the twins"." "And you guys are friends with them both?" I asked.

"Sure," said Rachel. "We're friends. It's quite a big crowd of friends we share. All the girls are from our res and the guys from this one. We're all going to the dance tonight. You coming?"

"Ja," I said. "I'm coming with Kimberly." I thought I saw Rachel's eyebrows lift in surprise, but maybe I misinterpreted the expression. "So Kimberly is quite an influence on Kim?" I asked.

"More like the other way around," Rachel said. "I mean, Kimberly is res mother, so she's kinda in charge, you know? But she really listens to Kim." "Really?" I asked, surprised. "In what way?"

"Well ..." Rachel looked at Andrea, as if asking for backup. "Like, Kimberly will go with Kim's suggestions for how to manage the res," she said.

Andrea chimed in. "And we always do what Kim thinks we should do," she said.

Rachel spoke again, "And she wants Kimberly to take up hockey with her." "And she thinks Kimberly should break up with her boyfriend," said Andrea. They both stopped and looked at me with shock as they realised Andrea's gaffe. They had been so caught up in describing Kim and Kimberly's relationship, Andrea had forgotten who she was talking to. I took a second to compose myself.

"Excuse me?" I said eventually. The two girls were silent, not wanting to give away any more. "Kim thinks Kimberly should break up with me?" The two nodded silently. "Why?" I asked. They were reluctant to speak again, considering how much they had already inadvertently given away. "Come on!" I was exasperated. "You can't tell me something like that and not give me the details!" Rachel and Andrea looked at each other. I thought I saw Rachel give a shadow of a shrug.

Looking back at me, she asked, "You'll keep this just between us?" I nodded. "You promise? No telling Kimberly!" I nodded again.

"Well ..." Rachel sighed and clasped her hands in front of her. "She thinks Kimberly's relationship with you is keeping her back."

"Keeping her back?" I was stunned. "How?"

"Um ..." Rachel was avoiding my eyes, she examined her shoes as she spoke. "I don't know. Kim's just always telling Kimberly how she needs to "spread her wings", you know? How Kimberly mustn't feel obligated to stay with you." Rachel looked up at me. Guilt and pity were written all over her face. Andrea picked up where Rachel left off.

"She reckons Kimberly would be happier with someone closer, someone more available to her ... like, someone in her circle, you know?" I didn't know. All I knew was that Kimberly was being encouraged by Kim to end it with me, and the thought made me furious. How dare she?

"And is there someone else?" I asked. "Another guy? Someone "in her circle", as you put it?" The girls looked at each other and shook their heads.

"You're sure?" I asked again, watching them squirm under my scrutiny. "Mm-hmm," they both nodded, their mouths sealed tight, as if afraid of spilling more beans if they so much as parted their lips. They made to rapidly depart.

Going to the dance with Kimberly now felt like a bad idea. I wondered if there was someone else, another guy, someone "from her circle", who might be there, watching as Kimberly paraded me like a lamb to the slaughter. Reluctantly, I prepared for the event in Harald's room, showering and shaving before pulling on the same blue suit which had seen service at my graduation and my sister's wedding, and doing up my tie. I looked in Harald's mirror. The face returning my gaze was someone I didn't yet know, a slender, tanned man with broad shoulders – all traces of boyishness erased from almost two years in the army. Deciding I looked rather dashing, I braced myself for meeting Kimberly. As I made my way out of Harald's res, I caught the approving glances of a couple of girls who were there visiting, and my confidence was buoyed.

Kimberly, done up in her finery, took my breath away. Her hair was swept up off her face and a pair of long beaded earrings brushed at her jaw line. The crisp white of her strapless gown accentuated her olive brown skin which positively gleamed with youth and vitality. Her beauty made me ache inside. It seemed so strange to me that she might be considering ending our relationship when the last weekend with her had felt so much like old times.

She smiled radiantly at me and took my arm. In the coolness of the spring twilight we walked the short distance together from her res at Girton Hall to the auditorium where the dance was being held. Kimberly took hold of my upper arm with both hands, leaning into me and hugging me to her as if to warm her bare skin with my body heat. She was excited for the evening, and chattered away animatedly about the afternoon preparations and the evening ahead.

At the entrance to the venue, a photographer was taking pictures of the couples as they arrived. I encircled Kimberly's waist with my left arm, holding her left hand in my right, and smiled into the camera. As the photographer clicked the shutter open to capture the moment forever, I thought I felt her pull away from me ever so slightly.

In the hall, Kimberly was electric. Several people stopped her to talk as we made our way towards the main table where we were to be seated. Eventually, I left Kimberly chatting and made my way to the table ahead of her. Seated at the table, I waited for what seemed like an age. Other couples arrived, including Harald and Kim. Before I had a chance to confront Kim, she departed to traipse and trail along with Kimberly to all and sundry sitting at the various tables, leaving Harald behind. I engaged Harald in some small talk, but the longer I waited, watching Kimberly swanning about the room like the lady of the manor, the more vulnerable and ill at ease I became. Harald, not being a drinker of alcohol, declined my offer to fetch him some punch. I made my way over to the punch table and filled up a glass each for Kimberly and me, downing one and refilling it before returning to our table.

Harald, in the meantime, had left the table to tag along with Kim and Kimberly – I was certainly not going to join them in this social roundabout! The other couples at our table were deeply engrossed with each other – they ignored me and I was happy to ignore them. I was hoping the alcohol would help take the edge of things and relax me a bit. Feeling the need for something stronger and more manly, I returned to the bar a couple of times to get a beer before Kimberly eventually arrived, grateful to feel the drink soothe my troubled mind.

There were speeches and some accolades which meant nothing to me, followed by dinner and dessert. Then the dancing started. After dancing once together, Kimberly refused to dance again, telling me there were still other people she needed to talk to about important res matters. I was a bit at a loss. I looked around for a familiar face, but seeing none, I consoled myself with more beers as I watched the couples on the dance floor.

It was a relief when Rachel and Andrea appeared, taking empty seats either side of me. They had clearly been partaking of the punch themselves, they were relaxed and chatty and decidedly flirtatious. They didn't seem to have partners. Andrea asked me to dance, and I was happy to join her on the dance floor. Soon, Rachel joined us, and the three of us were having a good time. We stopped our dancing when we got thirsty, and I made my way towards the bar with a pretty girl on each arm. Refortified by a beer for me and a glass of wine each for the women, the three of us were making our way back to the table when Rachel indicated to me that I should come closer so that she could speak into my ear. I leant down and she whispered from behind her hand.

"Why don't we ditch this place? Come with me to my room." I thought I had misheard her, snapping up to look at her in confusion, but she smiled invitingly and looked up at me through her eyelashes, leaving me in no doubt as to what I had heard. Before I could respond in any way, I was grabbed by the arm and tugged from behind. Turning to see who had taken hold of me, I looked into Kimberly's steely face.

"It's time to go, Michael," she said.

It was like my sister's wedding all over again. Kimberly had paid me no regard until she saw me having a good time with Rachel and Andrea, and now she was jealous. I was more than a little confused by her.

I had hoped to have a good heart-to-heart with Kimberly on the way to Pietersburg, but when I arrived to fetch her on Saturday after lunch, she was waiting for me with her long-time varsity friend, Amanda who was also going to the party. My distaste for the adventure grew. Not only would it feel like I was returning to Mabiligwe, but with a stranger in the car, I would have no opportunity to talk to Kimberly. I was feeling a strong urge to talk, to talk like we hadn't for a long time. I needed to understand where Kimberly was, to let her know how the two years of national service were crippling our relationship, and find out what her experience of my absence was. I really needed to resolve with her all the doubts and anxieties I was feeling about our relationship.

At the party, I happened to bump into a friend of Kimberly's I knew. "Hey, Dezi!" I greeted her warmly, relieved to see a familiar face. "How are you?" Dezi was taken by surprise, obviously not expecting to see me here. "Oh. Mike." She blinked, looked around. "Hi." She was unsmiling and awkward. I leant against a wall, settling in to chat.

"Long time," I said. "What have you been up to?" Dezi tucked her hair behind her ears.

"Listen, Mike," she said. "I've got to go. There's a friend of mine over there ..." she pointed somewhere behind me, "... uh ... I must ... anyway ... bye." She shuffled off as if she couldn't ditch me fast enough. I was left feeling puzzled.

The morning after the party, Kimberly wanted to stop and visit someone who lived in Pietersburg. On meeting Mrs Cohen, I realised that she was the mother of a guy who was at res with me, about a year behind me. I hadn't been friends with him, and I couldn't understand why Kimberly would want to see this woman, or how she knew her. Kimberly and Mrs Cohen, who was decidedly Afrikaans despite her very Jewish married name, chatted away like they were old friends, and I slowly began to feel very uneasy about the whole episode. In the car on the way home, I asked Kimberly how she knew Jimmy and his mother, and she told me she had met Jimmy at some event in Joburg, and had wanted to drop off something he had given her for his mother.

Following the pleasant weekend we had spent when she had fetched me from the Sterkrivier training base, I was again confused and disturbed by the strange events of the last two days with Kimberly. When she asked me to drive her to Natal to visit her folks who had recently relocated to Pietermaritzburg, I jumped at the chance of spending more time with her and hopefully resolving some of the issues that were occupying my thoughts. We departed at lunchtime on Monday under an overcast sky, and as we drove through the northeastern Orange Free State towards the Natal Midlands, the clouds became very heavy and black. There had been unprecedented rainfall in Natal over the weekend, and we were fortunate to encounter the rain only sporadically on our trip.

Kimberly was tired after the busy weekend. She dozed on and off as I drove, and I decided to let her be and not press her with my concerns about our relationship. There would be time in the coming days. I slotted the tape of our favourite album, *Tango in the Night* by Fleetwood Mac, into the tape deck, losing myself in pleasant memories of Kimberly and me as the music played over the car speakers. Passing by Howick on the N3, not far from Pietermaritzburg, I saw that the Umgeni River was inundating the riverside properties of the small tourist village just below the Midmar Dam, almost reaching their back doorsteps. I wondered when the rain would let up. As we exited the highway towards Pietermaritzburg, I wished I could have kept on driving. Kimberly and I could have made our way straight down to Durban and spent a couple of days at the beach.

Her parents greeted me warmly enough when we arrived at their house late in the afternoon, setting me up in the garden flat at the back of the house. The evening meal was a bit stifled, Kimberly's folks seeming unfamiliar to me in an unexpected way. I slept alone in the flat that night, listening to the rain hammering down incessantly on the corrugated iron roof.

After breakfast on Tuesday, Kimberly and I decided to venture out to Howick to take a look at the effects of the floods. Opening the door of the Escort, I stepped into an inch-deep pool of water in the foot well. I took a closer look, and discovered the wind deflectors attached to the doors, which must have affected the normal aerodynamics of the car, had pulled the door frames away slightly from the roof, and the rain had poured all night long through the gaps. Mopping up as best I could, we settled giggling into the damp car and made our way out of the driveway and back towards Howick, the soggy carpets at our feet misting up the windows.

The road into the town was lined with cars and people looking out over the devastation. A number of the houses we had seen on the way down the day before had now been flooded, the Umgeni River having broken its banks overnight. The rain by now was over, and we stood on the bridge amongst the crowd of onlookers. I could see stockyards and factories under water. We drove to the Howick Falls and walked close to the now cordoned off lookout point at the top of the waterfall. An immense volume of muddy water was pumping across the overhang, appearing to crest the edge horizontally before cascading nearly a hundred metres to the pool at the base in a haze of water droplets. The sound of the water was thunderous, and we had to shout into each other's ears to be heard. I was mesmerised by the power and ferocity of the falls.

We stopped at the little restaurant near the falls for coffee and cake. It was packed with people. The floods had produced an electrified atmosphere in the town, and people were animated with awe and thrilled with excitement. So enjoying this time with Kimberly, I was again reluctant to broach the subject of our relationship with her, so I let it rest for another day, engaging her in small talk and banter instead. That night, Kimberly sneaked out of the house to kiss and cuddle with me in the garden cottage.

Reassured by how Kimberly seemed to warm to me during our time in Pietermaritzburg, I began to wonder if my time away was as hard on Kimberly as it was for me. I was comforted to think that perhaps, when I returned to my life and began to forget these difficult years of my national service, Kimberly and I would return to our old ways and I could shake off the apprehension that had become my constant shadow. Tentatively, I began to think of our future with the same enthusiasm I used to.

At the end of the week, Kimberly and I left Pietermaritzburg for Pretoria. Her mother travelled with us, wanting to visit her daughter, Kara and her family, in Pierre van Ryneveld in Pretoria. The presence of Kimberly's mom in the car made conversation awkward, and I got the impression that Kimberly was relieved not to face the prospect of talking to me for the duration of our journey. I could have kicked myself for putting off discussing the difficult subject of our relationship for so long – now the conversation would be postponed again.

Approaching the Midmar Dam wall, where the N3 North crosses the Umgeni River, we were diverted by traffic officials to the eastern bridge downstream. Stopping to find out what was going on, I learnt that the raging torrent of water coursing down the flooding Umgeni had battered the concrete supports of the bridge. With the water still swollen and showing little sign of abating, it wasn't possible to assess the damage to the bridge, and concern about the stability of the structure at the height of the flood led officials to closing that side of the highway.

Passing through Harrismith, the car began to steam severely. Between the compromised radiator, which had become a factor not long after purchasing the car, and the trip up Van Reenen's Pass under the weight of the three of us and our luggage, the overworked engine was severely strained. North of Harrismith, I pulled over onto the side of the N3 near a farm, which had a small dam I could see from the road. I was relieved to have an empty two-litre plastic cold drink bottle in the boot, due to the often-experienced radiator problems, but I cursed myself for not filling it before we left Pietermaritzburg. Bottle in hand, I scaled the fence and jostled with a herd of cows to get to the water, but not before Kimberly had sighed deeply and with irritation at the inconvenience I and my car had caused. Her mother, huffing, made the suggestion that I should have been better prepared for such an event.

Perhaps Kimberly was steeling herself for another goodbye — there were so many during my time of national service. Perhaps she found it as hard to send me off as I found it to leave her. Whatever it was that caused the discomfort, Kimberly and I were again separated by a distance that felt impossible to negotiate as I prepared to return to Mabiligwe. I still hadn't had the chance to have a heart-to-heart with her, and it was with great frustration and pain that I took my leave of her after a single day back in Pretoria. I kissed her on the lips, not wanting to let go of her, and felt already that her mind was far away.

It's a cold winter day on the Highveld. The sun is shining from a clear blue sky, but a blustery wind brings with it the suggestion of snow from some landscape higher than Pretoria. The photograph of Kimberly and me at the dance is pinched between my thumb and forefinger, our youthful faces lit up by the brightness of the camera's flash, and I am reminded of that balmy evening in the springtime of 1987. There we are in the foyer of the Linder Auditorium, both smiling into the camera, Kimberly smiling more widely than me. Carefully printed on the cover of the photograph's sleeve in Kimberly's neat hand I read: "Thank you for a wonderful time — I really enjoyed the evening". The note bears no name, no address or signoff, and no assertion of love or care. Why didn't I realise then what is so clear to me now?

I put the photograph aside, and return with my younger self to Mabiligwe.

The camp was a quagmire of doom and gloom on my arrival: Lieutenant Psycho had sent word that he was coming back. He arrived shortly after me and life basically picked up from where we had left off with him in July. We were told to pack up our gear and leave the base. I was deployed with my platoon to the Kruger National Park, close to the Pafuri Gate entrance where my friend the game ranger was stationed. I made regular patrols past his gate, and I would send the troops to go and take it easy under the nearby trees — out of sight of tourists and SADF personnel — while I had long chats with

Mark. We still tracked spoor along the dirt roads, fighting off the Mopani flies which were more numerous by the day. Lone antelope and troops of vervet monkeys were our constant companions in the dense bush and tall trees.

"Ag, please, man, Mike!" It was Dries Bekker. "Let me take your car! You don't need it while you're here, man. I really want to get home quickly to see this girl I'm keen on." This wasn't the first time he was nagging me to loan him my car for his upcoming pass. I had already refused him politely several times. Once, on a good day, when I was feeling particularly positive about the world and life in general, I came close to agreeing to let Bekker take the car. But Gavin had wisely intervened, taking me aside and warning me not to.

"Mike, think very carefully, man," Gavin had said, when we were out of Bekker's earshot. "What if something happens to the car while Bekker has it? If I was you, I wouldn't do it, Mike. Don't lend him your car. Take it from me." But Bekker's nagging was wearing me down. This time he had cornered me when I was alone, probably aware that Gavin would do his best to persuade me not to, had he been around.

"Dries," I said, trying to be light about it. "How many times have I told you

"*No?*"

"Okay, listen," his voice became conspiratorial. "How's about this?" He sat on the chair next to me, leaning forward eagerly and speaking with his hands. "How's about I take the car to a mechanic buddy of mine while I'm in Pretoria? I'll have him take a look at it for you, fix whatever is making it misfire. Hey?" He smiled, "What d'you think?" I knew it would be a good idea to have a professional look at the car – sooner better than later. And if Bekker had it fixed for me, the car would be driving well for when I next went on pass. He must have seen me thinking about his offer, because he took the opportunity to press me further. "Tell you what," he said. "Let me take the car, I'll take it to my mechanic friend to get it fixed, and I'll throw in a six pack to sweeten the deal." He spread his arms and cocked his head. "You know that's a good deal, Mike," he said smiling. "You know you're making the most out of that kind of a deal!" I eyed him for a minute or so before finally relenting.

"Okay," I said reluctantly. Dries whooped and did an air punch. "But you take care in it, hey!"

Bekker was gone for ten days. On the day he was scheduled to return to camp, I stuck close to the main Pafuri road in the Kruger Park with my section, patrolling one particular dirt track that had a good view of the tar road back to Mabiligwe. I was relieved that afternoon when I saw the car drive past in one piece, under its own, unhindered power. Bekker claimed he had taken the car to his mechanic friend, but I had my doubts. When next I drove the car, it still had the misfire, and I thought it even seemed more pronounced. Gavin gave me a single *I told you so!* look when I complained about it though.

Time passed fairly quickly over this period. Psycho hadn't really been too much trouble. I had been out of the base so much, I hadn't had to deal with him face-to-face a great deal. Plus, I had been able to spend many a day visiting with Mark. Before long, towards the end of October, we were informed that the troops were to be given two weeks off and we would be given the same. It couldn't have been better! It was just over a month since my last pass, and now I was going to go home again. The troops were seen off in the SAMIL convoy down to Giyani and Letaba Ranch, and then we left the base, leaving a skeleton crew of NCOs and a few looties to look after the base and do patrols.

Chapter 27

I arrived at the Johannesburg College of Education at lunchtime on Friday. Being in Kimberly's presence was like quenching a thirst. It was so good to kiss her, to feel her in my arms. We walked to the canteen for lunch, the October sun dappled under the slowly waking jacarandas. It felt good to be back.

I reached for Kimberly's hand, wanting to connect with her in this moment. She chuckled nervously and skipped out of my reach. I looked at her, puzzled.

"You know I shouldn't, Michael." I didn't know what she meant. "What?" I asked, surprised. "You shouldn't hold my hand?" "Yes," she replied.

"Why?" I asked, looking at the student couples scattered about the campus: walking hand-in-hand, lounging in each others' arms. One couple on the grass under a tree were getting positively x-rated. I was confused.

"I'm res mother," she said. I didn't understand how it was relevant. "And?" I said.

"Well ... I should be an example to the others," she said. "I shouldn't be intimate with you on campus." I couldn't see the logic of her reasoning, but I wasn't going to argue.

As we entered the canteen, I saw Jenny, my mother's cousin, at a table with some friends. Kimberly set off to queue for our lunch and I made my way to say hello to Jenny. After her polite enquiries about the army, Jenny leant over her apple juice, grabbed my arm on the table and pointedly turned her back to Kimberly.

"Mike," she spoke in an exaggerated whisper. "Mike, do you know?" I had no idea what she was talking about, but her dramatics made me smile.

"Pardon me?" I said. She exchanged glances with her friends. "Jenny! What do you mean? Do I know what?" Jenny raised her eyebrows and rolled her eyes towards Kimberly.

"Your girlfriend," she said. "She's been messing about behind your back!" This time I knew it was true — there was no doubt, no denial — but it was a shock all the same. I tried to stay composed. I took a deep breath, avoided Jenny's eyes. I watched Kimberly's back as she fished through her purse. I had to find out more.

"Do you know who?" I asked after some time. Jenny didn't seem surprised by my calm.

"It's that dark-haired, Jewish chap from your old res," she said. "I've seen them together here a couple of times." Jimmy. I should have known. "It's been going on for most of this year. Just ask my friends," she indicated to her companions at the table with a nod of her head. "It isn't exactly a secret around here."

I felt ill. I wanted to escape. It took all the strength I had to stay, to hold my pose and force a smile. Internally, I was furious. *Bloody bitch!* I couldn't stop my angry thoughts. *How many times is she going to two-time me? Does she have no shame?* In that instant, Kimberly, my Kimberly, the love of my life, turned into a Jezebel in my imagination. Thoughts of her unbridled lust played through my head, and I was repulsed.

Kimberly returned to the table. "Hi Jenny," she smiled. Jenny gave her a cold hard stare. I stood quickly, led Kimberly to an empty table. "What's up with her?" she asked.

"I think Jenny's just having a bad day," I answered. Lunch passed in awkward silence. I tried not to choke on my food, I kept retching. I felt my whole being seem to reject me – it was like having an abject out-of-body experience. It was the most awful, deeply hollow feeling I've ever had. Blackness, a deep and indisputable blackness, seemed to engulf me, dragging me down.

We walked back to the res in silence. My hands were clenched in my pockets, my legs felt leaden beneath me. Kimberly greeted some mates hanging around in the reception hall on the ground floor. As res mother, she occupied a large suite on the first floor, complete with kitchenette and lounge area. I was about to walk up the stairs to Kimberly's rooms when she stopped me.

"Michael," she said. "You can't come up with me." I was aware that entertaining men was strictly forbidden at the res. But I knew that Kimberly must have had Jimmy up there. I suspected the other girls knew what she had been up to, too. I wasn't going to be fobbed off in front of them.

"Just make me a cup of tea, Kimberly." I turned back to the stairs and began climbing them, two at a time. Kimberly sighed and trotted after me.

I sank into a chair in the lounge, feeling mentally and physically drained from the revelations of the last hour or so. As Kimberly put the kettle on, memories of all the years we had shared, the friends we had made, the good times we had had together were cascading one into the next in my head. I was totally overwhelmed.

With bile rising in my throat, my thoughts turned to Kimberly's repeated transgressions. Ian during high school, Barry at orientation week. The rumour about her and Damon. And now, Jimmy. This was different, though. This time, Kimberly was pursuing another relationship, not indulging in a fling. I had felt the growing distance between us; I had known that something was wrong. But I had always put it down to the distance wedged between us by my national service, imagined she was suffering from lack of attention from me. I had always made the decision to trust Kimberly, to remain committed to our relationship and the future I had envisioned for us. I had always reasoned that this was the leap of faith required of a devoted partner. Now I knew – there really was someone else. And it had been going on for months.

Hatred rose within me. But I loved Kimberly, I adored her. My hatred was not aimed at her. My hatred was for the things she had done to me. I heard my name being repeated, as if from a distance. I shook the thoughts away and tried to take hold of my sanity. "Michael?" Kimberly was speaking from the kitchenette, "Michael?" I stood and walked towards her. "How many sugars?" This harmless question angered me. After seven years, could she no longer remember how many sugars I took? I was offended, but tried not to let it show.

"Two," I said. I held the proffered mug of hot tea between my hands, feeling ice cold inside. I couldn't look at her. I stared ahead, not focussing. "Are you okay, Michael?" Kimberly kept asking. I don't know how I got through that afternoon with her.

Later, as twilight settled into the corners of the room, I tried to reconnect with her. She was distracted and unsettled, but I caught her by the hand and led her to the bed. Perched on the edge of the bed beside her, I took her face in my hands and looked into her eyes. I kissed her gently on the mouth. "Let me stay here with you tonight," I whispered. She looked away from me, took my hands from her face.

"Okay," she said, "but you must sleep on the couch." She made as if to walk away, but I stopped her.

"Kimberly," my voice was gruff with unshed tears. "Kimberly, stay here." I sat her back on the bed, swept her hair from her face, kissed her again. There was no response from her, no reaction.

Despite all I had learnt about Kimberly and Jimmy, I clung to the fact that she had not yet ended our relationship. I convinced myself that she still loved me, that she still had hopes for our future together. Perhaps her reticence, her coolness, was because she was feeling guilty about Jimmy. Perhaps I just needed to reassure her that there was so much to fight for after seven years together. Perhaps I just needed to remind her of all we could look forward to in the years to come.

It was with thoughts of our future in my mind that I drew Kimberly closer to me, wrapped my arms around her and tried to reignite our physical love for each other. I needed to feel close to her, to satisfy my need for intimacy.

But my mouth and hands were met with cold. I kept trying to reach her. I kissed with more passion, pulled her closer, stroked her stiff back. The more I tried to get close to her, the more the distance between us seemed to grow.

Eventually I realised that all my efforts were going nowhere. Every attempt at intimacy I made was met with indifference and the whole episode began to feel empty and meaningless to me. Frustrated and dejected, I abandoned my search for our connection. I didn't know what to make of the situation. I didn't know what to do next.

Later, I convinced her to let me share her bed. I lay next to her, listening to her regular breathing as she slept. I couldn't rid myself of images of Kimberly with Jimmy, and the thought of them together repulsed me. In the early hours of the morning I fell into a fitful sleep.

In the morning, Kimberly suggested we go into Hillbrow for breakfast. These days, Hillbrow is nothing but a ghetto, filled with vagrants, junkies and illegal aliens from the north. But in those days it was a safe and vibey place the students would frequent. Kimberly and I had spent many a night out in Hillbrow, partying 'til the early hours. We went to Big Al's, our favourite place. There were several couples already seated, chatting intimately. I suddenly had the urge to avoid any intimacy; afraid of the hypocrisy of her actions towards me. I led her to an open table, away from the intimate booths for couples and we placed our orders.

Kimberly was stirring her coffee absent-mindedly. "Michael," she hesitated. She shook her head slightly, put the spoon down and rested her arms on the table with resolve. "Michael," she spoke a little louder. "I have something to tell you."

"I know," I said. She looked up, stared at me with wide eyes. "How can you know?" She was incredulous. I kept my voice low.

"About you and Jimmy?" She recoiled. "I know," I repeated. I almost enjoyed her shock. Kimberly returned to stirring her coffee, now with some vigour.

"How long have you known?" Kimberly asked me. She must have wondered why I hadn't confronted her.

"I've known something was wrong for ages," I said. "Someone has finally been honest with me, though." I couldn't help being satisfied by her almost invisible cringe at my barb. "Jenny told me yesterday." I watched Kimberly compose herself, study the cup before her. Some minutes passed in silence.

Eventually, Kimberly spoke. "I still love you, you know." I raised an eyebrow. "I still love you. But I also love Jimmy." It was the dumbest thing anyone had ever said to me! Kimberly wasn't looking at me, didn't see my disbelief. She continued, "I'm caught between the two of you." Part of me wished she would just shut up. I kept quiet, though, listened to what she had to say. "I love you both equally." I stared at Kimberly as if I was seeing her for the first time: she was like a stranger to me!

"Impossible!" I exploded. I had never heard such nonsense before. "You can't be serious! Surely you must feel more for one of us?" She started to cry. I felt emotional, too. She babbled on. "I do. I do. I love you both! What must I do?"

"You have to choose," I replied. "This isn't the first time you've done this to me, you know!"

"I know," her response was feeble. "Please don't remind me. But it's so hard to make a decision ..." I couldn't believe her response. Did she not care for our relationship? Did she not care for the time we had been there for one another? It had been seven years!

I wasn't ready to consider my relationship with Kimberly over. In spite of the turmoil, in spite of the hurt, in spite of the revulsion, I couldn't shake my commitment to her. I still loved her and wanted to believe in our future together. I thought we would only need some time to work it out.

Kimberly was almost finished with her final exams. I suggested she come to my parent's house in Pretoria the following morning. She could do some quiet studying there, and later we could discuss our predicament further. I dropped her back at her res and made my way to Pretoria – to sanity. It was a heart-wrenching drive for me, but I had to think my way through this one carefully. I didn't mention my dilemma to my folks, but it felt good to be back in the family home. Wanting a break from my circling thoughts, I called up some school mates and some of the other looties also on pass. Six of us met at the Farm Inn later.

The place was pumping! Filled to the rafters, a stream of gorgeous women passing by, the DJ had the place rocking. Several beers later, I had forgotten about Kimberly and my problems. With Parfitt, I hit the dance floor. The deafening music and Dutch courage combined to make me feel invincible. I was having a great time. Before long, we were joined by some girls. The music reached a frenzied pitch and, on impulse, I lifted one of the girls over my head, sitting her on my shoulders, gripping a thigh each side of my head. Once she overcame her surprise, she shrieked with enjoyment. We were the centre of attention on the dance floor as I bobbed and swung to the music. Before long there were other guys doing the same, I had started a craze! I felt like a king: I had broken through to another, better place.

The song came to an end and I lowered the girl to the floor. An attractive auburn-haired girl approached me, held my arm and shouted into my ear to be heard above Michael Jackson claiming he was *Bad*. She was brazen: "I want to go on your shoulders!" she said with a grin, "It looks like fun!" I grabbed her by the waist and hoisted her over my head, as she straddled my neck with her thighs. Soon, her blonde companion was on the shoulders of another guy about my height and the four of us were having pure, unadulterated fun!

Two songs later, I lowered the girl to the floor and beckoned for her to follow me to the bar. "Can I get you a drink?" I asked. She was flushed from the dancing, her eyes shining.

"Hunters," she nodded. I ordered a beer and a cider from the barman, handed over the cash. I passed her the cider, ice cold and in the bottle. "What's your name?" I asked.

"Allura," she replied.

"Pardon me?" I thought I had misheard her.

"Allura!" she said, raising her voice.

"Allura?" I repeated. She laughed, obviously used to this puzzled exchange. "Yes, Allura. What's yours?" I introduced myself, clinked my bottle to hers.

"Pleasure to meet you, Allura!" We smiled at each other. "Your name is truly winsome!"

We chatted a bit. She introduced me to the blonde who turned out to be her sister. She laughed at my jokes, looked sideways through her lashes when I asked her questions. I got the impression she was totally enamoured with me. What a feeling!

Like all good things, the evening came to an end. I walked her to her car, a little pink-mauve 1600 Ford Escort. She sat in the driver's seat and scratched through her handbag. She scribbled her number and address on a scrap of paper and handed it to me. We said goodbye and she sped off. I stood for a moment and watched her taillights disappear, feeling the slight coarseness of the paper between my thumb and forefinger in my pocket.

I had just woken, still sleepy and a bit groggy from the previous night's jol, when Kimberly arrived. I went out to meet her in my slippers. She had parked a borrowed cream Audi 100 on the pavement and was emerging from the driver's side as I approached. We greeted each other with a non-committal peck on the lips. I took the bag of books from her shoulder. "Whose car is this?" I asked as she locked the door, thinking it must belong to a buddy from res.

"It's Jimmy's mother's," she said, as if unaware of how inappropriate it was. I couldn't believe her audacity. She must have seen it on my face and was immediately defensive. "Well, how was I supposed to get here, Michael?" she bristled. I dropped the subject, not wanting to start the morning with a fight.

I settled Kimberly in my room where she wouldn't be disturbed. She refused my offer of breakfast, accepted a cup of coffee. I bathed, dressed, then I made myself breakfast and took it through to where she was sitting.

She paused in her studies to keep me company as I ate. "Did you go out last night?" she asked. I nodded. "Where'd you go?" I knew she was only making conversation, but her questions irritated me.

"Farm Inn," I said.

"With Trevor?" she asked. "Ja," I said, "and some looties."

"You have a good time?" I tried to be cool, shrugged a shoulder.

"It was okay," I said. I was feeling uncomfortable, so I changed the subject. "What are you writing next week?" I asked, pulling a text book closer to me.

"Geography," she wrinkled her nose, pulled a face. "It's my last exam". For a second, it felt like I was with the old Kimberly again, my high school sweetheart. I smiled at her.

"You'll do great. As always." We sat in silence as I finished eating. My mind kept returning to the evening before, I couldn't get Allura out of my mind. I rose with my empty plate. "Hey, you study," I said to her. "I'll go out and pay a friend a visit."

"Okay," she said, picking up her pen.

"See you later," I kissed the top of her head and left.

I found Allura's house in Waterkloof, a very up-market suburb southeast of Pretoria. I rang the doorbell with some excitement and a little trepidation. When Allura came to the door and saw it was me, her face lit up and she greeted me warmly. Taking me into the house, she introduced me to her mom and her sister – the blonde from the night before. Her sister greeted me with a knowing grin. After a cup of coffee and some small talk, Allura took my hand and led me to her room.

It had been so long since I had even looked at a woman in this way, other than Kimberly. Allura had put my nervous mind at rest with her welcome, but I was still surprised to be in her room, the door closing behind us. It was odd, but I was game for anything. She pushed me onto the bed and began to undress. She unzipped her white shorts, revealing a glimpse of panties below. Whoa! I was keen, but this was over the top. I stopped her, pulled her onto the bed next to me and kissed her on the mouth.

"Hey!" I said, holding her chin in both my hands. "I'm happy to see you, too, but slow down!" She giggled, took my hand and kissed the palm. "Why?" she asked innocently.

"Well," I held her hand. "I like you." She smiled. "I'd like to get to know you better ..." I let the last sentence hang. We kissed again slowly. It was strange to kiss a girl who wasn't Kimberly. Strange and exciting!

I managed to convince her to stop before we had gone too far. This was all too soon for me, too fast. I managed to preserve her honour and my dignity. Returning downstairs, we giggled over another cup of coffee. She kissed me as I left, and I drove back home feeling over the moon. It felt good to be filled with excitement and passion again.

It was with a spring in my step that I returned to Kimberly. She smiled as I entered, "I'm done," she said. "Shall we talk?"

"Yes, let's talk," I said, feeling buoyed by my time with Allura. I sat down opposite her, drew a breath. I decided to get straight to the point. "You know I love you," I said. She smiled. I continued, "but I can't accept what you've done." I hesitated, wondering if I should tell her about Allura. I decided against it. "This isn't the first time you've hurt me like this," Kimberly lowered her eyes, bit her lip. "I'm telling you that you're free to love only ... him," I couldn't bring myself to speak Jimmy's name out loud. "I'm telling you that you don't have to make a difficult choice." Kimberly looked perplexed. "You don't have to choose who to love," I continued. "I'm making that choice for you." Kimberly was taken aback. I wondered what she expected. Did she expect me to continue taking her back despite her betrayals? Did she expect to continue stringing me along while she took advantage of me? A tear welled up in Kimberly's eye, then spilled over her lower eyelid and made its way down her cheek. *She's still beautiful,* I thought. *I still love her.* Before long, tears were streaming down both her cheeks.

"Michael ..." Kimberly spoke through her tears. "Michael, please ... don't do this ..."

"What?" I was flabbergasted. "What did you expect, Kimberly?"

"I ... I don't know ..." She was breathless. "... But I love you, Michael ..."

"You love me and you love ... him," I was annoyed with her. "Yes, so you've said. But I refuse to continue to be strung along by you, Kimberly. I'm done. It's over."

"Please, Michael, please. Please don't do this," she was sobbing now, a note of desperation colouring her speech. "Please ... Please don't leave me ..."

"It's over," I said again.

We were witnessing the demise of a seven-year relationship. This was a heavy business. She was beside herself. Tears were welling up in my eyes, too. But I stood firm. I had made up my mind, and I wasn't going to allow her to change it. At last I knew what I had to do. At last I knew that my relationship with Kimberly was finally and irreparably over. I couldn't take her promiscuity and deceit anymore. When she realised I was not budging, she packed up her books quickly and left, weeping.

I followed her out to the car on the pavement, concerned that she was too upset to drive all the way back to Joburg. She was sobbing uncontrollably. She said something incoherent about still loving me, got into the car and sped off. I stared after her as she disappeared around the corner at the top of the street. We had travelled that corner so many times together over the years. So many times I had stood here, waiting for Kimberly to come around that corner with her engaging smile, so that I could give her a lift to school on my motorbike, her thighs resting warmly against mine. I was saying a final goodbye to my high school sweetheart, the woman I had thought was my soul mate.

I was filled with a deep sadness. I was not sad to see Kimberly go. In the final analysis, I was not even sad to face the end of my relationship with her. I was sad for myself, for wasting so much of my life by taking Kimberly back after each of her thoughtless dalliances.

Chapter 28

The remainder of my pass was spent in the company of Allura. She lived in a different society to me, a world I knew little about. But in the whirlwind of activity that was her life, I managed to forget almost entirely about Kimberly. Allura didn't seem to have a job – she probably didn't need one. Her family was clearly quite well-off. Every night we would party at one of the nightclubs in Pretoria. Days were spent visiting friends or engaging in some or other activity. Once or twice I accompanied her to the Pretoria Country Club driving range, where she would practice her swing, sending the gardener to collect the golf balls she scattered about the driving range and practice green. One weekend that pass, we went windsurfing and skiing with my school mates at Bon Accord Dam, a popular venue for water sports, north of Pretoria. On another weekend, I took her along to a braai put on by an old mate of mine. My mates and their girlfriends seemed to like Allura, and welcomed her into the circle, which made me feel good about her and us. But she seemed to always need to be somewhere, to be doing something, surrounded by others, as though she felt she was going to miss out on something special if she didn't attend every function. It was difficult to pin her down for a decent conversation.

She introduced me to several of her friends. One of her friends, Martin, turned out to be an old class-mate of mine from primary school. He was always around, always popping up wherever we were, and I began to wonder if he was my competition. Still raw from Kimberly's betrayal, I found the thought disturbing. Eventually, I confronted her, asking if there was anything going on with Martin, but she laughed the suggestion off, insisting that they were just friends. It was hard for me to let go and trust her. She must have perceived my concern, so to show some kind of conciliation aimed at pacifying me, I got a keepsake accompanied by an affectionate kiss. The keepsake was a photo of her, clearly taken recently.

Wearing only a pair of light blue jeans, she was lying on a carpet in a model's pose, her right arm discretely hiding her naked breasts, her left arm propping up her head. She smiled provocatively into the camera. I took the gift to mean something, and I was happy to receive it. I never did think to ask who took the photo.

I met Allura's family. Just like Kimberly's household, the siblings counted four sisters in all. They lived comfortably with Allura's mother in a mansion in Waterkloof, serviced by several maids and a gardener. I got the idea that the parents were estranged; Allura's father always seemed to be away on the family farm near Tshipise. Allura's older sister turned out to be dating a guy called Ben, who I discovered on meeting him was an ex-boyfriend of Kimberly's sister, Roberta, from a couple of years before. Small world!

When I told her I was going back to Mabiligwe, she suggested that I meet her at the Tshipise Overvaal family resort in a couple of weeks, when she would be up there to visit her father. I liked the idea, and she gave me the dates she planned to go.

During my last weekend in Pretoria, I got a phone call from Kimberly. She pleaded with me to see her one last time in Joburg. I don't know why I agreed to it, but I did. I met her in a little coffee shop we both knew in Hillbrow. She smiled at me as I made my way to the table where she was waiting for me. I had to control the urge to lean down and kiss her lips to say hello, a gesture which had become habit in our seven years together. We exchanged an awkward greeting. It was strange to see her after the events of the last two weeks.

Kimberly asked how my pass had been, and I answered her with a vague, "Fine." I asked about her exams, and she responded similarly.

"So," I said, not wanting to waste time on trivialities. "What did you want to see me about?" She rearranged herself on her chair with a sigh, avoided my eyes.

"Oh, Michael," her voice was strained. "I just wanted to find out how ... to see if there is a way ... to ask you what I must do to fix this ..." She looked up, made eye contact with me. "... Us." I didn't speak. She rushed to fill the void. "I don't want to lose you, Michael," she said. I was irritated by her desire to patch things up.

"You've already lost me, Kimberly," I said. "There's nothing left to fix." She looked hurt.

"That can't be true," she said. "We've been together for so long. Don't you want to make things right? To save what we have?"

"What do we have? What are we saving? In any case, why would I want to do that?" I asked her. "You betrayed me. More than once. I don't want to go through that again."

"You won't, Michael." A note of pleading was in her voice. "I promise you. Give me a chance to make this right. I won't hurt you again."

"How can I ever trust you again, Kimberly?" I asked, "After what you did to me?"

"Please," she said. "Just give me a chance." I was resolute. I shook my head.

"I'm sorry, Kimberly," I said. "I've given you so many chances already. I won't do it. Not again. I know it would only be a matter of time before you deceive me again." I watched as tears welled in her eyes. "I'm not prepared to try again." She put her head in her hands. "Besides, I've met someone else." She looked up at me then, turning ashen, shock and disbelief on her face.

"What do you mean?"

"I've met someone else," I repeated. "Who? When?" she asked.

"Her name is Allura," I answered. "We met at Farm Inn at the start of my pass." Realisation dawned on her.

"You mean, the weekend we broke up?" "Yes." She was floored by this revelation.

After some time she asked, "Is that why you broke up with me?"

"No," I replied. "I had only just met her, then. I broke up with you because you cheated on me. You cheated on me repeatedly, Kimberly. Meeting Allura just gave me the courage to do what had to be done. What I should have done a long time ago."

When we parted company, it was amicable, but sorrowful.

Singing along loudly to U2's *Joshua Tree*, I drove back to Mabiligwe with a renewed passion for life. There was a new woman in my life, the countdown to the end of my national service had begun, and I had the invigorating sense that I stood on the threshold to a new chapter in my life. Arriving back at camp, I discovered, to my great pleasure and relief that Cappie had returned. What a welcome surprise! We greeted one another warmly. That evening, Cappie held a braai for all us loots, a celebratory event. We had now all returned to base for our last stint as national servicemen.

The *min dae* countdown had begun. Traditionally, national servicemen started counting from forty days to go. We didn't yet have confirmation of when we would be discharged, but we knew it would be sometime around the second or third week of December. What satisfaction it was to mentally check each day off as it passed. I faced my last month with some enthusiasm, wanting to make the most of the time I had left there.

A day or two after my return to camp, most of the troops had returned by SAMIL. Deployed once again to Mabiligwe and the Kruger Park, we were visited regularly by Cappie, who would come by in the SAMIL 20 to drop off extra food and meat and generally boost morale. The troops really loved this man. He kept things fresh during those weeks by rotating platoons and sections on a regular basis. It was really pleasant again. When we were back at Mabiligwe base, we made liberal use of a pool that had been constructed to cool us down on those hot days. A massive, thick, blue plastic liner had been pulled tight over sandbag sides with a part corrugated iron, part camouflage netting roof as protection against the brutal rays of the sun, and made for a wonderful splash and paddle in about two feet of water. With beers in hand we lazed about in the tepid water like wallowing hippos – man, it was good to wind down like this!

It was somewhat late, considering my national service was almost over, but one day during this time, Cappie dished out our Pro Patria medals for operational duty of sixty days or more on the border in South West Africa, from the year before, when we had deployed with Infantry School. We laughingly called it the ProNutro medal, but I know the medal was important to those who went through hell on the South West Africa-Angola Border, or the families of those who had died in the Bush War. We didn't rate the trinket as much. For one thing, I'm not sure the training we did up there was strictly "operational duty". Besides which, I know that we were not even there for sixty days. And talk about getting it late. What a joke! The medal was accompanied by a standard roneoed letter, in Afrikaans, bearing the photocopied signature of PW Botha, which congratulated the recipient on carrying out his duty in defence of South Africa.

In the middle of November, I got permission from Cappie to visit Allura at Tshipise for the weekend. I left the base on Friday, driving to the entrance to Tshipise Overvaal family resort where Allura was waiting for me. I was happy to see her and hugged her close, but I got the impression she was ill at ease. Driving behind her car, I followed her to her dad's farm close by. On those dirt farm roads, my car began to act up. It felt as if the engine was close to cutting out, and I had to keep the revs up to keep from stalling.

On our arrival at the farm, Allura's father greeted me in excellent English coloured with an unmistakeable Afrikaans accent. A thickset, mountain of a man who certainly looked the part of a *Boer*, he seemed to me to be much older than Allura's mother. He was a man of few words. After sharing lunch with Allura and me, he said goodbye and set off to take care of the business of his farm.

Now that Allura and I were alone together, Allura seemed especially awkward. It was as if she was unsure of what to do next. We took a walk around the farm, a pretty piece of land with several large citrus orchards. Later, we had supper and watched the news on TV.

When it was time to turn in, I was surprised to discover that Allura and I would be sharing a large dormitory, two long walls lined with empty single beds. I guessed this was to accommodate large groups passing through the farm – school tours, perhaps, or church groups. All day I had found Allura to be very unresponsive to me, and now, sharing a dorm, we weren't intimate at all. I was slightly confused by her strange behaviour, but reluctant to make the first move. I wondered if Martin – or someone else – was the reason for her cold shoulder, but perhaps my anxieties were just the after-effects of my experience with Kimberly. As I drifted off to sleep, alone in an unfamiliar and uncomfortable bed, I decided to disregard Allura's coolness and see what the morning would bring.

She awoke on Saturday as chipper and cheerful as you may, as if nothing was wrong. A bit taken aback, I began to wonder if she was affected by deep mood swings. I decided to ride the changeable moods – make the most of the ups and enjoy her company; leave her alone during the downs and find something else to keep me occupied. In this way, a bizarre weekend passed, leaving me wondering what Allura's expectations of me were and whether I was still interested in pursuing a relationship with her.

When I began to take my leave of Allura on Sunday afternoon, my car stubbornly refused to start. I couldn't understand it. The battery was fine and the engine was getting fuel, but nothing I did to try and fix it worked. We laughed at the absurdity of this turn of events, but I was annoyed by the delay. I would have to call Cappie.

Allura drove me to the nearby Messina Sector Head Quarters, where I contacted Cappie by radio from their signal room. He suggested he come by to fetch me and the car. By the time he arrived by SAMIL about an hour or so later, the sun was just beginning to set. He arrived with a driver and some of the loots. I introduced them all to Allura and we chatted for a bit before rigging the Escort up to the back of the SAMIL 50 by a long tow rope. I said goodbye to Allura and we lumbered off to Mabiligwe. It must have been quite a sight: that large army truck pulling my little white car!

That evening, Cappie pulled me aside for a confidential chat. "Mike," he said. "Tell me about Allura. What's she like?"

"Well," I was caught off-guard, still confused myself after the strange weekend I had just spent with her. "She's a great girl," I said. "Fun and easy-going. She's always game for a dare, and I like that about her." I paused, thinking of the weekend. "Although, to be honest, Cappie," I went on at last, "I find her a bit unpredictable." He nodded his head.

"Mm-hmm," he said. "And is it serious? With her, I mean." I felt a bit uncomfortable thinking about it.

"Well ..." I hesitated, trying to formulate an answer in my mind. "It's still early days, you know. Plus, I'm out here ..."

"But you're interested in her, are you?" he asked.

"Sure ..." I tried to convey a confidence I didn't quite feel. "I'm interested in her."

"You know," he said, smiling reassuringly at me. "You are a good guy, Mike. I can tell you would make a great boyfriend for the right girl." I felt a bit self-conscious, but I was pleased by Cappie's words. "I know some girls lovely girls – from Clapham High School. They were pupils of mine there, you know. They've finished with school; some are working and others are studying at varsity. They would love to meet someone like you: a stand-up guy, responsible and hard-working. Plus, I reckon you can be quite the charmer, hey?" With this last question, he chuckled, a twinkle in his eye. "When we get back to Pretoria," he continued, his index finger wagging like the *Groot Krokodil*, "I'm going to introduce you to some stunners," he said and smiled. I knew that Cappie and I shared a special bond. I think he liked my new-found determination and willingness to break the mould. Parfitt had once told me about a conversation Cappie had had with the other loots. Apparently he had told them that he was certain that I would be very successful. He saw me in a corporate environment, Cappie had said to them, wearing a fancy suit. I liked the idea. And Cappie as it turned out – would be proven right. Well, almost.

Not long after our little chat, Cappie approached me late one Friday afternoon. He was grinning with glee. "Hey, Mike," he said. "How'd you like to come to Pretoria with me?"

"What? Now?" I asked.

"Yup. There's a plane waiting for us." He was positively bursting with excitement.

"You're joking, aren't you, Cappie?" I didn't want to get wound up for nothing. It seemed like a dream. He shook his head.

"Hurry up, let's go!" I didn't need much encouragement. I had barely been back from my weekend pass to Tshipise, and now I was off again!

Coordinates: 22°22'32.51"S 30°52'58.69"E

Gavin accompanied us on the adventure. The three of us jumped into a SAMIL 50 and the driver started out west down the sisal barrier service road, turning off to the south onto a gravel road within twenty kilometres. Just a few minutes later, we arrived at a tarred airstrip for SAAF planes. There on the Madimbo runway, engines running, stood a camouflaged SAAF Douglas C-47 Dakota, or "Gooney Bird".

Boarding the "workhorse of the air", I recognised the pilot – a kid I had known at Waterkloof Primary School, who had always, even back then, dreamed of becoming a pilot: Mark Embleton, now "Captain". Cappie was immensely impressed that I knew our pilot!

We settled down across from each other on long hard benches and Captain Mark Embleton throttled up the engines. As he began taxiing for takeoff, I had to shout to be heard.

"How did you get us this ride, Cappie?" Cappie's face was a picture of delight.

"I heard it over the radio at Messina HQ. They said there was a Gooney Bird in the Madimbo Corridor airspace to offload supplies. So I requested the pilot wait for us here." With that, the noise of those turbo-prop engines drowned out all possibility of further conversation, so we just grinned at each other as we lifted off into the cloudy sky of early evening dusk. Homeward bound!

It's about 550 kilometres as the crow flies from Madimbo to Pretoria. At a cruising speed of about 260 kilometres per hour, I calculated that we would land in just over two hours, assuming there was no other air traffic. We sat on our slatted wooden benches without speaking as the bird made her way southwards, only standing every now and again to relieve the ache in our backsides. Mark must have really gunned those engines, maybe there was a tailwind to assist him, because in an hour and a half we were flying over the evening lights of Pretoria. What a sight – what a feeling! We landed shortly before 19h30 at AFB Zwartkop at Snake Valley, southwest of Pretoria. We disembarked, thanking Mark, and Cappie reminded him that we'd meet him at the same bay on Sunday afternoon for our flight back. My ears were ringing.

Cappie had organised a lift for us. En route to my parents' house, he suggested we should spend the evening with some of the girls he knew. He asked where we should take them, and I had the answer, no problem: Farm Inn! I agreed to meet Cappie there at 21h00.

My mom couldn't believe her eyes when I stepped through the front door of the house. I told her about the trip back as she prepared my favourite dinner: steak and chips – what a treat! Having eaten my fill, I quickly changed clothes and freshened up, before starting up my mom's blue Volkswagen Jetta and making my way towards Farm Inn. As I was driving there, I wondered if I would run into Allura, and whether I should have let her know that I was in town. *So what!* I thought.

When I arrived at Farm Inn, Cappie was already there with two girls. Cappie introduced me to them, Danielle and Karla. Karla's foot was in a cast. She was a very attractive blonde and Danielle a good-looking brunette. Both greeted me warmly, as if they already knew me. I wondered if Cappie had been talking about me and what he had said.

I was quite drawn to Karla, and we talked at length, getting to know one another. She told me that she was Czechoslovakian, having escaped communism to come to South Africa with her parents as a young child. After we had been chatting over drinks for some time, the music got underway and I suggested we dance. She looked puzzled, giving me a *What now?* look, holding up her crutches. I laughed.

"Hold on," I said. "I'll show you." I helped her to climb carefully onto the couch we had been sitting on, and then hoisted her onto my shoulders as I had done with Allura before. She loved every moment of dancing on my shoulders, and soon other couples were doing the same. With the DJ playing songs like *Livin' On A Prayer* by Bon Jovi, *La Bamba* by Los Lobos, the live version of *Mony Mony* by Billy Idol and *Everybody Have Fun Tonight* by Wang Chung, the evening was a blast! As Cappie left to take the girls home, I suggested to Karla that I should make contact with her some time. She gave me a parting kiss and a hug, and as they left I was beaming from ear to ear.

I phoned Allura in the morning to let her know I was in Pretoria and make a plan to get together. To my surprise, instead of eagerly agreeing to meet immediately, she told me she was only available to see me that evening. Suppressing my disappointment, I made an arrangement to meet her at a nearby suburban club after dinner.

The early evening news reported that a South African Airways Boeing 747 Combi, known as the Helderberg, had crashed into the Indian Ocean off the coast of Mauritius in the early hours of Saturday morning. My parents and I watched in a state of shock as the news anchor described the disaster as the result of a massive fire on board the plane. There was some debate and speculation between us later as to what might really have happened.

My evening with Allura was nothing special. Perhaps I had already decided that she was nothing but a friend. Perhaps, after meeting Karla, I had realised that there were many beautiful and interesting women out there for me to meet. Whatever the reason, we chatted a bit about the air disaster and some of our own mundane personal issues, and parted saying, "See you soon." But I left with the distinct feeling that Allura was not the woman for me.

I spent Sunday with my parents, sharing a Sunday roast and catching up with their news. My dad dropped me off at AFB Zwartkop where I met up with Cappie. Cappie spoke animatedly about the Helderberg disaster as we boarded Mark's plane, speculating that it must have been sabotage; perhaps those terrorists had gotten lucky. Not for a moment did we believe our own government may have been implicated in the tragedy. Thoughts of the Helderberg disaster made the flight back a little unpleasant, but we landed safely at Madimbo Airfield just before dusk, where our driver awaited us in the warm bushveld air that hinted at imminent rain. It was surreal. For a moment, we had stepped out of this life into a better one for a brief respite, only to return all too soon to the same ol' same ol' again ...

The next morning, the last Monday of November, Cappie sent me to Messina to pick up a few supplies. I sent Phiri to collect orders and cash from the troops, while I did the same for the officers and NCOs. I then hopped into the only vehicle available for this excursion, which happened to be Corporal Chauke's armoured Casspir Rinkhals Ambulance. Phiri and three others climbed into the back. The Rinkhals is an odd vehicle. The driver sits cocooned in his cabin and the passenger side is confined and claustrophobic. Chauke, with me behind him looking over his shoulder, peered through the thick armour-plated glass which tinted the view with a shade of purple-blue. As this vehicle had been modified for use as an ambulance, the mounting for the 20 mm cannon was never used, in accordance with the treaties of the Geneva Convention. Its only armour was its skin. Designed as a mine-protected vehicle, the Rinkhals has a distinctive V-shaped hull and weighs close to twenty tonnes.

The going was slow on the tar road, the ambulance tracking as badly as a honey badger drunk on fermenting maroela fruit. I thought Chauke was severely deficient in driving skills as we veered towards the edge of the road several times, until I felt the play on the steering wheel and realised our wavering course had nothing to do with the vehicle's driver. We arrived in Messina just as the sun began its descent.

We made our purchases at a little supermarket, and then I took the opportunity to phone Allura from a public payphone. The phone was answered by the maid who called Allura. I had to drop a couple more coins into the slot while I waited for her to pick up. Eventually, I heard her voice on the other end, "Hello?"

"Allura!" I said cheerfully. "It's me, Mike. How are you?"

"I'm fine," I waited to hear her ask how I was, but the question never came. My excitement turned into disappointment.

"I'm in Messina," I said. "I thought I would take the chance to call you from the payphone here. What have you been up to?"

"Oh, nothing much," she said. Again, the conversation fell into silence.

"It was nice to see you on Saturday," I said. "I thought I would just check in to see how you are doing." More silence. "Um ..." I was reaching for something to talk about, trying to generate conversation. "We don't get much news up here. Has there been any more news about the Helderberg crash?"

"I dunno," she replied. "I haven't really been following the story. I don't watch the news much, you know." Her tone changed, "Listen," she said. "I have a visitor. I should go."

"Okay," I said. "Well, stay well."

"You too," she said. I was puzzled by her indifference. I wondered who was visiting her, and whether that was the reason she was so distant towards me. I decided this girl was like a wild mustang mare. Perhaps she was untameable. Perhaps she wouldn't settle down easily into a relationship. Cappie was right: Allura had been fun, but she wasn't the one for me. She loved being part of the in-crowd and the centre of attention; she was a party-gal. It was clear that we should be no more than friends.

As we left Messina, the sun had already set, leaving a faint glow to illuminate the horizon. The dusky light of twilight and the poor headlamps of the Rinkhals made the road difficult to see through the thick glass of the windscreen, but on we rolled in the ungainly vehicle, past the Tshipise resort. About halfway to Mabiligwe, I saw a herd of cattle standing in the road about two hundred metres on. It didn't seem as though Chauke had seen it, as he continued without hesitation, hardly braking. The herd slowly dissipated from the road as we neared it, but a lone calf stood transfixed in the beams of the Rinkhals's headlamps. At the last moment, I tried to grab the steering wheel from Chauke, trying to pull it towards myself in an effort to avoid the calf. With all that play on the wheel and the massive lumbering weight and momentum of the vehicle, it hardly moved. I heard a dull and sickening thud as we collided with the animal. Chauke braked hard and the ambulance eventually came to a stop. Changing gear, Chauke reversed quite a distance, then aimed the headlights so that the beams shone over the scene of carnage. The calf had been hit so hard that it lay in the grass next to the fence, way over on the left-hand side of the road, several metres from the point of impact. I shakily got out and went over to it, Chauke and the guys following behind.

"It's dead," someone said. Bending down and looking into his one wildly staring eye, I could hear the poor creature's lungs wheezing as blood bubbled from its maw. It was dying, not yet dead. I was overcome with pity and anger – pity for the poor beast and anger at Chauke, who could have avoided this had he been more aware.

We were unarmed, our R4s left behind at camp as required by army policy. I asked around for a knife, but none of us had an implement with which to end the suffering of the animal. Reluctantly, we left it dying, gasping the last of its breaths as a family of mourners started to gather around, lowing in lamentation and impending loss. The remainder of the journey took place in palpable and poignant silence.

During our last week at Mabiligwe, we sent sections out on their own to patrol. It was clear that we were gearing down to vacate the base. The weather had started to build up again in anticipation of the dry turning to wet, but not with the same intensity as it had in December of the previous year. Expecting that any day the Limpopo River would come down in flood, we waited anxiously for the message to come from Messina Sector HQ that the floodwaters had passed Beit Bridge. The water came sooner than expected, with no prior warning from Messina Sector HQ. On Friday 11 December, the day before we were to leave Mabiligwe Base, the river started to flow once more. The approach of the water was less spectacular than when we had first watched it almost a year ago, but it was still a sight to behold. As it swallowed up the dry riverbed, the river flowed just a few inches high and was less turbulent than before, moving sluggishly. I guessed that this was probably a localised event upstream, which explained why the warning from Beit Bridge hadn't come.

We had already received news that another company was about to take over from us, and now, with the rain pending and the river already starting to flow, we had several legitimate excuses to pack up and leave.

Chapter 29

Early in the morning, Saturday 12 December 1987, Gavin and I walked down to the Limpopo River – a kind of farewell, I suppose. The river was substantially deeper and faster than the day before, and just as muddy as it was at the beginning of the year. The sound of the agitated waters seemed to hush the usual sounds of the bush around us. Our conversation ceased, each of us now preoccupied with our own thoughts as we watched the river in companionable silence.

On our return to camp, all the troops, under instructions from their NCOs, had packed everything up, broken down their tents and were mustered, ready to leave Mabiligwe base. We had to make a plan to remove my lifeless car. Attaching one end of a long towrope to my car and the other to a SAMIL 50, I navigated my little Ford Escort behind the lumbering behemoth, a diminutive insect at the tail-end of the convoy. As we exited the base, I looked down towards the river on my left. It was flowing steadily. A sudden feeling of loss, a sense that I would miss this place, washed over me, and I was surprised by the unexpected emotion. How could I be sentimental about Mabiligwe? I supposed I was going to miss the rugged beauty of this place we had called home for so long!

Cappie had decided that we should drive through the Kruger National Park, as everyone wanted to see the place, maybe catch a glimpse of the animals. The stifling heat of the early morning had given way to cold, and the change was dramatic. As we entered the park through the Pafuri Gate, the sky was heavy with imminent rain. I greeted my game ranger friend for the last time. Mark stood outside his caravan at the gate, waving goodbye to our disappearing column. Soon, we came across a large herd of elephants standing on the road, languishing in the heat radiating off the ground. As we approached the herd, the beast in front turned to face us: a massive bull. For some time he stood nose-to-nose with the SAMIL 50 in front, swaying slightly from side to side, ears flapping, trunk raised, taking stock of us. Eventually the size of the trucks and the rumbling of their V6 diesel engines intimidated him enough, and he grudgingly gave way to us.

As we passed the herd, a large *plop!* landed on my windscreen, shortly followed by the splatter of many more. The elephant dung being thrown up by the tyres of the truck towing me stuck all over my windscreen, and now I was desperate to look through the few gaps that were still left. It made driving extremely difficult and hazardous. I knew that if I put my wipers on I would be done for – it would smear the windscreen completely. After driving a few kilometres peering through the gaps in the crap, once I knew that the truck's tyres had sprayed the last, I risked sticking my head out of the side window and drove like that. Ahead of me I could see the faces of the Nkuna twins and Phiri: they were laughing uncontrollably and loving every minute of my ordeal! Eventually we stopped on the side of the road and I quickly made a plan to use the little remaining water in the water truck to wash the windscreen off to the echoes of the troops' laughter. I was laughing myself.

Around midday we reached Phalaborwa, attracting stares from people on the sidewalks. I dropped my car off at the Ford agents just before closing time. With a brief explanation of what I thought was wrong, I asked when I could expect it back. The two polite Afrikaans gentlemen on duty said they were extremely busy at that time, and because I had arrived unannounced and without prior appointment, I would have to wait at least a week, possibly two if they had to order a part from Joburg. I had no choice but to leave the car in their hands. I handed over the keys and they saw me out of their air-conditioned offices. As I departed, I asked, "Please would you give the car a good wash?" and pointed it out to them. They were aghast at the sight of the car, all caked in brown and green elephant dung!

Finally we were off on the last twenty-odd kilometres to 113 BN at Letaba Ranch. Back in base we unpacked the trucks, got the troops back to their lines and went to our mobile homes, positioned under those shady trees near the river.

We spent that last weekend relaxing in the camp. We found the ubiquitous coffee and rusks at the officers' mess. The greasy eggs, bacon and fried tomatoes were still on the menu a year later, but we didn't mind. The camp was quiet and peaceful, with the troops relaxing in their tents on the far side. With all the PFs out of camp, we wore our civvies. We played pool and drank beer in the officers' recreation hall. We sat on the patio of the officers' mess, watching fish jumping and antelope drinking. We looked on as the sun sank slowly over the Great Letaba River.

We would soon be going home. What lay ahead was anyone's guess. For now, we were marking time, for the last time. We were about to *klaar* out. We would be free men.

The new intake of national servicemen officers was due in camp that weekend. They would start their year with 113 BN, do their duty at Gumbu Mine, Mabiligwe and the Kruger National Park and retrain at Sterkrivier. As we relaxed in camp during those last days, we reflected on the year that had finally come to an end. There was great camaraderie between us loots, but we knew in our hearts that soon each one of us would be moving on into a life of his own.

It was during this second year of my national service that I came to realise that I had to just accept what I had to do. In Apartheid South Africa, there was no viable escape from conscription – not for me, anyway. In the army, there is no room for defiance. Non-cooperation from a conscript had its consequences. Being *slapgat* in combat could mean paying the ultimate price.

I knew I was fortunate to be posted to 113 BN. I managed to overcome the shortfalls of my training at Infantry School and ended my second year in the army with a sense that I had been able to forge relationships and make a difference here. I also knew that this army experience had been invaluable to my own personal growth.

My thoughts of the second year were undoubtedly coloured with relief that I was never forced to do township duty. I knew that performing duties in the township would have been contrary to my recently-formed understanding, and I could not imagine the trauma of being caught up in the conflict raging there. Can you imagine witnessing the horror of a necklacing? I suspect many rational national servicemen and campers who served in the townships hated it for this very reason.

The training I received at Infantry School had not prepared me sufficiently for the leadership role I was expected to take at 113 BN. I would hear later from many other national service officers that they had the same experience. Newly-ranked officers posted in the South West Africa-Angola operational area were thrown in the deep end on arriving at a unit, facing far greater danger than I did in the fairly low-key conflict on the Zimbabwe-Mozambique-South Africa border. Even as I contemplated the year from the lookout patio of the officers' mess at Letaba Ranch, it occurred to me that I might have benefited from some on-the-job training before getting rank. As a potential officer, I could have been posted to my allotted operational unit for the last month, maybe two, of Infantry School, ensuring that I was better prepared for the tasks and responsibilities that were expected of me at 113 BN.

Here, I was expected to lead a totally different class of soldier compared to the men I had encountered at Infantry School. The black men of this battalion weren't fighting against their compatriots because of differing philosophies. These men were fighting to keep their jobs in the SADF, to keep hunger at bay and take care of their families. They were faced with inequality at every turn: second-class citizens in their own country. Dismissed as traitors or sell-outs by other black South Africans. Second-rate soldiers in an army which didn't provide them with training on par with white conscripts, would never consider allowing them to achieve commissioned leadership ranks in the organisation, and even sent the discarded battle gear from white battalions for their use. My training had definitely been inadequate to prepare me to find common ground with these soldiers, to motivate them to fulfil their duties, or even to engage with them in a mutually respectful way. I remembered the dreadful two-pippers we had encountered at Letaba Ranch at the beginning of the year. How had my men ever endured such arrogant and bigoted individuals?

A feature of my second year of national service is how I came to know myself so much better. Through the ordeals and challenges of my experience at 113 BN, I came to realise that I was sometimes impatient, that I had an uneasy relationship with authority, and that I was often stubborn. I had to learn to be patient with my troops and occasionally hold my tongue with senior ranks. Although I was resistant to orders which seemed unreasonable, I learnt to choose which battles were worth taking on. When faced with a dispute I couldn't ignore, I learnt how to challenge my seniors with well-crafted arguments and appeals to reason. Gradually, I had to learn to be a little more flexible, a little more accommodating.

This creeping maturity led me to seek a mode of leadership that was based on mutual respect. I wanted to help my men to grow personally and to achieve more than even they could have imagined. I never wanted to become like the racist PFs, or the bullying black NCOs, or the hard-nosed and bigoted Afrikaner looties that I had come across in the army. I chose to stand for what was reasonable, moral and logical.

I started the year with a dim view of the Afrikaner PFs in the SADF, but my time at 113 BN really cemented for me what a bunch of hardnosed and arrogant men they were. I don't know whether the climate of the army just attracted this kind of person, or if serving in such a *verkrampte* institution and being responsible for carrying out the orders of the Nationalist Government brought out the worst in some people, but the PFs that I encountered seemed to be a species lacking in human compassion. I knew I would have to face PFs again during camps in the upcoming years, but the knowledge that I would not have to face them daily anymore was heartening. I reserved a special kind of contempt for these boneheads!

Many of the positive aspects of my national service would only appear some time after I had finished. Like many ex-soldiers, I did better at work and at studies. I had self-discipline. I had a more mature approach to life. I was probably thought of as a good employee. Unfortunately, like many ex-soldiers, I also tended to be a bit foul-mouthed, sometimes moody, and generally insensitive!

More than anything else, my time with the men of 113 BN changed my flawed perceptions of black people. Let's face it, I am a product of Apartheid – what South African man my age, regardless of his race, education or political leaning, can claim to be anything but? Living with my men day-by-day in the bush challenged my preconceived and unconscious assumptions about black people. I was fortunate to have the opportunity of getting to know these guys, learning each man's uniqueness and character traits, and have them get to know me similarly. For the first time I caught a glimpse of the thread of common humanity between me and these men so different from myself, and it was a gift. It was because of this experience that I was able to really start looking past my own created and assisted prejudices, and begin building an image of humankind as a single conceptual entity. I began to see the necessity of eliminating man-made constructs such as race and culture in the mind, in order for us to live side-by-side in mutual respect. My preconceptions had been challenged, and the walls of prejudice were slowly being taken apart, brick by brick.

All in all, my second year of national service was a far better experience than the first. Soldiering with the men from 113 BN had been a privilege. I was placed in a situation few white officers would ever find themselves, and I wouldn't have swapped it for the world! Even before I left, I knew that the wonderful memories of my time at 113 BN would stay with me forever.

A few new one-pippers arrived that Sunday, and we greeted them like long-lost brothers, wanting to make them feel at home. We wanted to be different to those condescending men we had met a year ago in that camp, and we were. I could see that these new looties were a bit unsure of our munificence and sociable approach to them, but they soon sensed that we were genuine. We drank beers with them and played pool. By mid-Monday, all the new looties had arrived.

That Monday and Tuesday morning we had the standard mustering on the parade ground, Roll Call, day's orders and Sick Report, but now with the new guys watching our every move in camp, much like we did a year ago. After morning parade there was free time for all of us, most of it taken up with the handing in various items of kit, such as our rifles and webbing, and the filling out of numerous forms and registers with the affable civvy ladies. In those last two days, we totally relaxed, slowly packing up our bits and pieces, so that only the essentials remained at hand, with one set of civvies laid out for the final day. I phoned the Ford agents in Phalaborwa on Tuesday, but they said that they'd had to order a new distributor and that the car would only be finished at the earliest by Friday.

On Tuesday 15 December, the day before the public holiday, the Afrikaners' Day of the Vow, we had our last parade. We didn't wear our step-outs, only our browns. If this was our *Uitklaar Parade*, it was a really low-key affair. We saluted the orange, white and blue flag for the last time.

Following the parade, we said our goodbyes to the troops, who would soon be going home for their December pass. These guys had really crept into our hearts. Sure, we had our favourites, but overall, these were men much like ourselves, caught up in a system which cared little for any of us. Us looties were forced to defend Apartheid by conscription; these troops were caught up in the economic dilemma of having to provide for their families when jobs were scarce. Side-by-side we had worked, one day at a time, defending a system we had no part in constructing, but one that, in the end, forced us to look out for one another.

All my men came and shook my hand warmly, saying that they would never forget me. I was never to forget them, too. The Nkuna twins, one smiley, one grumpy, and their unforgettable incident with the buffalo. Mabunda, who nearly shot me accidentally. And Phiri, who had hated me initially, threatening to shoot me, but with whom I had come to share a mutual respect.

We changed into our civvies and went to say our farewells to the other staff members and to the civilians working there. We said goodbye to the one-pippers and wished them the very best for the year ahead. Lastly, we came to take leave of Cappie.

He had tears in his eyes. *"Julle ouens,"* he shook his head and smiled. "You were the best men ..." he paused as if for emphasis, "the best men I have ever had the pleasure of meeting and soldiering with." We all shifted uncomfortably, I looked down at my sneakers in the dust, blinked. "I will miss you all terribly." He gave us each a miniature model replica of a Ratel

Armoured Personnel Carrier, and had hand-written a small plaque on the body of the vehicle, inscribed with the words, "Regards, from Cappie". I still have that memento to this day.

We all turned to walk slowly towards the cars waiting to take us away. I walked beside Cappie.

"Hey, Cappie," I said. "Let's keep in touch."

"Of course, yes. Of course. We will keep in touch," he replied, earnestly. "After all," I stopped at Parfitt's car, turned and held my hand out. "You know the best girls in Pretoria!" He chuckled and shook my hand warmly.

I slipped into the passenger seat of Parfitt's car, Gavin and Maas took their places on the backseat. The car started, and we slowly pulled out to take our place in the mini convoy of vehicles leaving the base. An anxious silence descended as we each looked out our windows, watching the familiar landscape pass us by. I was mightily relieved to be leaving, but I couldn't help wondering what now lay ahead for me in life.

The boom to 113 BN was opened for us by the broadly smiling Shangaan guards who saluted us as we drove past, despite the fact that we were in civvies. This gesture, I felt, was executed as a genuine sign of respect for us as officers. We waved goodbye and smiled, knowing we had forged good relationships amongst these men, relationships built on respect and genuine affection.

As the boom closed behind us, Parfitt picked up speed, gunning it out of there. I held my breath and barely looked back for fear that somehow the top brass had sent an order for us to stay, to spend another year in defence of Apartheid.

Acknowledgements

I would like to express my thanks to the following people for their invaluable contribution to the production of this book: To Charmaine Higgins, for her assistance in the initial development of the book's framework. To Shellique Carby, for research and early edits of the original preface and border sections, and for proofreading the final manuscript. To Fiona Ingham, for her research, many rewrites and considerable edits.

And finally, I am indebted to Sarah McGregor, who stuck by through thick and thin, tirelessly working on this manuscript, and for her substantial research, significant and numerous rewrites and extensive edits, her concise proofreading and invaluable assistance in publishing, without which the book would not have seen the light of day.

42405059R00231

Made in the USA
San Bernardino, CA
09 July 2019